Production Management Handbook

Production Management Handbook

B. H. Walley

Gower Press

Published by Gower Press, Teakfield Limited,
Westmead, Farnborough, Hants, England

British Library Cataloguing in Publication Data

Walley, Brian Halford
   Production management handbook.
   1. Production management
   I. Title
   658.5   TS155

ISBN 0-566-02133-1

Typeset in Times Roman by
Pintail Studios Limited, Ringwood, Hampshire
Printed and bound in Great Britain
at The Pitman Press, Bath

Contents

Illustrations

Preface

This is not a conventional book on production management, although it covers in detail the techniques needed within the function. Its chief objective is to present, to production and other managers who can influence the operation of manufacturing units, a way of looking at environments and the production system that will help them determine an appropriate series of alternatives for each unit's change strategy. The subject is a vital one, and a serious look at it may represent the difference between organisational life and organisational death in the next decade.

The view from the factory gates for most production managers is uninspiring. In the UK at least, industry is not held in high regard. Its productivity is comparatively low, while national economic policies seem at times to deny the capital investment needed for its improvement. Social attitudes appear to be fostered which make it difficult to use either the carrot or the stick for increasing productivity.

My own experience in industry suggests that it is not for the want of trying that UK production performance remains obstinately low. Most production managers can point to a long list of activities they have been involved with — work study, budgetary control, production planning, cost control. Yet the fundamental problems remain the same. How can the labour force be motivated adequately? How can conflicts over responsibility, authority and power between trade unions and management be resolved? How can change be undertaken without a major upset in the industrial relations situation?

Perhaps it is not the solutions that have proved inadequate but the way the problems were analysed in the first place. The profound social and cultural changes now taking place must continue to affect the shop floor more and more. A prime requirement of any production manager therefore is an ability to analyse his external environment and then determine what changes he must introduce in order not to be overwhelmed by external influences.

A second reason why productivity continues to stay low may lie in the training of production managers. They often seem to be technique-orientated — work measurement, incentives, labour control systems, and so on. The techniques have usually been applied piecemeal, without regard for their effect on the production process generally.

So what this book suggests is that the production activity should be seen as a system, conditioned by its environment and only capable of being improved if all the factors making up the system are taken into account. These, it is suggested, can be regarded as a framework comprising work organisation, methods of motivation, the resources needed in production and the systems of planning and control. One element of the framework cannot be altered without some effect on the other parts.

While every production unit is unique in some way, this approach provides a radically different way for looking at and improving production efficiency.

B. H. Walley

PART I

The Production Framework

1

The production framework

1.1 THE PRODUCTION FUNCTION

Production management is one of the most onerous functions of a manufacturing organisation. It is often, too, one of the most criticised. If costs are successfully contained, this may only be at the expense of the flexibility which marketing people say is essential for an increase in sales. Improved output may lead, on occasions, to greater pollution and waste disposal problems and attract complaint from local environmental groups if not from the local council. Activities designed to increase output and improve quality, reliability and delivery performance, may affect the level of shopfloor earnings and cause trouble with the trade unions.

Yet considerable and rather depressing evidence has been collected to prove that UK production managers do not carry out their highly complex task of utilising and balancing resources very well. [1]

1 As a result (or is it a cause?) the whole production function tends to have a low status, attracting few business school graduates. [2]
2 Its pay compared with other management functions is emphatically on the low side. Its 'perks' are few.

The last two decades have seen drastic changes in the economic, social and educational environments in which companies have to operate. Some notable products have disappeared and some marketing strategies have had to be changed. But the environmental changes have been felt most severely on the shopfloor. Government legislation has imposed constraints on production management on a scale previously unimagined. The power of trade unions has grown, making obsolete many theories on organisation and motivation. The 'will to work' seems to be disappearing.

Yet there is every likelihood that in the next decade an increase rather than a decrease in change of all kinds will be seen which will vitally affect the production function. How can change be accommodated with the extra problems it will inevitably produce, when so far we seem to have made exceedingly heavy weather of improving productivity substantially, solving our industrial relations problems and generally meeting international competition?

1.2   PLANNING THE PRODUCTION FUNCTION

Faced with increasingly difficult environments in which to operate, a natural response is to consider long-term plans to accommodate them. Yet, production management tends to be excluded from profit or corporate planning. New product development is considered, or research and development, or even manufacturing capital investment, but not the social planning needed on the shopfloor. The nature of the production manager's traditional role is largely to blame. He is expected to think in the short term. For example, an immediate industrial relations problem must be solved; action must be taken quickly to counter the effects of a machine breakdown; one or two orders are urgently required and production schedules must be changed to meet them. The performance of production managers is usually judged by how well they can balance the conflicting interests of marketing people, management accountants, trade unions and even environmentalists. While this kind of activity produces short-term benefits, it allows little time for longer-term planning. The nature of production management in the UK is to achieve short-term benefits at the expense of well planned future improvements in production performance. Well founded manufacturing plans are the key to improving production effectiveness and so to ensuring that enough wealth or value is created to satisfy most demands of employees, managers and the nation at large.

1.3   DIAGNOSIS IN THE PRODUCTION SYSTEM

A starting point for a production plan (as for any other plan) is to carry out a diagnosis of the present situation. To begin with, production managers might like to consider their function as a 'system' — a complex grouping of human beings and machines joined together to achieve a goal or goals (Fig. 1.1). The production system, like any other, has inputs and outputs; it has feedback mechanisms, which inform those who have control over the inputs what changes they must make to achieve desired results. It is an 'open system', for it must relate to the rest of the organisation. It is also influenced by the external environment and must adapt accordingly.

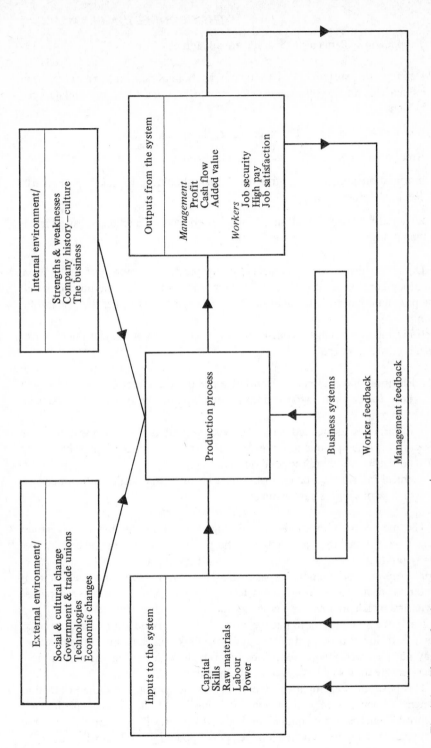

Fig. 1.1   The production system

Thinking in systems terms has several advantages:

Defining the system helps to define its boundaries and the things that influence it and so eventually what has to be done to accommodate such influences.

It should help to clarify the objectives of the system.

Areas of potential conflict should be highlighted.

Information needed to control the system should be revealed, particularly 'feedback information'.

It should help to aid analysis of why the production function is less effective than it might be.

Despite evidence to the contrary, many production managers still believe that they control, or at least have a primary influence over, the functioning of the production system. It might be useful to explore this rather dangerous illusion.

If production managers believe that the system is totally under their control then it must follow that:

1   they must have complete knowledge of how the system works. They will know, for example, what and how much input to the system will produce a given output;
2   all variables associated with the system must be known and under the control of the production manager. The variables must be alterable at will in order to produce a required output;
3   control information or feedback must be such that needed adjustments to the system's inputs can be made.

The most casual examination will suggest that production managers no longer have either this knowledge or the power, if indeed they ever had. Yet many production managers still behave as if they expect to control the system. For example, production departments even now sometimes erect firm hierarchical structures which tend towards rigid control and an impersonal style, and which are unable to adjust to rapidly changing demands.

It might also be useful to put the 'power' of the production manager in perspective. If power is defined as 'the ability to make other people do things they may not necessarily want to do', he has very little, if any, as the system now operates. He may well have even less in the future.

This position is exemplified by considering the outputs from the production system as being purely 'management'. This is not at all true, as the 'job security, high pay' etc. quoted in Fig. 1.1 suggest. If all outputs from the system are not recognised then a large area of potential conflicts will exist.

1.4 ENVIRONMENTAL INFLUENCES ON THE PRODUCTION SYSTEM

The boundaries of the production system lie firmly in the national, social, political/trade union environments. Influences from these sources provide a challenge to the power and authority of production management and indeed to the whole basis for the production system's existence. Training in environmental analysis and the making of contingency plans to cope with changes must therefore be a key part of every production manager's role.

The production system is also part of the overall business system. It is an important part often assailed by problems which managers in other parts of the organisation do not always appreciate. Emphasis on marketing has misled many senior managers into believing that flexibility in production is a key requirement for profitability. While in the longer term everything is flexible (the company could collapse), government legislation on employment protection, trade union power, and limits on capital investment, all mean that manufacturing is fast becoming a fixed not a flexible resource. Profit planning within the business needs to start with this premise. Environmental influences and their effect are unique to each nation; indeed to each company. It is quite unrealistic then to believe that a solution to industrial problems used successfully in Sweden or Germany will work equally well in the UK. Even 'participation' or 'industrial democracy' mean different things to different people. There are no ready made solutions which can be equally well applied everywhere.

1.5 PRODUCTION PERFORMANCE IN THE EIGHTIES

If more than marginal improvements are required in production performance, far more fundamental solutions must be sought. Within the production system, goal conflict has to be reconciled, the production organisation will have to be adapted to take account of changes in authority and power, and there is a real possibility that the system will have to cope with scarcity of inputs such as capital, materials, skills and energy.

It is a habit of British management to embrace some technique or procedure which offers to solve all immediate problems. There have been countless examples — management by objectives, job enrichment, operations research techniques of various kinds, computers and, once upon a time, even work study. Any one of these techniques may solve one problem, but it invariably throws up others, while also tending to disturb, if not distort, the whole production system. Obviously a wider view is needed. If the system as a whole is to be improved then the complete framework of the production system will have to be considered. The system has four parts:

the resources it requires;

the internal organisation of production;
how hard and effectively people work to make the system productive;

and finally

the methods of planning and control which bind the system together.

This framework is shown in Fig. 1.2.

Each of the factors is closely related with the rest as Fig. 1.3 suggests. They cannot have an independent existence, as is suggested in much writing on management. A brief discussion of some of the factors which are quoted will confirm this.

The eighties are likely to see diminishing supplies, and therefore increasing costs, of all kinds of raw materials and perhaps of power. Resource planning systems need to adapt to such situations, to analyse the limiting factor and to organise operations accordingly. The absorption method of costing, so long practised in the UK, seems unlikely to give the necessary information, and direct or contribution costing should quickly be established in its place.

Numerous examples of the effective use of this type of analysis occurred during the 'three day week' which British industry suffered some years ago. By concentrating on products which gave most profit contribution or on machines which produced most profit per unit of power consumed, many organisations found that their overall profit fell only slightly.

What happened in a crisis may need to be carried out largely as a routine, certainly if interruptions in power supplies, raw materials and other inputs to the production system increase.

If labour has to be treated largely as a fixed cost, the production variables will need to be controlled much more closely. Unfortunately in the past labour has often been controlled much more tightly than material even though the cost of the latter was often two or three times higher. Materials and power look like being more vital in the future. The increase in the proportion of fixed to variable costs suggests that profit planning will have to be directed towards maximum utilisation of existing resources. This has repercussions on planning, especially marketing strategies, but also on the expansion of manufacturing activities.

With increased fixed cost and a break-even point at a high level in production volume, new capital investment must be considered very carefully. Unless new equipment can operate at a high utilisation right from its introduction it will prove a poor investment.

It is difficult to say how much longer Taylor-type incentives will dominate motivational practices. They suggest something about a worker — that his service can be bought, that money is the only true motivator and that he cares little about other aspects of his working life — none of which is true.

An alternative to individual payment by results schemes can be found in what are being called 'second generation incentives'. [3] These are based on

Production resources
Capital Machines Material Labour: Management   Employees Power Stocks & work in progress Production services

Work organisation		Motivation and reward systems

Structure:
   Power–authority–
     responsibility
Resolution
Job design
Resolution of goal
   conflicts
Work groups & teams
Socio-technical
   systems design
	Production system	Traditional 'Taylor'
		   type incentives
		Multi-factor incentives
		Measured day work
		Second generation
		   incentives
		Non-financial incentives
		Staff status
		Motivation

Resource planning and control systems

Measurement of
   performance
Added value
   contribution
Resource planning &
   control systems
Computer use
Modelling

Fig. 1.2   The production framework

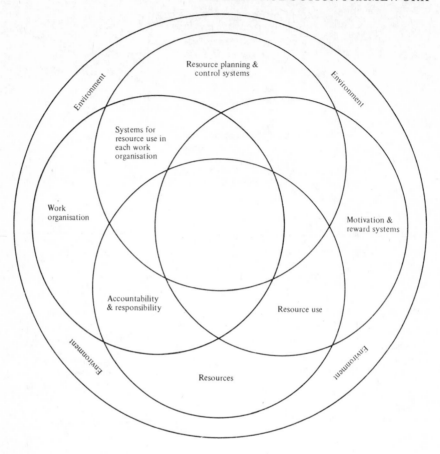

Fig. 1.3   **Interrelationships**

profit sharing, or the sharing of gains in added value. They recognise the need to promote co-operation, economic realism and understanding of the business. They also recognise that workers have real power to influence the performance of the company.

It would certainly be a pity if these incentives were treated purely as another mechanistic way of attempting to raise productivity. The more successful applications appear to have utilised the full production framework (Fig. 1.2) in a practical way.

The reward system has been based on well considered work measurement and management accounting practices.

Work has been organised for the most part on the basis of fairly small work groups, where autonomy to improve added value has been given, meaning that control over the use of resource has also gone to those groups.

Discussions have taken place on the objectives of the production system. For example, if job security is to be maintained at all times this will be at the expense of the added value which can be shared. Such discussions seem to have lessened the potential conflict concerning the objectives of the production system. Information concerning the productivity of the work organisation has been produced, developing, instead of MIS (management information systems), WIS (workers' information systems).

As Fig. 1.3 suggests, resources, resource planning and control systems, motivational systems and work organisation, all have to be seen as interdependent elements in the production framework. Either by environmental pressure or government legislation, 'participation' will inevitably increase. There is a great danger that this too could be misapplied, if discussions only centre around the objectives of the production system or 'who gets what?'. As a shop steward once said 'If participation means that we argue about the same old things round a more highly polished table, then it's all a waste of time'. He went on to ask how the culture of the factory could be changed so that everybody could be better off.

By 'culture' he meant that workers should be rewarded not just for their effort (as a Taylor-type PBR system operates) but also for the value which they contribute to the company generally. At the same time he wanted his people to be given more responsibility — for quality, for setting up machines and perhaps job swapping.

In adopting such an approach, a re-appraisal of the resource planning and control systems and how they could be made to operate effectively in a new kind of work organisation is required. If improved production performance is to be achieved, therefore, all the factors in the production framework have to be considered.

Interdependence is also a vital factor in the future role of production managers, particularly first line supervisors. With their power decreased, supervisors need to adopt supportive or even consultative roles in their local work groups to improve the planning of work and the measurement of performance, to get resources for the group and finally to determine rewards for the group and individuals within the group.

Interdependence, not independence, of the various elements in the production framework is the key to improvements in production efficiency. Introducing a technique or application whether it is computerised production control or product rationalisation can only make marginal improvements if the changes are not seen in the context of the production system and how they might influence it. Improved production control, for example, may improve delivery performance, but by decreasing work in progress or altering the product mix, it may upset existing reward systems and work groups.

Life for production managers is not going to get any easier. However, a careful analysis of environments, followed by a search for interdependent alternatives to provide a production system framework which makes sense in terms of the history, attitudes, skills and objectives of each individual organisation, should be the basis of a plan whereby improvements in efficiency can be achieved.

NOTES

1 See for example: *'The Mismanagement of Production in the UK',* The Production Management Action Group.
2 *The Business Graduate in Britain,* A Business Graduates' Association Report, 1973.
3 See for example: 'Getting Double Value from Added Value', *International Management,* January 1978.

PART II

Environmental Analysis

2

The production audit

2.1 INTRODUCTION

The measurements quoted in this chapter will help to indicate the efficiency of the production function. However, a word of caution needs to be given. Any question such as 'How good are we?' can produce a misleading answer unless the results are seen in context. The 'context' in this instance is the internal and external environments with which production managers have had to operate. There is therefore no easy answer to a 'What is our efficiency?' type of demand. For example, is the measurement to be confined to whether predetermined objectives were achieved, even though these objectives may have been unrealistic when account is taken of the internal and external environments? Is resource utilisation the most important aspect of the production audit, or is it some other function such as good industrial relations, which may be considerably more difficult to define and measure? Such problems need to be borne in mind when carrying out a production audit.

2.2 KEY DATA

While all useful data are 'key' in that they should help to measure performance, the starting point should be to determine 'what production business are we in?' as follows:

2.2.1 Production processes

What kind of production process is being considered:

Batch/jobbing
Process
Line
One-off

or a combination of two or more?

2.2.2   Policy constraints

What policies constrain the production process, e.g.:

  Direct order acceptance from the customer
  Making for stock
  High machine usage, due to capital intensiveness
  Small or large product range
  Fast delivery times
  Total flexibility to meet marketing requirements
  Low cost production to meet national or international competition?

2.2.3   Demand patterns

  Steady throughout the year
  Seasonal
  Random
  Nature of demand — rising/falling for all products or only part of the
  product range (if so which part)?

2.2.4   Competition

Are competitors better than the company in the following:

  Production costs
  Delivery lead times (and especially their reliability)
  Quality and reliability
  Product range and ability to produce special items
  Back-up service including spares availability?

2.2.5   Machinery and plant

  Age
  Quantity
  Utilisation and breakdowns (time spent on maintenance)
  Type and where purchased
  Comparisons with competitors, if available
  Availability of better equipment — give both cost and performance.

2.2.6   Industrial relations

  Size and composition of the work force
  Age breakdown

Industrial relations record (strikes, absenteeism) — compared with other factories if possible

Consultation and participation schemes in operation. Comparison with other similar sized companies will be necessary

Wage rates compared with companies in the same industry and other companies in the same area.

2.3   OPERATIONAL INFORMATION

Operational measurements should help to provide an indication of how the production process operates within the business. Trends over the last three years would be useful.

2.3.1   Organisation

Type of organisation (hierarchies, autonomous work groups, etc)

Actual organisation — breakdown by departments and functions, levels of management

Definition of roles
   authorities
   power
   responsibilities
of both shopfloor personnel and management. Job descriptions may be helpful.

Objectives. How these relate to roles would also be useful.

2.3.2   Resource utilisation

Machines:
   Technical maxima
   Standard performance (what might be expected if standard conditions applied and why this differs from the previous item)
   Bottlenecks and potential bottlenecks
   Ratio of downtime to production time
   Flexibility in making different products or performing different tasks
   Replacement criteria — which are used and how effective do they appear?
Material (most used types):
   Material yield for materials used in all major products
   Average material yield of remainder
   Operational and technical material losses
   Major areas for material loss
   Substitutions
   Quality standards

Labour:
Quantities — male, female, skilled, unskilled, fulltime, part time
Average efficiency
Ratio of effective hours to clocked hours
Utilisation
Ratio of direct to indirect workers
Ratio of direct to administrative personnel
Overtime — its quantity and value
Turnover and absenteeism.

2.3.3   Production and products

Deliveries on time as a percentage of all orders produced
Lead times
Batch sizes and size of orders
Numbers of orders handled per month
Number of items in the product range
Effect of product range on
    deliveries on time
    machine utilisation
    tooling
    productivity by labour and material.

2.3.4   Cost information

Product costs
Production and/or operation costs per hour
Contribution per hour of key machines
Material costs
Labour costs — direct; indirect; general works overhead
Service costs of all kinds (materials handling, maintenance, etc)
(see Chapter 8 for definitions).

2.3.5   Productivity

Added value per
    product
    machine hour
    labour hour
    direct worker
    indirect worker
    wages paid
Labour efficiency and utilisation
Machine efficiency and utilisation.

2.3.6 Hours worked

Overtime
Teabreaks and other agreed allowances
Ratio of direct labour to indirect labour
Ratio of administrative labour to direct labour.

2.3.7 Systems in production

(a) *Production planning and control*
Quote effectiveness in:
Ensuring orders are produced on time
Matching capacity and demand
Minimising costs of all kinds
Maximising production resource utilisation
Controlling performance, i.e. enabling out-of-course events to be corrected
Achieving flexibility in production.

(b) *Management accounting*
Quote effectiveness in ensuring planned use of:
Plant and equipment
Operations
Labour
Material
Services.
Are measurement, planning and control facilitated? Time scales for control information produced should be recorded. What is the elapsed time from an action taking place and a control report being produced which records it?

(c) *Quality control*
Where does inspection take place? Does this provide appropriate control? How are quality and rejection rates reported?
What reject rectification or improvement is attempted as a result of a quality control procedure?
What is the percentage of rejects to output?

(d) *Systems of reward*
Incentives — quote type; i.e. individual PBR, measured daywork, etc.
When were the schemes introduced?
How were the standards established?
What rates are now earned?
How much do the schemes cost to run and maintain?
How much wages drift occurs?
Comment on the possibility of loose values and on overall effectiveness.

(e) *Payment systems*

What records of work output are in operation?

What records of productive and non-productive time are made?

How is the calculation of bonus carried out?

What relationship is there between good work produced and work paid for?

Does a pay policy exist? If so how was it established?

(f) *Works documentation*

Copies of works documentation should be collected and reviewed as follows:

Who makes out the documentation?

What is its purpose?

What is its effect?

What would happen if any document was discontinued?

Can any documentation be simplified, combined or eliminated?

2.3.8   Space and factory layout

What space is utilised for
production
work in progress
general storage
maintenance
quality control?
The non-use of space of any kind should be calculated.

2.3.9   Other data

What are work in progress costs?

What are finished goods costs, compared with work in progress costs?

2.4   ENVIRONMENTAL LINKS

2.4.1   Technology

Describe the technology or techniques used in the company.

How do these compare with the best practice in the industry?

What is the product life-cycle of major company products?

What are the chances of changes in the technologies used?

What investment would be needed to change company technologies?

2.4.2   Cultural change

Is cultural and social change recognised in any formal way?
How is such change accommodated?
Can cultural change be accommodated by considering
   job turnover
   absenteeism
   decline in output standards?

2.4.3   Government and trade unions

How has the company absorbed government legislation on employment protection, redundancy, health and safety etc?
What further legislation is likely and how can this be accommodated?

2.4.4   Economic considerations

How has the company handled the various economic changes which have occurred in the last few years?
What economic trends must be considered in the next 2 to 3 years, i.e. inflation, wage rates, gross national product changes, market rises and declines, international trade?

2.4.5   The company and the outside world

The following key ratios should be determined for all national and international competitors and compared with the company's own ratios:

Operating profit
Capital employed

Sales revenue
Capital employed

Sales revenue
Numbers in the work force

Cost of sales
Net sales turnover

Added value
Numbers in work force.

These are all figures which can be gleaned from the normal published accounts. While there will always be some variables which will upset comparison, the data will provide a broad indication of comparative efficiency.

2.5 SUMMARY

Having recognised the need to consider the main influences on the organisation, does the company:

Have strategies which cope with such changes?

Provide the means for change in production systems, technologies and investment within a profit planning system?

Provide the means for production managers to play a leading part in establishing production objectives in their units?

Provide appropriate information for shop stewards?

2.6 CORPORATE PRODUCTIVITY — AN INPUT–OUTPUT MODEL

In Chapter 25 added value is recommended as a means of measuring productivity and the effectiveness of productivity payment systems (though not all economists and accountants agree that added value is a complete measurement of corporate productivity).

Added value is the difference between inputs (such as raw materials, power, packaging etc.) and outputs — usually expressed as 'net sales revenue'. But while the difference between inputs and outputs can be regarded as corporate productivity several qualifications are required and they complicate what otherwise is a simple calculation. For example:

1 Sales — these should be net sales, after discounts and bad debts have been taken into account.
2 Distribution costs are really part of the sales activity and may justifiably be deducted from sales revenue.
3 Inventory levels — production is often retained as finished goods when sales are below production. Accountants normally value this stock at sales value or cost of production, whichever is the lower. This may not reflect the possibility that selling the products may be some way off. All changes in inventory levels are important and should be part of the input–output equation.
4 Raw materials and work in progress are 'stock' and should be treated accordingly. (WIP has always been difficult to value, but normally a figure relating to a percentage of completed value is used.)
5 Capital — this is divided between 'fixed' and 'working' for the purpose of making an input–output measurement. Depreciation or some charge for using the capital is the usual way to ensure that it is embodied in a model. Fixed capital will include land and buildings as well as machinery or plant. Working capital will include stocks of all kinds, cash in the bank, accounts receivable, etc.

6   Labour — labour costs should include all salaries and wages paid plus all on-costs (pensions, national health insurance etc.).

7   Bought-in items — these should comprise all the items which the company has to pay outsiders to provide (including power, packaging, consumable stores of all kinds, insurance, telephone rentals, etc.).

8   Inflation — because inflation acts on both inputs and outputs, and on salaries and wages as well as capital replacement, there are many who say that it can be ignored. However, as inflation may be greater or less on imported raw materials than on products sold in the home market, a differential rate of inflation needs to be included.

Once such factors have been considered and any associated problems resolved, it is possible to provide a productivity model, based on inputs to the production system and outputs from it.

2.7   CONCLUSIONS

This fairly simple audit of production should help to indicate the following:

Where there are problems in production.
What weaknesses and strengths are obvious.
How effectively the production function has coped with pressures from inside and outside the company.
Whether production efficiency is rising or falling.
Whether the company is as efficient as its competitors.
Where changes in the production function's activities are needed.

However, while such indications may be invaluable in deciding how well production is run, the possibility exists that the problems and weaknesses which are discovered may not be solvable within the production framework. There may be overall company policies and strategies to which production management will — rightly — have to conform.

NOTE

1 B. W. Taylor and K. R. Davis, 'Corporate Productivity — getting it all together,' *Industrial Engineering*, March 1977.

3

Major environmental influences

3.1 INTRODUCTION

No factory can remain isolated from the national and local environments which impinge on it. There is no production unit which never has to take account of what goes on outside the factory gates.

In the last two decades, many organisations appear to have adapted, in some way, to external influences almost without conscious effort. A spate of government legislation may temporarily have overwhelmed them, but social and cultural changes seem to have been absorbed without the need for planning. Yet many companies have gone out of business; production efficiency has not, by any standard, improved at a satisfactory rate and any production manager will admit that his job is now immeasurably more difficult than it used to be.

In some ways the gradual unplanned absorption of external influences is the best way of changing to accommodate major environmental influences. However, the possible future effectiveness of this approach should be judged against the following factors:

1 The pace of change is increasing, particularly in social and cultural aspects. In the past, changes which occurred might have been accommodated without formal planning but as the whole process speeds up, will informality suffice?

2 Of all the influences external to a company, the technical one has generally been accepted as being the most important. This could have been due to the predominance in industry of trained engineers and technologists, professionally concerned with technical improvements. Industry tends not to employ people who are trained professionally to appreciate what could be even more important — social and cultural changes.

3   Many organisations now employ, even if in a rudimentary fashion, some form of profit planning. This process was originally designed with a financial bias, intended to ensure that planned profit, cash flow, sales revenue and costs were achieved. To allow an organisation to respond informally to important social and other changes is to throw away most of the benefits which profit planning should produce. The financial bias is not enough.

4   While some environmental analysis is carried out within profit planning, experience suggests that this is not often directly related to production planning and the way social change is affecting the shopfloor.

The production manager is not, as a rule, asked to provide 'organisational development' plans, related to the external environment.

5   The key to planning the production function lies in appreciating what changes in the external environment might occur. Consider the following for example:

Government wage policies
Trade union influences on wages policy, wage rates and systems of payment
Legislation on safety at work, employment protection and equal pay
Efforts by the EEC, the government and trade unions to effect 'participation'.

In some ways these are the tip of the iceberg and other social and cultural influences may have even more importance, particularly on work organisation, motivation and wage payment systems. Not to plan for them in as much detail as is necessary has obvious dangers.

3.2   THE FUTURE

It is surprising that so many writers on management and industry are prepared to state categorically what they expect to happen in the future. 'Futurology' is a growing profession attracting many people, even though their forecasts are so often wrong. In forecasting the future, however, several truths appear to be immutable. There will be a decline in the availability of all raw materials — particularly fossil fuels. At the same time there are rising expectations of all kinds in the Western world and increasing population in the developing world.

While production managers are unlikely to consider that they alone can solve such problems, they *must* recognise:

1   the discontinuities which will occur in plant technologies and production line effectiveness;
2   the need to use ever more effectively the resources which are available;
3   the changing objectives of the work force.

The following suggestions on possible environmental changes and their effects are intended as indications of general trends. Anyone who has attempted to forecast the future will be aware of the associated dangers.

(a)   Social and cultural change

Activity
   Increased violence
   Improvement in educational standards at all levels of society
   Enhanced expectations of employees in working and private lives
   Greater condemnation of organisations which spread pollution and damage to the environment
   Changes in the balance of power between employees and management
   Rise of white collar unions. Rising recruitment of white collar unions (ASTMS, TASS, etc) shows that white collar people recognise the need for group strength through union membership
   Breakdown in traditional values, such as 'deference' and 'loyalty'
   Decay of the work ethic
Impact
   Greater job mobility
   Decline in loyalty to one organisation
   Personnel will take many cues on discipline and work values from outside the organisation
   Demand by all employees for the same facilities as management
   Greater power of shop stewards and perhaps a desire to negotiate with senior rather than middle or junior management
   Loyalty of junior and even middle management and many white collar specialists is no longer solely to the company
   Ill discipline such as refusals to carry out legitimate requests
   Abdication of leadership/management role by many first line supervisors
   Low morale of such people
Possible solutions and contingency plans
   Organisational change of job redesign which will help to create a desire to work as a team
   Management style is likely to change from authoritarian towards co-operative
   Pollution control will be a key factor in production
   Greater stress on involvement and participation will be necessary
   Rate of technical change slowed down to match that of employees' expectations may be demanded
   Resource teams
   Workers educated in company problems
   New negotiating procedures
   Disciplinary problems will have a high priority in participative agreements

First line supervision to take part in and belong to autonomous work groups
Spread of 'supportive management'

(b)   *Government and trade unions*

Activity

Greater penetration of government into industry through legislation and investment aid
Trade union pressure on government to legislate on industry
Trade union pressure for membership of boards and other 'ownership' requests

Impact

Company must accept and implement legal obligations

Possible solution

Need to employ specialists in government legislation and its implementation
Need for training
Control systems to ensure conformity
Industrial pressure on government, to counter trade union power

(c)   *Technological change*

Activity

Continuation of rapid technological change of all kinds
Increasing use of computers
Enhanced size of companies
Greater fixed cost required

Impact

Difficulty of raising money to fund investment
Turbulence in production
Tasks within the organisation will need greater flexibility and technical competence
More specialists required

Possible solutions

More co-operation between organisations operating in the same industry
Closer co-operation with technical institutions and trade associations
Management of change will be principal training requirement for production managers
Introduction of rational problem solving
Flexible organisations

(d)   *National and international economics*

Activity

Inflation continuing at fairly high levels
Unemployment to remain high and perhaps increase

Decline in the availability of raw materials and higher prices
Less cheap power
Impact
Measuring performance through traditional accounting methods less important
Conventional methods of reducing labour probably redundant
High direct production costs
Possible solutions
Inflation accounting necessary
Investment directed towards providing:
   better working environment
   less pollution
   more interesting work
   better use of raw materials and power
Materials management and limited factor analysis required

3.3   DILEMMAS IN PRODUCTION MANAGEMENT

While not being an exhaustive list, the following serious dilemmas face production managers because of environmental influences:

1   The comparatively low status offered to production managers has led to low morale. At the same time it has prevented many good recruits from coming into production. Production management, for many people, is not an attractive occupation. Yet production is at the heart of the economy. Done well, the nation prospers. Done badly, the nation declines. Status will accrue to production managers who do their jobs well and let others know that the job is well done.

2   Breakthrough and control. A classification of types of people has used 'breakthrough' and 'control' as labels. Production managers often have to behave in a 'control' manner. The nature of their job and the short term objectives they have to achieve ensure that their time is largely spent on the day-to-day running of their factory. However, as this book suggests, serious and wide ranging changes have to be considered and introduced. These really need a breakthrough personality. Is it possible that one production manager can have both kinds of personality in sufficient quantity and quality? It certainly seems unlikely.

It may be necessary therefore, for a breakthrough personality to be seconded to the production function. This will raise all the problems of relationships between line and services people and between senior people with quite different personalities. The solution of this dilemma is crucial to ensuring progress and high future performance.

3   Innovation and insecurity. It is a truism that change is usually resisted in some way. Certainly change seems to bring insecurity and so will be resented and probably challenged. How change is introduced therefore, is extremely important.

4   Technology can be exploited at human cost. The introduction of new machinery is often based on the elimination of some of the work force as this is the only way it can be justified economically. If it is introduced on this basis there will be human problems. If, because of such problems, it is not introduced at all then it is certain that competitors — international and national — will introduce it, so there will be a competitive decline. In the long run it is the economic viability of the organisation which is really crucial. How can this be maintained by introducing new technologies without too much human cost?

5   Innovation and government legislation. The government legislation on employment protection and equal pay has in some ways restricted innovation. For example, if labour cannot be dispensed with easily how can new technologies, demanding lower manning levels, be introduced?

6   Balance of power. This is discussed more fully in Part IV, but it is clear that many production managers have the responsibility for obtaining results without the power.

3.4   ASPECTS OF CHANGE

While environmental influences are having a general effect on production, there are several aspects of the process which the production manager might need to consider in greater detail:

1 Automation

The word 'automation' has been around for a long time. It seems to have lived down its bogy image. However, it is still with us and its importance is growing. Automation is difficult to define as it has been considered to cover many different kinds of operation and activity. Initially it was used to describe purely automatic machines where something (occasionally highly complex) was done without the need for manual intervention. The term has become slightly debased, in that it is now used for activities where some manual intervention is necessary.

Production managers, when reviewing 'work organisation' might consider the following when automation is introduced:

(a)   people will become monitors, not workers in the physical sense. Their attention to dials and other controls will replace physical effort. Training is needed in this process;

(b) as fewer people could be involved in the process (with more automated machines to look after) there may be reduced social interaction;

(c) while some monitoring of the monitors may be necessary the traditional range of chargehands and foremen may not be appropriate;

(d) the process largely defines the quality of the product, so that this is no longer under the control of the operative. This in turn could lead to some disaffection;

(e) redundancies or labour deployment to other jobs will be necessary. To do this effectively needs well thought out plans.

2   Social responsibility

Many companies already have had to face severe tests of their social responsibility. For example drug manufacturing organisations are usually under social pressures of some kind, not just to supply drugs but to ensure that the drugs they make do not have undesirable side effects.

There is a serious ethical problem. Is it right to make profits (perhaps high profits) at the expense of environmental pollution and the public in general?

The overall problem may not be in the hands of production management but, even so, production people should have views on the possibilities of trading off high profit against environmental pollution.

3   Role of management

Managers have expected and accepted deference to their status. An office holder expected the power due to the office itself, irrespective of his own competence. While there may have been some withholding of deference, the status of the job was what mattered.

The considerable changes which have occurred in society and industry have produced a situation where deference to a job holder is no longer automatic. Deference, if given at all, falls to those who show positive and superior skills, which the less skilled can utilise.

Management, therefore, has to earn respect. It can no longer be expected as the right of a job holder. This has considerable influence on the role of production management, perhaps as follows:

(a) the skills of a production manager must be seen to provide the basis for holding down his job;

(b) skills must be demonstrated, not just in paperwork or planning, but in face to face contact with shop stewards, operatives and first line supervisors. It is increasingly necessary for production managers to demonstrate their ability where it matters — on the shopfloor, or at least in discussion with people who work there. The quiet office-bound production manager who manages solely by analysing control reports and production statistics may gradually become obsolete — if indeed he still exists.

4 Multi-disciplines

A production system can be analysed and its defects recorded and eventually corrected through the production framework. This approach requires a multi-disciplinary team. The behaviourist is no more important than the engineer or computer systems analyst. They have to work as one unit. How they are organised so that they can all use their specialism effectively will largely dictate the progress which is made. The accountant or operations researcher who believes he can go on largely working in happy isolation is a danger to himself and his organisation.

5 Objectives

What should the objectives of the production system be? High profit, job security, job enrichment, low costs, high output? Is it now possible to divorce management's objectives from those of employees and the nation or must they all be seen to be interdependent?

6 Management stress

Life in many production units can be extremely stressful. Partly this seems to stem from frustration. The game can be played but chances of winning often appear to be in doubt. Losing the game might cause dismissal. Promotion can increase stress and job workload, but owing to taxation the financial reward is rarely commensurate with the extra stress incurred. Production managers (like other managers) must learn to create situations that reduce stress, not by switching off or contracting out, but by trying to win only those battles which can be won. They must develop 'coping mechanisms'.

7 The computer chip and microprocessors

The silicon chip will have a major impact on industry in the next ten years, especially in low cost data processing. It is cheap. Probably the computing power which needed a roomful of equipment in the early 1960s can now be provided by a box of ten cubic inches. The cost of the same computing power is now approximately 100 times less and sinking all the time. Silicon chips in microprocessors mean that there is now a possibility of eliminating many dirty and boring jobs, such as repetitive machining. In some instances complex assembling without manual intervention is now a practical proposition.

It is likely that a whole range of skilled workers will be affected: draughtsmen, machine setters, toolmakers, etc. There are already indications that important structural changes in organisations and jobs will have to be made if full use is to be made of microprocessors.

While governments can provide capital to develop uses of microprocessors and even help to overcome some of the problems of introducing them, the production manager will eventually have to bear the brunt of the microprocessor explosion. Its effect on employment could provoke serious unrest through dislocation of jobs.

The view that unions will not allow fundamental changes to occur has to be seen against the likely introduction of microprocessors on a large scale in Japan and the USA. Competition will ensure that all countries will have to follow suit — or become non-competitive over a wide range of their industries.

Production managers will need to consider how structural changes in employment and skills generally can be made acceptable without massive dislocation.

So the forward thinking manager must take account of the following:

What analysis is required to ensure full understanding of the microprocessor revolution?

What links to government and industry, resources and equipment suppliers are needed to ensure that the company will benefit from current and future equipment and gain experience in using it?

What manufacturing planning process must be introduced to utilise microprocessors fully?

What manpower planning needs to be done to avoid changes which will create labour unrest?

What new investment will be required to make sure that the company remains competitive?

3.4   THE LAW AND THE PRODUCTION MANAGER

More and more government legislation covering industrial practices of all kinds is being introduced. Some of this is obviously necessary, if only to codify existing practices.

While production managers may bemoan what often seems like a torrent of government interference, the law has to be obeyed. Some of the legislation which has been introduced (and more might be introduced in the future) is complex. Shop stewards and trade union officials often know the legislation thoroughly. Production managers fully occupied in trying to run their factories might designate one of their staff to be the 'management lawyer' on appropriate legislation, to draw up check lists and other means of ensuring that production management applies government enactments.

Current legislation

In the last few years, production managers have needed to contend with all the following in the UK:

> Disabled Persons Acts 1944 and 1958
> Factories Act 1961
> Industrial Training Act 1964
> Race Relations Acts 1965 and 1968
> Redundancy Payments Act 1965
> Equal Pay Act 1970
> Industrial Relations Act 1971
> Contracts of Employment Act 1972
> Employment and Training Act 1973
> Social Security Act 1973
> Health and Safety at Work Act 1974
> Trade Union and Labour Relations Act 1974
> Employment Protection Act 1975
> Social Security Pensions Act 1975
> Sex Discrimination Act 1975
> Employment Protection (Consolidation) Act 1978

3.5 PLANNING FOR ADAPTATION TO ENVIRONMENTAL CHANGE

A cardinal part of the manufacturing plan should be concerned with planning adaptation to environmental change. Mainly these might be contingency plans which can be re-edited from time to time. Training can be started, new job descriptions written and proposed procedures recorded. The application can then be activated as and when the appropriate conditions arise.

The following is a brief contingency plan of the type envisaged:

CONTINGENCY PLAN NO 7

Planning for environmental change   Date: 1.7.79

TITLE: WORK GROUP CHANGES

1 Environmental influence

Changes occurring in the educational, social and cultural life of the nation are producing a greater demand for jobs with an increased thinking content. While technological changes may eliminate many of the more mundane and routine jobs, there will still be some left which are hard and comparatively dirty. Various industrial psychologists have encouraged a belief that 'enrichment' of jobs is a possibility and should be actively pursued, if the full potential of the workforce is to be achieved.

The possibility of enriching a single job in our kind of manufacturing process is limited. If greater opportunities for self-fulfilment are to be offered to the shopfloor, they will probably be best achieved through the formation of small working groups with local autonomy. Job interchange and greater authority for the group over aspects of quality, or even output, is to be considered desirable.

Autonomous work groups have been tried in numerous organisations mostly with some success. It is recommended that such work groups be explored and, if there is agreement with unions, introduced on a trial basis in part of the pressing shop.

2 Strategy

The industrial strategy recommended, therefore, is the establishment of work groups with limited autonomy based largely on our current 'section organisation'. First line supervisors can play a supportive role to aid the work group to achieve agreed objectives. 'Supportive management' is defined as the aiding of employees of a lower status to perform their jobs more effectively.

3 Plan

(a) Work organisation

Work organisation will be established and based on current sections. The responsibility given to these groups will include:
   job rotation;
   wage payment (how the total payment is to be shared);
   quality of products;
   the production of certain control information required for management accounting purposes.
Responsibility for final plan — Production Manager

(b) Measurement of the work organisation

·Input–output statements will be used.
Agreement is needed on the format of these and the measurement needed.
'Output' will be credited at standard cost — this will need to be confirmed with group members.
Responsibility for measurement — Cost Accountant plus Work Study Manager

(c) Training

 (i) Training for supportive management;
 (ii) Role of first line supervisors;
(iii) Work Group Training.
Suitable training programmes for each of these activities are required.

Introduction would be 3 to 6 months before work groups are established.
Responsibility — Training Officer/Personnel Officer

(d) Wage payment
Wage payment will be based on the difference between inputs and outputs of the group as a ratio of wages paid.

It should also be based on agreed work measurement and job evaluation. Systems should be specified in detail, ready for implementation, as soon as possible. Monitoring of wage performance on this basis should begin immediately.
Responsibility — Work Study, Personnel and Wages Office Managers

(e) Trade union negotiations
The timescale for recording the proposals and gaining agreement is thought to be six months prior to date of intended implementation.

A trial period would have advantages and this should be negotiated if possible. Initially it is intended to operate the scheme on one production line only. This too needs to be negotiated. Choice of the line must be a management prerogative.
Responsibility — Personnel Officer/Production Manager

(f) Production control
Required amendments to the production planning and scheduling activity need to be discussed and agreed.
Responsibility — Production Controller

(g) Other functions
Service functions — maintenance, production planning etc. — may also demand similar work group structures. This possibility needs to be discussed with the managers of all service departments.
Responsibility — Personnel Officer. To co-ordinate discussion and help prepare appropriate contingency plans.

(h) Physical measurements of inputs
Some change in the physical measurements of inputs may be necessary in order to ensure accurate control.
Responsibility — Production Manager

(i) Objectives of the new work groups
Objectives of the work groups should be discussed with them. They should be established to ensure that corporate strategy — or tactics — is not disregarded.
Responsibility — Production Manager/Personnel Manager

4   Action Plans

Action plans will be prepared by each of the nominated personnel and be available by 1.9.79.

These should be updated at six-monthly intervals following discussions with members of the Board.

PART III

Production Resource Planning and Control Systems

4

The internal environment

4.1 INTRODUCTION

The internal factory environment in the UK has been subjected to considerable government legislation, notably the Factories Act of 1961 and the Health and Safety at Work Act of 1974. This latter Act imposes severe penalties for non-compliance including imprisonment for managers who do not conform.

'Internal environments' therefore should be treated carefully, though in considering them there is much that is only the application of common sense and working practices which any good employer should introduce.

4.2 THE LEGISLATION

The principal piece of legislation which covers health and safety (i.e. the Act of 1974) is an enabling Act, which does not go into minute detail. It gives power to the Secretary of State for Employment to draw up regulations and codes of practice on any health and safety matters. It is likely therefore that health and safety provisions will flow fairly freely from the Act.

It does not invalidate any previous legislation such as:

The Offices, Shops and Railway Premises Act 1963
The Factories Act 1961
Fire Services Act 1947
Building Act 1959
Fire Act 1959
Public Health Act 1961
Fire Precaution Act 1971
Clean Air Act 1956
Mines and Quarries Act 1954

The Act imposes new general duties on employers:

1   To establish the maintenance of plant and associated methods of work which are safe and carry no risks to health.
2   To provide appropriate information, instruction, training and supervision which as far as possible will ensure the health and safety of employees.
3   To consult employees on matters of health and safety. At the request of elected or appointed trade union officials, to establish safety committees.
4   To prepare written statements on safety policy.
5   Workers' safety representatives have to be given facilities to carry out inspections of work areas on a quarterly basis at least. They will be allowed to visit a machine or activity where a notifiable accident has taken place. They will be allowed to look at any document or record relating to health and safety kept in the company.
6   Organisations have a responsibility to inform the public about any potential hazards to health and safety.
7   Premises as well as machines must be safe.
8   Premises of a prescribed class must use the best possible means of preventing emission of toxic fumes and waste.
9   Designers of plant, machinery and premises must take account of the Act and provide safe equipment etc.
10 Expenses incurred under the Act must be borne by employers, not employees.

The Act unified various inspectorates (i.e. factories, quarries, mines, etc.) into the Health and Safety Executive Inspectorate (HSE).

The Act identifies 15 criminal offences. These range from the contravention of any regulation to a failure to take action when an inspector has served an improvement notice on the employer.

Appeals against improvement orders and prohibition orders (i.e. where it is deemed that an activity or operation should stop immediately) can only be made to an industrial tribunal. The penalty for non-compliance with the Act could be a fine of £400 for each offence in a magistrate's court or, in a higher court, a term of imprisonment coupled with an unlimited fine.

Besides legislation, a number of detailed codes of practice have been produced. It is often these that inspectors attempt to see implemented.

Apart from the Health and Safety at Work Act there are other key pieces of legislation. The Factories Act of 1961 lays down regulations covering the guarding of machinery, removal of dust, and the provision of lighting, heating, fire escapes, washing and toilet facilities etc., as well as various safety measures. The Offices, Shops and Railway Premises Act 1963, covers the working conditions in offices etc.

4.3 SAFETY POLICY

One of the most useful ways of ensuring that government legislation is introduced effectively is to state a safety policy, in leaflet or booklet form issued to everyone in the organisation. Even comparatively small production units need this approach if compliance to legislation is to be assured.

The booklet might comprise the following:

1 Introduction

A statement which sets out that the company and the company management is responsible for safety, especially for injury prevention, the promotion of occupational hygiene, fire prevention and fire control, the control of situations likely to cause damage to property and plant and the thorough investigation of all accidents which do occur.

If a safety officer is employed then his place in the management team should be stated. His role should be recorded, particularly in his responsibility for monitoring the safety policy.

2 Safety organisation

The Health and Safety at Work Act stipulates that safety committees must be established where safety is discussed formally. The committee should recommend action which improves safety. The role of the chairman will be important and should be carefully recorded.

How the committee's and the safety officer's roles can be mutually supportive should be settled within the organisation.

3 Safety training

Safety training should be an integral part of normal company training. No one should be employed in operating any machinery or equipment where unsafe acts are possible without being trained in all the safety aspects. The hazards and precautions needed to be taken should be stressed.

Management training too needs to be effective.

4 Management procedures

The major management procedures which need to be set out will include:

Plant inspections. All plant which needs compulsory inspection should be listed.

The various plant and equipment with mechanical and electrical devices should also be recorded.

5   Safety operating procedures

The procedures which should be recorded will include 'permits to work' listing personnel who can operate certain machinery or undertake safety routines on it.

Codes of practice

These will normally be concerned with industry practice, e.g. in the Rubber Manufacturing Industry.

Accident investigations

All accidents should be followed by a rigorous investigation as to their cause followed by recommendations for their prevention in future. The procedure for this should be standard.

6   Hazard control

This heading might cover factory housekeeping, plant and machine hazards and personal protection.

Good housekeeping routines and what is expected from employees in this respect should be recorded.

The machine hazards will often be covered by law. This law might be considered the minimum in hazard control — for example in putting guards on machines.

Personal protection will include clothing and safety shoes.

7   Health and hygiene

The provision of health services might be recorded. This will include first aid and perhaps a well established surgery with a medical practitioner in attendance.

Other factors which could be included might be the problem of noise and how it can be suppressed. In some factories the handling of toxic materials may be a problem and how these are to be handled should be laid down.

8   Fire prevention and control

Three factors need to be recorded in the policy document. Fire prevention, detection and evacuation procedures should be stated. Fire fighting and fire prevention training should form a major part of the appropriate policy.

9   General

Under this heading: how visitors to the plant are to be treated or contractors' personnel when employed inside the plant.

4.3.1 Safety of individual machines or equipment

While general and perhaps wide ranging policy statements need to be made which cover all the plant and its operation, it is vital that major pieces of plant or equipment have their own safety codes. For example, the ubiquitous forklift truck might have some of the following safety factors recorded in a safety and maintenance handbook for the use of operatives:

1. Who can use trucks. Normally only fully trained operatives who have undergone a requisite course should be allowed to drive a truck.
2. Starting checks — on brakes, battery, tyres, horn and all controls — should be carried out at the beginning of each shift, to a strict routine. Faulty parts must be replaced immediately if they constitute a hazard.
3. A properly trained mechanic should carry out parts replacement and general maintenance.
4. Loading of trucks. Weight and type of material being lifted and carried, the position of the load, should all be supplied.
5. Method of driving the truck should be stipulated carefully, e.g. speeds, when to hoot, avoidance of jerky progress, sharp turns, etc. No overtaking should be allowed. When parked, the brake must always be applied and controls set in neutral.
6. The conditions under which the use of the truck might be hazardous should be stated, e.g. in wet weather when used out of doors, on oily surfaces, etc. State where the truck is to be used.
7. Parking in front of fire exits or where the truck will be a hazard should be forbidden.
8. No passengers should be carried on the truck.
9. No alterations or additions to the truck should be made without contacting the suppliers.
10. Lifting and towing procedures should be carefully laid down.
11. General maintenance should be regular and carefully carried out by trained personnel. A maintenance manual should cover each vehicle.

Suppliers of equipment (e.g. Lansing Bagnall in the case of forklift trucks) will usually supply a safety and maintenance handbook. Occasionally this will need supplementing. It should form part of the operative training programme.

4.4 THE WORKING ENVIRONMENT

4.4.1 Ventilation and air pollution

The possibility of air pollution in a factory environment has been enhanced with the introduction of new technologies.

The Factories Act states only that adequate ventilation of work rooms must be secured by the circulation of fresh air. All practicable measures, it is stated, must be taken to protect workers against the inhalation of dust, fumes and other composites likely to be injurious or offensive. Local exhaust ventilation must be provided and maintained where practicable.

Government inspectors lay down maximum amounts of pollution in the atmosphere. These are threshold limit values (or TLVs).

1   Pollution

The main causes of air pollution are:

Oil mists (the TLV is fixed at 5 milligrams per cubic metre of atmosphere)
Dust
Fumes and gases of various kinds.

Oil mists arise from the use of cutting oils which vaporise during use. Any factory that uses automatic lathes, drills, grinders, honers, broachers, etc. will have some oil mist pollution unless adequate control has been introduced. The high speed of automatic lathes seems the most dangerous source of such pollution.

The total elimination of oil mist pollution would mean the full enclosure of a lathe or other machine with no exhaustion of air to the general factory environment. This is obviously impractical and, normally, splash guarding is used to prevent the most serious emissions. Self-cleaning air filtration units are being introduced in most modern factories where oil mist presents a hazard.

Dust is generally defined as particulate matter in sizes of 1 to 100 microns. The finer the dust the more hazardous it is likely to be. The smallest dust speck to be seen with normal eyesight is of 50 microns.

There are various regulations covering quarry dust and the use of asbestos. The Asbestos Regulations of 1969 for example state that immediately an emission of dust is made it must be extracted.

Prevention of dust is often achieved by suppression, through the use of wet manufacturing processes instead of dry ones. Total enclosure of dust producing areas, where operatives can wear masks is also a possibility.

Fumes and gases are also potential polluters of the factory environment. Lead fumes produced during smelting and burning are a well known hazard. Various fairly common factory activities produce fume hazards — for example welding, and degreasing with trichloroethylene.

Separation of fume producing processes into areas which can be sealed off and have extra ventilation is perhaps the only practical way of reducing if not eliminating fume hazards.

2   Ventilation

Ventilation is necessary even where fume and dust hazards are minimal, if they exist at all. Ventilation implies that fresh air will constantly replace stale air and at the same time remove contaminants in the stale air.

The Institute of Heating and Ventilating Engineers in its *Guide to Current Practice, 1965* recommends that air changes of between $1\frac{2}{3}$ and $3\frac{3}{4}$ per hour should be installed depending upon the height of the factory roof. If no mechanical ventilation is installed, there should be five square feet of openable windows either on walls or in the roof for every 100 square feet of floor space.

The air changes should be adjusted for winter and summer external temperatures.

Natural ventilation is often impossible and an electro-mechanical system is then used. For some plants in city locations, air conditioning may be necessary; otherwise a recirculation system may be better.

Adequate air filters will usually form part of the ventilation system. There are various types available and their use will depend upon the degree of air cleanliness required:

Dry filters — these depend upon a screening action produced by very small openings in the filter through which the air passes.

Filter banks — formed by fixing individual cells or frames together.

Viscous impingement filters

Automatic self cleaning filter units

Electric filters — either ionising or charged media types.

Air washers, though not used primarily as filters, are often introduced into the ventilation system.

3   Humidity

In designing a ventilation system, humidity should be planned not to fall below 40 per cent or exceed 80 per cent in either winter or summer. Ventilation causes heat loss and this should be taken into account in designing a system. Factories with windows facing south or south west are most likely to need good ventilation.

Warming air from 0°C to 22°C increases the air's capacity to hold moisture fourfold. Employees who feel cold at temperatures of 22°C are most likely suffering from heat loss due to evaporation.

To provide an environment which is satisfactory from heat and general ambience viewpoints may need some mechanism which changes the humidity. (Humidity refers to the general moisture in the air. Absolute humidity is the weight of water vapour contained in a predetermined volume of dry air.) The general level of humidity best suited to provide a stimulating environment will be about 55 per cent.

4 Decreasing temperatures

An optimum working temperature is around 17°C. In a badly ventilated factory, where machines or processes give off considerable heat, temperature could rise to 30°C. In summer it might well be 33°C or 34°C. From every $15\frac{1}{2}$ square feet of glass the sun can produce as much heat as a 1kw electric fire.

It has been calculated that at 30°C a workforce is 20 per cent less productive than at 17°C. The chances of having an accident also rise with rising temperature.

A key part of any ventilation system, therefore, may be concerned with keeping temperatures at reasonable levels.

4.4.2 Lighting

The Factories Act of 1961 states that there must be suitable lighting in every part of the factory where people are working or passing. The minimum lighting level is laid down as 6 LX/sq ft (60 Lux) (i.e. lumens per square foot for which Lux is the metric equivalent).

The Illuminating Engineering Society recommends a general level of 40 LX/sq ft (400 Lux) with washrooms, lavatories, warehouses, stairs and lifts at 150 Lux.

1 Natural light

Natural light is thought to be superior to that produced artificially. Factory design, location and layout will play a big part in deciding how much artificial light is needed and in what areas.

2 Light measurement

Light meters cost about £30. Production managers might each have one.

3 The need for illumination

The quantity of light needed will be determined by three factors:

The tasks being performed. Generally the higher the degree of accuracy of the task, the higher the illumination needed.

The factory environment. Dark, dingy walls with few windows, and low windowless ceilings will demand more extra light than factories which are naturally well lit.

The age of operatives. Older operatives need higher quantities of light than younger people.

Illumination standards should be corrected to compensate for dirt and deterioration in lamps. A factor of 1.75 should be used for this purpose.

4 The quality of light

Quality of lighting is as important in many instances as quantity. For example if the available light produces glare and considerable reflection, it will have adverse effects. Quality of light will depend upon glare, contrast, diffusion, direction, colour and brightness.

Glare can be reduced by providing a lighting system which does not produce shadows but gives even distribution. Shiny surfaces should be avoided if possible. Many small lighting fittings will tend to provide more glare than fewer larger fittings. Light fittings with a lowered or prismatic base and opaque or semi-opaque side panels directing most of the light to a ceiling will produce the least glare.

Glare from outside the building may be a problem.

5 Lighting systems

Most systems will be a mixture of natural light, general artificial lighting and supplementary lighting.

In single story buildings the window area should be at least 30 per cent of the floor area if possible.

Artificial light should be of good colour, free from flickering, heat, fumes, and reliable and safe.

General lighting is usually fixed at about ten or twelve feet above working height and is often fluorescent, with either lowered fixtures or some other means of ensuring a good quality light with little glare.

Low-loaded ranges of fluorescent lamps should be investigated to minimise lighting cost (though with lower lighting quality).

The problem with fluorescent lighting is that to be economic it should not suffer from repeated switchings on and off. Once on, such lighting needs to be left for half an hour or more.

The lighting system should not inhibit the relocation of stores or machines. Generalised lighting should be established with this in mind.

Filament lamps suffer from high cost per Lux produced and often the shading used is not as effective as fluorescent lighting in reducing glare.

Areas of light should overlap, so preventing shadows and giving uniformity of illumination.

Lighting units can be:

Direct — these project light downwards and are usually shielded by plastic louvres.

Indirect — these send light onto the ceiling so minimising glare and harsh illumination.

Semi-indirect — 60–90 per cent of total illumination is directed to the ceiling.

General diffuse — these shine light equally upwards and downwards. Glare and shadow may be troublesome.

Semi-direct — most of the illumination is directed downwards.

Generally the more direct the illumination the more likely there will be shadows and glare. While in many production activities this may not be significant it can be tiring and sometimes causes much fatigue.

Two lighting installations may be required — one for daylight and another for hours of darkness.

The following might be a useful method of determining what lighting system is required.

(a)   Analyse the production operation being carried out and determine the level of illumination required. Type of operation, age of personnel, condition of building will all need to be taken into account.

(b)   Select the lighting system which provides glare-free but effective lighting.

(c)   Consider the economies of the system in terms of:
      Maintenance
      Independent switching
      Failure of main source of power
      Use of sunlight.

(d)   Determine the coefficient of illumination, i.e. the ratio of illumination that will reach the required operation with that emitted by the system.

(e)   Calculate the number of luminaires or lamps required.

(f)   Determine their locations.

6   Reducing lighting costs

According to the Lighting Industries Federation, lighting accounts for about 15 per cent of all electricity costs used in industry.

Localised rather than overall lighting will have immediate advantages if there are periods when only parts of the plant are in use. Block or area switching will be useful.

Regular cleaning of lighting fittings is essential, perhaps every six months.

Painting the production area in light colours is advantageous.

Full use of outside and natural lighting should be made. Windows should be kept clean.

Existing lighting systems should be kept under review and replaced when necessary.

At the end of its useful life a fluorescent lamp will probably be giving 10 to 15 per cent less light than when it was new. There seems a case to be made for lamp replacement at regular intervals, rather than when they stop functioning. Planned replacement is recommended.

4.4.3   Heating and energy usage

What constitutes a reasonable temperature to work in is as much in dispute for manual workers as for office personnel.

The Factories Act states that in each workplace, where most work done is either at a bench or sitting down, the temperature should be at least 16°C after the first hour. The Woodwork Regulations state that the temperature should be at least 13°C.

Heating cannot really be discussed without considering ventilation. The two very often go hand in hand.

The design of heating systems should begin by considering two factors:

Heat gains and how these can be utilised in the overall system. Gains will come from external sources and internal machinery.

Heat losses due to conduction through walls, roofs and windows. Ventilation too will cause losses.

1   Types of system

The site of the factory will often be crucial in designing the system. Minimum (absolute) mean and maximum temperatures should be known. Wind direction and velocity will also be important. The amounts of solar heating should also be taken into account.

All heating systems will comprise three elements:

A heat source. This may be anything from a Lancashire boiler to independent local heaters run by electricity;

A heat distribution system. The longer the transfer system the more important the prevention of heat losses becomes;

A heat dissemination system. This could be a series of convectors, radiators, or grills in a hot air system placed in the areas where heat is needed.

Hot water or steam systems have predominated in most factory heating systems though hot air systems come a close second. Hot water systems normally have an inbuilt 'extra' capacity of approximately 25 per cent to cope with severe climatic conditions. No other system has this inbuilt capacity.

Central and unit systems need to be considered. In the former one main central heat-generating unit is supplied, e.g. a steam boiler. Unit systems can be operated independently and therefore have greater flexibility. There is a chance however that their control will be more difficult than a central unit's.

Usually heating and ventilation systems are designed as one unit.

From time to time gas-, oil- or coal-fired boilers have each proved to be the most economical. Likely energy trends in the future need to be considered in deciding which energy source will prove to be least costly over the life of the heating system. It may be advantageous to attempt multi-fuel systems, where switching from one fuel to another is a possibility.

There is clearly no one best heating system which can be recommended but the following might be considered:

(a)   Boilers have an efficiency of 65 per cent or more but this sinks rapidly if correct maintenance is not carried out at stipulated intervals.

(b)   Control over heat losses is nearly as important as providing heat. The two should be seen as part of the energy use/cost calculation.

(c)   Heating has to have a certain flexibility. For example fairly rapid heating before the start of a shift may be necessary.

(d)   Factory organisation — the type of shift systems worked, and the siting of machines and process plant may have a crucial influence on the need for heating.

(e)   Maintenance may be a problem and the system should be designed to minimise it.

2   Heat/energy conservation

It seems certain that future energy costs will continue to rise unless some unforeseen energy source is discovered. Conservation of energy will become progressively more important. The following comments are made to help in establishing a heat/energy conservation plan.

(a)   Improve the building structure by providing more insulation — in the roof, on the walls, possibly the windows.

(b)   Repair or improve the building generally. Eliminate draughts for example. Provide self-closing doors. Keep entrances and exits to the minimum required by the Factories Act.

(c)   Install efficient thermostats which will control unit heating apparatus. Ensure that they are well maintained and set correctly.

(d)   Localise air extraction (ventilation) to suit local conditions.

(e)   Recover heat where possible and re-use within the system.

(f)   Insulation of steam and water pipes and hot air ducts is essential.

(g)   Boilers may need to be replaced well before their actual life is finished if maximum energy conservation is to be achieved.

(h)   Idle equipment and lighting should always be turned off.

(i)   Factory scheduling in shift working and machine usage should have energy conservation in mind.

(j)   Leaks in the system could cause considerable loss and should be repaired as soon as possible.

(k)   It may be possible to use waste products and other waste as fuel.

4.4.4   Noise

Surveys made by the UK Factory Inspectorate in 1971 and again in 1973/4 suggested that more than one million workers are exposed to excessive noise for some part of their working day. Noise is recognised as a prime health hazard and cause of fatigue.

Acceptable levels of noise are difficult to determine. Noise is measured in decibels or phons. A decibel is a measurement on a logarithmic scale designed to measure the pressure of sound waves. On the decibel/logarithmic scale, up to forty-five decibels is considered normal. Excessive noise can begin for most people at seventy decibels, and beyond ninety (common in some factories) serious hearing deficiencies can result from mere months of exposure. Beyond 100 decibels is considered to be a point where extensive and permanent damage to hearing can occur. A code of practice published by the Department of Employment giving guidelines to factory inspectors states that ninety decibels is a permissible limit. (This is for continuous sound.) Where noise fluctuates (and this may be even more deleterious) new limits need to be calculated.

An approach to considering noise and its suppression might be:

1   Identify areas, activities or machines which appear to make excessive noise. Measurements in decibels are required.

2   Can these machines be noise suppressed in any way, for example by:
    Silencing machine exhausts
    Enclosing machines in sound proofed covers
    Better maintenance
    Redesign of equipment.

3   If suppression is not possible can noisy machines or processes be isolated?

4   If neither 2 nor 3 is possible are operatives provided with ear protectors — plugs, valves or muffs?

5   Can jobs in noisy areas be rotated so that for part of the time employees work in non-noisy areas?

6   Can rest rooms be separated from noisy areas?

7 When new equipment is purchased or leased is noise taken into account?

8 Are local engineers trained to measure noise and as far as possible eliminate it?

9 Employees who are subjected to high noise levels need audiometric tests carried out at fairly frequent intervals.

4.4.5   Fire

1 The 1971 Fire Precautions Act states that fire certificates are needed in industrial premises in the UK wherever highly flammable substances or liquids are used and stored or where more than twenty people are employed (ten if they work above ground level).

2 The local fire authorities normally will determine fire escape needs, their type and location and the escape routes from places of work to exits.

3 The fire certificate will also state how the building is to be used, the restrictions on use and the number of people to be employed in it. Occupiers must inform the local fire authorities of any change in the structure and use of the building. In high risk production activities the factory will be inspected by the factory inspector.

4 Doors in occupied rooms must remain unlocked. Doors leading to escape stairways and corridors must open outwards.

5 Wherever highly flammable liquids and/or liquefied petroleum gases are in use in premises covered by the Factories Act, the Liquefied Petroleum Gases Regulations apply. These state that all highly flammable liquids should be stored either outside the factory or in special storerooms in appropriate containers. Only a minimum of such liquids should be used on the shopfloor at one time. Strict smoking regulations should apply where flammable liquids are stored and used. Notices marking highly flammable areas have to be in use.

6 Fire exits have to be marked and kept free from obstruction. In areas which have a fire risk, there must be more than one exit. In multi-story buildings there must be at least two staircases. Working areas must be closed off from them by fireproof doors.

7 Employers must make sure that their employees know what action to take in case of fire. The fire alarm must be audible in all parts of the factory and tested every three months.

8 Suitable fire fighting equipment must be available and ready for use. 'Suitability' will depend upon the potential fire hazard — i.e. water, foam etc.

9 Hoistways and liftways in side buildings, built after June 1938, must be completely enclosed with fire resisting materials. Access to them must be through fire resistant doors, except where the hoist is unvented (when material enclosing the hoist must be easily broken).

4.4.6 Factory amenities

Slowly the standards of amenities provided in factories are rising. Seating, cloakrooms, restrooms, lavatories, changing rooms and washrooms are all being enhanced. The one-time gap between office and factory employees is closing quickly. People who work in adverse environments should surely have amenities equal if not superior to those who work in reasonably pleasant surroundings.

1 Seating

The Factories Act states that sitting facilities must be provided where this is not detrimental to the work being performed. Seats should be of a suitable design, with foot rests if these are necessary for comfort.

2 Cloakrooms, changing rooms and showers

A statutory obligation on employers is to provide space for clothing not worn during working hours and also an area for drying wet clothes.

While the Act states that 'adequate' provision is necessary for such facilities it is likely that:

separate lockers,
provision for drying clothes in a specially constructed unit,
adequate space and facilities to change clothing,
high standard of cleanliness,
adequate lighting and ventilation,
precautions against theft and
showers or baths

will be needed if an employer is to provide reasonable facilities.

3 Lavatories and washrooms

Section 7 of the Factories Act, the Offices, Shops and Railway Premises Act and various other regulations lay down legal requirements for lavatories and washrooms.

For example, where women are employed there must be one toilet for every twenty-five employees.

Every lavatory must be ventilated, under cover, and have properly locking doors. The lavatories must be easily accessible to everyone who works in the factory.

A supply of clean running hot and cold water must be supplied as well as soap, clean towels and other means of cleaning or drying. The factory inspectorate recommends that one washbasin should be supplied for thirty workers.

The regulations do not appear to be at all generous in laying down provision for lavatories and washrooms and good employers might like to consider two washbasins for every twenty workers and an appropriate increase in lavatory facilities, say one for every twenty people.

Drinking water, says the Act, must be wholesome with an upward jet convenient for drinking or suitable drinking vessels with suitable facilities for rinsing them.

4   First aid

First aid boxes or cupboards of prescribed standard must be provided. An additional box is required for each extra 150 people. The boxes must be placed under the charge of a competent person. If more than fifty people are employed, this person must always be ready, during working hours, to carry out first aid.

4.4.7   Clothing and safety equipment

Protective clothing should include overalls, safety shoes, gloves, aprons. Equipment covers ear plugs and muffs, helmets, goggles, flameproof clothing and respirators.

While it is not a legal requirement for employers to supply overalls or safety footwear, most good employers now do so. (In some industries — asbestos for example — it is compulsory.)

It has been found that the best way to achieve proper protection is to have three sets of overalls which are changed at least once a week and are dry cleaned (not wet washed).

Some 14 per cent of all accidents happen to toes or feet and approximately three million working days are lost each year as a result. The TUC estimate that only 20 per cent of all workers in the UK wear safety footwear and that 90 per cent of that worn is bought privately, though many employers provided some kind of subsidised scheme. [1]

There are many reasons for skin disease and skin trouble causes approximately 900,000 lost working days per year. The results of skin contamination range from dermatitis to skin cancer. Hands are only one of the parts to be affected but they are a main factor. Gloves and appropriate barriers and cleansing creams are essential where substances which remove natural oils (like turpentine or petrol/chemical irritants like acids or alkalis or mineral oils) come into contact with the skin.

Eye protection is legally enforceable in some industries — grinding, some building operations, chemical and cement works, foundries and welding.

Goggles or glasses or some other eye protection shields must be provided free by employers.

Where dust is a great hazard, as in the asbestos industry, respirators must be provided. If blue asbestos is being used only air-line breathing apparatus will give the protection needed.

Other types include:

Canister respirator. The canister contains absorbent chemicals which remove atmospheric pollution. The absorbent material is quickly exhausted and must be correct for the pollution being excluded.

Filter respirator. The filter traps dust particles which endanger health. The respirator covers the mouth and nose and is known colloquially as a 'pig's snout'.

Cartridge respirator. The cartridge absorbs gases and vapours.

Positive-pressure powered respirator. This works by having air driven through a filter to the face mask by a battery powered air blower.

4.5   GENERAL SAFETY PROCEDURES

1   The Factories Act is specific about general safety procedures, particularly guarding and fencing. Every part of transmission machinery and every dangerous part of other machinery and all parts of electric generators, motors, rotary converters, and flywheels directly connected to them must be securely fenced.

Methods of machine guarding:

Fixed guards will prevent contact between the operation and the operator's body, no matter what operation is carried on.

Interlocking guards should ensure that openings to machines are closed automatically while the machine is operating.

Trip guards which automatically drop into place if there is a likelihood that a machine operator will be injured.

Automatic guards. These are usually operated by photo-electric cells during a machine's operational cycle.

One of the greatest dangers exists when either management or operatives ignore machine guarding in order to gain high output and good operative earnings.

2   Cranes and lifting gear are also subject to rigorous government legislation.

A register of all chains etc. is required and appropriate test certificates must be kept.

All parts and working gear of cranes, hoists, lifts, chains, ropes and lifting tackle must not be used unless of good (mechanical) construction, sound material and adequate strength. Hoists, lifts, chains, ropes and lifting tackle must be examined by a competent person every six months. A thorough examination of cranes must be made every fourteen months.

The equipment must not be used for any load exceeding its stated safe working load, which must be shown on the crane, hoist or lift.

3   Floors, steps, stairs, passages and gangways must be soundly constructed, properly maintained and so far as reasonably practicable kept free from obstruction and any substance likely to cause people to slip. Where wet processes are carried on, adequate means for draining the floor must be provided.

4   Cleaning and maintenance of machinery can be particularly hazardous. Many accidents happen when machinery which is stopped for maintenance is suddenly started by someone who is unaware that a maintenance man is in a position of danger.

A 'permit to work' that specifies how a machine due for maintenance has to be isolated before work commences is essential. The same applies to erecting scaffolding, locking off steam pipes or the provision of temporary machine guards.

'Young people and women must not clean a prime mover or transmission machinery when it is motion, or any machine if there is a danger when it is moving.'

5   Welding is another potentially dangerous activity because of burns and the hazard of fumes and gases. 'Eye-flash' can occur if appropriate shields are not used. Excessive exposure to ultraviolet radiation may cause burning of the skin.

6   Overcrowding is forbidden by law. Each worker must have a minimum of 400 cubic feet of space.

4.6   HOUSEKEEPING

Factories, declares the Factories Act, must be kept clean. Accumulations of dirt and refuse must be removed daily from floors and benches. The floors of every production area must be cleaned at least once a week, inside walls, partitions and ceilings washed every fourteen months if they have a smooth impervious surface or painted at seven year intervals or less (and also be washed every fourteen months) or colour washed every fourteen months.

1   Cleaning policies

Cleaning policies turn round two subjects:

How to clean
Equipment to be used

(When to clean is stated in the Factories Act.)
'How to clean' might start with deciding whether to use one's own or contract cleaners. The latter have cleaned offices for many years and seem to be making inroads into factories. The advantages of using contract cleaners appear to be:

They have cleaning expertise.
They can purchase cleaning materials more cheaply than would a small factory, owing to bulk purchasing.
The bill is easily budgeted.

Cleaning equipment continually becomes more complex. Industrial vacuum cleaners now have both back-pack types and powered floor sweepers. The former can be used to clean girders and other parts of the factory structure as well as lighting and heating arrangements.
Most powered vacuum cleaners are battery operated and many can handle a variety of graphite and flaky materials, and can operate on irregular surfaces.
A variety of neutralising detergents are on the market to help in the cleaning of toxic wastes of all kinds.

2   A housekeeping check list

The Health and Safety at Work Act provides the framework for good housekeeping. It may be useful to have a check list which covers all factors associated with health, safety and housekeeping. The following might be extended to suit local conditions:

Cleaning
Do we know the regulations?
When did we last paint the factory?
Do we accumulate dirt and waste for excessive periods before it is removed?
What cleaning policy do we have?
Is it effective?

Heating
Are temperatures maintained at prescribed levels?
Could the heating system be improved — to make it more effective
                                                        to make it more economic?

Ventilation
Is there appropriate ventilation without the need to open windows?
Does the extractor system eliminate polluting emissions from the production process?
Does the ventilation system provide sufficient air changes?

Lighting
Is the lighting sufficient for tasks being performed, age of employees and condition of factory?
Is the quality of light appropriate?

Toilets and washing facilities
Are sufficient provided as per the Factories Act?

Noise
Does the noise level in the factory comply with the accepted code of practice?
Are we attempting to reduce noise levels — if so how?

Accidents
Are all accidents recorded and reported to the Inspectorate?
Is the general register well kept?
Do we record the causes of accidents and as far as possible eliminate them?

Guards and fencing
Are all transmission and moving parts of machinery, generators, motors, conveyors etc. fenced off in accordance with the Factories Act?
Is all machinery properly guarded and not misused by operatives?
Is transmission machinery fitted with means of cutting off the power immediately?
Are safety regulations concerning cleaning always followed?
Do we issue 'permits to work' with rigorous care?

Hoists, lifts and cranes; steam boilers, air receivers
Do we have such equipment inspected at the legally required intervals by competent personnel?
Is the safe working load indicated on all necessary occasions?
Is maintenance properly carried out?
Is there a system of preventing travelling cranes from approaching persons who are within twenty feet of the wheel track?

Construction of floors
Are all steps, stairs and passages of sound construction, properly maintained, free from obstruction and substances likely to cause a person to slip?
Are all fully lighted?

Fire and safe access
Is the fire certificate up to date and in line with the current factory layout?
Are proper fire exits available — free from clutter and properly marked?
Do doors leading to escape stairways etc. hinge outwards?
Are doors kept unlocked during working hours?
Do we have regular fire drill with the fire alarm sounded at least every three months?
Do employees know what to do in case of fire?
Is fire fighting equipment supplied and well maintained?
Are employees instructed in how to fight a fire?

Safety clothing and equipment
Do we provide adequate safety equipment for:

   Welding
   Use of abrasive wheels
   Power presses
   Use of toxic fluids?

Do we conform to all requirements in storing, handling and venting to avoid hazards from toxic fumes?

Welfare
Do we provide adequate:

   Toilet and washing facilities
   Dressing and drying rooms
   Water drinking facilities?

Is there a first aid box or cupboard for every 150 persons employed or less? Is it accessible?
Is a responsible person in charge of the first aid box?
Is that person trained in first aid?

External environment
Do we emit polluting dust or fumes to the general atmosphere which can harm the general public?

5

Information systems

5.1 INTRODUCTION

It is confusing that the word 'system' has acquired two meanings. Its most common use covers paperwork systems — production planning, machine scheduling, inventory control and management accounting. In a broader context it can be defined as being organisational — 'the complex grouping of human beings and machines, joined together to achieve a goal or goals'. (The term socio-technical system is also used for the same thing.) To establish control over the 'organisational system', production managers need to have knowledge of how this system works. They must control (if they can) the variables of the system and need information for this purpose. They need to know when the system is going out of control. For all these purposes paperwork systems are needed. Inevitably production management will have some information on which to base decisions — late order reports, labour efficiency statements, machine breakdown data, total cost of production etc. It may be produced in a timely way and enable corrective action to be introduced if things are going wrong. Yet in most cases this is not what happens. The information available will not usually have resulted from a coherent and well thought out plan, which relates the information to the objectives of the managers of work groups in production. Usually information will have grown up more by chance than design.

5.2 CROSS FUNCTIONAL SYSTEMS AND OPERATIONAL PLANNING

1 The 'broad production system' is only part of the overall company system. While the production function may have the majority of the resources in

the organisation, it cannot exist as an independent activity. For example, if production control is mainly concerned with the use of production resources and how these relate to inventories and market demand, then it is essential that the related paperwork systems have to be cross functional — covering production, marketing, stock control and distribution — if they are to be truly effective in their purpose.

2 The interdependence of functions shows the need for resource balance. For example the relationship between production capacity usage and inventory levels is often vital. This suggests the need for short term or operational planning where the various resources are planned in order to achieve tactical goals.

5.3   MANAGEMENT AND MANAGEMENT INFORMATION SYSTEMS

1   Management and organisational roles

The term 'management information system' has had a long but not always distinguished history. Why in fact do managers need information? What information is required and at what intervals of time? These questions can only be answered and understood by suggesting the needs which information should fulfil. The role of production management (and others of course) can be stated in four words — measurement, planning, control and motivation. The last is not directly concerned with paperwork systems but can be instituted or directed as a result of providing 'management information'. The other three represent the basic needs for production paperwork systems.

Measurements — THESE are the key to understanding how the production function operates. They will include speeds of machinery, material utilisation, costs of all kinds, and especially what will happen if more or fewer resources are provided for the function. What are the important marginal measurements which a production manager should use?

Planning — Production managers should be involved in two levels of planning. The first level concerns the routines which are called long range or profit planning and mainly concern the renewal, reduction or reapplication of production equipment and technology. The second level refers to operational planning, the fairly short term balancing of the use of resources which should achieve tactical objectives.

Control — Within the overall production system 'control' covers information required for determining how well the system is operating and where corrective action needs to be taken. Production management will mainly use control information to compare the results being achieved with those planned.

2   Management hierarchies

No matter how democratically the production function is structured, authorities and responsibilities will differ between managers and supervisors; one work group and another; one department and another. Hierarchies in the accepted sense of the word may not exist at all, but management of resources of different types and scale certainly will.

There will be a need, therefore, to identify hierarchies (if these exist), authorities and responsibilities, and relate management information, its type and how often it is produced, to them.

5.4   RESOURCE SYSTEMS

If the overall production system is concerned with the 'complex groupings of men and machines', the paperwork systems should be mainly, if not completely, concerned with 'resources' — inputs to the system and how these resources affect the outcome of the system, helping to measure, plan and control resource use.

In most manufacturing companies the resources which are fixed and nearly permanent are by far the most valuable. Plant or machinery can be sold off. Normal wastage and 'nil recruitment' can gradually reduce the work force, but the ability to rapidly reduce either is no longer present. Direct labour, for example, was once considered by management accountants to be a variable cost, but now it is as fixed as the administrative staff and perhaps, with strong trade unions, even more so. Management accounting systems based on absorbing the fixed cost and presenting standard costs to production managers, comprising both fixed and variable elements, do not help in maximising the use of production resources. They tend to hide the desirability of maximising the difference between the variable costs that are incurred in production and the sales revenue received for the products which are made. (This topic is discussed more fully in Chapter 8.)

5.5   INFORMATION NEEDS — THE BUSINESS APPRAISAL

Anyone who has the opportunity to redesign or introduce new production systems should initially carry out a business appraisal of the production function and its relationship with other parts of the business. There should be an environmental analysis of the production function. The following should be covered:

1   What important changes will occur, or are likely to occur, in the next few years? These could include the setting up or closing down of production

lines, the use of new equipment, the establishment of new work organisations, greater emphasis on some aspect of resource utilisation. Each factor will need a new or developed paperwork system to ensure that full benefit is being or will be obtained from it.

2   What are the overall objectives of the business (both now and in the future)? What impact do these have on the production function and on production management? Can objectives be established in a hierarchical way? Do objectives relate to resources which have been allocated to production managers at all levels?

3   What are the greatest problems facing the production function? What might be done to put things right or to improve the situation?

4   Is it likely that improved systems will be of benefit in any of the situations described in 1 to 3 above? If so could the benefits be quantified so that the cost-benefit of development can be calculated?

5   If systems are to be changed or new ones introduced, what priorities should be established?

The completed appraisal should specify where systems development is required, so among the more important elements in the report will be:

6   Where serious discrepancies have come to light between objectives, resource allocation and information available to measure, plan and control such resources.

7   What key businesses, business elements and business decisions have been identified.

8   What opportunities and benefits will exist from improving management information.

9   What obvious advances in production efficiency could be obtained through the use of computers, and particularly modelling, which will help to answer 'what if we did this?' types of question.

The following is an example of a business appraisal of the type recommended.

5.5.1   Objectives of the appraisal

These were:
1   To determine the minimum paperwork systems and information requirements which will aid the production function in measuring, planning and controlling its resources, so that the function will help to achieve either wholly or in part the following corporate objectives:

Objective	Current	1 year	2 years	3 years
Return on investment	15%	16%	18%	18%
Profit	£16m	£17.8m	£20.6m	£22.6m
Added value	£26m	£29m	£31m	£36m
Wages/AV ratio	1.726	1.842	1.842	1.842
Direct wage/AV ratio	1.961	1.961	1.961	1.961
Admin. wages/AV	1.640	1.700	1.750	1.800
Materials yield	78%	85%	88%	88%
Finished goods stock level	£7m	£8m	£8.5m	£9m
Work in progress	£1.2m	£1.3m	£1.5m	£1.6m
Labour: direct	2146	2200	2200	2200
indirect	1126	1100	1100	1050
admin.	2200	2000	2000	1800

2   To highlight the benefits which better systems and improved information will help to achieve. These should include:

Identifying the changes which are occurring and are likely to occur in the production environment — especially the external environment — and ensuring that appropriate adaptation within the production function is carried out.

Achieving corporate objectives, particularly the wages/added value ratio.

Planning the strategic as well as the tactical use of production resources.

5.5.2   The business appraisal team

This comprised the following personnel:

Works manager
Production managers of fabrics and pressing
Production trainees (2)
Systems analysts (one senior, one junior)
Shop stewards — where appropriate.

5.5.3   Method of appraisal used

The following were identified:

The production business

(a)   Products (product differences), machines, capacities
(b)   Relationship between product markets and current capacities
(c)   Future product markets v future current capacities
(d)   Relationships between stock values and capacities
(e)   Contribution per product type
(f)   Cost, profit/volume relationships
(g)   Relationship between work organisation needs and overall business requirements

Information needs

These were seen to be concerned with:

(a)   Measurement — product line statements
(b)   Planning — operational planning
(c)   Control — by responsibility and resource
(d)   Motivation — general motivational systems

Current systems

The following were recorded in detail:

(a)   Planning and machine scheduling systems
(b)   Labour efficiency systems
(c)   Material control systems
(d)   Wages payment systems

Systems improvement was considered essential for the following activities:

(a)   Operational planning — all aspects
(b)   Materials productivity
(c)   Role identification and design of appropriate systems, especially for:
     Production management hierarchies
     Resource allocation
     Work organisation
(d)   Adaptation to external environment

5.5.4   General problems

(a)   Lateness in producing reports of any kind, particularly management accounting control systems, is prevalent.
(b)   Administrative cost of supporting production system is high.
(c)   Lack of computer support in systems is preventing production managers from adequate decision making in many instances.
(d)   There is a need to develop closer links with other parts of the business, through strategic and tactical planning.
(e)   Resource allocation based on inadequate plans and control systems has to be strengthened.
(f)   There is a need to develop new performance measurements to ensure that operational planning is effective — e.g.:
  added value
  contribution
  material yield
(g)   Inadequacy of available data was evident.

5.5.5   Needs of production management and work organisations

These were identified to be:

(a)   Closer links between production and other parts of the business systems to ensure better balance between capacities, stock levels and customer demand
(b)   The introduction of interactive systems to answer 'what if?' types of question
(c)   Improved information flow to shop stewards and shop floor personnel, so expressed that it is understandable
(d)   Better 'money' information to ensure that management and supervisors are aware of financial implications of decisions they make
(e)   An ability to relate information to objectives

5.5.6   Potential benefits in improving management information systems

The principal benefits appear to be:

(a)   Closer links between the production function, its organisation and its external environment, will ensure that sufficient adaptation is made to improve industrial relations, create a good motivational ethos, and ultimately ensure survival of the business.
(b)   Improved use of production resources, by preplanning production (through a cost model) which could gain cost savings in resource utilisation by up to £1 million annually.

(c) Improved materials productivity, so saving up to £150,000 per annum.
(d) Much improved management effectiveness; the precise monetary benefits are doubtful, but substantial all the same.

5.5.7 Priorities

(a) Undoubtedly, enhancing operational planning is a first priority. Production management tends to think in a tactical rather than strategic way. This makes decision making rather short-sighted. Enhanced operational planning will provide the means to plan production resources in a superior way to that now possible.
(b) To achieve better operational planning, a considerable improvement in information will be necessary. This means, not just collecting data (an essential prerequisite to any production system's development) but so recording it that it can be used as the basis for decision making.
(c) The appraisal team believes that it is essential that production control in its widest definition must be improved with emphasis on the ability of production management to co-operate better with marketing and distribution managers.

5.5.8 Action plans

Once the team's conclusions have been discussed and agreed by the Board, formal action plans need to be drawn up to commence systems analysis and data collection. The action plan should record the resources and time needed to carry out the actions required, as follows:

Action	Personnel responsible	To be completed by
1 Review current production scheduling system	GAT SAM	1/9
2 Review data available and extend where necessary	BSM	1/12
3 Define system for production scheduling and stock control interface	GHB FOD	1/1
4 Consider and report to the Board on an operational planning system to cover 'X' production line	GHB FOR GAT	1/1

5.6   SYSTEMS AND THE PRODUCTION ENVIRONMENT

It is important not to design systems that will become rapidly obsolete. (Some obsolescence is inevitable.) The following check list should be used as the basis for systems development:

1   What major changes are envisaged in the company's long range plan which affect:
    New products to be manufactured
    Changes in design of products currently made
    Changes in methods of manufacture
    Major changes in capital investment?
2   What major problems will occur as a consequence of implementing the company's long range plan? How might these be accommodated within the systems plan?
3   What big changes in the production environment are likely to occur in the next five years? Can these be accommodated by appropriate systems?
4   What changes are likely to occur in the next five years in systems application and data processing equipment?
5   What objectives will the production function be asked to achieve over the next five years? How can systems be designed which help to achieve these objectives?
6   What changes in organisation are envisaged? Will the roles of production management be changed? Will this mean that systems will need to change also?

Answers to these questions will help to define a systems development strategy. This should cover two prime elements.

The development plan
The justification for carrying out the plan.

As Fig. 5.1 suggests, the design process should be encompassed within the production framework.

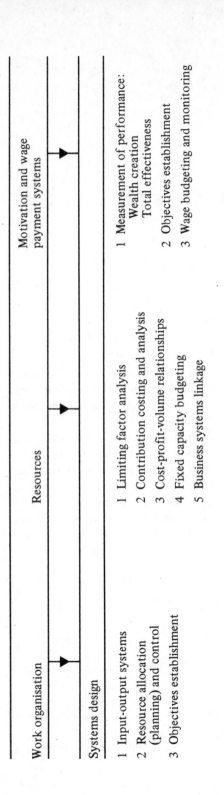

Work organisation	Resources	Motivation and wage payment systems
Systems design		
1 Input-output systems	1 Limiting factor analysis	1 Measurement of performance:
2 Resource allocation (planning) and control	2 Contribution costing and analysis	Wealth creation
	3 Cost-profit-volume relationships	Total effectiveness
3 Objectives establishment	4 Fixed capacity budgeting	2 Objectives establishment
	5 Business systems linkage	3 Wage budgeting and monitoring

Fig. 5.1 The production framework – systems design

6

Data for production systems and data bases

6.1 INTRODUCTION

Many production systems suffer from a lack rather than a surfeit of information. Often the limited information available is apparently accurate but a test — particularly when computers are used to process the data — proves it inadequate in some way.

It is surprising that much common information concerning production and machine or operation capacities is needed throughout a business system. For example, production capacities are needed for strategic as well as tactical planning purposes, for plant scheduling as well as in promising deliveries to customers, for stock control as well as management accounting use.

These common usages suggest that gaining and using information for one purpose only, say plant scheduling, will not make the best use of the data files which are needed.

6.2 INFORMATION

6.2.1 Production control

For production control purposes, two sets of basic information will be required. These are:

(a) Operational data: information about capacities, machine constraints, potential bottlenecks, etc.
(b) Products — product specifications — sizes, technical details, tolerances of various kinds.

6.2.2 Operational planning

Largely, operational planning should be concerned with maximising the use of current resources measured by either 'contribution' or 'added value' or perhaps some other way. It will be necessary to have three measurements:

(a) The technical maximum resource usage. For machine usage this will normally be the speeds at which the machine was originally designed to operate. This will be an engineering or technical decision.

With some operations, it will be occasionally found that basically similar machines — possibly purchased or modified at different dates — may have dissimilar technical rates of production.

(b) Standard capacity. Starting with the technical maximum, the various standard allowances are recorded and deducted. For example, there may be regular meal break interruptions, setting and starting up times etc. which can be calculated. The standard sales mix will indicate the number of change-overs needed.

(c) Current capacity. This is the capacity currently being obtained. For various reasons it may differ considerably from the standard capacity — e.g. lack of orders, sales mix deterioration, excessive machine breakdowns, etc.

It is likely that operational information will be changing most of the time. It may be possible to issue to all production managers and supervisors a line status report which shows in bold terms the current capacity situation. The current potential or actual bottleneck operation should be clearly shown. These 'limiting factors' need to be established so that appropriate resource planning and usage can be decided.

6.3 PRODUCT INFORMATION

The information needed for products will probably be established under a product category or code or both. Weight and material yield will be important, so that product size and raw or semi-finished material origins will need to be quoted.

The production processes through which the product has to pass should be recorded and processing times per 100 products calculated. The information should be set out so that batching is possible in production and maximum resource utilisation settled.

6.4   PRODUCTION COST INFORMATION

The costs produced should support decisions on resource utilisation. For example the contribution which each product makes should be known. This can be determined by adding together all marginal costs (usually the direct expense) and deducting the result from the net sales revenue obtainable for the product.

For bottleneck operations it may be necessary to calculate a contribution hour rate so providing the basis for priority scheduling. This limiting factor analysis will be described in Chapter 8 which describes management accounting systems in detail and further reference should be made to this.

6.5   COMMON INFORMATION SYSTEMS/DATA BASES

Many people have fallen into the rather painful trap of designing systems as if functions within an organisation have independent existences. Where this information is on a computer file, cross functional access to it is very difficult.

Data is a valuable commodity in any organisation. Using it for one process only can largely be avoided if a 'business system' viewpoint is taken in designing information systems. Fig. 6.1 shows the need for common data in what would appear to be several disparate systems.

The cost of storing data was once high. Relatively, with new computer technologies, it has become cheaper. The separate files usually designed for independent systems have been based on maximum usage of data store, so as to provide least storage. Now that is not so necessary.

The traditional approach to computer systems design has been to computerise existing systems. While this has often proved satisfactory, it has not generated cross functional data usage. While production managers may feel this is mainly a problem that should be solved by systems personnel, the nature of the problem should be fully understood by production people, especially where they have been seconded to lead systems development teams. It also happens that line managers are often much more aware of the type of data needed to run the business than are systems analysts. Given that a data base is necessary, line managers should designate what it will comprise. Systems personnel should translate required data to a technical data base form.

6.6   DATA SHEETS

The various data sheets (Figs. 6.2, 6.3, 6.4) associated with this chapter indicate the type of information required and which might form the basis of a production data book.

	Information						
System	Operational capacities	Production constraints	Product information	Planned production costs	Order progress	Budget of performance and costs	Actual costs incurred
Market/product planning	✓✓						
Operating plan		✓✓					✓
Plan control					✓✓		
Forecasting	✓				✓✓		
Administration							
Financial accounting	✓			✓		✓	✓
Payroll	✓	✓	✓	✓		✓	✓
Budgeting	✓	✓	✓	✓		✓	
Management accounting				✓			
Personnel							
Manpower planning	✓			✓		✓	✓
Industrial relations				✓		✓	
Manufacturing							
Process design	✓	✓	✓				
Machine loading	✓			✓	✓	✓	✓
Performance monitoring	✓					✓	
Buying							
Purchase of raw materials			✓		✓	✓	
Stock control	✓	✓	✓		✓	✓	
Warehousing			✓		✓	✓	
Distribution			✓		✓	✓	

Fig. 6.1   Common data requirements sheet

6.7   DETAILED INFORMATION

Details of the information quoted are as follows (using a practical example):

Capacity assessment and sales forecast (Fig. 6.2)

Col 1 — Plant item

A brief description of the plant item together with plant number and the number of machines.

Col 2 — Bottleneck rating

The known bottleneck item will be rated 1. The near bottleneck items will be rated 2 (and possibly 3). Only these machines will be given close attention.

Col 3 — PG

PG (product group) will be liberally interpreted and sub-groups will often be used depending on production control criteria.

Col 4 — Technical maximum output

The technical maximum output of a machine is the maximum rate possible at the present state of development of the plant running continuously for 120 hours per week in which one floor to floor to cycle succeeds another without a break or the purchase specification rate whichever is higher. The month used throughout is the standard month of $19\frac{2}{3}$ working days.

Col 5 — Time loss to standard performance

The details of the production losses which reduce the technical maximum to standard (see below) are given in Fig. 6.3 which is a detailed sheet giving each loss cause and its quantitative effect. Some of these can best be expressed for calculation purposes as straight time and others as a factor. These losses are those which arise from strategic or business policy decisions.

Col 6 — Standard performance

The standard performance is the best obtainable for the zone if all improvements within the power of the Works Division are made.

Capacity assessment

Section: _____

Zone: _____

Page no. _____

Date _____

1	2	3	4	5	6	7	8	9	10	11
Plant items	Bottle-neck rating		Technical maximum ('000 pieces per month)	Time loss to standard performance (hours/month)	Standard performance ('000 pieces per month)	Time lost from standard performance (hours/month)	Current performance ('000 pieces per month)	Forecast requirements ('000 pieces per month)	Forecast utilisation (% of standard performance)	Current utilisation (% of standard performance)
Description	No. off	P.G.						78 79 80 81	78 79 80 81	

Fig. 6.2 Capacity assessment data sheet

Reasons why the technical maximum is not achieved

Section _____   Zone _____   Bottle-neck machine _____

Technical maximum output ('000 pieces per month)	Addition losses	Multiplication losses
	Total	Total

Standard performance =   '000 pieces per month

Fig. 6.3   Production loss – cause and effect

Reasons why standard performance   '000 pieces are not achieved

Productive time loss reason	Losses		Potential improvements	Cost	Benefit	New output '000 pieces/ month	Action plan number
	Addition (hours/month)	Multiplication					
Total							

Fig. 6.4   Time lost from standard performance

Col 7 — Time lost from standard performance

The time lost from standard performance to bring it to the current performance will be listed in Fig. 6.4 which will show the most important losses. The addition of cost and benefit columns in money terms will enable the most advantageous actions to be decided upon and given a reference number for the Action Plan. The new output can be calculated. All the improvements would be within the capacity of the works.

Col 8 — Current performance

The current performance will be the average over the last 6 months provided the method of production has not changed.

Col 9 — Forecast requirements

The forecast requirements will be in the simplest case figures taken straight from the sales forecast. However, often assumptions will have to be made about the proportion of a product group using a bottleneck machine and these assumptions would need to be stated. An extra document may be needed for this.

Col 10 — Forecast utilisation

The forecast utilisation as a percentage of standard is intended to give an alert to the danger of long term capacity problems.

Col 11 — Current utilisation

The current utilisation is intended to indicate what readily available capacity is being under-used.

7

Production objectives and planning

7.1 INTRODUCTION

In Chapter 3 an analysis was made of the some of the external and internal environmental factors likely to cause problems to production managers. Their impact was suggested as well as the actions needed to accommodate them. This activity is a precursor to considering production objectives.

7.2 GOAL CONFLICT

The production system has two distinct sets of requirements which have a considerable potential for generating conflict. One is mainly concerned with management objectives — output, profit, high productivity, low costs, etc. The other is related to employees — increased financial awards, more satisfying jobs, improved benefits of a non-financial kind, job security.

Some of these requirements will clash: for example, there may be no way of reducing costs except through redundancies. Others are potentially complementary: enhanced job satisfaction might well be a positive aid to achieving higher output.

In the past, economic objectives have tended to dominate profit planning and objectives setting. Profit margins, costs of all kinds, stock levels, etc., have tended to be the bones of the planning system. This assumes that the system is basically an economic one.

Enough has been said previously about production systems to suggest that this is not necessarily so, though economics are still very important.

So any attempt to solve the potential conflict in the requirements of the production system needs to start with recording all possible objectives, e.g. economic and social, employees, managers and the company. In Figs. 7.1, 7.2,

Objective	Direction	Method	Areas of application	Data needed	Improvement possibilities	Constraints
Increased profit	Increased volume		All production lines	Current capacity usage Line status: Technical maximum Standard capacity Current capacity	From marketing/sales plan Application through production control system	Sales plan
	Better use of current volume	Application of contribution analysis	All major products	Profit/volume ratios		Available cost data
		Limiting factor analysis	Key machines (i.e. actual or potential bottlenecks)	Contribution hour rates at each bottleneck	Application of contribution costing	Application of data within product/market policy
	Decreased costs	Investigate asset utilisation	Materials Productivity	Operational & technical losses at each stage or process product material yield	Materials productivity Improvement campaign	—
			Labour Productivity	Effective hours/clocked hours Incentive results Absenteeism	Work organisation New incentives Planning & control	Company style & organisation
			Machine utilisation and efficiency	Current capacity used/availability efficiencies	Production control improvements Tighter shop-floor control	Data processing
		Service functions utilisation	Administration	Admin/added value produced Total cost	Work measurement Use of E.D.P. Work simplification	
			Maintenance	Maintenance/added value produced Total cost	Planned maintenance Better maintenance control	
			Power	Power consumed per production unit	Contribution analysis of contribution per kilo/hour etc.	

Fig. 7.1 Production objective – increased profit

Objective	Direction	Method	Areas of application	Data needed	Improvement possibilities	Constraints
Improved fixed asset utilisation	Plant utilisation	Strategy in corporate plan	All production plant	Planned usage Cost/profit/volumes	Planned use Resource allocation and control systems	Sales performance Product/market environment
		Current utilisation	All production plant	Current usage Cost/profit/volumes Productivity	Incentives Production control system Limiting factor analysis	
	Plant layout	Space utilisation	Production areas Non-production areas		Methods study	Structural deficiencies in factory and limitations of factory site
		Materials handling	All areas where materials handling occurs	Type of equipment used and usage Effectiveness in movement: speed, breakages, etc.	Methods study Application of materials handling principles	
		Offices	All	Utilisation and space needed per person and function	Elimination or reduction in function Space utilisation programme Office layout changes	
	General assets	Warehouses	All	Utilisation Space per product/customer	Better layout and materials handling Faster order processing	Sales policy
		Lorries	All	Utilisation Mileage and breakdowns	Better maintenance Improved control Bonus system for lorry drivers	

Fig. 7.2 Production objective – improving fixed asset utilisation

Objective	Direction	Method	Area of application	Data needed	Improvement possibilities	Constraints
Maximum cash flow	Raw materials	Stock control	All stocks	Stock levels and type/monthly production requirements		Long term application
		Range: standardisation and variety reduction (policy)	All stocks	Range of types, varieties, qualities	Production rationalisation	
	Work in progress	Production scheduling	All production lines	W.I.P. quantities and values at each machine and for total line	Planned W.I.P. to be part of scheduling activity Scheduling geared towards reducing W.I.P.	Trade-offs between least cost production and minimum W.I.P.
		Production monitoring	All production lines	Planned W.I.P. quantities	Enhanced reporting of W.I.P.	
	Finished goods stock	Stock policy	All stocks	Current levels of stock Planned levels to achieve desired service levels	Production requirements planning Better forecasting payment and creditors	
		Range	All stocks	Number of items Sales per year Times turned over Items—contribution	Production rationalisation Changed sales policy	Customer service and marketing plan
		Stock control	All stocks	Stock levels in type 'ABC' categorisation Turnover/stock ratios	Application of inventory control principles Order–procedures improved Forecasting improvements	

Fig. 7.3   Production objective – improved cash flow

Objective	Direction	Method	Areas of application	Data needed	Improvement possibilities	Constraints
Improved employees' conditions	Financial	Incentives	First generation Second generation Incentives	(1) Current incentive applications and effectiveness (2) Measurement data	Added value, profit sharing, M.T.M., measured day work, P.B.R., etc.	Skilled work study personnel Agreement timing Outside influences: national wage agreements, inflation, etc.
		Straight pay increases	Hourly rate	Possibility of increase i.e., through wage budgeting system	Offset against possibility of: improvement in quality improvement in timekeeping improvement in absenteeism etc.	
	Job structure	Job enrichment	Job redesign	Current job descriptions Principles of design	New forms of incentives Method changes	Possibility of job enrichment Technology of industry Local management style
		Work organisation	Work groups	Current organisation Work organisation principles	Link with participation and discussions on methods of improving productivity New forms of incentives	
	General conditions	Considerable cost	Major changes in (a) working hours (b) environmental conditions (c) Benefits in kind	Expense to be incurred Loss of profit	What can be gained by management for costs incurred?	Company profit Relative deprivation of management and trade union strength
		At no or minimum cost	(a) abolition of irritants	What irritants exist?	Smoother industrial relations	
			(b) Evening up of status differences	What status differences exist?	– – –	
	Job security	Minimum labour force No redundancies	All labour	Profit product market	Forecasting Manpower planning	

Fig. 7.4 Employees' objective – improving their conditions

Major goals	Sub-goals	Linkage	Dichotomy
Increased profit	Increased volume	Incentives – more pay for employees	Type of incentive Share of extra earnings
	Better use of volume	Improved company performance Enhanced job security	Increased labour flexibility
	Decreased costs	Job security	Job security – redundancies Need for improved flexibility
Improved cash flow	Raw materials	Job security Corporate prosperity	Concentration on materials productivity may reduce output
	Work-in-progress	–	Less pre-operation buffers may cause increased set-ups and lower output: incentives will need to be geared to cope with this
	Finished goods stock	–	Need for lower finished goods stock may decrease batch sizes and lower output
Improved condition of employees	Financial	Methods of wage payment and relationship of productivity and payment	Possibility of lower share of added value going to company
	Job structure	Improved performance at lower levels in the company	Undermining of traditional methods of organisation and control
	Job security	Worker satisfaction Good morale Improved company performance	Clash with 'decreased costs' and improved profit performance

Fig. 7.5   Goal conflict – linkage and dichotomy

7.3 and 7.4 some typical objectives are considered under several headings. It is suggested for example that increased profit can be achieved through increasing production volume, better use of current production volume and decreasing manufacturing costs.

Determination of methods for achieving such objectives is an obvious next step in the process; to be followed by decisions as to where the methods could be applied. Data will be needed, as suggested in the figures, to decide on the potential of the application. This will also help in recording the improvement possibilities. Finally the constraints likely to prevent the application of the method are recorded.

The procedure is recommended for any discussion of production objectives. It is a useful method to determine the feasibility of such objectives and how they might be achieved. It is a discipline which should prevent the indiscriminate allocation of objectives which cannot be achieved no matter how hard production management tries.

The same procedure can be used for testing the feasibility of employees' objectives, as Fig. 7.4 suggests.

The potential conflict between company and employee objectives is set out in Fig. 7.5. The principal objectives are tested by links with other objectives and the likely conflicts which could ensue.

7.3 SETTING OBJECTIVES

1   'What is our business?' is a key question, not just for the business as a whole but also for the production function. The nature of the business, the type of products it makes, the degree of flexibility needed to meet sales demand, even the size of orders which are accepted, will be reflected in the efficiency of the production system. Conversely, therefore, production management should express views about the business and how it might be changed so that production efficiency can be improved.

Production objectives should reflect the adopted business strategy and tactics and where possible the relation between the two shown. For example if the company is prepared to accept orders of any size (especially small ones) the cost in terms of machine set-ups and production generally must be known.

2   Investigation of current production performances will provide the basis for discussing objectives. Are these good enough? Could they be improved? One key evaluation lies in analysing the difference between current and technically possible performance of various activities as follows:

Area	Evaluation	Comment
Machine utilisation	1 Technical maximum 2 Standard capacity 3 Current achievement	How far is it possible to move from current achievement towards the technical maximum? What must be done to achieve this?
Materials production	Current yield. 100%	Can we use materials productivity techniques to improve our yield?
Manpower utilisation	1 Current 2 Possible	Do we need to improve or extend our incentives and production control to improve manpower efficiency?

Setting new standards of performance might be conditional on:

(a) the use of techniques — value analysis, product rationalisation, work study;
(b) the acquisition of capital equipment;
(c) the solving of industrial relations problems;
(d) the improvement of production control systems;
(e) the application of new forms of work organisation and incentives.

The application of one or all of these needs either experience or money. In either case the value of the resource to be used and the probable result is required.

3   The production function may be asked to consider certain levels of performance if required company profit is to be achieved. This will usually be a request to achieve a certain level of output at a stipulated unit cost. The method shown in Figs. 7.1, 7.2 and 7.3 should be used to test the possibilities.

7.4   MANAGEMENT BY OBJECTIVES

M.B.O. should be seen as not just the establishment of standards of performance which are monitored regularly. The activities to pursue include:

1   the evaluation of strengths and weaknesses of people involved;
2   the evaluation of environments;
3   the writing of job descriptions, which can be used to allocate resources and responsibilities;

4   performance appraisal routines;
5   appropriate training and general development plans to improve perfor-
    mance.

It is axiomatic that:

6   objectives be discussed and agreed with managers, following the type of
    analysis suggested earlier;
7   measurements of performance be instituted.

Chapter 16 provides appropriate detail for these procedures.

7.5   RELATED PLANS

Planning within the production function should be concerned with two aspects:

1   the translation of production strategies into well defined action plans;
2   the application and monitoring of agreed objectives.

The timescales of either 1 or 2 could differ considerably.

3   the whole manufacturing plan might constitute the following:
    (a)   an analysis of the environment of the manufacturing unit with the
          likely impact of economic, social and cultural conditions. Likely
          changes in work organisation, incentives, systems and resources and
          their allocation needed as a result of environmental analysis;
    (b)   both current and planned capacity utilisations on each production
          line;
    (c)   both current and planned costs per production line;
    (d)   action plans to cover changes envisaged. The following headings
          need to be used:
              Action to be instituted
              Improvement envisaged
              Person responsible
              Resources allocated to carry out the action
              Timescales
              Reporting mechanisms
    (e)   organisational changes. Succession planning;
    (f)   management supervisor development programmes;
    (g)   systems development plans;
    (h)   capital investment.

These plans are not detailed, as individual elements are recorded in each of
the appropriate chapters.

8

Costing production

8.1 INTRODUCTION

For many production managers, costing is the concern of cost or management accountants. The costing system is usually designed by costing personnel. The information which emanates from it is often that which cost accountants believe production managers require.

Despite the fact that decision making in the production function mostly needs monetary evaluation, production managers tend not to challenge the figures which the accountants produce. Yet costing systems are fairly easy to understand and to design. The principles are simple. The applications are usually complicated only because too much is attempted in producing over-accurate data.

Information produced by a typical management accounting system is historical. It reports on events which have happened days, weeks, even a month or two in the past. Costs are often given which are not under the direct control of local production management. For example, many systems use absorbed costs. (That is, all the product costs contain a proportion of fixed overhead which is not within the responsibility or control of the production manager.) Such costs often confuse rather than explain what is happening in production. Vital analysis is frequently missing. For example, information on limiting factor use is not often given.

8.2 COSTING PRINCIPLES

8.2.1 Base data

Like production control, a costing system has to be based on information about the production process. The starting point is the same, e.g.

The technical maximum output of a piece of plant or production line;
Standard output;
Current output;
Labour manning;
Material yield;
Power consumed;
Other controllable elements, i.e.: packaging, consumable stores etc.

It should be noted that information is usually collected under two headings:

1 operational, machine or production line;
2 product.

8.2.2 Standards

Most production managers will be aware of 'standards' within a 'standard costing system'. (This is the type of system normally used in manufacturing organisations.) 'Standards' are merely predetermined levels of performance, in output, material yield or cost, which in normal circumstances should be achieved.

A standard product cost therefore is the planned predetermined cost of a product when it is manufactured under normal conditions (though 'normal conditions' may have to be defined).

A standard hour is an important measurement. It is the unit of time in which all output can be expressed. For example:

Machine A can produce the following:
Product X at a rate of 50 per hour
Product Y at a rate of 100 per hour
Product Z at a rate of 150 per hour

The following output has been achieved:

X – 100
Y – 300
Z – 450

The credit in standard hours is:

X – (100/50) = 2
Y – (300/100) = 3
Z – (450/150) = 3

Total standard hours achieved = 8

The main purpose of a standard costing system is to establish an adequate yardstick against what actually has happened compared with what has been planned or budgeted.

8.2.3 Budgets

Budgets are closely related to standards. A budget can be both a forecast and a target. It can be either financial or non-financial. It can refer to a single item of planned cost or the whole of the plan which records a company's planned revenue and expenditure.

An important element in budgeting is the establishment of budget or cost centres. These are parts of an operating unit, often a section or a series of machines where it seems to make sense to establish control. Too many cost centres will produce too much paperwork. Too few will not provide the control necessary. (Cost accountants often generate too many rather than too few.) As a rough rule of thumb cost centres should relate to the responsibilities of first line supervision and should be established to provide the base for improvements in performance. So it is important to recognise where

1   operations or processes can be separated from each other;
2   material or product flow in and out of the processes can be counted or measured;
3   costs associated with a process or operation can be identified accurately;
4   monitoring of performance is possible.

For most production managers a budget will mainly refer to the annual assessment of costs which will be incurred in making certain numbers of products, perhaps of different types.

Usually the process is non-dynamic. The previous year's budgets are examined, an addition for the current inflation rate is added and a new one calculated. Attempts to challenge budgets in a rational and comprehensive way are increasing but are far from universal.

8.2.4 Types of cost

Cost is a word which should rarely be used without some form of qualification. ('Standard costs' have already been described.)

The first and perhaps main distinction in costs is between those which vary with production and those which do not. (Some vary partly with output, but for the time being can be ignored.)

The variable costs are usually power to drive machinery, materials or components and various consumables such as cutting oils or tools. 'Direct labour' was once automatically included as a variable cost but with the advent of government legislation there is a tendency to treat labour costs as more fixed than variable.

Variable costs are often called 'direct costs'. Normally a 'variable cost' varies both directly and proportionally with production (though this definition may not be acceptable by some management accountants).

While direct labour may not come into this category the marginal use of labour is important, e.g. what extra output would be gained from employing extra men?

Non-variable or fixed costs, conversely, do not vary with production and are often referred to as 'overheads'. These costs are usually sub-divided into groups which allow control and evaluation to take place. For example, there are works' indirect costs — which are costs that cannot be directly allocated against production but would normally be under the control of junior production and facilities or services managers.

Some examples of types of cost which have been mentioned are:

Variable (or direct) or prime cost:
    Direct materials (materials consumed in production)
    Components needed to complete a product being made
    Power
    Packaging
    Consumable stores (consumed in production)
    Labour (but there is some doubt about this)
    Dies and tools
Indirect cost:
    Maintenance in all aspects
    Supervision
    Scrap collecting
    Materials handling
    Quality control
    Superannuation
    Stores and storemen's wages
    Despatch
    Heating and lighting
    Cleaning
    Health and safety
    Clerical labour
    Training and retraining
General works costs (these normally will be fixed and could be classified as manufacturing overheads):
    Welfare and surgery
    Canteen
    Rents, rates and insurance
    Production management

    Depreciation
    Works furniture
Administration costs (these are usually fixed):
    Salaries and associated costs
    General office expenses — heating, lighting, furniture, cleaning
    Stationery
    Postage
    Telephones and cables
    Office equipment
    Computer costs
    Insurance
    Donations
    Depreciation
Sales costs:
    Salaries and associated costs
    Travelling
    Advertising
    Marketing
    Entertaining
Research and development costs:
    Salaries and associated costs
    Depreciation on equipment
    Capital expenditure
    Consumable materials
    Heating, lighting and general building costs

In the long run all costs of any kind are variable. If the company goes bankrupt nobody will be employed. Even in the fairly short term 'fixed costs' can be eliminated — R & D can be closed down; administrative clerks dismissed; sales budgets cut by eliminating certain travelling and entertaining. But normally, in taking a one-year view there are variable and fixed costs.

To add some difficulty to what might appear to be a simple situation, some of the indirect costs may also vary with the levels of production or output achieved. For example, maintenance may have to be increased if more use is made of machines, as breakdowns may grow with greater strain on equipment. Scrap collecting may increase if production is raised.

In some costing systems such costs are referred to as 'semi-variable' and the variable element is included in the variable cost.

8.2.5   The process

1   The sales budget

Once appropriate cost centres and cost breakdowns have been established, the

Sales budget 1980–81
Product type: C.A.S.L.

Cost centre 2204

Product category	Market	Total	Monthly forecast	Contribution	Speed	Standard hours
A	OE export	10,640,000	886,666	£4.27	12,600 per hour	70
	Replacement	12,600,000	1,050,000	£6.87	—"—	83
B						
C						
D						
E						
F						
G						
H						
J						
Totals						

Fig. 8.1   Sales budget

sales budget can be used by production management to determine:

Operating costs of all kinds
The degree of plant utilisation which is envisaged.

The sales budget should set out product requirements in a manner that will facilitate the calculation of the data shown in Fig. 8.1. The total and market product requirements are shown plus the monthly forecast; the contribution to be obtained is calculated; the machine speed used to determine the standard hours needed to meet each product category requirement is also recorded.

'Contribution' is the difference between the sales revenue to be obtained for each product and the variable or marginal costs which will be incurred in making the product. Where different products are made on one machine or where the same product is sold in different markets, the contribution obtained in each case is very important in determining plant usage.

To calculate budgeted contribution will need the standard net sales revenue from each product market and the standard variable cost. ('Contribution' will be discussed in greater detail in the 'Developments' section, pages 111–119.)

2   *The manufacturing budget — schedule of capacity usage*

The standard hours needed to make the forecast or budgeted sales demand can be determined by using the currently accepted standard speed of machines or output at each cost centre and dividing it into the product quantities required. Fig. 8.2 shows an appropriate form.

Normally less than 100 per cent efficiency is accepted in determining 'current expected standard speed' and various allowances will be built into it (e.g. set-up and change-over time, down time, cleaning etc.).

The monthly budgeted standard hours can be compared with the normal monthly capacity available.

Any difference between normal monthly capacity and the budgeted standard hours should be a cause for concern and discussion between production and marketing personnel. Whether production capacity is apparently to be over- or under-utilised has obvious importance.

3   *The manufacturing budget — schedule of cost*

Once agreement has been obtained on capacity utilisation and initially the sales mix, production management should complete their budget detail sheets for each cost centre and if necessary for each product group. Figs. 8.3 and 8.4 suggest how this might be done. Data Book information should be used to provide the performance standards appropriate to the mix and the current state of the production line.

Manufacturing budget 1980–81

Schedule of capacity usage

Product group	Standard hours	Monthly budgeted standard hours	Normal monthly capacity	Capacity usage %
A	153	180	240	64%
B				
C				
D				
E				
F				
G				
H				
J				
Totals				

Fig. 8.2   Manufacturing budget schedule of capacity usage

Normally it should be possible to work out:

(a)   a direct labour hour rate, i.e. the cost in labour to operate a machine or cost centre for one hour;

(b)   a cost centre or machine hour rate.

With the latter figure it should be possible to calculate any direct cost centre — product cost if the time taken to make a product is known and material costs are added.

As well as direct and indirect costs, it will be necessary to budget for general works expenses — i.e. those included in section 8.2.4.

In times of high inflation, it may be necessary to build in an appropriate allowance. Common practice is to decide — or forecast — the annual inflation rate and suggest what costs will be at the midpoint of the budgeted period. So,

Manufacturing budget 1980–81
Schedule of variable cost   Cost centre _____

Product group	Capacity per hour	Item	£
A	12,600	Materials	£2,400
		Power	620
		Packaging	40
		Consumable stores	10
		Direct labour	520
	Cost centre	Cost	£3,590
Cost from previous operations			£7,200
		Total	£10,790

Fig. 8.3   Manufacturing budget – schedule of variable cost

half the year will be overcosted and the other undercosted — each cancelling the other.

4   Allocation of overheads

In an absorption costing system fixed costs are apportioned to production cost centres in a way which should provide a logical basis for cost recovery.

The reason for applying absorption costing is that the costs which are eventually determined will be full and complete. If budgeted output is achieved then, with absorbed costs, full cost recovery is probable.

By using absorption costing, cost accountants suggest that all production and other managers will be fully aware of all the costs being incurred by the company, and consequently every effort will be made to recover them by making the products which have been budgeted at standard cost.

The allocation of overhead is usually made using a form similar to the one shown in Fig. 8.5. The total overhead budget is shown on the left hand side. An appropriate method is agreed and used to spread the overhead. In the case of the canteen, for example, the spread of costs is done on 'a number of employees basis'. The cost centre with the most employees (who all probably

Manufacturing budget 1980–81
Schedule of indirect cost   Cost centre   _2204_

Indirect cost item	Cost per cost centre hour £	Proportion considered to be variable £	%	Monthly cost £
Maintenance	64	32	50%	£20,480
Supervisors	15	—	—	4,800
Scrap collecting	12	12	100	3,840
Materials handling	8	8	100	2,560
Quality control	19	19	100	6,080
Superannuation	12	12	100	3,840
Stores	17	5	29	5,440
Storemen's wages	10	—	—	3,200
Despatch	40	20	50	12,800
Heating and lighting	120	100	83	38,400
Cleaning	20	10	50	6,400
Health and safety	7	—	—	2,240
Clerical labour	12	—	—	3,840
Training and re-training	8	4	50	2,560
Total cost	364	222	61	116,480

Fig. 8.4   Manufacturing budget – schedule of cost – indirect

use the canteen) will bear most of the canteen cost.

The provision of cost centre costs will help to provide an accurate assessment of work in progress for financial accounting purposes. Products half way through the production process can be valued at the calculated cost at the end of the cost centre the products have just left.

5   Costing rates

Once the budgeted expenditure has been allocated to cost centres the total expenditure can be divided by the budgeted standard hours (see Fig. 8.2) to

Account	Allocation basis	Total budget	Cost centres				
			1	2	3	4	5
Welfare and surgery	Employees	£34,000	£7,000	£11,600	£6,800	£3,500	£5,100
Canteen	Employees	£40,000	£8,300	£13,000	£8,500	£4,100	£6,100
Rent and insurance	Floor area	£17,600	£2,000	£1,500	£1,500	£10,000	£2,600
Production management	Employees	£96,000	£20,000	£32,000	£21,000	£10,000	£13,000
Works furniture	General						
Works clerical	General						
Salaries	General						
General office expenses:	General						
Heating	General						
Lighting	General						
Furniture	General						
Cleaning	General						
Depreciation	Plant & value						
Insurance	Plant & value						
Totals							

Fig. 8.5   Allocation of overhead

Cost centre			Cost per standard hour		
Description	Std hrs	Cost	Total	Variable	Fixed
ASSEMBLY	16,410	Direct	£96	£96	—
		Indirect	£120	£50	£70
		Gen. works	£320	£60	£260
		Admin	£460	—	£460
		Total	£996	£206	£790

Fig. 8.6   Costing rates

give the standard hourly costing rates. Each costing rate produced is the total planned cost for running a cost centre for one hour under normal operating conditions. Fig. 8.6 shows how the calculation is done.

6   Product costing

Once costing rates have been established it is possible to cost products. This can be done using a form similar to that shown as Fig. 8.7. Material is issued from the raw material stores at a standard cost predetermined to provide an appropriate recovery for the full budgetary period. Then in each cost centre the standard time to make (say) 100 products is calculated and the result multiplied by the standard hourly cost rate. To this is added the material cost.

The total for one cost centre is added to the next one until the end of the process is reached.

Where the product range is large the usual practice is to cost the items which make up 80 per cent of the range and provide cost divisions for the remainder.

The need to separate fixed and variable costs is important.

7   Operation of the system

Costing should be seen as part of the production control system. While it has to have an independent existence, especially with its links with financial accounting, the decision making facility which a good costing system provides must be an intrinsic part of production resource allocation and control.

8   Recording what happens

This is one of the most difficult aspects of a costing system to get right.

Product cost sheet   Per 100 products

Cost centre	Product A		Product B		Product C	
	Hrly rate	£	Hrly rate	£	Hrly rate	£
Material issue						
2 Mixing						
Material		£620		£510		£720
Direct cost per hr	£50	£620	£55	£510	£50	£720
Direct cost per hr	£50	75	£55	55	£50	62.50
Indirect cost per hr	£120	180	£120	120	£120	150
G. Works cost per hr	£300	450	£300	300	£300	375
Admin cost per hr	£600	900	£600	600	£600	150
Total		£2,225		£1,585		£1,457.50

3

4

5

Total

Fig. 8.7   Product cost sheet

Insufficient importance is usually given to recording accurately what has happened and then ensuring that the record is eventually used in the costing system. As a result 'work booking fiddles' often exist, material wastage is allowed to go by default, machine downtime is reported inaccurately so that actual costs incurred are distorted and give a far from true picture.

What needs recording? Everything that gives production management the information needed to plan, control and replan production to improve performance:

Production:
  Output by —
    cost centre
    product type
    products
    rejects
    recoverable material
Material:
  Input at each cost centre
  Output
  Recovered
  Recoverable
  Scrap
Labour:
  Clocked hours per cost centre
  Planned hours per cost centre
  Achieved hours (i.e. production divided by standard performance)
  Allowance given and the causes of the allowances
Machines:
  Running time available
  Planned running time
  Efficiency
  Running time used for production
  Downtime and causes
Work in progress:
  Finished goods:
    Finished goods sent to warehouse
    Stocks of components
  Budgets:
    Actual costs incurred against budgeted amounts in each cost centre.

(a) Methods of recording
Most manual methods of recording have an inbuilt capacity for mistakes — by either genuine error or design — wherever possible verification needs one record to be supported by another. For example, work booked in one cost

Quarter ending   SEPT. 1980

Directs _____

Budgeted standard hours/week __720__

Week no.	Clock hours Normal	O/T	Total	Cred hr totals Eff	Prod	Paid	Performances Eff	Prod	Paid	% development of direct hrs	Activity ratio Actual eff/budget	% efficiency eff/paid
R.P.	620	50	670	750	40	790	NA	NA	NA	10	—	—
21	640	—	640	720	20	690	710	620	680	10	100%	95.7%
22												
Total												

Week no.	Productive credit hours CO SU	M/c clean	Re-main	Un meas	CO SU etc total	Std Meas UM	Non productive credit hours Non std UM	Rect Meas UM	Stop Code 1	2	Policy	Average Dev	Rem	Stab	M/up	Total
R.P.																
21																
22																
Total																

| Week no. | Examining Hours | | | Servicing Hours | | | Cleaning Hours | | | Remainder Hours | | | Total Hours | | | % dev ind hrs |
	Clock std	Non std	Pd	Clock std	Non std	Pd	Clock std	Non std	Pd	Clock std	Non std	Pd	Clock std	Non std	Pd	
R.P.																
21																
22																
Total																

Cost centre summary

Week no.	Total pay in CC	Cost per Clock hour	Cost per Eff hour	Cumulative production	Eff hours per products	CO & SU clean etc.	Excess hours per effective hour Non productive Average Dev	Excess hours per effective hour Non productive Average Other	Remain	Indirect	Total	% development
R.P.	£3,600	£2.261	£2.140	16,000	—	120	60	21	10	21	112	10%
21	£3,700	£2.300	£2.210	15,900	2,239	136	60	21	15	—	96	9%
22												
Total												

Fig. 8.8   Weekly summary of manufacturing performance

centre should always be checked into the next one. It seems particularly important to have an independent record of products received into the finished goods
warehouse and compare it with the work booked on the production line.

Methods of recording include:

Log books — usually completed by senior operatives or first line supervisors
to show the production achieved and machine downtime. Log books are
mostly used in production units where individual incentives are not in operation.

Day cards or work booking cards — these are completed by either
individual operatives or supervisors.

Machine logging — usually by means of a small computer or data logger,
which is attached to the process being monitored.

Shop floor data collection — this term covers an important and potentially
very accurate method of data logging by electronic or mechanical means. A
terminal or job reporting equipment is provided and linked with a central
processor.

(b)   Operating statements

The term 'operating statement' is used by cost accountants to cover a series of
documents and reports which record the operating performance of the
organisation and particularly the production function.

There are two types of statement. One is based on units of output and hours
utilised and another giving monetary evaluation of performance compared with
the budget.

The statements are usually designed to facilitate 'management by exception',
i.e. only those factors which are important in control or restoring control are
highlighted.

The data given on the statements normally relate to the objectives which
production managers have accepted.

(c)   Efficiency reports

An efficiency report should record the performance achieved by a machine,
work centre, zone, production line or factory in a way which shows production
management where things have gone and are going wrong. While financial
statements probably are best produced monthly or at the most weekly, daily
efficiency reports may be appropriate.

Simplicity is often preferred to complication as this will aid recording and
evaluation of data. In this respect Fig. 8.8 may be slightly too detailed. Most of
the information shown originates from the day cards or workbooking sheets
completed by operatives. The results are compared with budgets and expected
efficiency.

Section performance statement

Week no.	Programme			Efficiencies		Cost of production						Loss or gain
	Programmed hours	Achieved hours	Hours clocked	Programme	Overall	Labour		Material		Other		
						Stand	Act	Stand	Act	Stand	Act	
21	510	500	450	98%	111%	£1,100	£1,060	£5,100	£5,000	£26,000	£24,500	+£1,640

Fig. 8.9   Section performance statement

Where a production schedule is issued, a simple statement similar to that shown in Fig. 8.9 may be more useful. It records the hours of programmed work, the amount achieved (i.e. standard hours), hours operatives have clocked and then the calculated efficiency variances. Costs of production can be added if these can be calculated simply.

(d) Input—output statements

Where a production line can be split into sections or operating units under a first line supervisor, monthly cost performance or input—output statements are a useful way of showing how well local management is achieving its objectives.

'Input—output' implies that performance will be judged by how well raw materials or partly finished products have been converted. Output will usually be given a standard cost or value agreed with local management. Conversion will be achieved by the expenditure of labour, material and some overhead as shown in Fig. 8.10.

Actual inputs to the section are adjusted by work in progress changes and by comparison with the standard value of actual output.

The input—output statement might take the form shown in Fig. 8.11. The standard output is 'real output' monitored as it leaves the section. Variances are shown by work in progress and the standard output.

The budget might eventually be a quarterly or even monthly rolling budget, forming part of the rolling update of the company's profit plan.

One index figure can then be used to determine total efficiency:

$$\text{Standard cost of output} - \text{Standard cost of input} = X$$

The index is then

$$\frac{X}{\text{Actual direct costs incurred}}$$

Two ratios will complete the picture:

Output actual — output planned ratio
Orders on time — orders delayed ratio

It should then be possible — if standard costs have been produced uniformly — to compare one section, line or factory with another and to determine comparative efficiencies.

(e) Product line operating statements

Product line operating statements are usually produced monthly using information from efficiency reports and the section performance controls. Fig. 8.12 shows a typical example. The first column lists the budgeted standard hours.

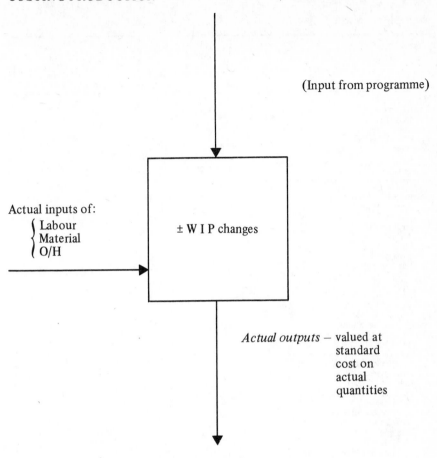

(Input from programme)

Actual inputs of:
  { Labour
  { Material   ± W I P changes
  { O/H

Actual outputs – valued at
                    standard
                    cost on
                    actual
                    quantities

Input–output statement compares:

Actual inputs ± W I P changes
with
actual outputs at Standard

Fig. 8.10   Input–output statement for section

The difference between hours budgeted and hours planned will be a sales volume problem and any major discrepancy is the responsibility of the sales manager. The difference between planned hours and hours achieved is the responsibility of production management. Where the difference is substantial a separate form may be needed to explain why the difference has occurred.

Costs, both standard and actual, can be shown for labour and material and 'others'. Again, if 'others' is significant a more detailed report may be necessary.

Monthly statement

	Budget	Actual inputs adjusted for WIP changes	Std outputs	Variances	Standard hours Budget: xxxx Output: xxxx Activity: %
Material:					
Good output					
Class I to misc.					
Class II rejects					
Class IV rejects					
Waste					
etc.					
Total material					
Direct labour:					
Productive standard					
Rectification					
Change over and set-up					
Meal and tea breaks					
Allowances					
Make-up/stabiliser					
Shift premium					
Rates of pay					
Total direct labour					
Variable overhead:					
Overtime premium – dir. labour					
Indirect labour					
Examining labour					
Holiday pay					
NI and graduated pensions					
Pension contributions					
Compensation (loss of earnings)					
Protective clothing					
Indirect material					
Production tools:					
Material					
Labour and overheads					
Hand tools					
Machine tools:					
Material					
Labour and overheads					
Tool repairs:					
Material					
Labour and overheads					
Primary services:					
Electricity					
Gas					
Other					
Training					
Maintenance and repairs:					
Stores					
Purchases					
Labour and overheads					
Sub contract					
Production tool setting					
Sundries					
Cleaning materials					
Plastics, cellophane, paint, shot					
Bandsaw blade sharpening					
Hire of plant and machinery					
Sub contract processing					
Total variable overheads					
Grand total					

Fig. 8.11   Section X: input–output statement

Product line operating statement

Budget prod'n hrs	Plan'd hrs	Act hrs ach'd	Std man hrs	Act clkd hrs	Costs						Efficiencies		Variances			
					Material		Labour		Other		Labour	Plant Utilis'n	Contribution earned		A V per £1 wage	
					Std	Act	Std	Act	Std	Act			Bud	Act	Bud	Act
600	510	550	560	620	£120	£150	£1,560	£1,720	£5,400	£5,000	90.3%	108%	£7,200	£6,200	£1.760	£1.621

Fig. 8.12 Product line operating statement

Efficiencies may be extended beyond those quoted (i.e. labour and plant utilisation) but these will often be sufficient to provide a requisite degree of control.

The variances may concern contribution and added value. To calculate these, sales revenue figures will be needed. Where 'making for stock' is usual, stock transfer values could be used instead.

(f)   Overhead or fixed cost control

As well as the direct or variable cost controls which have been described, monitoring of overhead or fixed costs will be required. This will usually take the form of a comparison between budgeted costs and actual costs incurred.

(g)   Costing profit and loss statements

The final statement which most production managers will need will be a report covering 'costing profit and loss'. A typical format will be as follows:

> Budgeted sales revenue
> less
> Budgeted direct manufacturing costs
> Budgeted gross contribution
> Add or deduct the following variances
> from standard due to sales performance:
> >   Sales, volume
> >   Sales, price
> >   Product mix
> >   Market, mix.
> Add or deduct the following variances
> from standard due to manufacturing
> performance:
> >   Direct labour:
> > >   Efficiency
> > >   Rate
> >   Material:
> > >   Usage
> > >   Rate
> >   Variable overheads
> >   Contribution before adjusting for:
> > >   Finished goods and work in progress
> > >   Movements
> > >   Actual contribution earned

Set out in this way it will be easily seen who is responsible for what variation in contribution. The manufacturing product line efficiency and operating statements can be used as supportive documents.

8.3   DEVELOPMENTS

The foregoing sets out the principles of a costing or management accounting system and how they can be applied to a manufacturing unit. Some of the inadequacies of costing systems likely to be met by production managers have been stated, but some of the more important and desirable developments have been left till now.

8.3.1   Marginal/contribution costs

In the costing principles which have been outlined a strict division between variable or marginal and fixed or overhead costs has been proposed. The method of absorption costing which has been common in the UK accepts the basis that overhead costs have to be recovered by loading them on to production units.

In practice this proves to have three serious drawbacks:

1   the system has to be comparatively complicated. It tends to hide more than it discloses;
2   the responsibility for incurring, controlling and reducing costs is not always clear cut;
3   production management, in consequence, has not always been able to suggest and carry out policy decisions on the planning and use of production resources as well as they might have done.

It is logical to have a costing system based on the assumption that it facilitates rather than hinders cost responsibilities and policy-resource planning in production. So it is desirable to have costing systems where only those costs directly incurred by production are used by production. Industry in the USA has utilised such direct costing methods much more than in the UK and it has to be assumed that they have gained commensurate benefit.

Variable or direct costs, therefore, should be assumed to be part of the total costs which a production manager might regard as his own. Fixed costs (or overheads) should be regarded as policy costs incurred by senior management in running the total business.

Direct product costs should always be separated from policy or organisational costs and the costing systems developed accordingly.

It is important to know, therefore, the amount which can be gained in sales revenue over and above the costs which are incurred in actually making the products being sold. This figure — known as 'contribution' (because it contributes to overheads) — is a vital calculation in resource planning.

Marketing personnel are obviously responsible for deciding product market allocation of production capacity, but production management is in the business of selling contribution. To this end discussions within the overall

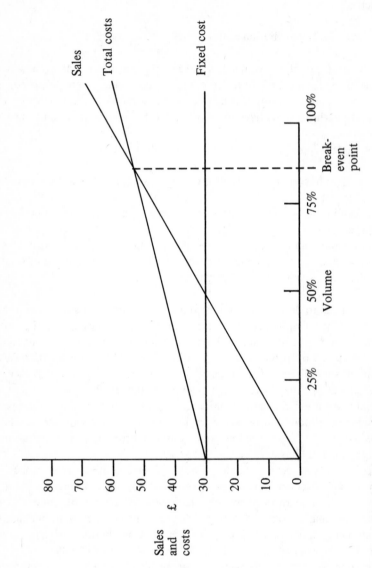

Fig. 8.13 Break-even chart

business system need to determine how best contribution can be maximised. This should certainly determine how, largely, production resources are utilised.

8.3.2 Cost–profit–volume relationships

The previous section has indicated the importance of contribution and the need to consider 'contribution maximisation' as one of the most important production objectives. The discussion can be taken further by reference to Fig. 8.13. This is the well known break-even graph. The fixed cost element apparently remains static, irrespective of whether a 25, 50 or even 100 per cent production volume is being achieved. The fixed cost and variable cost are added together to provide the total cost. Sales revenue is represented by a straight line in the figure and this and the total cost line cross at a point where volume is approximately 80 per cent and it is beyond this point in production volume where profit is made.

The graph shown is an oversimplification of the cost–profit–volume relationships of most if not all manufacturing organisations. Sales revenue is not usually obtained in direct proportion to volume. Fixed costs would rarely be so fixed at low production volume. However, the graph does indicate the need for production to be kept at the highest possible volume. (This will help to determine policy towards wages payment and stoppages in production.)

C P V calculation

Date: 1/1/80
Production line: B.C.L.

	Production volume						
Item	40%	50%	60%	70%	80%	90%	100%
Units made	800	1000	1200	1400	1600	1800	2000
Sales revenue	£1.7	£1.9	£2.5	£2.8	£3.2	£3.6	£3.9
Variable cost	£1.0	£1.2	£1.3	£1.5	£1.8	£1.9	£2.0
Contribution	£0.7	£0.7	£1.2	£1.3	£1.4	£1.7	£1.8
Fixed cost	£1.2	£1.2	£1.2	£1.2	£1.2	£1.3	£1.4
Profit/loss	(£0.5)	(£0.5)	–	£0.1	£0.2	£0.4	£4.5
Unit cost	£2800	£2400	£2100	£1900	£1900	£1800	£1700

Fig. 8.14 Cost–profit–volume calculation

Fig. 8.14 indicates more realistically what might be the state of a production line at various volume levels. Sales revenue rises from £1.7m at 40 per cent volume to £3.9m at 100 per cent. Variable costs rise, but not necessarily in proportion to production volume. Fixed costs rise at 90 per cent volume, due perhaps to taking on more administrative personnel to handle more orders.

Even at 40 per cent capacity some contribution is being earned. Profit is not made until 70 per cent capacity is achieved. Unit costs decline from £2,800 at 40 per cent volume to £1,700 at 100 per cent.

There is, then, great importance between costs incurred, production volume and profit subsequently earned.

8.3.3 Costing and wage bargaining

The cost–profit–volume ratio described in the previous section indicates the sensitivity of the production process to:

1 changes in volume;
2 variations in standards of performance of all kinds;
3 requests for increases in wages and salaries.

There are obvious limits to the total amount of wages which can be paid. While wage rates are determined by a variety of factors, not least the national economic environment, whether the company can afford to pay a particular rate will depend upon:

4 the volume of production capacity being used;
5 the possibility of gaining extra contribution to compensate for the wage rise;
6 the general state of the cost–volume–profit ratio.

When wage bargaining is undertaken it seems important that appropriate C.P.V. information is available.

8.3.4 Limiting factor analysis

A 'limiting factor' is something which, over a period of time, will restrict the achievement of corporate objectives and the operation at maximum efficiency of production facilities generally.

Usually the limiting factor is a production constraint, often a bottleneck, where a machine or process cannot produce a higher output than is already being obtained. However, there could be other limiting factors — labour, material, power, some form of packaging, working capital, warehouse space etc.

If profits are to be maximised a short term aim will be to ensure that the limiting factor is utilised so that the best possible contribution is gained.

Fig. 8.15 shows a simple application of the principle. The drying capacity of a production line has been totally taken up by required production and is now a

Limiting factor analysis   Date   1.1.80
                                                          Machine: Drying

Product	Output rate per hour tonnes	Direct machine running cost per hour	Total marginal cost per hour	Sales revenue per process hour	Contribution per hour	Production priority
A	100	£30	£100	£150	£50	2
B	100	£30	£110	£160	£50	2
C	100	£30	£130	£170	£40	5
D	110	£30	£110	£160	£50	2
E	120	£30	£110	£180	£70	1
F	130	£30	£110	£120	£10	8
G	140	£30	£120	£150	£30	6
H	140	£30	£130	£160	£30	6

Fig. 8.15   Limiting factor analysis

bottleneck. What can be done to ensure that contribution is maximised?

The output rate likely to be achieved for each product is quoted in the first column. The next column quotes the direct machine (i.e. drying) cost which will be incurred in running the machine in each hour. It is assumed in the example that the same hourly costs will be incurred no matter what products are being dried — in practice this may not be so.

The next column shows the total marginal cost of the product. Normally the major extra costs incurred over the current machine cost will be the total of previous direct machine costs and the cost of material.

Sales revenue should then be recorded. To obtain such information may not be so easy as it seems as, normally, a product will be sold to numerous customers often in different markets, even different countries and each at a different price. So often a standard price is used.

The contribution per hour which each product gives is then calculated and a ranking in order of production priority determined as is shown in the example.

Such analyses can be carried out for any limiting factor. For example power could be crucial at some stage. It would then be necessary to calculate the contribution earned per unit of power consumed. (It will be necessary to calculate total power used throughout production and not at one machine.)

It is more complicated when there appears to be more than one bottleneck — say power and a labour shortage — but often one is more important than the other.

The need to be aware of contribution earnings and the potential bottlenecks which will affect them suggests that to have appropriate information from which limiting factor analysis can be carried out is always desirable. The need to change the product mix must be discussed with sales management and it may not always be desirable to make rapid alterations. Production personnel, however, should always be aware of the contribution being earned.

Capacity budgeting for 1980–1981

Date: 1/1/80

Production line: B.C.L.

Product group	Current capacity in units	% capacity of tech. max.	% capacity of std capacity	Possible change		
				3 months	6 months	12 months
A.C.L.	120,000	72%	61%	+2%	+10%	+12%

Total

Fig. 8.16 Capacity budget

8.3.5   Fixed capacity budgeting

The degree of flexibility in the use of labour which is available to a production manager has declined considerably, particularly through the increasing power of the trade unions and the introduction of government legislation concerning employment protection. It has become increasingly difficult to change capacity levels without incurring inordinate increases in labour costs.

It seems realistic, if not absolutely desirable, that the establishment of the profit plan should start with the assumption that production capacity is, within narrow limits, fixed in the short term. Production managers might consider completing the form shown as Fig. 8.16 to indicate the degree of flexibility which is available. The 'fixed capacity' can then tell sales/marketing personnel the extent to which production can meet product market demand. This is then the starting point for the budgeting process.

8.3.6   Budget validation and cost reduction

The budgeting activity, very often, has little to recommend it. While it is often said that a budget is a 'chart for a voyage', usually it is the same old journey growing progressively more costly. Last year's budget plus 10 per cent (or any figure which could seem to account for inflation) is the widely accepted method of arriving at a new budget. Sometimes a bit more is added on with the certain knowledge that senior management will take it off during budget scrutiny. So setting budgets is more often a game than a hard financial appreciation of what it will cost to run a department or a machine, with competent management.

Budget validation, therefore, should be introduced as a means of ensuring that the budgets which are set are at the lowest possible level which will still enable required results to be obtained. The validation should be a major part of any line management planning activity.

Methods

1   Some organisations have introduced a continuous assessment of budgets and budget performance — i.e. actual costs set against those that have been budgeted. A team is established of line and specialist cost reduction personnel (e.g. work study or internal consultants) who investigate the budgets of all manufacturing departments and suggest where cost reduction techniques might be applied to reduce the intended budget or correct out of course results.
2   Line managers are taught cost reduction and value-for-money procedures (i.e. value analysis and value administration) and have to confirm that they have undertaken a requisite validation before the budget is accepted.
3   A committee is established to vet all budgets before they are accepted. A criterion of value-for-money is used to determine whether the budget is truly needed at the level proposed to achieve corporate objectives.

4   Potential input and output indices are used to determine where budgeted costs appear to be too high.

8.3.7   Budgeting — backward iteration

The traditional method of arriving at a budgeted profit has been to total up all budgeted costs and then deduct them from budgeted sales revenue. This process is acceptable if it leads to an outcome of desired profit. However, in practice this rarely happens.

There is a more dynamic and eventually more satisfactory method of carrying out what could be the same process called 'backward iteration'.

The choice of profit or other principal objectives is made and then the steps taken are backward into the resources, standards of performance, costs and revenues, which must be achieved if corporate objectives are to be gained. The required levels of performance are established and then compared with what local line managers believe they can achieve. A debate concerning the discrepancy between the two is then carried out.

If some local performance requirements are agreed at a level lower than that required to meet corporate objectives, other performances must be enhanced — if this is possible.

8.3.8   Cost-modelling

The need for backward iteration to establish levels of performance which come nearest to achieving required corporate objectives suggests that cost-modelling needs to be developed.

A model is a representation of a whole or part of the characteristics of a real life situation. In production, useful systems models will comprise a series of mathematical equations which are manipulated to simulate a real life system.

Usually a system's model is used to predict the outcome of decisions to be made to affect the real process. 'What if we did this …?' is the type of thing.

Cost-modelling, therefore, could be useful to any production manager who is involved with budgeting and objectives setting. It could also be used for the purpose of forecasting likely contribution earnings. Costing and management accounting generally have been based on providing comparisons of actual with standard performance, sometimes long after the event which is being reported. This has the drawback of being wise after the event. The possibility of making significant improvements is restricted to still unmonitored future activities. There would obviously be advantages in considering these from a future-potential cost-earnings point of view. A cost-model could provide information from which order sequencing, machine manning levels, machine utilisation, etc. could be so established that contribution earnings might be maximised.

8.3.9   Zero-budgeting

Zero-budgeting roughly covers what has already been described but there are some differences. Like budget-evaluation and backward iteration, it starts with the premise that traditional budgeting is not very effective as it provides insufficient information for budget approvals and does not, as a rule, suggest an appropriate means for measuring performance.

Zero-budgeting focuses on two main areas of cost — discretionary overheads and non-capitalised development expenses. The former covers costs not directly associated with production — accounting, maintenance, quality control etc. The latter are the research and development activities which occur in the works on an ad hoc basis.

The zero-budgeting method starts with a belief that money spent on discretionary costs (i.e. they can be accepted or not) has to be seen to produce more in value than is spent.

The true costs of providing any service are then calculated. Marginal analysis is used to measure the relationship between input and output.

Traditional budget or cost centres are redesignated 'decision units'. (Cost centres may be split to provide a decision unit.) The managers of the decision units carry out an analysis which is directed towards reasons why the unit exists. The analysis will help to suggest (i.e. if the unit is to be maintained) the minimum amount of money needed to give a required service. Any addition to the service must be viewed marginally, i.e. the value gained must be greater than the money spent.

All managers of decision units then submit their plans or budgets to their superior who directs resources to the units which will give most reward for the marginal costs incurred. The direction of resources needs a ranking of all activities.

9

Production control

9.1 INTRODUCTION

Definitions of 'production control' are various and occasionally disconcerting. For present purposes it is suggested that 'production control' covers all the functions and activities which process orders and, at the same time, have a fundamental effect on production resource utilisation and efficiency.

Fig. 9.1 indicates the likely activities which are considered under the title of 'production control'. (It will be seen that only a proportion of these will normally be under the control of a production manager.) Production control is concerned with both marketing and production, linking the two together; so that while there is efficient production planning, marketing people respond to production situations.

9.2 PRODUCTION CONTROL OBJECTIVES

The following may all be considered simultaneously as suitable objectives for production control:

X per cent of orders produced on time;
X per cent of orders produced within Y weeks;
Increased production by X amount;
Reduction in production costs — for example reducing set-ups and idle time and so increasing machine and labour utilisation;
Reduction in overtime;
Reduction in shopfloor labour;
Improvement in cash flow by reducing work in progress, raw material stocks and finished goods stocks;

Improvement in production — market flexibility, to ensure increased competitiveness;

Maximisation of added value;

Minimisation of industrial relations problems.

The achievement of one of these could be at the expense of others. For example, the majority of orders could be produced on time but this could lead to minimal order batching, which in turn will increase production costs. More finished goods stocks could help batching, but cash flow will deteriorate.

It is important, therefore, that production and other managers be able to calculate the advantages of accepting one or other of a series of objectives; they must be aware of the need to consider 'trade-offs' and have the information on which to do it.

The objectives of a production control system will help to determine:

1   The type of system required. For example if the organisation is dominated by a need to provide product market flexibility and a speedy response to customer demands, then the production control system must have 'flexibility' as an overriding design consideration.

2   The data needed, judging by the relative merits of undertaking one as opposed to other courses of action and deciding upon order sequencing rules on which production scheduling is based, require appropriate data. .

3   How the system is operated. For example, a manual system will have a limited capacity to handle large quantities of information. It may be restricted also in providing sufficient flexibility.

4   The degree of interrelationship needed within the production control system. Links between inventory control and production planning can be strong or weak depending upon the importance of ex-stock deliveries.

9.3   TYPES OF PRODUCTION ACTIVITY

It has become traditional in describing production control to suggest that systems design will largely be determined by the type of production process being controlled — i.e. batch, job shop, process or flow line. While these factors may play a major part in determining the type of production control system, it is often even more important to consider whether the production process makes for stock or to customer order. If customer order manufacturing predominates, are orders made to a customer's own design or are they repetitive or non-repetitive, expensive or of low value?

The analysis of these latter types of production activity (i.e. made for stock or customers) will help to determine:

1   the strength of the linkages in the system between order input, stock control and factory scheduling;

2   the need to improve forecasting and relate the results to capacity planning;
3   the emphasis which needs to be built into the system — e.g. flexibility, responsiveness, need for control, good customer delivery performance, low cost manufacture, cash flow requirements etc.

9.4   DATA FOR PRODUCTION CONTROL PURPOSES

A key factor in production control systems is the availability of relevant data and the way it is structured. The fixed data required will include:

1   operational capacities (technical maximum, standard and current capacities);
2   manufacturing methods. Each product should have an operations layout or routing sheet prepared for it which shows the machines and operations, its production route, tolerances, other making particulars which need to apply.
3   Bill of materials. The components of a product are usually referred to as a bill of materials, where component relationships are established (i.e. what is used with what). Historical data for this purpose is usually filed under one of three headings:
    (a)   separate definition of each part, with a unique number;
    (b)   the finished part number and a variant that is given to every component;
    (c)   standard variants with alternatives based on 'add to' or 'take from' the standard variant.
    Bills of material can provide alternatives when parts are out of stock as well as 'kitting lists' when the product is not stored in its assembled form.
4   Part, product and operational costs. Emphasis must be on direct or variable costs which are controlled by production management.
5   Included with product data may be:
    Recommended 'batch with' information
    Alternative resource uses ⎫   which can be used when
    Alternative operations   ⎬   limiting factor analysis
    Alternative routes   ⎭   is required.

Organisation of the data is extremely important. It must be easily accessible, for either retrieval or updating. Different users may need the information, so multi-user access is required. Responsibility for data accuracy and integrity must be clear. Where large volumes of data are needed, the use of computer facilities is practically mandatory.

In most moderate to large systems, the establishment of a product/production control data base system is essential. A data or specifications department is often required. A good part numbering system is another important aspect of controlling data and will often aid computer use.

In passing, it is recommended that rigorous product rationalisation and standardisation will pay dividends both in simplifying the data requirements for the production control system and in reducing the overall product/production control complexity.

9.5 ASPECTS OF PRODUCTION CONTROL

It is impossible to suggest a system that will suit all types of production process and all variations in 'make to stock', 'make to order' etc., but there are standard operations which should be considered in designing, redesigning or auditing a production control system. The importance of each function and the internal emphasis within each function will largely be determined by local objectives.

A typical production control system is shown in Fig. 9.1. The main functions are quoted along the middle line — capacity planning, production requirements planning, material requirements planning, production scheduling and sequencing, and performance monitoring. These functions can be regarded as building blocks which are used to complete the whole system. They have, so far as production control is concerned, links with other systems — management accounting, inventory control, maintenance, and so provide the means of planning and control of all resources within the production system.

The building blocks may not be of equal importance. In some companies strict capacity planning may not be necessary, as capacities are rarely, if ever, full. There may be a strong need, however, to control work flow very closely as adequate cash flow is crucial. Then the most important production control blocks will be scheduling and control.

Each building block is now described and one practical application recorded.

9.5.1 Capacity planning

Capacity planning relates product/market requirements and production capacities in the longer term. In some organisations it may be possible to do this for several years ahead and embody the result in the long range plan. In other companies capacity planning may be possible only on a quarterly basis, owing to the dynamic nature of the business.

Objectives for the production system should be established during the capacity planning stage. For example:

Production capacity to be utilised
Levels of finished goods stock to be carried
Delivery service required
Product/market allocations of capacity
Production cost levels

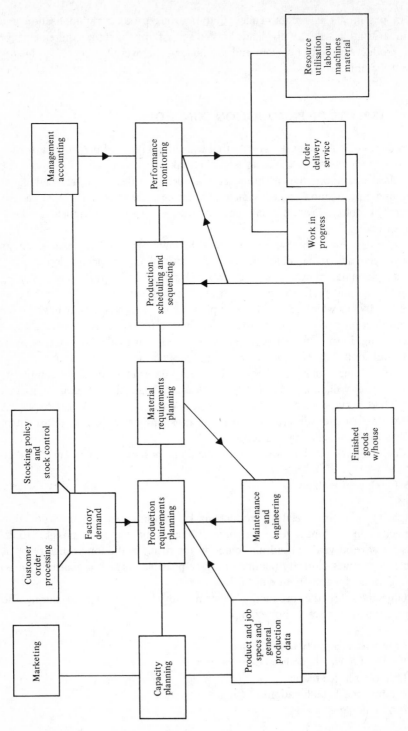

Fig. 9.1   A typical production control system

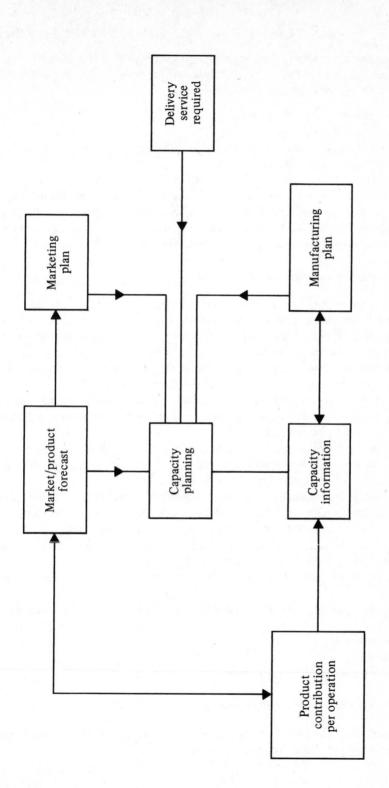

Fig. 9.2 Capacity planning

Such objectives should then be embodied in the organisation's budgets.

There is also a need at this stage to calculate the possible outcome of various alternative uses of production resources, i.e.:

Contribution per product market
Contribution per product item
Value of finished goods stocks when related to reducing factory costs
Added value improvements.

Acceptable solutions may be derived only after considerable juggling with alternatives. The 'interactive' nature of the process is emphasised in Fig. 9.2. Until capacity planning has been undertaken it is unlikely that an appropriate marketing or manufacturing plan can be established.

9.5.2 Production requirements planning

Capacity planning is the process of considering how production facilities are utilised in the longer term to achieve corporate objectives. Production requirements planning is the shorter term application of the same rules with additional information on the current state of the order book, the pattern of ordering, the needs for cash flow and profit, the state of the production unit, breakdowns, engineering problems, labour difficulties etc. (See Fig. 9.3.)

Capacity planning may have been carried out at a time when the product market and production situation looked very different from when production requirements planning takes place.

Capacity planning is often strategic; production requirements planning is more tactical with a comparatively short time horizon. It has to adapt the capacity plan to make sense of the current situation.

In many organisations production requirements planning is based on a monthly plan which takes account of current constraints. It may be necessary to carry out limiting factor analysis at this stage (i.e. the maximisation of a resource of some kind which is limiting output). An ability to redesign the output arrangements of the factory and perhaps consider the short term implications of lack of a raw material or some labour problem is also necessary.

Capacity planning will have suggested how quickly changes can be made to:

Production levels
Sales mix
Performance in deliveries and cost

9.5.3 Materials requirements planning

Materials requirements planning (see Fig. 9.4) will follow from carrying out capacity and production requirements planning.

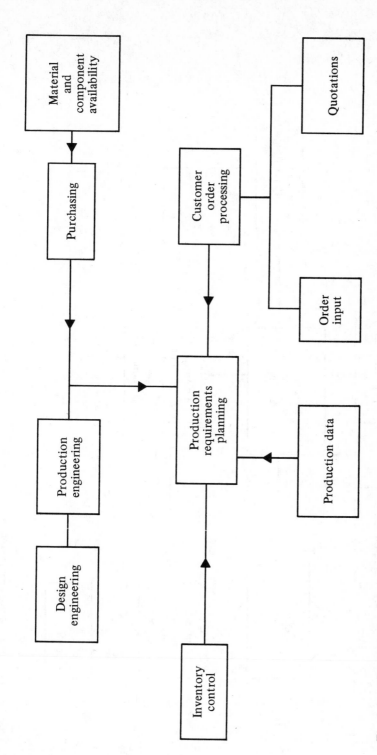

Fig. 9.3   Production requirements planning

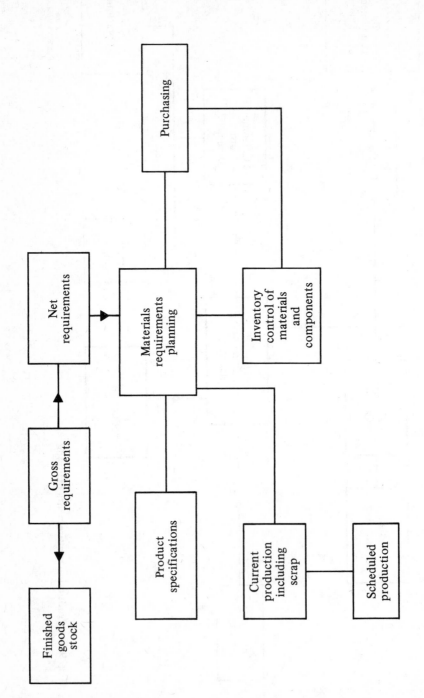

Fig. 9.4   Materials requirements planning

At the capacity planning level longer term plans for raw materials and components will be established (long term contracts should be made for example). In the shorter term material requirements will be matched against current stock levels and potential (and actual) changes in demand and production.

Material purchases account for between one-third and two-thirds of total cost in many organisations and are key factors in cash flow considerations. So a separate material purchase and control plan is usually made which fits in with production planning and also takes account of current cash flow requirements. Often the whole of material cost is controlled under one manager. These costs include finished goods stock, raw material and component stocks, work in progress and even consumable stores. An appropriate set of sub-systems is required to handle this arrangement. Such systems will need to be:

Flexible enough to handle quickly changes in order input and production levels. (Reaction time is very important.)

Able to synchronise material purchases and material stocking to meet production requirements and yet still maintain required stock levels.

(Manual systems are not always flexible enough to provide information for them to control the interaction between stocks and production.)

9.5.4 Production scheduling and sequencing

Both capacity planning and production requirements planning will make use of simple scheduling rules when production capacities are related to order input. Priorities are established which determine the use of production equipment and the sequence in which orders will be manufactured. Materials planning will help to determine which products can be batched to run together and what batch sizes might be appropriate.

Scheduling of production (often called operations scheduling) therefore rarely starts with a clean sheet of paper and the question 'how shall we sequence these orders on the factory?'. It is, however, important that the scheduling and sequencing rules agreed at capacity and production requirements planning levels are made explicit and expanded to ensure that scheduling is as effective as current constraints allow. Fig. 9.5 shows the main elements involved.

In scheduling, current capacities are matched against available order input and an order operational sequence determined which, it is hoped, will achieve required delivery dates. Predetermined scheduling rules, current capacities, queue lengths, factory work load (i.e. work already scheduled and sequenced) and delivery dates are used to determine when and how work is loaded to the production lines.

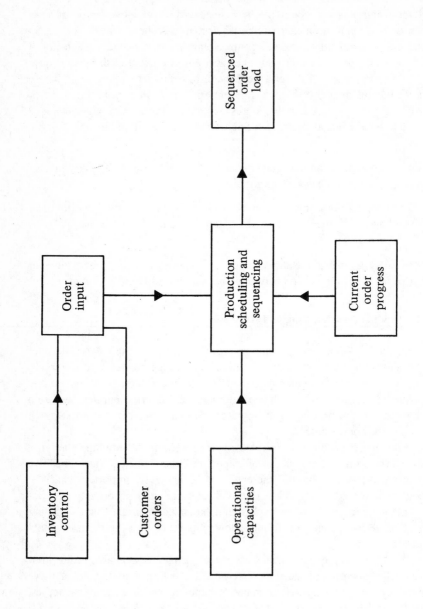

Fig. 9.5   Production scheduling and sequencing

A scheduling technique is used which matches corporate strategies. The technique will usually be chosen by taking account of:

1   The production system, i.e. whether manufacture is repetitive or one-off. A batch manufacturer may plan each operation item by item. A company operating a flow line may only need careful control over order input. The degree of matching between capacity and order input will probably require to be developed in greater detail for high cost, high production value machining than for comparatively simple production processes.
2   Degree of control required. In many production units first line supervisors carry out a scheduling activity allocating work to the machine operatives under their control. Consequently, planning the machine zone may be all that is required. The potential use of a machine operation is also important. If the operation normally lasts longer than a shift, minute by minute control may not be necessary.
3   Other uses of scheduling systems. Many scheduling systems are used for purposes other than scheduling work. For example, they may need to record input to a production section and form part of the management accounting system. Tool ordering may be an important part of the programmes or schedules which are issued. Confirmed customer delivery promises may be taken from the schedule.
4   Priorities. The system of order priorities must be reasonably disciplined, if scheduling rules are to be effective. Within limits there must be an element of discipline in establishing priorities. The constant leapfrogging of orders will only cause chaos and the probable breakdown of the scheduling system.

Three major scheduling methods are commonly used. These are:

Priority scheduling

There are numerous methods of establishing an order's priority — e.g.:

1   Latest start date — taking account of process time, free or float time available in the plant and the number of operations.
2   Latest finish date.
3   Earliest start date.
4   Time to complete the order.
5   Value of work in progress represented by orders etc.

In priority scheduling actual start and finish dates and times for each operation and product are not calculated. The order priority on which the shop floor should operate only is indicated.

However, in priority scheduling operations must not be overloaded. The total operational time available must be greater than the priority load. A calculation of the total production line load and capacity is usually made to ensure that work in progress is kept at a minimum level.

Ensuring operational balance (i.e. that the right mix of work is always available at each operation at all times) could be difficult.

Serial scheduling

In serial scheduling, orders also are given a priority sequence. Machine operations are loaded in priority order. Once an order is completed it is transferred to its next operation. Only if orders (individually) fill each operational capacity, will maximum resource usage occur.

Parallel scheduling

The essence of parallel scheduling lies in maximising machine use.

Orders to be scheduled are allocated the earliest and latest finish dates at each operation in order to achieve their final delivery date. Then 'float' is calculated, i.e. the difference between the earliest and latest finish dates less manufacturing and set up time.

Resource availability is calculated, and then according to the priority order sequence, orders are loaded until resource availability is taken up.

Combination of systems

Perhaps the best scheduling system will be a combination of priority and parallel scheduling, which will provide maximum machine use and a basis for delivery date processing.

Scheduling systems can be highly complex depending upon the product mix and control needed. Other considerations to be taken into account include:

1   The time span of a schedule. In most organisations it is a week, or at most a month. Work is set out in the form of a production programme. Weekly schedules give a facility for fairly speedy schedule redrafting, where current production performance can be taken into account.
2   The scheduling of time. This can be done in discrete units — e.g. shifts or days. Where close control is needed standard hours are often used.
3   Network scheduling is used where assembly of components into one product is carried out.
4   Backward and forward scheduling. Either of these methods might be used. Backward scheduling uses a plan based on the latest date for an order to achieve its delivery time. This gives little or no time to recover late orders, but should ensure that work in progress is minimised.

Forward scheduling fits orders into production as soon as a space becomes available. This may raise work in progress and finished goods stock, but should achieve a high percentage of orders delivered on time and minimise delivery lead times.

(The output from a scheduling system is often referred to as a programme or work-to list.)

9.5.5 Performance monitoring

Performance monitoring is a term used to cover all recording activities which take place on the shop floor once a work schedule has been issued. The simplest way to do this is to record achievements against the schedule or programme and institute corrective action once out of course events have been recognised. (This assumes that the format of the schedule is such that it allows close control of this type.)

Schedule checking, however, may leave out a considerable number of 'performances' which will need careful monitoring:

1   Order location and status

It will not be sufficient usually to report that an order is standing in a particular production zone or work centre. The number of products being made will be required. In a multi-operation shop, some may have been rejected at a previous operation and the amount still being produced will be important when considering order cover and the priority being given to the order for production purposes. An indication will also be needed of the length of time the order still has to stand before being worked on.

Both actual and potential delivery delays need to be reported and, where necessary, action taken to ensure that delayed orders are given priority.

Locating every order at every operation may not be possible. Reporting points that correspond to the end of a responsibility zone can be instituted as an alternative.

2   Work in progress

The order location and status data should be aggregated to provide information to monitor work in progress. This will be particularly useful where production personnel tend to buffer production to improve the possibility of batching.

3   Shop output and plant utilisation

Aggregation of order achievement provides the basis for calculating shop output and plant utilisation. Orders produced are converted into standard hours, or some other measurement and used to compare actual with planned output. A calculation of plant utilisation can also be made.

The reasons for not achieving planned machine utilisation should be known. This information may have to be sought from operatives' work booking documents and machine log books or machine charts which directly monitor machine running.

Occasionally maintenance document data will need to be used to determine reasons for breakdowns.

4   Cost monitoring

Cost performance monitoring has obvious links with the management accounting system. Conversion of achieved production into standard hours will be needed, to which a standard cost can be applied. Actual costs of labour utilised (data from the payroll), material consumed, and power and other variable costs incurred can be added together and compared with the standard cost of production.

A wider and more significant cost monitoring will be needed to confirm the rightness of decisions made concerning the 'trade-offs' related to production control objectives. For example, has a rise in finished goods stock brought more benefits from reduced set ups than the extra carrying costs of the increased stock? This kind of performance monitoring and that normally recorded in a management accounting system may need different data requirements.

5   Material utilisation and quality control

The material requirements planning and material control system will require records of material input to the production process, product outputs, work in progress and material losses. This information will be the same as that required for the management accounting system (so each event should be reported only once). Quality control data will help to evaluate operational losses being incurred in the process. Often quality control is pursued as if it were a function separate from materials requirements planning and indeed, on occasions, as an activity divorced from the production process as well. Information must be provided in a way which helps to improve materials productivity, not merely preventing reject material being sent to the customer.

6   Tool control

Tool performance is often an important part of ensuring that the production process is running efficiently and orders are being produced on time. Tool control is, therefore, important:

Tool availability — is a tool available for production purposes?

Tool condition — how long has a tool been in use? Can it be assumed it will fail in X more hours or days?

Tool progress — if a tool has been sent to the tool room what priority has it been given and when is it likely to be returned to production?

Standard tool performance should be known, and control exercised over tool room activities. The latter are not usually considered to be part of the main stream of production control.

9.6 PRACTICAL APPLICATION OF PRODUCTION CONTROL PRINCIPLES

The previous section suggested that production control can be approached and appropriate systems developed from a building block viewpoint. It was also suggested that there are general production control principles which can be applied no matter what manufacturing activities are being performed. Systems design will depend upon:

the environment in which the production system operates;
the objectives of the production control system;
the comparative importance given to the 'building blocks' within the production system;
local expertise in systems design.

The present section gives a practical example of the application of production control theory in a job shop, where approximately 2,000 product orders are made each month from a total product range of approximately 7,000. [Figs. 9.6–9.12].

The headings used and the relevant production control building blocks are as follows:

Heading in the practical example	*Building blocks in production control theory*
1 Establishment of operational report capacities [Figs. 9.6 (1) and (2)]	1 Production control data. Data base
2 Alignment of production capacities with order input [Figs. 9.7 (1) and (2)]	2 Capacity planning
3 Work acceptance [Figs. 9.8 (1) and (2)]	3 Production requirements planning

4 Control of planning documentation
   [Figs. 9.9 (1) and (2)]

4 Not listed as such but obviously
   important

5 Load breakdown — initial factory
   scheduling
   [Figs. 9.10 (1), (2) and (3)]

5 Production scheduling and
   sequencing

6 Factory scheduling
   [Figs. 9.11 (1) and (2)]

6 Production scheduling and
   sequencing

7 Order control and work in progress
   [Fig. 9.12]

7 Performance monitoring

8 Performance monitoring

8 Performance monitoring

1) ESTABLISHMENT OF OPERATIONAL CAPACITIES

Method	Control	Origins of control data
(a) Aim To establish technical maximum, standard, and currently achieved capacities. To record how such capacities can be improved/decreased. To highlight constraints and time scales which inhibit changes in capacity levels.	The line status report updated monthly.	*(a)* Data provided by local Production Section Management and Production Superintendents.
(b) Procedure A line status report which sets out the above information will be updated each month. The figures recorded should be agreed by local Production Superintendents and Section Managers. Works Planning Management will vet the capacities recorded and where necessary, discuss the need for change with the Production Line Manager.		*(b)* Data collected and collated by Data Department and issued to the Production Director, Works Planning Management and Product Line Management.

Fig. 9.6(1)   Establishment of operational capacities

Month _____

Zone	Machine/operation	Output rates			Bottleneck and potential bottleneck	Operation/machine status
		Technical maximum	Standard output	Current output		

Fig. 9.6(2) Line status report

Method	Control	Origins of control data
(a) Aim To agree production capacities with Distribution and Sales personnel which accommodate current demand. To arrange for capacity changes which will take place in an agreed time period.	*(a)* The Product Line, Forward Load statement which shows current agreed capacities by product type and capacity centre, the current weekly allocation of capacity by product market, current orders awaiting manufacture and queue lengths.	*(a)* Current capacities agreed monthly between Production and Distribution/ Sales Departments.
(b) Procedure A monthly meeting will take place between Production and Works Planning Management and Sales and Distribution Management, where current capacities and order demand are discussed and, where necessary, arrangements made to change them (to either increase or decrease them.) Changes in capacity should only be carried out within agreed lead times, to ensure that factory resources are not under utilised. Current demand will be calculated as 'queue weeks' i.e. the amount of work, at current capacities, available to be issued to the works.		*(b)* Order Department will provide information on demand and queue lengths. *(c)* Document provided by Order Department.

Fig. 9.7(1)   Alignment of production capacities with order input

Month:

Product category	Product description	Current capacity	Market allocation of capacity		Five month moving average of market demand	Current load content	Queue data		
			Market	Capacity			Items in queue	Queue weeks	Current delivery offered

Fig. 9.7(2)   Order input – current capacity report

3) WORK ACCEPTANCE

Method	Control	Origins of control data
(a) Aim To ensure that orders accepted by Works Planning Department match current capacity. This should ensure that delivery promises, based on order queue sequence and current capacity, will be kept.	Load Report Data Sheet agreed by Works Planning Dept.	Distribution (Order) Dept will supply:— Production category item requirements Reissues Order items Size of orders and present it on the Load Report Data Sheet.
(b) Procedure Distribution Department will agree overall capacities with Production Management. There will then be an agreed distribution of this capacity between Product Market Managers.		
As orders are received, or raised via the stock control system, they will join a queue held in Order Department.		
The priorities or sequence of items in the queue will be determined by Sales and Distribution Department, not by Production personnel.		
The queue will be built into loads, which match current agreed production capacities at key capacity work centres.		
At agreed intervals, a work load (given a code letter) will be sent to Works Planning Department.		
A speedy analysis of the load will then be carried out by Works Planning personnel to ensure that:		
1 The load of orders matches current capacity, particularly by product categories, at key work centres.		

Fig. 9.8(1)   Work acceptance

Method	Control	Origins of control data

2 The mix of product orders is as agreed with distribution department.

3 Order size mix is in line with that agreed.

4 Approximate delivery dates have been established. Delivery dates will be determined by reference to the place or sequence an order is given in the queue and current capacities.

The load queue in Order Department
There will be agreement on how long (or short) the queue has to be before the factory capacity is changed.

Fig. 9.8(1)   (*Continued*)

Load data sheet

Load reference

Date:—

Load element	Target		Works backlog	This load	
Product category	New orders	Re-issues		New orders	Re-issues
A					
B					
C					
D					
E					
F					
G					
H					
J					

Fig. 9.8(2)   Load data sheet

4) CONTROL OF PLANNING DOCUMENTATION

Method	Control	Origins of control data
(a) Aim To ensure that all order documentation in Works Planning Office is handled effectively, expeditiously and completely. To avoid any order being mislaid.	Weekly document control sheet.	Each planning function completes a batch control slip, each time orders are passed from one function to another.
(b) Procedure The requirements of Distribution Department are converted into works order card sets. (The production of the numbers of card sets takes account of materials handling constraints in the Works.) As each batch of cards are sent from one planning function to another (i.e. materials issues, loading, scheduling etc.), they are counted and signed for. The results are published on a document control sheet each week, the total order quantities being accounted for at each section. Mislaid items are 'chased'. Inputs to the computer are also handled by a batch control system where 'batch-counting' is carried out. Orders are date stamped where necessary when they leave each planning function.		

Fig. 9.9(1)   Control of planning documentation

Document control weekly report

Week ending ——————

Details	Load no.			Load no.			Load no.			Load no.		
	F33 cards	ST2 fact sets	ST1 fact sets	F33 cards	ST2 fact sets	ST1 fact sets	F33 cards	ST2 fact sets	ST1 fact sets	F33 cards	ST2 fact sets	ST1 fact sets
Load requirements												
Balance o/s Control 2 Document control												
Control 3 Material allocation												
Control 4 Typists												
Control 5 Stage 1 loading												
Control 7 Stage 2 loading												
Total balance												
Issued to factory F33 cards filed												
Total balance plus issued to factory												

Fig. 9.9(2)   Document control weekly report

5) LOAD BREAKDOWN – INITIAL FACTORY SCHEDULING

Method	Control	Origins of control data
(a) Aim 1 To ensure that orders are assembled and batched in a way which minimises operational set ups and machine/tool changes on the works. 2 To ensure that the issues to the works will provide 'zone balance' i.e. the right amount and kind of work, will be available in each part of the factory at all times. Allowance for potential breakdowns and other contingencies is built into the load. 3 To provide the possibility of changing the load sequence if a breakdown occurs.	1 Planned set ups and tools as a proportion of machine operating time, should be in line with agreed standards. 2 The factory load statement, which compares weekly forward load quantities with agreed capacities. Also included are delayed product quantities and items in each work capacity centre.	Loading section in Works Planning Department
(b) Method Product category requirements are analysed and segregated into weekly quantities equal to the current work centre capacities, throughout the plant. Products are batched to relate their size and quality characteristics to production tooling and operational constraints. Rough order sequencing is established which will achieve standard non productive/ productive time ratios. The factory is divided into zones which comprise a series of operations, one or other of which will be the potential bottleneck. Recognition of this fact will be made in establishing zone completion times, i.e. the time which each order will clear each zone.		

Fig. 9.10(1)   Load breakdown – initial factory scheduling

Load number:—

Work centre/zone	Agreed standards	Weekly plan			
		Planned week no.	Planned week no.	Planned week no.	Planned week no.

Fig. 9.10(2)   Load breakdown report

Date:—

Work centres	Sales forecast	Agreed weekly target	Arrears on the factory		Weekly loads								Output needed to complete arrears and week load
					Week no.		Week no.		Week no.		Week no.		
			Pieces	Orders	Pieces	Orders	Pieces	Orders	Pieces	Orders	Pieces	Orders	

Fig. 9.10(3)   Weekly load statement

6) FACTORY SCHEDULING

Method	Control	Origins of control data
(a) Aim To ensure that order sequencing is established and records of this are made, so that product/operations are carried out in a way which achieves minimum set ups and re-tooling, while achieving predetermined delivery promises.	Planned non-production time/ production time for each production line.	Programmes issued to the Works.

(b)
To provide work in units/ values equal to required quantities, for payment purposes.

(b) Procedure
Work is issued to the factory on a programme. The programme lists the order number and quantity to be achieved and the sequence in which work is to be carried out. A calculation of work content of each order and of each programme is made which ensures that a complete match is achieved between programmed work and available operational capacity.

The programmes are accepted by local production management and are checked daily and weekly to determine whether achievements equal planned requirements.

Fig. 9.11(1)   **Factory scheduling**

Load no.

Work centre/zone	Standard weekly quantities	Standard set up/ production ratio	Weekly schedules							
			Per week no.		Week no.		Week no.		Week no.	
			Planned	Achvd	Planned	Achvd	Planned	Achvd	Planned	Achvd

Fig. 9.11(2)   Factory scheduling and control

7) ORDER CONTROL AND WORK IN PROGRESS

Method	Control	Origins of control data
(a) Aim To ensure that orders are completed on time.	1 Tabulation from the computer.	1 Data processing department.
(b) Procedure Reporting points have been established in Works Planning and the factory, and are used to report order progress. When orders pass a reporting point, order numbers are transmitted to the computer via the Works Planning Office. See-Check equipment.	2 Delayed order counts carried out in the zone control system. 3 Delayed order summary list provided by the computer.	2 Provided by local production management. 3 Completed in Works Planning Office.
Tabulations of Work In Progress are printed by the computer. These show order delays in each zone.		
The zone control system operating in the works, provides local management with information concerning orders delayed in the zone.		
Programmes are checked daily and weekly to ensure that all orders are completed on time.		

Fig. 9.12   Order control and work in progress

Materials requirements planning is not considered as such, but in practice it has links with capacity planning and also with production requirements planing.

In this practical application the most important of the production control building blocks is scheduling.

9.7   IMPROVING PRODUCTION CONTROL

Production control is at the heart of any manufacturing organisation. If it is done well then nearly inevitably the whole organisation will do well. The benefits that can be obtained from improving production control, therefore, are considerable.

The following suggestions might be useful when improvements are considered:

1   Production control covers functions which traditionally many managers have thought to be independent, not interdependent. Designing separate systems for each function will be counter-productive.

It is usually impossible to develop a total production control system at one time. It would be wasteful of resources and probably produce chaos when implementation started. It seems quite feasible to take the most important of the building blocks in production control and start from there. (The starting point will obviously be dissimilar in different organisations.) However, the overall system must be designed or at least be seen and understood in principle, if not in detail, before the individual systems (building blocks) are tackled.

2   Data is a vital factor in improving production control, particularly for production controllers and others who manage production control resources. They need to assess the various alternatives which are possible in using their resources and relate them to corporate objectives. For example, when should a machine be broken down and another item run on it? When can inventory levels be increased (and to what level) so that increased batch sizes can be run on the shop floor?

Most of the data which are needed to improve production control are already available somewhere in a company. What is often required is that it be collected and then recorded in a way which can be readily assessed so that the most appropriate alternative from one or more possible courses of action can be chosen. For example, if a more flexible approach to order acceptance and processing is required, or if inventories have to be reduced because improvements in cash flow are essential, then the probable impact on production activities should be quickly determined.

The implications of this suggestion are:

(a)   Data must be available on demand by all managers concerned, so that such options can be considered. All interrelated activities comprising production control, not just the parts of it directly concerned with manufacturing, need to be considered.

(b)   The data must be collected and eventually structured so that it can answer 'what if we did this?' types of question, which are fundamental to the best use of production control resources.

(c)   The discussion in 2 presupposes that the objectives of production control are always appreciated and everything possible is done to ensure that the correct choice is made. Some of the more important trade-offs have been listed previously but, perhaps to labour the point, there is often a bias built into the system which is not borne out in reality. For example, customer-service requirements may apparently dominate at the expense of least-cost manufacturing. This could result from an inadequate knowledge of the 'trade-offs' particularly in not considering contribution earnings from key customers.

Production control objectives are often unclear or even unstated. (Hence one difficulty in developing production control systems is making some assessment of the potential benefits. So inadequate systems resources are often deployed in the production area.) This lack of precision has influence on many production control staff who are often unsure of their role. They spend a considerable part of their time chasing delinquent orders, but insufficient effort to the planning activities which should optimise the use of production facilities.

A moderate production control system with clear cut objectives and a well controlled approach to applying them will always be better than a better system applied with inadequate discipline and unclear objectives.

3 Production control systems, like the overall production system, are influenced by the external environment and it would be unproductive to design systems which are not responsive to the environment. If this is true what important environmental factors need to be considered? Perhaps the following:

Planning time scales have, of necessity, to be much shorter than they were. The long term planning which was in vogue a few years ago may still be necessary to make diversification, acquisition or major capital expenditure strategies but comparatively short term planning is now probably more important to most companies. The difficulties of judging rates of inflation, the possibility of industrial action leading to a shortage of key resources (e.g. power), possible changes in product markets, especially overseas, will surely continue.

Flexibility in production control, therefore, is essential. If a raw material suddenly rises in price or a bottleneck changes in the factory, the potential impact on profit needs to be calculated very quickly. The product mix which gave maximum contribution a month ago may suddenly become inadequate for profit purposes.

Manpower flexibility has declined over the last few years. The power of trade unions has ensured that labour mobility is now less than it used to be. Dismissing part of a workforce is now much more difficult than it was. So, while increased flexibility is required to meet changing environments, there is a necessity to treat labour as more fixed than it has ever been previously. It is important therefore to ensure that the inanimate parts of a production control activity be carried out correctly. It is no longer possible to rely on the possibility that changes of all kinds can be buffered by manpower flexibility.

4   In an era when educational qualifications are valued highly it appears paradoxical to suggest that the calibre of people operating production control systems may actually be declining. At the same time, it is expected that the production control system needs to meet ever more demanding requirements. This incompatibility can only be met by the increasing use of computer data processing equipment.

5   The possible improvements to production control systems listed in 1 to 4 are general to all aspects of such systems. It may be useful to consider the possible improvements which might be introduced, under the headings of the main production control building blocks:

Capacity planning
Development might be concentrated on:

> Providing information on capacities that make sense to marketing personnel. Categorisation of products in a manner that allows calculation of product items into work-centre capacities could be worthwhile.

> Forecasting. This may need improving particularly in considering the external environment.

> Long term contracts which even out order flow. These will be beneficial in enabling a longer time to be taken than would be possible without them.

> Better marketing decisions which may use contribution analysis and statistical analysis on market profiles.

> Modelling which may be a useful technique to test assumptions about resource usage.

Production requirements planning
Development might concentrate on:

> Improving inventory management, especially in the provision of orders for the factory. Enhanced ABC evaluation may help in this respect. The re-order system should be based on a re-order cycle, where inventory replacement requirements are matched against an allocated capacity (see Chapter 10).

> Batching rules which may need to be extended, to provide an appropriate link between inventory levels and factory efficiency.

> Management accounting systems which provide information for choosing between competing resource usage and objectives.

Functions which restrict customer service and planning in general, e.g. design, estimating, purchasing, warehousing and delivery, maintenance. They should (according to their local importance) be linked into the main system.

Customer order processing which could be crucial if many orders are handled each day and the company's competitors provide a fast delivery service. Profile planning may provide rapid analysis of future work loads and resource requirements including cash flow.

Material requirements planning
Developments might be concentrated on:

Systems which encompass materials in all aspects — purchase, storage, stock control, order input, uses, quality failings, output to the finished goods warehouse.

Forecasting and links made between capacity and production requirements planning.

Updating of stock records and establishing their relationship with current and planned product-capacity usage. (This is a 'netting' procedure.)

Stock control which may need to be enhanced to link more closely with production scheduling. The levels of safety stock which need to be carried should be reviewed carefully so as to conserve cash, but not run out of stock.

Checking on material yield. Measurement of technical and operational losses may be worthwhile.

Performance monitoring
Developments might be concerned with:

Providing facilities which give 'immediate' (on line) knowledge concerning order progress and status.

Data collection equipment. This might be rejected by shopfloor personnel. Any system which involves shopfloor production personnel must be designed to take account of possible industrial relations problems. It may be worthwhile to develop performance monitoring procedures with, not necessarily for, shopfloor people.

Performance monitoring which provides a double check on production recording. Using one data source for several systems is useful.

Production scheduling and sequencing
Possible developments:

Choosing a scheduling and sequencing method which fits overall strategy requirements. The method may be simple or complicated depending upon the environment of the organisation and the production control system. The scheduling method must be a discipline which everyone concerned with scheduling should apply. The discipline it imposes on the production control system should be known by everyone involved with production control.

Linear programming and transportation techniques might be used to provide a suitable scheduling method.

9.8   A PRODUCTION CONTROL AUDIT

There is a variety of measurements usable to determine the effectiveness of production control. The measurement results, though, may not be good or bad in themselves. It is their impact on the business which matters. For example, provided delivery promises are kept, long lead times may not be serious from a business point of view. It is a major weakness only if business is lost to competitors because supplies cannot be obtained fast enough.

Delivery on time:
>   The percentage achievement of deliveries on time will reflect the effectiveness of the production control system. Any systems which cannot ensure delivery of at least 80 per cent of all orders on time must be inadequate in some way.

Lead times:
>   Excessive lead times can be defined as the times taken to deliver orders when they exceed those of national and international competitors. In some industries deliveries within days may be necessary. In others, weeks or months may be acceptable. Industry standards must be achieved where necessary. Long lead times may be compensated for by a high achievement of deliveries on time. Customers might prefer to wait three weeks longer in the knowledge that deliveries will be made as promised.

Set-ups as a ratio of production time:
>   This figure may not be meaningful unless it is given a monetary value and compared with the savings which are apparently being made by achieving a high set-up/production time ratio.

Work in progress:
>   A work in progress measurement should be in value and production units or standard hours of work. The latter measurement should be compared with standard available production time. This should be done both in total and at key operations, especially if they are bottlenecks. Any work in progress count which is more than double machine capacity is suspect.

Stock service levels:
>   The level of service can be defined as:

$$\frac{\text{demands satisfied ex stock}}{\text{total demand}} \times 100 \text{ per cent}$$

Defining 'demands' may be a problem, as some requests for service which are not met may not be counted in the demand figure.

Total stock levels:

An appropriate stock level might be calculated by considering replacement lead time (and the stock needed to cover this period), safety stock to cover splash demand, stocks required to cover batching and re-ordering rules, as well as normal demand. However, cash flow may be a major determinant of stock levels.

Stock imbalance:

A listing of ABC categories (i.e. popular, semi-popular and unpopular items) and stock levels should suggest whether serious stock imbalance is occurring.

Systems effort:

This may be excessive in terms of either manual (i.e. clerical) or computer time. The man/computer hours spent on each part of production control should be calculated and compared with the apparent advantage gained. Work study should be used to consider 'value administration'.

Production costs:

While it is difficult to determine precisely what costs can be reduced by effective production control, productivity costs should be known and set out in such a way that views about the efficiency of the production control system can be evaluated. Reporting of materials and labour productivity will be important.

10

Stock control in a manufacturing organisation

10.1 INTRODUCTION

The approach to stock control in a manufacturing company needs to be different from that in a trading or a commercial businsss. For a supermarket the main reason for holding stocks will be to provide good customer service. A high degree of such service will be required. If the cornflakes are out of stock, the customer will go elsewhere. The goods classed as 'stock' will mainly be finished goods, ready for sale. Ordering from suppliers will be done largely without considering the consequences on any manufacturing activity.

For a manufacturing company, stock control systems must take account of manufacturing activities. Inevitably there will be clashes or trade-offs between the level of stock carried, the service given to the customers, the cash flow involved in carrying stocks and the influence stock ordering policy has on manufacturing costs.

'Stocks' will cover finished goods stocks, but also raw materials, work in progress and components ready for use.

Defining the real need to carry stocks of finished goods may be a problem. For example, rarely, if ever, do any manufacturing companies divide stock into two categories — the portion needed for servicing customer requirements and the remainder which is carried because the factory has to make comparatively large batch sizes to ensure minimum factory cost. Yet in a manufacturing organisation this division is important.

This problem becomes clearer if a marginal approach is taken. For example, it is intended that stock values are to be increased by £250,000. The carrying cost, taking into account the cost of borrowing money, could be 15 per cent.

The annual cost of the extra stock is going to be £37,500 (higher, if obsolescence and other factors are considered). Savings in manufacturing costs or extra profit generated by increasing the stock by the proposed amount must equal at least £37,500.

If there is an alternative use for the money which increased stocks will take, then there should be competition for it. If a new machine will also cost a quarter of a million pounds, but yields a potential 25 per cent return, then investing in stock could be erroneous.

10.2 STOCK POLICY

A strategy or stock policy is a necessity. It should answer the following questions:

What items should be stocked?
What amounts of money should be invested in stock, e.g.:
   raw materials
   work in progress
   finished goods stocks?
For what purpose is stock required?
   To take account of lower purchase prices?
   To give a customer service which will attract a desirable level of sales?
   To reduce factory costs by minimising set-ups and change overs?
   To reduce paperwork?
   To take account of a seasonality in sales which only stock could accommodate?

The stock strategy should help to define:

The appropriate level of service which can be offered (i.e. how often is it permitted to be out of stock?)

The level of safety stocks which need to be carried to cover business eventualities such as unusual surges in sales demand.

All costs should be included in 'stock'. For example:

Stock holding costs — interest, storage, obsolescence, damage, insurance etc.

Buying, purchasing or administration costs

Setting-up costs at key machines

The degree of obsolescence which is likely to be incurred in carrying stocks

The cost of being out of stock (i.e. the profit lost if an item is out of stock for, say, two weeks)

Administration cost. This is often very high, perhaps £2 to £3 per order.

10.3   TYPES OF STOCK

While most stock control systems record, forecast and replace on an individual item basis, there is usually some indication of the comparative importance of the items concerned. Mostly the traditional ABC classification is used, but occasionally 'fast movers', 'slow movers' and 'others' are preferred.

10.3.1   A, B and C classification

The A, B and C classification is a value-based system, where a product's value contribution to the total value of stock carried is given a coding letter.

The A items are those which contribute most to the total. The B items contribute the second highest value. The C items contribute least in value terms.

This breakdown follows the Pareto or 80/20 rule which, when applied to stock control systems, suggests that only a small number of items will contribute most, but usually there will be a considerable tail of numerous items of low value.

The breakdown usually has the following pattern:

	Number	*Value*
A items	10 per cent	45 per cent
B items	20 per cent	35 per cent
C items	70 per cent	20 per cent

It will pay dividends to concentrate on controlling the A items where least effort will gain most rewards.

10.3.2   Semi- or part-finished stock

In many production units the products made tend to be uniform until late in the production process, when a variety of finishing operations such as painting, drilling or branding are carried out.

An important way of reducing the costs of carrying finished goods stock yet still retaining a good customer service, is to maintain a partly finished or semi-finished stock. This stock is held prior to the finishing operations so that fewer items in total need to be stocked. These can then readily be turned into finished stock.

In some production processes it may even be possible to have a series of cascade stock holdings which can grow progressively larger in numbers until the final finished goods stock is held.

10.4   FORECASTING IN STOCK CONTROL

Short term forecasting as used in stock control is usually based on trend analysis. The simplest method used is 'moving averages'. A year's data (e.g. sales demand) are collected, the monthly or weekly totals added together and divided by either twelve or fifty-two. The result is the forecast for the next period.

As each month or week passes, the earliest period is dropped and the latest one added.

The result — the moving average — will approximate to the midpoint of the period being covered. A recent change in demand will be absorbed in the calculation and so largely ignored.

To give greater weight to the more recent data in a series, a weighting or smoothing constant is often used. The method was first used by R. F. Brown in the 1950s. The smoothing constant is given the Greek letter α (alpha) and the value applied varies between 0.1 and 0.9. If variations in sales demand are low then a small alpha factor is used. So that if:

α = the smoothing constant at any value between 0.1 and 0.9,

let

m = the month's past demand

so that m_1, m_2, m_3 and m_4 are past months in order, then the average demand will be:

$$\alpha m_1 = \alpha[1 - \alpha]m_2 + \alpha[1 - \alpha]m_3 \ldots + \alpha[1 - \alpha]n - 1m,$$

which will become

$$\text{new average demand} = \alpha m_1 + [1 - \alpha] \text{ old average demand}$$

where m_1 is the most recent demand.

It is possible to calculate the trend in the data by subtracting each month's demand from that of the previous month. The trend average can then be determined as follows:

$$(\alpha) \text{ current trend} + (1 - \alpha)(\text{old trend})$$

A forecast can then be calculated by adding together the average demand and the trend.

The accuracy of the forecast can be checked by the use of a tracking signal. This is a quantitative method which measures the degree of error in the forecast and shows the degree of compensation for past errors which needs to be built into the new forecast.

Most sales demand is erratic to some extent. Some products will have exceptional (or splash) demand where a customer requires an out of trend requirement. Safety stock is designed to cover such eventualities.

The level of service required by sales personnel will also influence both stock levels and re-order requirements. 'Service' is the measure of stock availability to meet sales demand. High service levels will need high stock levels.

Lead time will also be a determinant in stock ordering. Lead time is the time taken from the ordering of a product until it arrives in the warehouse and is available for issue to customers.

The method for determining a stock replenishment quantity using the factors quoted is:

1 Calculate demand for an item by adding together the sales in a specific period.
2 Calculate a weighted average demand. The weighting should be carried out by multiplying the most recent demand by an alpha factor.
3 Determine a trend factor (found by subtracting current month from the latest weighted average).
4 Weight the trend in the same way as demand was weighted.
5 Find a forecast requirement by adding together the trend and weighted average.
6 Calculate the safety stock to be carried. The safety stock should be equal to 1.25 times the square root of the lead time multiplied by a statistical constant for the appropriate service level multiplied by the mean average error.
7 Stock to be ordered must be equal to the forecast demand multiplied by the lead time.
8 To this figure add the safety stock calculated in 6.
9 The stock requirement should be compared with the free stock available, plus any which is already on order.

10.5 RE-ORDERING SYSTEMS

The major difference in systems design between manufacturing and non-manufacturing companies will be in the method of stock re-ordering.

10.5.1 Re-order point system

When stock reaches a particular level a replacement order is raised. The amount to be ordered is calculated theoretically by reference to replacement lead times, sales demand, service levels and safety stocks needed for splash demand (i.e. requirements outside the normal demand pattern) or irregularities in replacement lead times.

10.5.2 Periodic review systems

Time, not stock level, is the major determinant in the re-ordering process. Stock levels are reviewed at fixed intervals when reference is made to replacement times, sales demand etc. to determine the amount to be ordered.

The system is also designated 'cycle re-ordering'. The 'cycle' is always the same — monthly, weekly, etc.

10.5.3 The roller-coaster effect in inventory control

In many traditional inventory control systems, there is a 'roller-coaster' effect which has a major influence on stock holdings. It operates in the following manner. The demand of a product rises. More orders are placed on the works. The number of back orders increases. The factory lead time lengthens, owing to the larger queue. The new lead times are built into the forecasting routines, with the result that more is ordered on the works to cover the increased lead times.

In times of decreasing demand the converse happens. Lead times decrease, fewer orders are put onto the works and the effect could be to cut back production at a faster rate than real demand is decreasing.

Any system which uses flexible lead times will operate in this way.

If, however, fixed lead times are arbitrarily set, and not altered, there could be considerable over or under stocking depending upon the relationship between order demand and factory capacity.

10.5.4 Which system?

Where stock replenishment is obtained outside the company then the re-order level system is the most useful. Orders can be accumulated in a way which minimises order placement costs. (Many suppliers, however, now stipulate minimum order quantities or order value.)

The periodic review system has advantages where the company's own manufacturing facilities are used and a periodic filling up of production capacity is carried out. Batch sizes are important to minimise set-up costs and any periodic review system should have a batch size calculation procedure built into it. The major difficulty in the system is to reconcile factory capacity with stock replenishment demand.

Either system tends to suffer from some or all of the following drawbacks:

1 Lead times tend to vary. Instability of lead times is probably one of the most important factors in producing stockouts, over stocking and perhaps mal-aligned stocks. A lead time variation of even one week in ten (which could be fairly common) has considerable effects on service and stock levels.

2   Future demand is misforecast. It is difficult to determine sales demand at any time and even the most sophisticated mathematically based forecasting systems fail in some degree.

3   Inventory analysis is often difficult. For example using A, B and C categories will initially divide a stock range into stock turnover categories, but they can quickly get out of date in a reasonably dynamic situation. Other analyses such as service level evaluation and stock turnover/gross margin calculations should enable a stock picture to be made which can be compared to the stock policy which is established.

4   Stock policy. It is logical to allocate the highest stock resources (in value) to those stock categories and items which will yield the most profitable business. A breakdown of the range should be made by group or product item contribution to turnover/profit. Where cash flow and other considerations impose a limit to the total value of stock carried, allocation becomes more important than the inventory control system, which ostensibly controls stock levels. This produces difficulties in most stock control systems.

5   Stock recording. Stock recording and counting (both into the stock area from a supplier or the factory and that outward to a customer) is a vital part of stock control.

     Unfortunately it is rarely done as accurately as is needed.

6   Information to make relevant decisions about stocks and stock levels is not always available.

10.6 PRACTICAL DESIGN

The design of a manufacturing organisation's system might follow these steps:

1   Production capacity should be established so that work centre capacities are recognised and loading of stock replenishment batches are facilitated. Family or product groupings should be established which will help to minimise set-ups.

2   The product groups or families should be recorded on stock records.

3   The anticipated monthly demand should be forecast for each product group.

4   From this forecast a monthly factory capacity requirement should be determined, taking into account constraints on factory capacity.

5   The actual current monthly demand of each product group should be recorded and compared with the actual amount of input to the factory.

6   A budget should be made to indicate the value of stock which should be held if service levels of a budgeted percentage are to be achieved.

7   Actual values of stock and service levels should be recorded and compared with those budgeted.

8   Orders should be issued to the factory to fill the forecast capacity requirement on a regular basis.

9   Batch sizes should be established for stock ordering purposes.

10   A performance sheet similar to the one shown in Fig. 10.1 can be used for stock level planning and monitoring.

10.7   DESIGN DETAIL

The broad system outlined in Section 10.5 might be introduced as follows:

1   Product groups should relate to the particular aspects of the production process which make them unique in some way — e.g. by their use of a particular piece of plant or special tool. Allocation of capacity of a commonly used machine may be necessary in some loading activities.

2   Budgeted stock values and service levels can be established by taking account of sales demand, lead times, the safety stock needed to accommodate out of line demand and lead times. This can be a complicated calculation, especially with a large stock range and a dynamic situation where a computer will be needed. It may be simple to assume that stock levels will be a two or three months' multiple of forecast demand. The service level can be calculated as follows:

$$\frac{\text{Total demands ex stock}}{\text{Total demands}} \times 100 \text{ per cent}$$

This could present difficulties where demand is not collected on a regular basis when potential customers are turned away through lack of stock.

3   The stock controller has another problem in determining what should be ordered from the works. It is possible to utilise the re-order point system and order an item when it has reached a particular level. However, it seems preferable to take each product group and the product items it contains and calculate the stock cover in each case, perhaps by using the re-order sheet shown in Fig. 10.2. Items can be recorded in ascending order of stock cover and orders placed until allocated production capacity is filled.

4   The recommendations in 3 imply that all items in one product category give the same benefit to the Sales department. In practice this is rarely so and it is suggested that within each product category A, B and C classifications be used which can form the basis for determining ascending stock cover. (An A category item would be more important than B and C etc.)

5   Stock re-ordering records similar to those shown in Fig. 10.2 could be used for re-ordering purposes as follows:

    (a)   The total capacity to be filled (column 1) is the allocated capacity for the whole product group.

    (b)   Current monthly demand is the forecast for the next few months. It

Month:

Families or Group	Anticipated Monthly Demand Ex Stock	Actual Current Monthly Demand Ex Stock	Factory Capacity		Budget		Actual		
			Schedule	Actual Input	Stock Value	Service Level	Stock Value	Service Level	Number of Stock outs

Fig. 10.1 Stock control – performance sheet

Product Group:
Month   :

Product Item	Current Monthly Demand	Safety Stock	Stock On Order	Total Stock in Warehouse	Allocated Stock	Free Stock	Week's Stock Cover	Order Requirements	Total Capacity to be Filled
	A	B	C	D	E	F	G	H	I

Fig. 10.2   Stock re-ordering sheet

can be determined either by visual scanning of past demand, the use of moving averages, or a forecast demand technique such as exponential smoothing.

(c)   Safety stocks can be calculated by determining splash demand or erratic lead times and recording the extra stock which would have been needed to cover such eventualities. The safety stock normally does not cover such situations totally, and some possibility of a stockout should be allowed.

(d)   Free stock F is determined by deducting allocated stock E from total stock in warehouse D.

(e)   The addition of stock F and stock-on-order C is divided by the current monthly demand A and weeks' stock cover calculated G.

(f)   Stock items can then be listed in ascending stock cover until production capacity to be filled has been reached.

(g)   Depending upon whether production capacity is over or under filled, the system should:

In an overfill situation, list the items not ordered and make an assessment of the subsequent queue in terms of week's production capacity. This information should be used to consider whether reallocation of capacity is needed or if production capacity needs to be extended in total. In an underfill situation, order one week's extra stock against each product item, beginning with A category items if the ABC listing is used, until production capacity is filled. The extra products and their value needed for this purpose should be listed.

The benefits of employing this kind of system are:

(h)   The allocation of production capacity to product groups and A, B and C items within each group should ensure that the best use is made of production capacity to service sales demand supplied ex stock. Capacity changes and reallocations should be facilitated.

(i)   The firmness of the lead time should help to reduce stock levels by keeping safety stocks at a minimum. Within a monthly production cycle system, it might be possible to state in what week delivery might be made (instead of what month).

(j)   The constant lead time and ABC classification should help to improve service levels of key items.

(k)   While the demand for one product may be extremely variable, the demand for a product group will be a good deal more stable. Forecasting, therefore, should be based on product groups and allocation of capacity made on the basis previously suggested.

(l)   A product group capacity allocation inventory control system should produce a more stable situation than one where individual items are reviewed on a re-order level system. The roller-coaster effect should be minimised if not eliminated.

10.8 CALCULATING BATCH SIZES

Each batch or order placed on the works incurs:

1 Cost of making out the order and processing it (the administrative and paperwork costs).
2 The set-up costs on the plant which are incurred in making the item.

(These costs imply that no batching is possible once the orders have been made out and passed to the works. In practice batching is usually possible.)

The annual cost of ordering will be:

$$\frac{R \times C}{Q}$$

Where R = rate of usage per year; C = cost of placing and making the order; Q = batch size.

Once the item has been made it will incur carrying costs (i.e. interest charge on the value of stock, insurance etc.) so annual costs can be expressed as:

$$\frac{Q \times C_c}{2}$$

Where Q = batch size; C_c = carrying cost for one item; 2 = appropriate factor because the average level of stock will be half the batch quantity.

Both placing and making carrying costs must be added together to provide the total batch cost as follows:

$$\frac{R \times C}{Q} + \frac{Q \times C_c}{2}$$

This can be established through a differentiating equation as:

$$Q = \frac{\overline{2R \times C}}{C_c}$$

To ease the calculations the order placing cost can be established for all items irrespective of type or quantity.

The set-up costs might be established for product groups, not individual items.

The formula produced is simple and can be applied as it stands. However, there may be reasons why the total number of orders to be handled each month should be restricted so that predetermined levels of productivity can be achieved. (The fact that set-ups are paid for in the product may not be the key factor.)

10.9   STOCK RECORDING

Accurate stock recording is essential to any stock control system. Money spent on ensuring that records are accurate is rarely wasted. Checks into warehouse from the works, on stock receipts, are essential.

'Recording' must then ensure that suitable information is always available as follows:

Reference

Units of measure

Cost of stock (average, standard)

Standard selling price

Units and value of stock held in the warehouse

Export, allocated and depots

Transactions:

1   Receipts: part numbers, quantity, price, order number, date
2   Movements: warehouse to depot; depot to warehouse; depot to depot
3   Sales: part number, price, quantity, order number, date
4   Stock adjustments: stocktaking; scrap and breakages; others
5   Back orders
6   Forward orders
7   Anticipated monthly demand by product group
8   Actual current demand by product group
9   Factory capacity: allocated; used
10 Budgeted stock value per product group
11 Budgeted service levels per product group
12 Actual stock values per product group
13 Service level per product group
14 Number of stock-outs per product group
15 Safety stocks per product item
16 Stock on order per product item
17 Total stocks per product item
18 Allocated stock per product item
19 Free stock per product item
20 Total capacity to be filled per product group
21 Factory performance in meeting stock replenishment requests.

Separate records for central warehouse and depots will be needed.

10.10   OTHER SYSTEMS DESIGN CRITERIA

1   The difficulties of individual product costing have not helped either the establishment of batch sizes (owing to problems of calculating set-up costs) or the maintaining of stocks which will give maximum contribution/profit.

If costing can be based on product group calculations or even size ranges within each product group, it seems likely that meaningful decisions on batch sizes etc. can be made.

2 Analysis is the key to determining whether stock control is as effective as it could be. The following analysis might be useful:

(a)   Stock items turnover rate — this will help to determine A, B and C categories of items

(b)   Stock turnover/gross margin analysis per product group — to help determine return on stock investment being achieved

(c)   List of slow moving items — items not moved for six months, one year etc.

(d)   Demand analysis by product group and major product item

3 A useful systems requirement will be the possibility of changing service levels and determining the levels of stock which will be needed to provide them.

4 It should be possible within the system to accommodate:

Planned increases in sales, including effects of promotional activities

Trends and seasonality

Competitive response

5 In any activity concerning profit planning the cost of company stock should be included in the analysis. For example, if £2 million of stock are carried to service export markets, then 10 per cent or 15 per cent per year of this stock value should be offset against the net sales revenue which exporting produces.

6 The job of the inventory controller should be to maintain levels of stock (including service levels) which have been agreed between senior marketing, production and distribution managers.

11

Use of computers in production systems

11.1 INTRODUCTION

Experience and evidence from published data suggests that the production function has proved particularly difficult for the application of computers. Successful computer based production control systems are still limited. This might be because:

1   Production is a difficult function to understand. Few systems analysts have actually worked in production. Some production managers are not fully aware of the computer's potential.
2   Because of the complex behavioural problems often encountered on the shop floor, production systems may occasionally 'defy logic'.
3   Much of the production process is often performed through experience or knowhow. 'Measurements', for example, are not set out in a formal way which can be used by systems analysts.
4   Paperwork systems are designed without considering the needs of the overall production and organisation system. Production control, for example, is considered to apply to production only.
5   The behavioural consequence of attempting to introduce (say) shopfloor data collection equipment is not always understood. Occasionally, these tip the industrial relations balance between management and operatives adversely.
6   Applying conventional management accounting or other traditional practice may have only limited value. On some occasions they may be counter productive, especially if a modelling approach is really required.
7   Applying techniques — e.g. linear programming — may also be counter productive, unless there is recognition of the overall need of the production function and the paperwork systems required to support it.

11.2   DESIGNING PRODUCTION COMPUTER SYSTEMS — A PROCEDURE

Because of the comparative complexity of applying a computer to production control there is a greater need for discipline and method in designing the system than perhaps in other systems development. The approach might take the following lines:

1   Use a diagnostic approach to discover whether all production people appreciate and understand the building blocks which make up production control, the parts of the overall system which would best suit the organisation, the parts of the overall system where the payback will be greatest and the apparent failings of the current system such as inadequate delivery performance, long lead times, high stocks, inadequate shop floor control, etc.

2   The likely benefits of using a computer should be determined — for example, improved deliveries, lower costs, etc. and these benefits compared with the likely development costs.

3   There may be a need for an educational programme on production control in all its facets.

4   An initial proposal should be prepared by one or two of the senior managers operating within the production control function. The problems as they see them should be stated and the likely way these could be overcome suggested.

5   A feasibility study should then be instituted where these problems are examined in some depth. A project manager will usually be chosen to carry out the study. He will normally be seconded from his line job and expected to lead a team of systems and line personnel which will design and introduce the computer system.

   The feasibility study team should:
      Within strict terms of reference, investigate the problems set out in the initial proposal.

      Record the associated systems in detail.

      Suggest new computerised systems, time scales for their introduction and likely costs.

      Outline the stages which might be followed in introducing the new systems.

6   The feasibility study proposals might be evaluated under four headings:

      Technical feasibility — Are the proposals technically feasible in terms of the equipment available and the skills which are needed?

Economic feasibility — Will the benefits which might be gained out-weigh the costs and if so by how much? Do the proposals seem a good way to utilise development resources?

Strategic feasibility — Do the proposals fit in with overall corporate strategy?

Social feasibility — Will the social structure be affected by the proposals, if so how?

7   Systems design. The first objective of any systems design will be to produce a system's specification, defining the processing logic of the system, the input and output media, clerical procedures and responsibilities.

Approval of the outline design will be needed before the next phase — data collection — begins.

Some of the data will be used to carry out a test of part of the system, after which the total system should be run.

The system should be documented and systems manuals prepared for everyone concerned with its operation.

User guides should be prepared.

8   Education and training. This is an essential part of the development.

9   Changeover methods should be designed to ensure that errors in the new system are quickly eliminated (systems must be tested). Parallel running will be necessary to prove that no snags in the new system exist.

10 Post installation review should be carried out about six months after the end of parallel running to determine whether the objectives of the develop-ment have been achieved at the original cost stipulated. The review should also indicate where more development is required.

11.3   THE BUILDING BLOCK APPROACH TO USING A COMPUTER IN PRODUCTION CONTROL

It is nearly inevitable that the use of a computer in production will be con-cerned with:

1   process monitoring;
2   production control.

Process monitoring is a special application usually needing specialised equip-ment. Small computers, or data loggers, are linked to a vital part of a process or machine, and, for supervision, either record the state of the process or control it in some way by instituting action which corrects an out of course activity.

Production control is potentially the most important application for computers within the manufacturing function though production control itself is cross functional. Within a production control system, there are several building blocks which make up the entire system:

Capacity planning
Production requirements planning
Materials requirements planning
Production scheduling and sequencing
Performance monitoring

There are other important sub-systems which will affect the building blocks:

Stock control
Management accounting
Raw material stock control
etc.

So in designing a production control system, there are two important decisions to be taken:

3   What are the building blocks in the system and how do they relate to each other? What total system is being investigated? What individual building blocks are most important? Which need to be improved?
4   What common information is required to ensure that the system is linked appropriately?

The first decision will determine the overall and individual design and the second should start the building of a common data base.

A diagram similar to that in Fig. 11.1 will be useful. The total production control system is shown and under each major component or building block three factors are highlighted:

(a)   Extensions required in the present system. These are improvements which would help the overall system.
(b)   Problems with the manual system. Normally these will be factors which inhibit systems improvement.
(c)   Benefits to be gained from using a computer. These should be expressed financially wherever possible. Once this exercise has been completed it is appropriate to choose one of the building blocks for development, with the certainty that any systems development will be compatible with the other parts of the system.

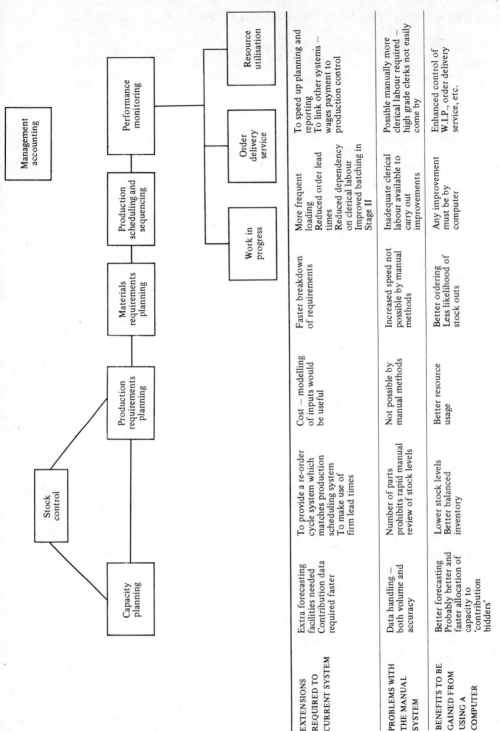

	Capacity planning	Stock control	Production requirements planning	Materials requirements planning	Production scheduling and sequencing	Performance monitoring
EXTENSIONS REQUIRED TO CURRENT SYSTEM	Extra forecasting facilities needed Contribution data required faster	To provide a re-order cycle system which matches production scheduling system To make use of firm lead times	Cost – modelling of inputs would be useful	Faster breakdown of requirements	More frequent loading Reduced order lead times Reduced dependency on clerical labour Improved batching in Stage II	To speed up planning and reporting To link other systems – wages payment to production control
PROBLEMS WITH THE MANUAL SYSTEM	Data handling – both volume and accuracy	Number of parts prohibits rapid manual review of stock levels	Not possible by manual methods	Increased speed not possible by manual methods	Inadequate clerical labour available to carry out improvements	Possible manually more clerical labour required – high grade clerks not easily come by
BENEFITS TO BE GAINED FROM USING A COMPUTER	Better forecasting Probably better and faster allocation of capacity to 'contribution bidders'	Lower stock levels Better balanced inventory	Better resource usage	Better ordering Less likelihood of stock outs	Any improvement must be by computer	Enhanced control of W.I.P., order delivery service, etc.

Fig. 11.1   Potential computer usage – production control

11.4 COMPUTER USE

A computer can, roughly, be used for three purposes:

1 simple interrogation of files;
2 simple updating of records and calculations;
3 complex manipulation of data.

Simple interrogation of files

It is normal in computer production systems design to develop 'product master and operations' files. These will comprise such data as:

Product reference
Product group
Unit weight
Number in a set
Materials or components to be used
Material yield
Product size — length, width, thickness, etc.
Tooling associated with the product — dies, jigs, etc.
Operational data —
    Operational sequence
    Key or bottleneck operations
    Work study values for each operation
    etc.

An important factor in setting up the computer system will be to determine the data to be contained on the product master file and the file format. For example, relationships between products using the same raw materials, components or tools may be required.

A further file should be concerned with order progress. It will list:

The part number
Quantity ordered
Order number
Delivery date
Zone or operation dates where appropriate
Reporting points
amongst other information.

The reporting points will be either zones or operations where order progress is monitored.

Operation information — work study values etc. — is often kept separately on an operational file. A separate cost file may also be needed.

The files will be looked up or interrogated. For example, it may be necessary to determine how many tools of a certain type and size are available to know whether a new order can be accommodated. Order chasing can be done by interrogation of the factory order load or order progress file.

Interrogation can either be on- or off-line. Off-line will be by the production of a tabulation (i.e. 'off-line' or disconnected from the computer). On-line normallly will be by use of a visual display unit, which will have direct access to the file contained by the computer. Hence it will be connected or 'on-line'.

Simple updating of records and calculations

(a)   The classic updating activity is usually concerned with the factory order load file. When an order is received it is put onto this file by 'inputting' the order number, part number, quantity ordered etc. onto the computer file. As the order progresses past predetermined reporting points it is removed from one zone, operation or location to the next in its manufacturing sequence. It is possible to do this on-line as recorded in 1 above.

(b)   As part of the fairly simple calculations which might be carried out it should be possible to:

   Calculate the labour content of a batch of orders (e.g. by multiplying work study values by quantities).

   Calculate material requirements for the same batch of orders.

   Provide management reports on order delay, by zone or operation and numbers of days or even weeks late.

   Compare standard material yield of finished products with that achieved.

   Calculate the standard cost of production for any achieved output.

Complex manipulation of data

The computer activities briefly described in 1 and 2 often will provide sufficient justification for the use of a computer. The most important, and at the same time the most complex, application is factory scheduling. It is often difficult because of the complex nature of the decision rules involved.

While there is danger in attempting to duplicate all the manual decision rules completely, a computer system must reflect reality. Unless the computer system can take account of the real world of scheduling, frustrated works planning personnel will soon cease to use it at all.

Using a computer in production scheduling, therefore, must not absorb too many resources or take up too much time, yet should produce something of significance.

How is the design process to begin?

The best starting point is to produce a logic diagram of the type shown in Fig. 11.2. This shows the scheduling of a production line, taking account of three factors:

1   The logic used in loading or scheduling the production line — i.e. the scheduling process which has been chosen.
2   The data required to be on file.
3   Data input to the system.

The logic diagram should duplicate — as far as possible — the real life scheduling which is being performed manually. It should show where the logic is faulty, or where the scheduling decisions made are indistinct. It will also show the iterative nature of the process: for example, having loaded current orders so as not to overload operational capacities, the result may not achieve a desired objective — such as 'production costs not to exceed £x per standard hour'.

The logic diagram can then be used to suggest whether the necessary iteration can be carried out. The nature of the process then becomes a 'model'.

It seems nearly impossible to get a production control system right the first time so it is useful to take a play it by ear approach in some areas, especially scheduling, in order to make sure that the system will provide what is required. To achieve this it may be best to reprocess a limited amount of data until a satisfactory solution is reached. Production planning personnel can readjust the outcome of each processing activity in the hope of arriving at the best solution.

To do this it will be necessary to have a terminal linked on-line with the operations and product master file. The controller should be able to run the systems and determine how far the order loading pattern produced meets production objectives. It should be possible to take out one or more orders from the sequence produced, post them into a different loading period and run the system again. This process can be continued until the result matches, most nearly, required production objectives.

This interaction with the computer will provide two main advantages:

It can compensate for the lack of programming or inaccuracy of systems design. Trial and error (in a sophisticated way) will be possible.

It will enable various solutions to be tried out to solve the scheduling problem at a comparatively small cost.

Data required on file	Load analysis and scheduling	Input required to system
Criteria for deciding which shop item will be made on		Order input and control tertiary quality quantity order no.
Conversion factors – items into batches		Shop records
Product line constraints		Batches required
Product – mixer data		Documentation – prepared – card sets
Load capacity data – mixer		Order data
Load capacity data – cooler		Product cooler – requirement

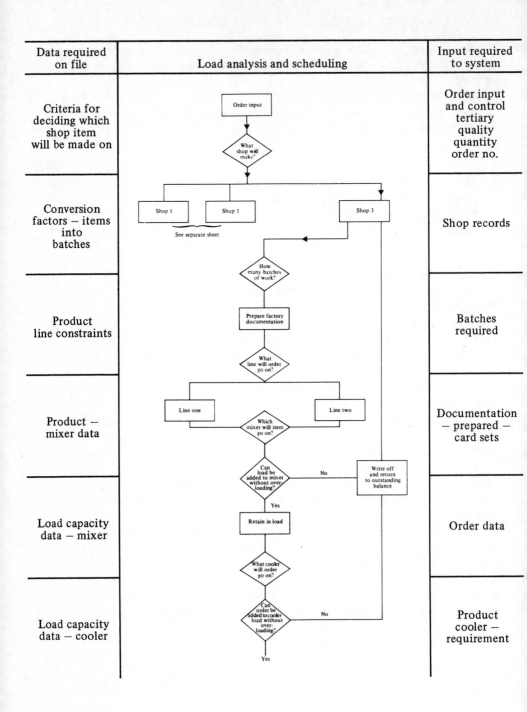

Fig. 11.2   A logic diagram

Data required on file	Load analysis and scheduling	Input required to system
Load capacity data grinding		Product/ grinding data
Budgetary data		Budget data
Service change over contribution data requirements		

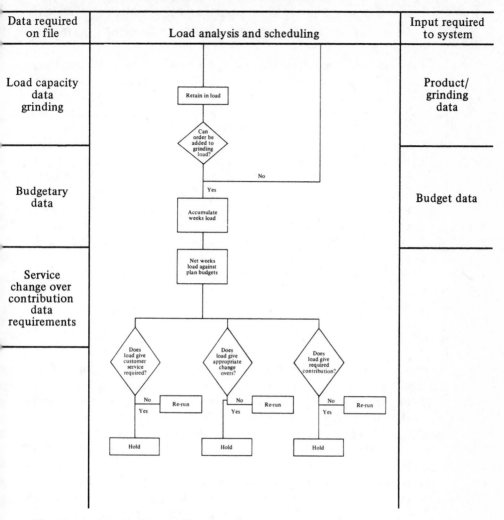

Fig. 11.2   A logic diagram (*Continued*)

Production scheduling, with absenteeism, quality failure, machine breakdowns and other imponderables, can be only comparatively inexact. The iteration proposed will be the basis for such an 'inexact' system.

The reports which a scheduling system might produce are:

1   Operation data list. This will be a record of the various pieces of data which are needed on file for scheduling purposes. Included will be the number of shifts the operations are scheduled to work, the man hours per shift, current capacity, set-up times, other non-manufacturing time allowances, standard cost per running hour, etc.

2   Order status report. This will show the order type, part number, operations
for manufacture, quantity to be made, required completion date, the start
date etc.
3   Material requirements list. This will be a schedule of required materials or
components which in turn may trigger off an order status report and a
scheduling activity.
4   Standard production cost report. This will summarise the production costs
for the manufacture of the orders on hand.
5   Capacity-order reports. These can be produced either as short or long term
views of the relationships between orders and operational capacity. The
longer term report should show the full queue of orders either in the
company already or forecast. The shorter term report will normally use a
scheduling system such as due date ordering, interdependence of operations, or earliest start date.
6   Work-to lists. These record the order sequence which must be carried out
at each operation if delivery promises are to be kept.

11.5   DATA PROCESSING EQUIPMENT

1   Shopfloor data collection

The booking of and payment for work carried out on the shopfloor is often a
problem for production management. It is usually subject to fiddling of some
kind, for which clerical controls are not always effective. As it is also important
to monitor order progress, some form of shopfloor data collection equipment
which can record accurately what is taking place makes sense.

In most production units the fiddles are concerned with the overbooking of
quantities and allowances such as set-ups or cleaning. To help to eradicate
work booking discrepancies, it is possible for a 'work-to list' or production
schedule to become part of a computer file. It can record the allowances
legitimately claimable and the order quantities which must be made.

The following equipment can be used to record information from the shopfloor:

(a)   Badge readers. Each operative uses a plastic badge to record his name
and number. Every time he starts or finishes a job he inserts the badge
into a recorder (several are appropriately stationed on the shopfloor).
These recorders are linked with a central computer which records the
badge and time.
(b)   Multi-input terminals. These will read an operative's badge as well as a
punched card if this is used as part of the works order card set. The
punched card can contain order number, a description of the item, and
the quantity. The computer can use stored work study values to calculate

the pay due to the operative when he carries out the operation shown on the punched card.

(c)   Multi-function terminals. These not only allow badges and punched cards to be read, but also permit the input of non-standard data. For example, it may be necessary for a supervisor to adjust the order quantity of a particular order stored on file because some products have been rejected. This data is input through an alpha-numeric keyboard. Some terminals of this type have a display panel, where information being input can be seen.

The terminals are normally designed for industrial environments and can work in temperature ranges from 0°C to 40°C, humidity from 0 per cent to 90 per cent and can operate in a dusty atmosphere (though see Chapter 4 on the Health and Safety at Work Act).

(d)   Visual display units. These are terminal systems where information display is important. They can be used in an interactive mode, as an 'intelligent terminal'.

(e)   Mini store equipment. It is often necessary to update multiple files, store information off-line and sort and merge records. Local mini store equipment, based on cartridge tape, can be used for this purpose.

(f)   Serial printers. These can be linked to an intelligent terminal to provide a printing medium for special reports.

2   Dedicated computers

These can act as local small computing devices (minicomputers) programmed to carry out specific tasks such as updating local work in progress files, checking operative attendance, calculating bonuses and general wage payments, costing production, calculating production efficiencies, etc.

Fig. 11.3 shows in a simplified way how a production unit might use local data processing equipment.

11.6   DISTRIBUTIVE PROCESSING

The arrangement briefly described in the previous section has been given the term 'distributive processing' by the computer industry. Production control systems more often than not need interactive data processing. Where the main computer is some distance from the factory this can be very expensive and distributive processing is to be preferred.

The local dedicated computer can be used to house part of the production data base while it is updated or interrogated locally. After this the data can be returned to the host computer.

The local computer should be compatible with the host computer; and distributive processing generally should fit in with the corporate computer policy. Apart from that, what other factors should a production manager con-

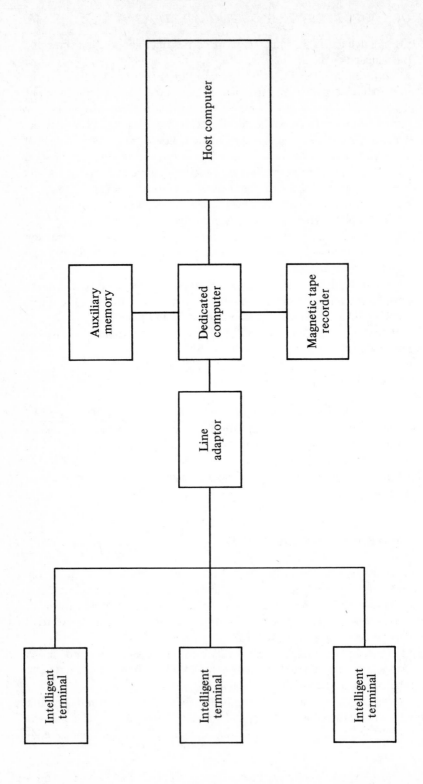

Fig. 11.3   Use of local data processing

sider in obtaining local data processing facilities? The following seem important:

(a) Software — operating routines etc., are very important. Will the computer supplier provide them? How effective will they be if he does?

(b) How will the computer be justified? If staff cuts are envisaged how easy will they be to make?

(c) Who will carry out the:
Systems analysis
Applications and systems design
Application implementation and programme
Design
Coding
Testing and integration
Conversion and operation of the installation
Training required
Controls and standards required?

(d) Who will write the specification covering the various applications? The following points will need to be covered:
General application of the system
Definition of the hardware
Description of the operating software
Input data definition
Service contracts will be important. How good are these?

(e) Who will operate the system after installation? Who will report on its performance?

(f) Who will perform systems testing to ensure that users will get what they have requested?

(g) The computer supplier might be chosen as a result of considering the following:
Corporate policies
Compatibility with other equipment already in use
Equipment performance/cost rate
Warranty offered
Servicing
General support offered.

11.7 EASING THE USE OF COMPUTERS

Computers are often well tended by programmers, operators and systems analysts, talking a language which is often alien to production managers who in consequence shy away from getting as involved as they should with computer technology. Two factors might be explored to reverse this tendency:

1   User languages

Computer languages vary in complexity. Some are reasonably easy to use —
such as APL which is a programming language supplied by IBM. It is a simple
language which could be quickly learned, the concepts are few and easily
understood. It enables a manager to communicate directly with a computer
without the need for a programmer or systems analyst.

While APL (and other similar languages) will be at a serious disadvantage in
large scale systems requirements, it is extremely useful where rapid development of an application is required and the need is not very well defined. It is
useful where the application is small and the specification might need fairly frequent change. APL is a 'conversational language' — i.e. it enables an interaction to be carried out with the computer. So 'modelling' is a possibility with
APL as well as financial calculations and analyses of data of all kinds.

The user of APL works in a workspace which can be approximated to a
blank sheet of paper. Through a terminal the workspace is used for writing in
the procedures and data which are required. In most applications, there will be
a 'question' and 'answer' session. Where the user can ask a question, the computer will reply and then 'ask permission to continue' by prompting the user in
some way.

Information entered can be validated and corrections made.

When APL is used, it can be taught as a new language with new terminology.
Once a function has been defined it can be used in any context. There are APL
application packages which are collections of functions or building blocks
which can be used in various combinations.

The drawback with APL (like packages) is that it tends to use a considerable
amount of core store of a computer. But this seems less important than it once
was. Ten years ago, people were comparatively cheap and computer time
expensive. Now the reverse is true. APL therefore (and other similar means of
using computers easily) is important.

2   Use of packages

Many companies have successfully used computer packages, especially for
such functions as payroll and financial ledger keeping, even capital expenditure
evaluation. By any standard, the applications have been fairly routine. In
payroll for example, it does not seem to matter what has been made or the type
of labour used. If the wage payment system is reasonably straightforward a
payroll package will often suffice.

Production systems are complex and dissimilar. They do not readily lend
themselves to packages. Some of the building blocks — inventory control for
example — may provide a better chance than, say, production scheduling
which is often nearly unique.

For example, IBM provide a scheduling package CAPOSS (Capacity Planning and Operation Sequencing System) and it may be possible to apply parts of such a package within one or more building blocks. There is a danger, however, that the total system could become distorted if too much reliance is placed even on parts of a package.

Using the whole package as it exists may not be possible or desirable in any organisation.

PART IV

Work Organisation

12

Work organisation

12.1 INTRODUCTION

The term 'work organisation' is used here to cover the establishment of tasks and goals and the structuring of individual jobs, work units, teams or corporate organisations, which can achieve these tasks or goals. Good work organisations recognise existing power relationships, the possibility of creating new ones and the appropriate allocation of authorities and responsibilities.

The following questions are relevant in considering new work organisations:

1   How is power to be recognised and if necessary created?
2   Can power and authority be largely interchangeable?
3   Can any conflict between power, authority and goals be identified?
4   Can jobs be designed which recognise the socio-technical factors in the overall production system?
5   How can the institutional techniques of industrial relations, collective bargaining, joint consultation and participation form part of the work organisation?
6   Can a work organisation structure be designed which is adaptive to changing environments?
7   Can improvement to personal and role relationships be achieved?
8   Can power be legitimised?
9   As far as possible can all workers in the organisation be given an intellectual commitment to their jobs?

12.2   CHANGING WORK ORGANISATIONS

Why should anyone want to change a particular work organisation? One or more of the following reasons may apply:

Management requirements:

Increased output, quality and quantity;

Enhanced productivity;

Reduction in or even elimination of industrial relations problems;

Elimination or reduction in the need for close supervisory control;

Reduction in turnover and absenteeism;

Improvement in working conditions on the shopfloor;

Introduction of change of some kind.

Worker requirements:

Enhanced autonomy and discretion;

Greater opportunities for self-organisation;

Increased wages;

Increased opportunities for training and skill enhancement;

Challenge of new jobs;

Broadening of contacts with other people;

Creation of close knit groups;

More work variety and less boredom;

Greater accountability;

Make work more worthwhile and interesting.

12.3   THE WORK ORGANISATION SYSTEM

1   The system

Work organisation is an intrinsic part of the total manufacturing system and as such is subject to the same environmental influences. Work organisation, however, influences other parts of the manufacturing system.

A representation of the work organisation system is given in Fig. 12.1. It shows that work organisation has an input of company resources, company style and management and worker requirements. The output is production, productivity and job satisfaction. The work organisation will be influenced by social, educational, political, economic and industrial environments.

The work organisation will itself influence the roles of management (especially first line supervision), shop stewards, and service departments such as work study.

Outputs from the system will be measured, and a feedback mechanism should ensure that adjustments to inputs to the system are made. Eventually, therefore, the work organisation may be altered to ensure that required outputs are reached. The feedback on job satisfaction may be possible through measur-

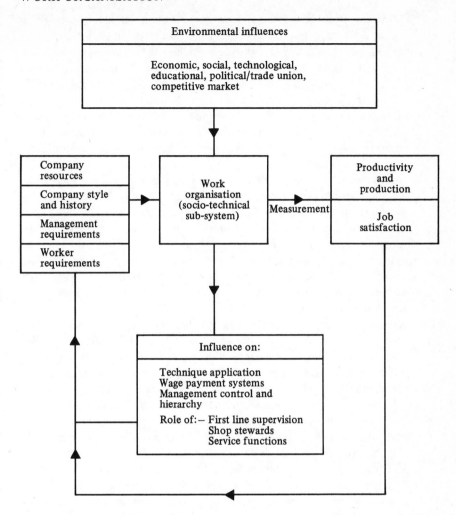

Fig. 12.1   Work organisation:— the system

ing such factors as absenteeism, morale (if this can be measured in a sensible way), strikes and industrial relations generally, co-operation (and the lack of it), productivity and attitudes towards the company.

2   Systems inputs

(a)   Company style and history: It will be difficult to escape from the way a company has been run for a long time. Usually if a fairly authoritarian régime has existed, its influences will have permeated most of the company. Even where there is a genuine desire to break away from the past, it is often difficult to do so. Habits of a lifetime do not alter easily.

Company style, therefore, will be an important influence, perhaps a major constraint on the possibility of radical change in the work organisation. It will dictate the pace at which change can take place even when it has been agreed at the highest level in the company. Intellectual acceptance of new ideas may be less important than emotional commitment to traditional methods of work organisation.

(b)   Management requirements: These might be stated as a contented workforce which achieves high productivity and output. There will be a minimum of industrial relations problems. Carrying out change of all kinds will be facilitated.

However, there will be many junior managers who will feel their position or job is gravely threatened if work organisations offering job enrichment or enlargement are established on the shopfloor. In the higher reaches of the management hierarchy the idea of greater worker autonomy may be viewed with more objectivity, especially if demands to share in senior management decision making are not made by the workforce. There could, therefore, be a strong dichotomy of view over the needs and merits of new work organisations between junior and senior managers.

(c)   Worker requirements: These may not be well articulated. Comments such as 'if you treat us like donkeys we will act like donkeys' may be made at shop stewards' meetings with management and these should be sufficient to stir some belief that a worker requirement is being expressed. Management, therefore, often has to act as an interpreter of events and construe them in a way that will indicate worker requirements.

(d)   Company resources: Company resources refer mainly to the traditional 'men, money and materials' which are common in most companies. It may be possible to increase these, but they will usually be restricted somewhat. The relationship between resource inputs and outputs can be measured, perhaps as added value. This measurement will help to indicate whether corporate productivity is as high as possible and so whether company resources are being utilised effectively.

3   Influences on work organisation

(a)   Wage payment systems: These have to fit in with the work organisation. For some autonomous work groups, for example, the only payment required may be for the number of products made by the group. How this payment is shared out could be entirely for the group to decide. To this end, a wage system based on a local contract is preferred — as happens in the coal mining and quarrying industries.

(b)   Management control: Within a hierarchical organisation, management controls are usually well developed — labour efficiency, machine utilisation, materials productivity, etc. They still need to be in existence under any work organisation but like wage payment systems will have to be adapted. Mostly the management controls should be centred on work leaving the work group (if some autonomy has been given). Cost effectiveness will still be a key factor and a control on money spent and value earned will be necessary.

Controls will be necessary for the work group itself. Designing these should be done in conjunction with group members. Training in their use will nearly always be necessary.

(c) Use of techniques: Paradoxically, companies who have recognised the need for improvement in production efficiency and consequently introduced various management techniques may be hindered from introducing organisational changes. For example, the application of job evaluation with its emphasis on individual job differences and the pay which should be allotted is typical of the techniques likely to constrain workers' wishes to change. The application of certain types of incentive also emphasises individuality and so, therefore, could restrict new forms of work organisation.

13

Traditional organisations

13.1 INTRODUCTION

Organisation has been defined [1] as that part of management which is concerned with the definition of the structure of:

1 The responsibilities by means of which the activities of the enterprise are distributed among the managerial, supervisory and specialist personnel employed.
2 The formal interrelations established among the personnel by virtue of such responsibilities.

Organisation is the formal way in which authority and responsibility are established so as to secure the participation and co-operation of all members of a company with the intended result of achieving objectives. It should have a linking effect on everyone's efforts.

Unfortunately the neat little boxes set out in a pyramid fashion which are often seen on organisation charts are rarely found to have any reality in practice. True power is not shown. Responsibilities may not be matched by an authority to achieve them. Organisations are 'more alive, more idiosyncratic, more irrational and much more human than those neat charted boxes suggest. Like individual human beings organisations are dynamic, self-adjusting systems'. [2]

13.2 SOME TRADITIONAL CONCEPTS

1 Corporate goals

What the organisation does is the most useful starting point for considering organisational structure. Some of the tasks will be simple and straightforward, such as 'X amount of output from machine A in T hours'. Others could be ill defined such as 'achieving good industrial relations'. When organisations appear to know precisely what they are doing the structure is often rigid with well defined authorities and responsibilities. Where the converse is true the structure may be loose. It is important to differentiate between tasks (i.e. what people actually do) and goals (what is really required). Even when goals are clear cut, an appropriate organisation may not be in existence due to past history, current environments and a lack of suitable people.

2 Specialisation

Organisations will normally be based on job specialisation. The degree of specialisation, including the employment of technologists and scientists, will depend largely upon the kind of operations the company carries out, the products it makes and the markets it serves.

Line and staff specialisation has become enshrined in organisational theory. Line organisations, it was stated, were the equivalent of infantry officers leading their troops into action. The staff function was to make the plans for the line people to carry out. This division assumed that the line officer had little technical planning skill (which is patently untrue in many instances in most modern industry). 'Line' and 'staff' interchange should be part of everybody's education.

Over specialisation has often led to people becoming divorced from mainstream company activities and even quickly obsolete. The narrow view which many staff personnel take is often counter productive to improving company performance. Specialists are often low on organisational loyalty.

'Line' and 'staff' divisions therefore, are anachronisms and should be discontinued wherever possible.

3 Organisational flexibility

Organisations by their nature are not flexible. Job holders, whether the manager of a research and development department or the head of cleaning services, want to retain their jobs. An appropriate organisation to them is orderly, structured and firm, with a well defined series of jobs and hierarchies, with them holding a key place.

Yet it seems that there was never a time when there was greater need for organisational flexibility. Environments are changing rapidly, long held power is being eroded, the basis for the existence of many organisations is disappearing. The last thing that many organisations require is inflexibility.

4   Organisations and people

The design of organisations is concerned with fitting people of varying ages, skills, personalities and psychology into a structure which will demand that they are treated as a resource within the organisational system. People see themselves as unique, irreplaceable, important. Their company buys the skill, energy and general ability of a manager or worker. That person also brings his individuality to the company.

This may not be conducive to achieving the goals of the organisation.

5   Functions in the organisation

Functional organisations unite line and staff personnel in carrying out a particular activity, perhaps under a general manager. A works manager who controls production, engineering, quality and production control is performing a functional activity — i.e. the organisation, planning and control of the works. The advantages of functional organisations should be to integrate and so make the best use of the skills of specialists and line personnel. However, responsibility is often diffuse and indeterminate lines of command and promotion may cause frustration, even animosity.

6   Span of control

This was a favourite theme of early writers on organisation. The crucial factor which concerned them was the number of people who could be controlled efficiently by a supervisor or manager. Numbers alone, however, are not necessarily important. A factory manager with six production managers reporting to him may be overwhelmed. A production manager responsible for one hundred operatives, working to a bonus system, may cope very easily.

7   Centralisation and decentralisation

It seems part of every organisation's history to have phases when centralisation predominates, only to have decentralisation come into vogue.

The style of the chief executive or general manager is often crucial in establishing one form or the other. It is comparatively easy to make a case for either. Centralisation should produce strong leadership and direction and well defined strategies.

Local autonomy has failed to produce the results which on-the-spot decision making was expected to give. Many quite large units have slowly disintegrated into separate, closely guarded groups where decision making is neither better nor carried out more quickly than with centralisation. Unless some cohesive, unifying method such as strongly based profit planning exists, then all the weaknesses of disparate decision making and selfish gaining and use of corporate resources may occur.

Yet decentralisation supports the man on the spot, local morale should be higher, span of control problems minimised, communications improved, decision making brought closer to the situation it is addressing. That none of these benefits actually occur when local autonomy is given needs to be a major concern of senior managers deciding upon a revised organisation.

8   Pluralism and organisation

Democratic societies generally operate through the interplay of conflicting groups, each of which has some power to influence the decisions which are made. In some respects an industrial organisation can be viewed in the same way. It is a complicated series of interlocking power groups. Marketing and production people have obviously different viewpoints in considering company organisation and the allocation of resources. Employees and managers, specialist and line personnel, perhaps even the young and old, will tend to have their own objectives and ways of looking at things.

13.3   HIERARCHIES

Traditionally most, if not all, production units have tried to operate within a hierarchical organisation, with fairly rigid lines of command. At each step in the hierarchy, there has been an implied increase in authority.

In reality the power of shopfloor workers, and particularly shop stewards, has grown at the expense of members of the hierarchy, often making the structure a hollow sham. It is unfortunate that production management has tended to stick to the illusion that the hierarchy still works well and that it is only through such a structure that production goals can be achieved.

13.3.1   The nature of hierarchies

If hierarchical organisations are appropriate for the production (as well as any other) function, then it is implicit that:

1   Authority and power largely lie with the members of the hierarchy.
2   Those higher in the hierarchy have greater power and authority than those lower in the hierarchy and their responsibility is commensurately greater.
3   Members of the hierarchy will try to control their subordinates in three ways:
    (a)   Coercive. Some method is used to ensure compliance to authority. In

the past dismissal has been the major coercive weapon. Suspension, loss of pay or some other less drastic means of coercion have been used where non-compliance has been of a major character.

(b)   Remunerative. Typically in management appraisals or job evaluation financial rewards play a key part. Money for achievements or 'merit' can be given or withheld depending upon some apparently objective assessment.

(c)   Normative. There are many factors surrounding a job such as status symbols and prestige, whose threatened withdrawal from someone who has been given them, could be a control mechanism.

4   People at succeeding heights in the hierarchy usually have higher prestige or status than others lower in the hierarchy.

5   Orders tend to be issued downwards, with minimum participation in establishing goals or tasks.

6   Specialisation of labour is usually a dominating feature.

7   The organisational framework tends to be bureaucratic and authoritarian. Flexibility is usually lacking. Rules are laid down for most activities.

8   The learning capability of the hierarchy will largely depend upon the ability of senior personnel to recognise the need for such learning.

13.3.2   Adaptation in hierarchies

Perhaps despite themselves hierarchies have had to undergo adaptation in the last few years. Those that have not responded to environmental change have been bailed out by either the Government or other agencies or have disappeared altogether. Amongst the changes which have occurred include the following:

1   There has been a slow introduction of participation procedures. Often these appear to be cursory despite Government prodding.

2   Efforts have been made to improve communications within the hierarchy — for example by news letter or issues of annotated copies of the company balance sheet.

3   There has been a spread of status or prestige symbols which were once the sole prerogative of the senior managers of the hierarchy — e.g. paid time off for sickness, increased holiday entitlement, new pension rights.

4   Discipline has been relaxed in many ways — e.g. in dress, deference and general behaviour.

5   Various techniques which help adaptation such as profit planning have been introduced.

Many of these changes have been caused by events rather than being carefully planned moves carried out by a senior management determined to break down the hierarchy.

13.3.3   Results of adaptation

The scars of change are very visible in most hierarchical organisations.

1   Conflict has not declined significantly (though Government wages policy may be a prime reason for the increase in industrial unrest). Industrial relations are still a big problem.
2   Because they see that their power has been eroded, the morale of first line supervision has declined. This trend is also obvious at junior and even middle manager level.
3   Though changes have been made, there appears to be little evidence that fundamental reviews of work organisation are taking place in many companies. While slow adaptation has attractions and, in some instances, may even be the most sensible and effective way of making requisite changes, is it in every case?

   To answer this question it might be worthwhile to consider the following environmental influences which are at work on hierarchies:
   (a)   The increasing power of the trade unions and shop stewards.
   (b)   Role conflict, especially in the lower parts of the hierarchy, where power in many instances no longer matches the responsibilities which have been given to first line supervision and junior management.
   (c)   Rapid technological changes of all kinds which must be accommodated on the shopfloor with goodwill.
   (d)   The tasks required from shopfloor personnel may need to become much more technical, complicated and unstructured, if competition is to be met.
   (e)   A higher degree of effectiveness and efficiency is required for the same purpose.
   (f)   Greater participation in decision making, particularly in establishing corporate and departmental goals and plans generally.

13.4   EFFECTIVE ORGANISATIONS

What is an effective organisation? The objectives stated earlier provide one viewpoint. The fact that the structure adopted extremely successfully by one company, is anathema in another, suggests there is no one correct organisation.

Debating the old ground of line versus staff or centralisation versus decentralisation could be barren. Analysis has to be more fundamental than that:

1   'Organisation' is part of the production system. It could be the backbone of it. As such it should respond to environmental pressures and conflicts

over objectives in the same way that the production system should do.

2   Increasing environmental pressures suggest that organisations need to be more flexible and less structured than in the past.

3   Like the production system, the organisation needs to reflect reality in the relationship between power, authority and responsibility.

4   Conflict, a considerable problem in the production system, must be lessened by the organisational structure or at least the organisation must provide the means for helping to resolve conflict — through participation or work organisation designed to provide more local autonomy.

5   Hierarchies, as a rule, do not provide the flexibility which is needed. They promote vested interests in the status quo which could inhibit change.

6   Job descriptions, performance appraisals (discussed in Chapter 16) may only put a firm line around jobs, which will prevent adaptation within the structure.

7   A major fallacy in organisations is that organisations apparently exist apart from the people involved. There is a 'scientific' approach which considered analysis can produce. People within the same grade, apparently doing the same kind of job, often have widely differing skills, drive and ambition. Unless the organisation can promote the use of different skills, then it is likely to develop a low average job performance and a corresponding low morale. The cult of equality of opportunity should not lead to equal treatment for unequal people.

     Organisations need, in large part, to be built around both the skills and wishes of the people in the company.

8   Managers concerned with organisational design should be aware of how powerful groups of various kinds can exert pressure in the company. Intergroup relationships might lead to a pluralist view of organisation. Groups and committees can hide individual responsibility.

9   Changes in technology may divide increasingly the thinkers from the doers. Planners may become divorced from those for whom they plan. Environmental pressures may divide rather than unite. Any organisation must be designed to unite people of different functions.

10   Which way the organisation points will be important. Will it be dominated by marketing personnel and made to jump at the whim of every salesman? Or will it be production orientated with the production system uppermost within the organisation?

11   The organisation chart need not — indeed perhaps must not — be pretty to look at. The neat lines of command, the boxes apparently showing status and authority, often reflect bureaucracy and rigidity. A good organisation, with a requisite degree of flexibility, must look slightly irregular with loose ends ready to be attached to demanding new activities.

12   Organisations largely exist within informal rather than formal relationships. If informal relationships are destroyed by too much organisational change, morale and efficiency will drop.

The succeeding chapters in this part (IV) will help to establish further criteria for choosing an appropriate production organisation.

NOTES

1 E. F. L. Brech, *Organisation — The Framework of Management*, Longmans, 1965 (Second Edition).
2 H. J. Leavitt, W. R. Dill and H. B. Eyring, *The Organisational World*, Harcourt Brace, 1973.

14

Conflict and its possible containment

14.1 INTRODUCTION

With the exception of some committed Marxists or Trotskyists, most people working within an organisation would wish to see it prosper. How the resulting prosperity is shared or even the way it is achieved would certainly not receive the same universal approval.

This chapter, therefore, starts from the basis that workers are not wreckers. Their attitudes to work may differ from those of their fathers. Their values and beliefs may also have changed, but the destruction of industrial society is not one of them.

14.2 CONFLICT — ITS NATURE

The nature of conflict seems to be changing. There is evidence, for example, that strikes are being used more and more as a means of attempting to influence the outcome of wages settlements and in industrial relations generally.

In the 1950s strikes in the UK were running on average at three million working days per year. When the Government of the day attempted to introduce the Industrial Relations Act of 1971, 24 million working days were lost. Currently (in the late seventies) the strike figure is around nine million lost days per year (10.14 million in 1977).

While some of the strike problems can be attributed to the interference of Governments in the collective bargaining process, either through wage freeze, restraint or statutory wage limitation, there is much more which is disturbing.

Administration and technical people irrespective of skills, trade, tradition or grade (within limits) are prepared to use the power of the strike to try to achieve their own objectives. Some strikes can be classed as political — for example challenges to Government legislation — but there is a wider significance to be seen in the strike figures. Dedication can no longer be taken for granted. A willingness to play industrial relations 'softly' may be dead. Ignorance of power and how to use it may be on the way out.

Production managers should consider the strike, therefore, not as something unthinkable, but nearly inevitable at some time, even in the best run factories.

Conflict does not necessarily manifest itself in an openly physical way. If a wider definition of conflict is a 'lack of compatibility' then it is possible that the elements of the production system are in conflict most of the time. Even senior production management is involved and the evidence of increased management stress suggests that there is incompatibility and conflict between personal and company goals and the resources available to achieve them.

Perhaps the largest area for potential conflict (using the 'incompatibility' definition) lies in the philosophy of a new generation of workers who have been brought up in an abundant society [1] or as some sociologists suggest, in a post-industrial society [2] where the work ethic has been undermined if not abandoned altogether.

14.3 SOME CAUSES OF CONFLICT

The causes of conflict within the production function are numerous and multi-dimensional. While pay and its associated troubles often seem to be a major cause of conflict, this could be because opportunities for fighting some other perhaps more fundamental battle do not exist. Pay is a convenient issue over which to quarrel.

This section covers possible causes of conflict other than pay, because these could in the long run be more important.

14.3.1 The political challenge

Marxists assert that as long as there are economically defined classes, conflict between them is inevitable. The Communist Manifesto begins 'The history of hitherto existing societies is the history of class struggles'.

Most Marxists will be able to quote further — 'Society as a whole is more and more splitting up into two great hostile camps, into two great classes directly facing each other, bourgeoisie and proletariat'. The bourgeoisie have a dominant position in society owing to their economic power and through it the means of manipulating ideas and culture and so ensuring their survival.

For Marxists there can be no justice or compromise while capitalism exists. Though the capitalist system can produce wealth it can never end the exploitation of the working classes which produce the wealth. This contradiction will eventually (says Marx) produce a revolutionary crisis when it will be possible for the capitalist system to be overthrown.

So inevitably there must be a polarisation between the workers and the capitalists. Managers are usually viewed as being the means whereby the capitalists largely retain power and so they should be regarded as 'class enemies' with all this implies for co-operation within the factory.

Marx (and presumably committed Marxists) scorns bourgeois democracy except to suggest that by establishing a form of co-operation, revolutionary parties may eventually be better placed to effect revolution. By attempting to integrate the objectives of various groups within one society democratic parties and other organisations are obscuring the reality of the class struggle, so therefore they too are enemies to be obstructed and eventually eliminated.

This concept of conflict and of Marxist ideology generally is useful in understanding the militancy of some shop stewards. The determination and dedication of most Marxists will ensure they do become, if at all possible, shop-floor representatives. It is essential for anyone who has to negotiate with shop stewards' committees to appreciate the political philosophy of some, perhaps a majority, of those who will become workers' representatives. Along with knowledge of production control, incentive schemes and engineering principles, Marxist philosophy might be part of every course for production managers.

14.3.2   The nature of work

Marx too is a useful starting point for discussing conflict which might originate from the nature of work. Marx suggests that because of capitalism man has become separated or estranged from his work, his colleagues and his true self. By being a small part of a large organisation a worker is no longer in control of his own life as he was before the advent of capitalism.

Blauner [3] describes alienation slightly differently. He suggests that four psychological conditions apply in modern industry — powerlessness, mean-inglessness, isolation and self-estrangement. He feels that these conditions have resulted from the technology of work, the division of labour, social organisation and the economic structure.

While the words that Marx and Blauner use are emotive and in some ways just jargon, the sense of frustration and boredom which they portray finds echoes on many shopfloors in unrest, strikes, unwillingness to co-operate, even in sabotage. Yet Blauner emphasises the importance of work because it 'influences a worker's opportunity for personal growth and development'.

All of which may leave a cynical production manager feeling that much was being made of little, especially in attributing feelings and beliefs to his workforce which they obviously do not have. People who have worked on an assembly line for, say, twenty years are used to it and put up with it even if they do not like it very much. At least they stick it out in preference to doing less well paid, though more interesting, jobs elsewhere.

Goldthorpe [4] seems to provide support for this view. In his survey of the Vauxhall plant at Luton, 62 per cent of the assembly line workers said that they would like to work elsewhere in the plant where the work was not so boring and monotonous. Even so, few did leave the line for less well paid work elsewhere.

The flow line therefore, may be taken as having high potential for alienation and conflict:

1 The process or line sets its own pace (i.e. management establishes the speed at which a machine or line works). In most industrial situations, the worker might normally wish to control the pace of his machine himself.
2 Once a few basic skills have been learned, there is little scope for skill enhancement. There is little need for special or divergent attention.
3 Tasks tend to be repetitive and so could induce boredom and fatigue. Some flow lines allow a change of occupation within a working group, but this tends to be within a restricted range of jobs.
4 Except for immediate contact with his local working group, a worker tends to be limited in his possibilities for social exchange. The nature of the flow line makes for isolation.
5 Noise tends to be high, so inhibiting conversation.
6 As a consequence of 1 to 5 it is likely that only a small part of a man's brain will be used actively in carrying out his job. There seems a strong possibility that he will feel alienated, ready to see work stop occasionally, if only to break the boredom of his day.

This last point is verified by the high number of strikes, stoppages and general unrest in motor car assembly plants. The tendency in the seventies has been for car plants to have approximately three times the number of working days lost through unrest than industry generally (though the linked nature of plants and the ease at which one stoppage in a factory has an automatic effect on many other factories must be stressed. The competence of management must also be a factor).

14.3.3 Power, authority and responsibility

Power can be defined as the means of making others comply to one's wishes whether they want to do so or not. Duverger [5] suggests that power 'is comprised of the entire range of social institutions which are concerned with the domination of some men over others'.

Barnard [6] states that for power to be legitimate it needs the ready assent of the individuals subject to power, plus the belief that the exercise of such power is not incompatible with the individual's personal interest and not inconsistent with the purpose of the organisation.

The problem of legitimising power therefore, could be a key one in reducing internal conflict and in creating a factory culture in which most people work willingly for a common goal. To stress this point further, the shopfloor and trade unions have gained power which effectively prevents management from totally controlling the production system. They have, however, neither been given nor perhaps want to take the responsibility of helping to ensure that the system works well.

14.3.4 Objectives

Perhaps the most obvious source of conflict lies in management's requirement of corporate success and an individual's desire to promote his own self-interest and ultimately that of the group with which he identifies and belongs. The company wants profit or efficiency (whichever is the local objective). The individual on the shopfloor might also want such things in an abstract way, but not at the expense of his own job security or pay. He will always prefer continuing employment in preference to high profit.

So the occasions when related conflict might occur are:

1   When company business declines and costs need to be reduced in some way — possibly through redundancies.
2   Any occasion when efficiency is improved at the expense of the employee — e.g. more output is expected with little or no increase in pay.
3   When new machines or methods are introduced which will decrease manning levels.
4   Application of procedures such as work study and improved output planned with only a minor part of the resulting benefits being given to employees.
5   When pay scales and pay awards do not keep pace with local or industry averages.

14.3.5 Culture

The nature of value systems might sound an implausible reason for conflict. Managers and shopfloor people have often had the same basic education, perhaps live in the same areas, even get nearly the same financial rewards. Yet the cultural differences between the two are often extensive. The word 'class' may sound archaic but it tends to sum up the relative position of many workers and management.

The application of participation usually serves as a good example of the cultural divide which tends to exist. The workers are often (but not always) less articulate, worker orientated and guarded in their approach. Managers are usually more articulate, they are more company orientated, and equally guarded in their approach. A full understanding of each other's position is rare.

Senior managers seldom live in a council house and do not usually have to make short term decisions based on a weekly wage. Their places of work are usually clean, well lit and relatively noiseless. It is infrequent that they have to work shifts or clock in. They have a degree of freedom in their jobs which would be intolerable to the discipline needed on the production line. Their social life is not usually centred around the local pub or working men's club.

There appear to be, then, considerable cultural differences between workers and management. Conflict to some extent, either through misunderstanding or an inability to communicate ideas and values, is nearly inevitable.

14.3.6 Relative deprivation

Relative deprivation is a term used to describe a condition where people or groups feel that their position, status, salary or pay is inappropriate when compared with other people or groups. This is a fairly common feeling in industry.

For example, shopfloor unions occasionally gain wage increases which technical or clerical personnel feel are unfair when compared with their own position. The shopfloor workers believe that management have much better conditions than they have and are resentful of them. Even though everyone has a reasonable standard of living and an adequate working environment, it is the comparison with others which can cause serious conflict.

14.3.7 Other considerations

So far the potential causes of conflict which have been given are 'vertical' — i.e. they probably result from people's places in a hierarchy. However, there are other causes which are horizontal. For example, the problems of demarcation between trades have still to be solved in many industries in the UK. There are frequent battles between skilled and unskilled workers. Sharing the available cake is far from easy.

There may also be frictional problems with organisations outside the company — suppliers, customers, the local council, Government. Some of the most important conflicts may arise from historical situations. For example, some decisions about how to increase profit taken years ago may only now be influencing jobs and job performance.

14.4 A SUMMARY OF SOLUTIONS

Some of the solutions which could help to resolve conflict problems are discussed elsewhere. For example, 'pay policy' and all that it means in the way of job evaluation and rewards for effort, skills, working conditions, etc. should help considerably in 'relative deprivation'.

There is a danger that conflict or potential conflict will not be recognised, or recognised too late for effective action to be taken to head it off. If conflict is manifest only in an unwillingness to co-operate, lethargy in carrying out prescribed tasks or just a failure to use production resources as well as they might be, then it could go on unchecked and unchanged for a long time. The need to recognise 'conflict', therefore, is important.

14.4.1 Pluralism

A school of industrial relations has grown up which suggests that it is important to appreciate that power in an industrial organisation is now diffused through several groups. Each group has some power but not enough to control the production system alone.

Fox [7] has summed up the essentials of the situation as follows:

'The enterprise is seen as a complex of tensions and competing claims which have to be managed in the interests of maintaining a viable collaborative structure within which all the stakeholders can with varying degrees of success, pursue their aspirations.'

This seems a realistic approach to conflict analysis as it recognises group power and group interests and selfishness. Equally it recognises the need to institutionalise pluralism in the way a political democracy attempts to do. A balance is struck between groups who have a potential for conflict, through mechanisms or institutions which allow a balance of power to be achieved.

Conflict can therefore be constructive rather than destructive. The production system brings together potentially hostile groups. A pluralist reply would attempt to unite them for the common good.

It is likely, however, that pluralism will only work if the competing groups have something approaching equal power. The problems of political democracies are relevant here. How far is a factory electorate educated to make a pronouncement on the government of the company? Even in a democracy the executive carries on with the day to day running of the country no matter what happens to the legislature. (Perhaps the two tier board comes closest to meeting this situation.)

Critics of pluralism might also suggest that no amount of institutionalised conflict will eradicate it. (Political democracies still have considerable internal conflict.) But is the total elimination of conflict a realistic proposition anyway?

14.4.2   The behaviourists' approach

Many production managers will be aware of the solutions to conflict which industrial psychologists have proposed. These, therefore, will be given only briefly. The debate should really be about how such proposals can be put into operation and how effective they will be eventually. Certainly there have not been many applications of job enrichment which have been completely successful. Production managers must use their own judgement and experience to determine how valid the competing claims are [8].

Herzberg [9] has suggested that many of the factors which traditionally might be considered to be 'motivators' and so conflict reducers, do not motivate at all. He calls these 'hygiene factors' — examples are:

Company policy and administration (i.e. how the company is run);
Supervision;
Salaries/wages;
Interpersonal relations;
Working conditions.

If these are not handled well they could act as de-motivators, but however well they are tackled, their motivational effect is limited.

There are, however, other factors which can act as motivators and amongst these are:

Recognition of achievement;
The work being performed;
Responsibility given to individuals;
Advancement and reward.

With McGregor's Theory 'X' and 'Y' [10] the approach is different but the end result (i.e. the application) might be the same. He suggests that managers adopt one of two different styles. If a manager believes his workforce is innately lazy and does not want to work and would avoid responsibility even if it were offered to it, then he adopts an authoritarian or Theory 'X' position. He will attempt to control tightly and allow little freedom.

Conversely if a manager believes that his workforce looks upon work as a potential source of satisfaction and that work itself is as natural as rest or play, then he is likely to believe that he can delegate responsibility and allow people to use their imagination, initiative and creativity in carrying out their work. This is Theory 'Y'.

Maslow [11] has suggested that a man has a hierarchy of needs starting with the most basic requirements. Once these have been achieved, needs change, as is shown in the familiar figure of 14.1.

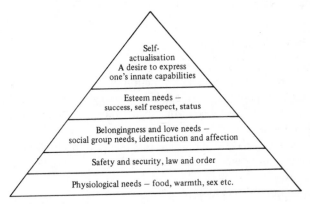

Fig. 14.1   Hierarchy of needs

While Herzberg, McGregor and Maslow all start off with different points of view, the application of their theories points in the same direction, and suggests an organisational structure with the following attributes:

1   authority is decentralised as far as possible;
2   maximum autonomy for local decision making and job enrichment is given;
3   the corporate style is participative and consultative;
4   as far as possible job enrichment is practised;
5   self expression and self actualisation are pursued for their own sake.

Those production managers who shudder at this kind of phraseology will no doubt be pleased to know that a critical analysis of the job enrichment theory as a means of motivation is given in Chapter 20 — Motivation.

14.4.4   Sticking to the rules of the game

As in football or cricket, it is assumed that fairly rigid rules can be agreed which can govern the conduct of everyone in an organisation. Every possible contingency which can arise has some agreed legislation which covers it.

Many organisations enshrine the legislation in a handbook or published notices — e.g. 'workers will not clock in or out for each other'; 'no-one will stop his machine until five minutes before the end of the shift;' 'no-one will leave his machine without the permission of his supervisor.'

Industrial dispute procedures are all recorded in detail and are expected to be followed to the letter. This, of course, does not always happen and short cuts tend to be taken. Legislation is effective only when everyone in an organisation sees the need for it and is prepared to follow it.

'Sticking to the rules', however, may only defer potential conflict until most of the procedure has been gone through. If underlying causes for conflict exist then having rules may only postpone conflict.

14.4.5   The organisation as a team

A company can be considered as a coalition of interests whose goals may conflict and which will only be reconciled if a unitary approach is taken to ensure corporate success. The essence of the 'team', therefore, and how it can thrive is to consider coalition goals and not management or employee desires alone. Coalition goals will have to be 'trade offs' — high profit cannot be earned if employee job security is to be maintained, high pay cannot be given unless high added value is achieved etc.

The team approach would need to:

1   Define corporate goals in a way which makes sense to everyone in the organisation. For example, explanation of why profit is needed and why a high return on investment will aid job security seems essential. Workers should worry most about job security when low profits are being made.
2   Make plans with coalition goals in mind.
3   Make the whole team — workers and managers at all levels — aware of the strategies needed to ensure that coalition goals are achieved.
4   Allocate tasks and duties, authorities and responsibilities accordingly.

The team should then play to its strength.

14.4.6   Is small beautiful? Organisational changes

Evidence suggests that days lost through strikes are about five times greater in companies employing above 1,000 than those which have less than 500. While special circumstances may exist — technologies or history — it seems likely that small companies will have less conflict than large ones.

Organisational changes which promote group solidarity, identity of purpose, good communications and common values should reduce the possibility of conflict, within a 'small company structure'.

14.5   CONCLUSION

Many production managers find it extremely difficult to bridge the gap between the writings and discussions of academics and their own experience of operating a production unit. Conflict — its causes and containment — is one subject where this applies. It seems too easy to advance an untenable theory in a facile way and so get it accepted as being valid on the shopfloor. Life is much more difficult. Yet many theories are pointing in the same direction — smaller units, operating with more autonomy than they have had in the past. Is this the way that conflict can be reduced?

NOTES

1   G. Huggin, *Scarcity, Abundance and Depletion*, Loughborough University of Technology, 1975.

2   E. G. Trist, *Urban North America — The Challenge of the Next 30 Years*, Tavistock, 1973.

3   R. Blauner, *Alienation and Freedom — The Factory Worker and His Industry*, University of Chicago Press, 1967.

4   J. H. Goldthorpe, D. Lockwood, F. Beckhofer, J. Plant, *The Affluent Worker — Industrial Attitudes and Behaviour*, Cambridge University Press, 1968.

5   M. Duverger, *The Study of Politics*, Thomas Nelson & Co., 1972.

6   C. Barnard, *The Function of the Executive*, Harvard University Press, 1958.

7   A. Fox, *Man Management*, Hutchinson, 1974.

8   See, for example: M. Fein, 'Job Enrichment — A Revolution', *Sloan Management Review*, Winter 1974.

9   F. Herzberg, 'One More Time — How Do You Motivate Employees?', *Harvard Business Review*, January–February 1968.

10   D. McGregor, *The Human Side of Enterprise*, McGraw-Hill, 1960.

11   A. H. Maslow. *Motivation and Personality*, Harper & Row 1970.

12   M. Argyle, *The Social Psychology of Work*, Penguin, 1972.

15

Industrial democracy

15.1 INTRODUCTION

Industrial democracy has been chosen as the title of this chapter as it seems to sum up many of the aspirations of trade union leaders and shop stewards if not shopfloor workers. The three main political parties in the UK (Conservative, Labour and Liberal) have common ground in believing that 'industrial democracy' needs to be introduced on a wider scale than currently exists. (They have less in common when they attempt to define the boundaries of industrial democracy.)

The term industrial democracy has been given a variety of meanings but all suggest that workers in an organisation should be given greater authority to influence the decisions which concern them. Everyone should be able to participate in the process of ensuring the success of the business and the way the rewards of success are distributed, so that in industry there should be the same rights to influence events as are found in local and national government.

The proposals for industrial democracy vary from enhanced joint consultation to workers' control. Not all trade unionists and shop stewards support industrial democracy. Some see it as a means of supporting capitalism and nothing more.

So what can be construed as 'participation'? The following appear to be relevant:

1 Joint consultation with management on working conditions, job opportunities, company welfare facilities and local conditions of employment.
2 Participation in management's tactical decision-making role — manning levels, activity and performance achievements and how to improve them,

work organisation and control. This might be called shopfloor democracy.
3   Participation at the highest level in the company (i.e. the Board) on strategic decision making. The decisions will be concerned with capital investment, plant closures, business opportunities, distribution of added value, etc. This might be called company democracy.
4   Ownership of the company either jointly with shareholders or government or entirely by the workforce. This might be called economic democracy.

15.2   WHY PARTICIPATE?

The example given later in this chapter (Section 15.8) provides some assumptions about the opportunities to be gained in introducing 'participation'. From a management point of view unless participation helps in overall problem solving and ensures that the business is more successful than it otherwise would be, then it is merely another burden which management has to carry. This should be said as often as possible.

Pressures for participation stem from:

1   The government. Many governments throughout Western Europe have introduced legislation which has forced companies to apply participation in one form or another.
2   The workers themselves and their representatives on various semi-official and government bodies.
3   Supra-national organisations, e.g. the EEC.
4   Trade unions.
5   Management theorists and writers.

For management the key problem is how to use constructively the power which trade unions undoubtedly have. How is it possible to work together for the benefit of the whole organisation?

15.3   PARTICIPATION — SCOPE AND TYPE

Formal participation has potential dangers. It could mean battle lines between workers and management drawn more firmly than they were before, with rigid and formal antagonism replacing informal sniping.

This seems to be one of the biggest dangers in imposing participation — the company may not be ready for it. Governments may propose, but company history, style and attitudes may dispose. Participation may also be influenced by the size of the company, its technology and the comparative education of its workforce.

In their day the following have all been given the title of 'participation':

Information giving — e.g. on company and product line performance.
Consultation — e.g. asking the shopfloor their opinion on time recording or canteen facilities.
Negotiation — e.g. joint decision making on, say, capital investment, incentives, wages policy.

Legislation has already been introduced in the UK in certain areas and for certain activities:

Health and safety
Pensions
Redundancy.

The practical example given at the end of this chapter indicates some of the problems and activities which participation can cover. In the instance outlined, there was a policy that anything could be discussed with the exception of the company's overall profit performance. This was considered to deserve a more formal structure than the one which was established.

15.4   STRUCTURES FOR PARTICIPATION

It used to be said that if informal joint consultation did not work then formal joint consultation would not work either. Setting up a structure in which discussions take place seems a trade union habit. It is something concrete which can be shown as evidence of their influence and power. Management, too, often tends to put trust in committees and discussion groups. The debate about participation has largely been about 'structure'. Following are some structures which have been either tried or recommended for participation:

1   Two-tier boards

These seem a favourite structure advocated by the EEC and applied in Germany. There is recognition of the need to separate the general day to day running of an organisation from the formal direction of the business in the longer term. Trade unions are represented on the senior but not necessarily on the management board. This leaves the managers still largely in control of the tactical activities of the company — though even at this level, there will be various participative activities.

2 Works or company councils

These are established to allow worker participation in the local decision making process, usually with representation on the local board. Tactical decisions are made concerning such subjects as capital investment, product changes, alterations to manning levels, etc.

3 Departmental participation groups

These could be the lowest level of a participation hierarchy and could concern activities such as output rates, production levels, overtime, local incentives etc.

4 Committees or problem solving groups

These are established to discuss and arrive at decisions about one particular problem — e.g. absenteeism, reject levels, labour turnover. Such committees will be needed for consideration of health and safety at work.

Membership of the committees, councils or Boards can be achieved in several ways. Election of members who are not shop stewards is rare. Normally shop stewards take a place on a committee as a consequence of being a shop steward. In some ways this may be a drawback and a separate election for some *ad hoc* committee may provide greater democracy than the automatic placing of already elected shop stewards.

Trade union nominations for the two-tier boards is a possibility and some government thinking points this way, though the 'trade union members only' rule will cause resentment irrespective of who applies it.

Large companies obviously have difficulties not found in small ones. The participation structures probably need to be hierarchical as well as more rigidly formulated than in small companies. The type of potential legislation on participation is well illustrated by the White Paper on Industrial Democracy published in 1978 [1]. This paper modifies considerably the proposals made in the Bullock Report which foreshadowed it. The White Paper proposed that:

1 Employees of companies employing more than 500 people will have a statutory right to discuss important changes which affect employees in the company. The important changes will include mergers, takeovers, substantial investment and fundamental organisational changes.
2 Guidance will be given on the form that industrial democracy might take by a code of practice.
3 Employees of companies employing more than 2000 people will have a statutory right for representatives to sit on the policy making board. Initially representation might be up to a third of all members on the Board.
4 Joint representative committees consisting of lay representation of independent trade unions will have a statutory right to discuss company

strategy or have representatives on a policy board by asking for a ballot of employees.

Industrial democracy, the White Paper suggests, will mean that all employees at every level will have a real share in the decisions made within the company for which they work, so thereby having a share in the responsibility of making it a success.

It is not intended (says the White Paper) that a standard pattern of participation in industry will be established by law.

Industrial managers may see the situation very differently. There is no adequate safeguard for the rights of managers, as such, and there seems to be a danger that decision making will become so diffuse and long delayed that it will be ineffective. People may be participating in decisions for which they have no competence.

Participation could be a considerable source of conflict.

15.5   UNION ATTITUDES TO PARTICIPATION AND INDUSTRIAL RELATIONS GENERALLY

Trade union attitudes seem to vary from outright opposition to participation to a recognition that trade union power will be enhanced by it, so it should be supported.

The TUC and various large unions have produced booklets [2] dealing with industrial relations and participation and some review of these may be useful.

At first sight these booklets make depressing reading. For example one of the key points which is discussed is 'mutuality' stated as a 'principle which means that all aspects of working conditions and pay should be permanently negotiable. Unless all agreements that are reached are considered to be essentially temporary settlements, arrived at by mutual agreement between employers and trade unions, a ceiling is put on members' standards of living, which can then be further reduced by rising prices'.

In another context the same point is again made. 'This paternalistic concept is the very opposite of all the union's objectives. There can never be anything fair about a master and servant relationship. All that any agreement ever achieves is a temporary acceptable day's pay for a temporary acceptable day's work. Both are always renegotiable.'

The possibility of unions wanting to renegotiate an agreement the day after it has been signed is not considered at all, nor is the lack of contractual justice. 'Mutuality' therefore is a curse in many union negotiations and management must insist that agreements have a time limit and during that time the agreement is not negotiable. While this may cause unrest, even strikes, it should still be a cornerstone of management—union negotiations. If a strike ensues so be it; the alternative could be anarchy.

The pamphlet published by the TGWU insists that 'trade unions seek to increase the workers' share of the cake. In practice, the degree of worker v management control over how much work is performed and the effort expended thereon are vital to this distribution conflict'. There seems to be no recognition that capital as well as labour has to have an adequate reward, otherwise the company may just go bankrupt.

There are concrete gains which should accrue to the workers in a bargaining situation, the TGWU states. These will be improvements in shop steward facilities, paid meeting arrangements, shorter hours, improved conditions, more satisfactory and less arduous work, increased job security, increased leisure as well as increased earnings. Again there is no indication of the give and take which is an essential part of participation.

A further point made by the TGWU is that every agreement should involve an extension of negotiating rights and trade union controls and facilities. Agreements, it is stated, should be as comprehensive as possible, because it is useful to 'consolidate the position that has been won informally, by putting the most favourable aspects of custom and practice into writing. Not only can this be useful to establish a floor on which to build in future negotiations, but it can also be used by members negotiating in other plants (and even in other industries) as a precedent.'

Production managers in many factories have come to despair of the phrase 'custom and practice'. Somewhere they have allowed some ill discipline to creep in by default; they have not controlled some activity as well as they should have done; something which would have been stopped had they had the time to do so has carried on. 'Custom and practice' sanctifies the procedures and management normally has — reluctantly — to accept them.

Second generation incentives seem to receive short shrift from the TGWU. 'The principal advantage of such schemes lies in making available to the union, facts and figures about productivity but if there is any doubt about the advantages they should be left alone ... care must be taken not to let members be persuaded by the employers that their interests are the same as those of the owners'.

This latter remark seemingly blows skyhigh the whole basis of participation where it is hoped that mutual interest might be generated.

The employee has apparently little responsibility for the work he produces. For example, in relation to faulty work, the following is stated. If some loss of pay is agreed while rectifying bad workmanship then 'Provision should be made that this will only take account of that work which is clearly 100 per cent the fault of that individual and not partly due to contributory negligence in previous operations, materials, machinery, tools, inadequate instructions or environmental conditions. The attribution of responsibility should be a question of fact, with the employee getting the benefit of the doubt.'

Change even when apparently accepted is often governed by a *status quo* clause, which will allow workers to revert to a previous method or procedure they were using. A *status quo* clause is often embodied in an agreement — 'If any change is implemented which the union subsequently feels to be against its members' interests and the union advises management accordingly, the *status quo ante* the change will be restored whilst the matter is being negotiated.'

Finally, to quote a TGWU policy statement — 'The history of collective bargaining between Employers' organisations and Trade Unions has been marked by a struggle between those seeking to maintain authoritarian management on the one hand and the aim of working people to control their own working environment.'

Enough has been said to suggest that:

1   No management can expect an easy ride over participation.
2   Even if management thinks that it is time to end the trench warfare, the union side may be far from wanting to debate rationally and carefully about enlarging the cake and ensuring the survival of the company.
3   What the union side may want to discuss as 'participation' could be totally different from what management would like to believe the discussions should be about.
4   Getting any kind of relevant participation started may take months, if not years, to achieve.
5   The degree of education required may be considerable.

15.6   A CODE OF PRACTICE

The 'Industrial relations code of practice' issued by the government in 1972 [3] was retained under the Trade Union and Labour Relations Act of 1974, and thus still seems to be a relevant and worthwhile document in considering participation. It makes the following points:

1   The code of practice is to give practical guidance in promoting good industrial relations. It stresses the need for freely conducted collective bargaining, orderly procedures for settling disputes, free association of workers and employers and security for workers.
2   Responsibilities. Under this heading both management and trade union responsibilities are discussed. For management, a principal role will be to develop effective industrial relations policies which command the confidence of employees, establishing effective arrangements for negotiation, consultation and communication. Responsibility for each group of employees would be clearly defined, particularly at supervisor level where appropriate training in industrial relations should be given. It is suggested that a key role for trade unions should be to ensure that the employing organisation prospers so ensuring job security for rank and file trade unionists. Officials and members should ensure that agreements are fully

observed; shop stewards should understand their power and duties; full time officials should be appointed in sufficient numbers to maintain adequate contact with management. Members of trade unions should be encouraged to attend branch meetings.

3 Employers' associations should promote those interests of their members which can best be served by co-operation at industry or other appropriate levels.

4 The individual employee has an obligation to his employer, to his trade union, and to his fellow employees. He has a contract of employment, many of whose terms are fixed by collective bargaining.

5 Employment policies. To achieve good industrial relations, clear and comprehensive employment policies are essential. Such policies should help management to make the most effective use of manpower resources and give each employee the opportunity to develop his potential. Manpower planning will be a key activity in working out manpower needs and ensuring future job security.

The employment policies should cover:
Recruitment and selection
Training
Payment systems
Status and security of employees
Working conditions.

6 Communication and consultation. In its everyday activities, management must ensure that information concerning the business is given to the employees and, conversely, that employees inform management of their views and opinions.

Consultation, the code of practice suggests, means jointly examining and discussing problems of concern to both management and employees. It involves seeking mutually acceptable solutions through a genuine exchange of views and information, by having systematic and structured consultative arrangements.

7 Collective bargaining is defined as a joint management and employee activity which establishes a framework for industrial relations. It is suggested that collective bargaining will normally take place at varying levels, the matters to be discussed at each level being arrived at by mutual agreement. The bargaining is conducted in relationship to a defined group of employees, though too many bargaining units will make it difficult to ensure that related groups of employees are treated consistently. A bargaining unit should be established after considering the nature of the work performed, the type of employees which might be covered and the interests they have in common, the wishes of employees, the matters to be bargained about, and the need to fit in with the pattern of union and management organisation.

Recognition of trade unions and their right to represent their members will be a key factor in any collective bargaining activity.

Collective agreements are defined as dealing with matters of procedure and substance which are of joint concern to management and employees. The agreements should be in writing, with regular discussions to determine whether they have become out of date.

A procedural agreement should stipulate the constitution of each bargaining unit, specifying the parties and matters to be bargained about.

Substantive agreements settle terms and conditions of employment.

The disclosure of information is a vital factor in collective bargaining as the procedure can only be conducted responsibly if management and unions have sufficient information on the matters which are being negotiated.

8   Employee representation at the place of work. Normally shop stewards will be employee representatives who will put forward the collective views of all employees to management. There are advantages to management in having a structured shop steward representation as it should provide a means for having a reasonable dialogue with the workforce.

Management should provide the means for the election of shop stewards and help to specify their powers and duties. They should help to stipulate the number of stewards required and any conditions for eligibility for the role.

Trade unions should give shop stewards written credentials, setting out their powers within the union including calling for industrial action.

Normally a senior shop steward or works convener will be appointed who will act as a co-ordinator of all other shop stewards. Facilities extended to shop stewards will result from agreements between the trade unions and management. Time off from the job normally extends to union meetings and should be given by the local production manager.

Training of shop stewards should be a joint management and trade union activity, especially in ensuring that stewards are informed about the policies of the organisation which employs them, the business position of the organisation and the agreements to which they are a party.

9   Grievances and disputes procedures. The code of practice is specific about grievances and disputes. It states that all employees have a right to seek redress for grievances relating to their employment and should be told how they can do so. Management should establish with shop stewards procedures for employees to raise grievances and ensure that they are settled as quickly as possible. The disputes should be settled as near to the place of origin as possible. The stages of the grievance procedure should be firmly established.

10 Disciplining procedures. Management should negotiate, with shop stewards, disciplining procedures which are fair and effective. They

should enable all mitigating circumstances to be taken into account. The following steps might be introduced:

An oral warning.

A written warning which may be substituted for the oral warning in severe disciplinary cases.

A final warning, suspension without pay or some other representative measure.

Dismissal.

In each stage of the proceedings the employee has the right to have his union representative to support him. In the case of a shop steward, a full time official of the union must be involved.

While the code of practice is not really about participation as such, it does describe the major facets of what generally comprises 'industrial relations'. It is appreciated that joint consultative machinery or even collective bargaining is not really participation as currently defined. However, how one shades into another is often difficult to determine as the introduction to this chapter suggests.

15.7 PRACTICAL PARTICIPATION — SOME BASIC QUESTIONS

The manager considering participation must obey the law if this stipulates that a participation structure has to be introduced. But it does not end there. If participation does not provide the means for a more successful enterprise than it otherwise would be, then it is of no value. So the following questions might be asked:

1 Can a greater commitment to the business be gained by introducing participation? If so, is it likely that this greater commitment can be actively used to ensure that the business is more successful in the future than in the past?

2 Can we avoid putting in some form of participation even if the government does not legislate for such a happening? People coming into industry are likely to demand more knowledge about the company than their fathers did and also a share in the way the company is run.

3 What can we do to ensure that participation is a success? How far can we establish work organisations with greater autonomy and self-discipline which might constitute a basis for participation at a higher level? Can we improve communication so that people understand the business better — its problems and how it might be made more prosperous?

4 Do our people appear to be ready for participation — employees and management? What training will be required to ensure that participation will be a success? When can we start the programme? Do we have to train work group leaders as well as shop stewards? Will it be more

important to train first line supervisors than say middle management? Will training courses differ?

5   Can we set up low level participation which will draw in ideas about how production should be organised or improved in some way?

6   Can we build on existing joint consultative machinery or are completely new structures required?

7   Employees may not actively desire participation, but active and ambitious trade unionists and shop stewards, more often than not, do so. How can this situation be accommodated? The 'union', 'shop stewards', and 'employees' may not at all be the same thing. Most workers would appear to want the power to prevent management from introducing changes which could affect them adversely, rather than help to create a more prosperous organisation. People cannot be ordered to participate positively.

8   Can experiments in participation be set up where various structures, philosophies, procedures can be tried out with no firm agreement on either side?

9   What about people in the company who may not be in trade unions — such as middle and senior management? Can they be included in participative arrangements? Do they feel they need to be involved?

10 How can the smaller unions in the company prevent themselves from being swamped — either in fact or psychologically by the large shopfloor unions? Will these latter always dominate participative proceedings?

11 In large companies with many associate organisations and perhaps worldwide manufacturing and trading facilities, where should participation take place? Will the local associate company, where people's security really lies, be the most appropriate place to develop participation?

12 What other things can be constructively discussed within the participation process, to make it worthwhile, which are not already discussed in some detail?

15.8   AN EXERCISE IN PARTICIPATION

The following report on 'problem solving task committees' covers a practical case of participation in a problem solving framework. It describes the approach taken, the benefits which were expected (and largely achieved) and the type of teams which were established.

During the exercise several facts emerged:

1   The shop stewards were more keen on the activity than were middle management.

2   The inclusion of shop stewards did not ensure that 'shopfloor democracy' resulted. There was a possibility that a management oligarchy would be

replaced by a management and shop steward oligarchy; shopfloor people still had no direct involvement with the committees. This is the problem of all 'democratic' structures. There is a limit on the degree of participation which is possible.

3 The benefits which result from such exercises are often more intangible than tangible. It is usually difficult to justify participation from concrete evidence.

4 The pace at which participation can be carried out depends upon attitudes, willingness and sincerity — perhaps in that order.

5 Considerable homework needs to be done to achieve sensible arrangements which are not just perpetually angry talking shops. Someone must provide the data for discussion in a way which everyone understands. A good secretariat is essential.

6 Training of participants — shop stewards and managers alike — is necessary. If management have been trained to communicate and make decisions at a high level, how can shop stewards hope to compete without similar training?

7 Starting participation at a reasonably modest level is advantageous in a company where industrial trench warfare has been the order of the day.

8 Far more management time is needed, if participation is to be successful, than is ever anticipated.

9 The whole process will become discredited if decision making is poor and decisions are not implemented when made.

10 Participation is as much for junior managers as shop stewards. Resentment will spread if first line supervision feel that they have been left out of the proceedings.

THE REPORT
PROBLEM SOLVING TASK COMMITTEES

For some time now management have been very conscious of the need to improve productivity and overall efficiency. At the same time it is appreciated that relationships between managers and employees are changing. External social and economic pressures suggest that new methods of achieving profitable change must be explored.

This report outlines the content of two meetings which took place on the 4th and 25th July between managers and shop stewards, when agreement was reached on an approach which it is expected will yield considerable benefits in changed attitudes and relationships and eventually improved production efficiency.

1   Opportunities which could be taken

It was agreed that the opportunities were:

1.1   To achieve a situation where the skills, knowledge and effort of everyone at the plant could be utilised to achieve benefits for themselves and the company.

1.2   To gain a fundamental improvement in working relationships so that change of all kinds will be accepted more readily in the future, including working conditions and job design.

1.3   To spread knowledge widely of the opportunities which exist to make substantial improvements in productivity, which are beneficial to everyone.

1.4   To provide a means whereby a continuous discussion on all aspects of factory conditions and performance is established between all members of the organisation.

1.5   To avoid disruption, ill feeling and low morale, which external influences may motivate.

2   Underlying assumptions in the approach taken

2.1   Some form of structural participation would help to gain the opportunities which are available.
   However, the activity for the time being should be in comparatively low key. The experimental nature of the approach should be emphasised.

2.2   Participation should not be handled through an extension of current consultative procedures as this would lead to a predominance of elected officials taking part, with only a minimum representation from other personnel.

2.3   As part of the process there must be an investigation designed to improve the position of first line supervision, suggesting how such personnel might play a more effective and challenging role.

2.4   The relationships between employees and management, although good, should be further improved before any desirable changes in payment methods are discussed.

2.5   The introduction of a low level resource allocation and control organisation would be considered if the problem solving task committees are successful. In the meantime, appropriate information and control systems for such organisation should be investigated.

2.6   When establishing task committees, participants should be drawn from as wide a source as possible. As far as it is feasible, task committee members should approach problems with fresh and open minds. For example, departmental managers should not be asked to chair a committee which is designated to look at a problem in an area or activity for which they are responsible.

3   Method adopted

3.1   Problem solving task committees have been formed consisting largely of non-management personnel, which will set out to gain knowledge about and suggest improvements in a matter of concern to both management and employees.

3.2   Three constraints have been imposed on the type of problems to be investigated:

(a)   The problem and any solution has to be self-contained within the plant.
(b)   The problem must be capable of solution and a positive result must emerge which could be of benefit to both management and employees.
(c)   Discussions of and investigations into payment schemes must be ruled out for the time being.

3.3   The composition of each of the task committees is:

One Departmental Manager
One TGWU steward
One hourly paid employee
One AUEW steward or other tradesman
One ASTMS steward or member
One ACTSS steward or member
One member of the monthly paid staff

plus co-opted members as and when necessary.

Managers have been chosen as committee chairmen so that they can use their general knowledge of the company, especially in knowing where specific information could be obtained so as to start the problem solving activity quickly and effectively. At some later date, committee members might elect their own chairman, when they are sure that this would enhance the spirit and effectiveness of participation in joint problem solving.

3.4   Composition of committees. Managers were asked to take part in the activity but other members of the task committees were volunteers. As the new method of problem solving proves successful, it is hoped that there will be continuous requests to become members of the task committees.

3.5   Resource utilisation and measurements. This problem, which is at the heart of low level resource utilisation, will be undertaken initially by a designated committee of Assistant Departmental Managers. This committee will obviously need guidance in solving the technical systems problems involved.

3.6   Operation of the committees. To achieve maximum effectiveness task committee meetings will be held once a fortnight for no longer than two hours. Each committee will decide which part of the problem they have been given should have priority. Committee personnel can, at any time, call upon assistance to help in producing solutions. All managers will be available for this purpose. However the committee will largely decide their own method of working, targets, time scales and solutions.

3.7   Reporting procedures. After four or five individual meetings it is proposed that managers and shop stewards meet to discuss progress and share experiences.

It is proposed that a special notice board in the canteen will be erected to record the following:

(a)   The membership of the task committees
(b)   The tasks being undertaken
(c)   Reports on progress.

It is anticipated that some problems will arise in presenting proposals. Secretarial assistance will be provided. Help in evaluating the feasibility of solutions will also be given. For example, detailed costings may be required which will need the aid of cost office personnel. It is hoped that the task committee will appreciate the cost/benefit of their proposals before a final report is prepared.

4   *Problems to be solved*

It was agreed between managers and shop stewards that the following problems would be tackled by the task committees. In each case reference points were raised which it was considered the task committee might investigate, but otherwise no terms of reference were written, as it was felt that these would be too constricting.

4.1   First line supervision/shopfloor relations
Reference points:
   Delays in dealing with complaints
   Excessive paperwork
   Reasons for pass outs
   Authority and responsibility
   Information which an operative should expect from his manager.

4.2   Flow of materials
Reference points:
   Loss of job cards
   Plant location
   Standardisation of handling equipment
   Identification of bottlenecks
   Material grouping.

4.3   Social facilities/relationships
Reference points:
   Investigate the gap between shopfloor personnel and managers and see how this can be closed.
   Examine the possibility of a club house.

4.4   Training
Reference points:
   Apprentice training
   Stepped training
   Instructor courses
   Availability of suitable instructors
   Joint courses/meetings between stewards and managers concerning performance requirements.

4.5   Rejects and quality
Reference points:
   Identification of cost centres where high rejects occur
   Rejects and discipline
   Material utilisation schemes
   Review of current quality control schemes.

4.6   Labour turnover
Reference points:
   Identification of cost centres where high turnover occurs
   Do some machine activities perpetually have high labour turnover?
   The possibilities of obtaining the real reasons why people leave
   Outside factors which contribute to labour turnover.

4.7   Systems of shift working
Reference points:
   Investigate possible alternatives to current shift systems, alternative times, handover problems and transport arrangements.

4.8   The environment
Reference points:
   Health hazards
   Waste disposal
   Dust extraction
   Noise.

4.9   The canteen
Reference points:
   Administration
   Staggered meal breaks
   Soggy chips.

5   *Comment*

The problems are mostly concerned with productivity and plant efficiency. They are in effect management supporting: constructive and not destructive. They indicate an awareness on the part of shop stewards of the possibilities for improving plant efficiency and a desire to see improvement motivated. Whether this view is reflected throughout the shopfloor is still to be fully tested.

It seems unlikely that major improvements will be made quickly. It is possible that each task committee's problem has to be broken down into more specific tasks.

The task committees are one alternative to the use of 'professional problem solvers'. They will not, as such, have the technical investigation ability of 'professionals' and some technical support may be necessary. However the implementation of agreed proposals should be facilitated considerably. The pace of profitable change should be improved.

The establishment of task committees could be a significant step towards achieving a unanimity of purpose between managers and shopfloor personnel, which should result in considerable benefits for both the company and employees.

It is still an experiment and considerable patience will be needed if all possible opportunities are to be achieved. Perhaps the most important outcome will be the improved relationships throughout the plant.

15.9   CONCLUSION

The participation style which has grown up in countries like Sweden and West Germany is often presented as the model which industry in the UK should follow. This belief ignores national characteristics, attitudes, history and social climate. If companies differ in these respects, how much more do countries?

Management in the future must in large part be by consent. How that consent is gained is really the dilemma facing managers, when considering industrial democracy. But before participation is started there should be some very clear cut answers given to the questions raised in this chapter.

Unions at national level and shop stewards in local organisations often appear to act in a negative way contrary to the increasing of national and local prosperity. Their restrictions on change or sheer obstruction of even minor improvements which would improve the job security of employees make many managers despair. Yet if the unions are not allowed to play, perhaps challenged to play, a positive role in ensuring increased prosperity then why blame them if they are constantly concerned with an 'us' or 'them' situation?

The most appropriate method of developing participation seems to be:

1 Develop communications about the business in general and local production and other efficiencies in particular.
2 Start low level participation, on an experimental basis.
3 Ignore the joint consultative committees, works councils etc. which already exist, and start afresh with new procedures.
4 Try to make participation into a problem solving, prosperity improving activity and move away from the sterile argument which is carried on in most joint consultation.
5 Attempt to make participation representative of all unions and people not in unions.
6 Participation takes up large amounts of management time. Management have got to be prepared to spend this time, otherwise participation will fail.

Finally two warnings are offered.

The morale of junior and middle managers is likely to fall rather than rise if participation is introduced without considering them deeply. In most companies this could be calamitous.

Secondly, the experiences of other companies, let alone other countries, may have little relevance in one's own company with its own history, style and culture. Like most other activities, participation procedures may have to be unique.

NOTES

1 *Industrial Democracy*, HMSO, Cmnd 7231, 1978.
2 See for example: *Plant & Productivity Bargaining*, TGWU 1969, *Plant Level Bargaining*, TGWU 1969.
3 Industrial Relations Code of Practice, HMSO, 1972.

16

Job study and design

16.1   INTRODUCTION

Job study covers several techniques or procedures which are used to describe and classify jobs, evaluate one relative to another and rate an individual's performance in doing a job.

It is possible that job study may in some respects be counter productive. This is despite its use as a major tool of personnel and line managers who have responsibility for assigning tasks and monitoring their performance.

Job descriptions can — in some instances — put a hard edge round a job, which will inhibit flexibility or change unless it is negotiated with financial inducements for the job holder. Management may feel that it is preferable to have fairly loose job descriptions with a correspondingly difficult process of performance evaluation.

Performance appraisal is often carried out half heartedly by a senior who feels that telling the exact truth to a subordinate may destroy morale. It is often argued that an annual appraisal is artificial and unnecessary when face to face contact with a subordinate occurs daily and there is an opportunity to debate job performance informally.

The subsequent sections should be read with these reservations in mind.

16.2   JOB DESCRIPTIONS

A job description is a formal mechanism for translating the essential elements in a job into factual information from which the job holder and others can determine the key areas of the job, its constraints, the resources it does or should command and the objectives it should achieve.

The job description might be divided into four sections:

1 Why the job exists

What in effect is its purpose? It could be to provide effective material control or ensure that 90 per cent of all orders are delivered on time. A useful aim might be to look at the job from a company objectives point of view and see how the job helps them to be achieved.

2 Dimensions of the job

The factors which will measure the magnitude of the job need to be quoted. How many people report to the job holder for example? What budget level (i.e. money) does the job holder control directly? A production manager might list:

Junior management reporting to him (numbers and grades)
Operatives under his control
Standard cost of output forecast
Budget for the year
Investment controlled.

A long list may not be required — just sufficient to place the job in comparison with others.

3 Nature of the job

The two previous factors may form the skeleton of the job. This section should put flesh on to the bones, giving the reader or job evaluator the means to assess the job's importance. The following need to be recorded:

How the job fits in with the corporate organisation. What significant internal and external relationships does the job holder have? Is there any travel needed to do the job? What committees does the job holder serve on?

The general composition of the management and staff who report to the job holder should be stated. This should include a brief description of the functions which will be planned and controlled. It should be stated where specialist knowledge is required by subordinate staff. Perhaps the type of problems which subordinate staff raise might be recorded.

The scope and restraint of the job should then be illustrated. For example it would be useful to know whether the job holder has freedom to recruit or dismiss; what amount of capital or current expenditure can be incurred; whether changes in production methods are possible; whether salaries can be improved.

In recording the 'nature of the job' therefore the main characteristics and importance of the job should be shown. How the bulk of the job holder's time might be spent would be a useful way to analyse the record.

4   *Key accountabilities*

Accountabilities or objectives should be stated succinctly and in a manner which can be used to measure job performance. The accountabilities should have an end result with headings as follows:

Establishing policy or policies
Directing the attainment of objectives — organising, staffing, communicating, movtivating
Measuring and controlling performance. Correcting out of course events
Promoting innovation
Developing people

5   *Skills, experience and qualifications*

The information produced under the headings 1 to 3 should provide the basis for the skills and qualifications which the job holder should have. These might be divided between 'essential' and 'desirable'.

6   *Comment*

Job descriptions have to relate objectives with resources. The two should be compatible, in that the accountabilities should be matched by the dimensions and nature of the job.

    The job description should be capable of being evaluated and having points allocated. It should therefore be written in a standard form which makes it easy to compare the importance of different jobs.

    A good description therefore should enable:

7   *Targets to be set*

8   *Job performance to be appraised*

9   *Controlled delegation of authority to be established*

10 *Identification of where more or less resources are needed to achieve required performance.*

16.3   PERFORMANCE APPRAISAL

Performance appraisals have a dual function. They should allow a corporate view to be formed of managers and management generally, how well it is carrying out its tasks and where there are strengths and weaknesses. It should also be used to indicate to individual managers how well they are performing and how their performance can be improved.

While many managers will be generally aware of how well they are doing their job, an objective view given by someone else is often valuable. There is a tendency to become subjective, even to blame others for personal failings.

An appraisal might begin by considering the various objectives which a manager should have achieved. These objectives might be implicit in the manager's job description or made explicit at the previous performance appraisal. The performance against each objective or task (and these may be three or four) should be assessed and perhaps graded from 1–6. Establishing the objectives therefore is the key element in carrying out a performance appraisal.

The appraiser needs to be aware of the reasons why the person being appraised has done well or badly. Perhaps the objectives which were set were too ambitious or not ambitious enough. Resources to gain the objectives may not have been available at the right time. Other factors — the failure of another function or manager — might have had a deleterious effect on the performance of the person being appraised. Success or failure is not an absolute. It has to be qualified in some way. The appraisal should not be a mechanical calculation of achieved results.

Once each objective has been assessed an overall view of the manager's performance is made: e.g. outstanding, good, satisfactory, poor. It might be useful to state 'too early to say' where some ambiguity about achievements exists.

The results obtained will indicate (perhaps only in part) the strengths and weaknesses of the manager concerned.

An assessment of potential either in the job holder's department or function or outside it, often follows. This is recorded as outstanding, considerable, limited or nil. From this assessment a position in the succession plan may be found for the job holder.

As a fundamental reason for the performance appraisal will be to inform the job holder of where he stands, the appraisal discussion should concentrate firmly on what can be done to improve performance. Training and development for example should be considered. Specific actions recommended should be recorded and an action plan produced.

The appraisal should end with an agreement between reviewer and job holder on the specific tasks that will be considered at the next review.

Performance appraisals are often intensely disliked by many people. The 'sitting in judgement' is usually disturbing, often offensive. Yet a review which does not get to the heart of the job holder's performance is a waste of time. Getting the best out of a review is difficult. Personal characteristics which have influenced job performance adversely need to be criticised, yet suggesting how they might be corrected is not easy.

It is too simple to provide an average assessment for most personnel. One departmental manager may mark all his personnel highly on the basis that 'if they work for me they must be good'. In practice people might be marked thus: four good, two very good, one outstanding, two satisfactory, and perhaps one unsatisfactory, or too early to say.

The following suggestions are offered to help to improve appraisal interviews:

1 Prepare for the interview. Subordinates may be disconcerted or depressed and their morale shaken if asked to discuss their job performances and future career prospects on the spur of the moment.
2 As far as possible the interviewee should do most of the talking, revealing successes and failings, strengths and weaknesses.
3 The interviewee might be asked how the interviewer could have helped him to improve his job performance.
4 Recognition of good work should be made.
5 The interview should always be carried out on an optimistic and positive note. Encouragement rather than criticism should be offered — unless job performance is so poor that criticism and warning are needed.

16.4 JOB EVALUATION

Job evaluation could be one of a number of methods which isolates job factors existing in a job and evaluates them in such a way that one job can be compared with another and relative salaries established.

The job factors can be considered under two main headings — the personal qualities needed for the job and the training and experience required. The job factors might differ depending upon the type of job being evaluated (for example, job factors for manual workers may differ from those for managers). Some general job factors might be:

Physical characteristics
   Manual dexterity
   Physical strength
   Endurance
   General health
   Co-ordination
   Sensory perception (visual acuity).
Working conditions
   Distractions
   Monotony
   Hazards — risk of accidents, industrial disease
   Posture
   Unpleasant conditions — noise, dust, dirt, fumes, temperature, humidity, illumination, etc.

Mental characteristics
    Special aptitudes — numerical facility, mechanical or artistic ability
    Initiative and creative ability
    Reliability
    Intelligence and response
    Judgement
    Powers of expression
    Determination and enthusiasm
    Co-operation
    Organising ability
    Leadership
    Temperament — coolness, tact, patience, adaptability, etc.
Responsibility (for)
    Material and equipment
    Records
    Money
    Confidential information
    Public contacts
    Supervision
        planning and development
        executive control
        recommending and deciding
Training and experience
    Length and time to become proficient
    General education required
    Technical/industrial education and training necessary.

For managers these factors might be simplified:

Job factor	Grade				
	Very large	Large	Medium	Small	Very small
Expertise					
Accountabilities					
Human relations					

Expertise might be broadened into:
    Technical
    Conceptual or problem solving
    Control/discipline
Accountabilities might be divided between:
    Absolute control
    Partial
    Small
Human relations might be further extended to include:
    Co-operation
    Leadership and motivation.

The principal methods of carrying out job evaluation are:

Ranking method
This involves the direct comparison of one job with another. Each job is given a rank, say from 1–10.

Factor comparison method
This considers a few important factors. Some fifteen or so jobs are selected — spread across the company and paid approximately fairly. The jobs are then ranked (not rated) factor by factor and a composite scale drawn up. Next, rating scales for each job factor are prepared. Rating scales and ranked factors are then brought together. All other jobs are fitted to this pattern and finally jobs are grouped into grades.

Classification method
A classification scheme is predetermined and each job is considered as a whole and fitted into the scheme.

Time-span of discretion
In this method there is discrimination between the discretionary and the non-discretionary parts of a job, taking into account the time periods over which these two elements are applicable.
   Those jobs with long period discretionary elements are rated more highly than the converse.

The points method
This is perhaps the most popular and widely used method of job evaluation. A list of job factors, similar to the one quoted earlier (16.4) is given a number of points. An overall number is first determined — say one thousand — and these are then split up to provide a suitable weighting for each job element.
   There will inevitably be some divergence of opinion concerning the weighting and this often causes some dissension.
   A coal miner, for example, would be quite scornful of say, twenty points out of a thousand given to 'risk of occupational disease'. A worker on a car assembly line might be equally upset at the same number of points being given to 'monotonous work'. The weighting should depend upon the type of industry in which the evaluation is being carried out.
   A committee of management — and often union — personnel then considers each job being evaluated and allocates points for each job factor after comparing it with the amount given overall. As the number of completed evaluations increases, similar jobs should be compared to minimise the chances of inconsistency.

16.4.1 Job evaluation and wage rates

When there are numerous jobs for which total points do not vary greatly, each job cannot be assigned a different wage rate. Grades therefore are introduced. For each grade a flat pay rate or a maximum or minimum is fixed. The last is the commonest approach and enables job evaluation to be integrated with merit rating.

While wage rates should vary with the number of points allocated to a job (perhaps with 'xp' per point) a base rate should be established which should be a 'living wage'.

If relative wage grades are determined first, absolute levels can be set by considering the levels the company can afford and the wage rates in the local area.

There are various problems which need to be considered. When new jobs and problems are constantly arising, can the evaluation committee ever be disbanded? When a job evaluation scheme is introduced and several groups of people earn more than their evaluated rate, are they left at the old rate or brought into line with the rest of the factory? In view of the rapid changes in labour and skill requirements should the job evaluation scheme be kept under constant review? How quickly can grievances and queries be settled? Like wages, 'systems drift' in a job evaluation scheme is always a possibility. How is it to be avoided?

16.5 MERIT RATING

Performance appraisal and merit rating have much in common. The latter perhaps is a more mechanistic way of assessing job performance and associated merit rewards.

The job holder is rated against a scale for the presence and degree of certain personal qualities. Usually a printed form is used both as a guide and to ensure consistency. Ratings are given as exceptional, good, average, fair or poor. A numerical scale can be linked to these assessments. Slightly different factors can be included for different employee groups (e.g. managers or labourers) although integration of factors and headings with job descriptions and evaluation is highly desirable.

Like general performance appraisal, the main weakness of merit rating is bias in the person carrying out the assessment. A merit rating scheme, no matter how well conceived, is only as good as the rater. The rater can:

Be too lenient
Allow general impressions to influence particular ratings
Allow one rating to influence another
Tend to give average ratings
Have favourites
Tend to overrate or underrate some characteristics

A typical set of merit rating criteria which might be used in a management merit rating system is:

1   *Initiative and creative ability*

The capacity for new ideas and initiative to develop them without being told
   Capable of routine work only
   Can develop ideas if given a lead
   Can develop ideas without guidance
   Can follow up own ideas with resource and persistence
   Exceptional resource and initiative.

2   *Reliability*

The capacity for producing dependable results
   Erratic and unreliable
   Makes some mistakes
   Reliable under close supervision
   Dependable without detailed supervision
   Outstandingly reliable.

3   *Intelligence and response*

The extent of capacity to grasp a situation and respond rapidly
   Very slow and laboured
   Slow, needs detailed explanation
   Grasps normal situations and responds adequately
   Quick on the uptake
   Outstandingly intelligent and responsive.

4   *Judgement*

The ability to assess a situation and draw sound conclusions
   Regularly makes unsound decisions
   Makes occasional unsound decisions
   Has sound judgement
   Good judgement allied to foresight
   Exceptionally good judgement and perception.

5   *Powers of expression*

The facility of clear, simple and concise expression in speech and writing
   Confused, verbose and inarticulate
   Fair clarity

Normal clarity and conciseness
Very clear, concise, direct and simple
Outstanding command of language and lucidity of expression.

6   Determination and enthusiasm

The ability to tackle work with keen resolution and to persist constantly. Speed of working to be taken into account.
Little enthusiasm; gives up easily in the face of difficulties
Not persistent; starts eagerly but peters out
Can work steadily with good spirit and overcomes ordinary difficulties
Enthusiastic and determined, attacks difficulties aggressively
Exceptional drive and infectious enthusiasm.

7   Co-operation

The ability to work smoothly with others
Difficult and unco-operative
Apt to be an individualist rather than a good team member
Co-operative and helpful
Inspires co-operation in others
Has outstanding qualities of co-operation.

8   Knowledge

Knowledge of the job and steps taken to improve knowledge and keep up to date
Knowledge poor and makes no effort to improve
Fair knowledge of job but does not improve
Good knowledge of job
Excellent knowledge and makes vigorous efforts to improve
Outstanding grasp of job combined with vigorous and resourceful attempts to expand knowledge.

9   Organising ability

Ability to plan and organise work in a systematic and effective way, including capacity for delegating responsibility
Poor and unsystematic
Copes with only minor problems
Handles well all normal tasks
A good and effective organiser
Outstandingly competent with exceptional organising talent.

10   Leadership

Ability to get the best from others and to inspire subordinates
   Poor — ineffective and overbearing
   Fair — sometimes leads but is erratic
   Good — a steady and consistent leader
   Excellent — subordinates respond well
   Outstanding — flair for leadership, sets very good example at all times.

16.6   TARGET SETTING

The essence of job study is to ensure that job responsibilities are clearly defined
and monitored in a way which will promote improvement. An essential part of
the process is the establishment of targets.

Targets could encompass 'output', 'machine efficiencies', 'material utilisation' and others of the same type, but might also include 'manpower development', 'better communications' and other factors which may not be precisely
measurable.

All supervisors and managers should have targets of some kind. However
how many, for what period of time, how easily they can be achieved, how
precise they should be, will all be debatable.

There seems little merit in setting targets which do not stretch people to
some extent. Asking a subordinate to suggest a target often, surprisingly,
produces one which is more ambitious than one achieved previously. Desirable
objectives are usually apparent (e.g. the overall cost reduction needed to
achieve planned profit) and these provide a useful starting point.

While precision is important in target setting (e.g. X per cent improvement in
material utilisation), there are many targets where such precision is impossible
or unnecessary.

A superior's targets should always be established before those of subordinates. Central targets or goals should therefore dominate.

Targets should indicate results required and not the activities which should
achieve them. A target is to reduce material losses by say 5 per cent, not to
carry out a material utilisation exercise.

The number of targets which are agreed with a manager need to be limited.
Too many will produce only diffuse effort and diffuse results.

17

Group job design

17.1 INTRODUCTION

Chapter 16 has been concerned with the design and appraisal of individual jobs. In reviewing the production system, it is possible that the design and evaluation of the performance of groups may be more important in many instances.

The term 'group dynamics' is widely used to describe an approach to consideration of group (usually small group) behaviour and how it might be influenced. It has come to have the flavour of a management technique like stock control or management by objectives. This seems to undermine the importance of considering groups and group job design within an organisation.

17.2 GROUPS — A DEFINITION

The term 'group' is often given a different definition according to whether it is being used by a sociologist or a psychologist. However, there are common themes between them. Groups are established either voluntarily or involuntarily. They often have group norms or codes of behaviour. They usually have group objectives.

Membership of the group is usually dependent upon an individual's acceptance of the group's rules, which are imposed upon him or her. By joining the group the individual gives up some individuality or freedom but in so doing hopes to gain more than is lost.

Various experiments carried out by social psychologists [1] suggest that wherever anxiety exists, groups form. (Anyone who has seen the rush of junior managers to join a trade union has an example of this fact.)

The standards of behaviour accepted by the members of a group may be partial or all embracing. Group output norms are usual on the shop floor. Anyone who breaks them invariably suffers from some form of penal sanction. This may be anything from a friendly word from a colleague to ease up, to social ostracism and worse.

17.3   WHY PEOPLE JOIN GROUPS

It is important for management to understand why there are groups or a group of people out on the shop floor who are prepared on occasions to act contrary to management's wishes.

Security

A prime reason for joining a group appears to be that the group provides security of some kind. Often this is against a readily identifiable danger — exploitation by management, fear of dismissal, fear of fellow workers breaking agreed limits on output.

2   Dependency

It often appears that people are very dependent on each other for social interaction. Few are genuine loners. Loose groups form wherever there is social exchange.

3   Reinforcement of prejudice

Where a person is already polarised towards a view expressed by a group, it is likely that receiving reinforcement of that view will be an enjoyable experience. This seems why people join political parties to some extent. 'Out groups' often provide a scapegoat to which all sorts of frustrations and bitterness can be directed — whether it is justifiable or not. History is full of examples of this fact. It is possible that shopfloor workers may see management as an 'out group'.

4   Self identity

Many if not most people appear to strive to give themselves a self identity. It must be a fairly common sight to see photographs of Manchester United or some other football club stuck up by the side of a machine. They do no harm and help to provide a self identity which operating a press may not allow.

17.4 DECISION MAKING AND GROUPS

As many production managers are only too aware, group decisions do not always reflect the rationally held views of the majority. Often it seems that fairly responsible workers vote together to take some (from a management viewpoint) irresponsible action. (Equally it often seems that where a 'cautious' management decision might be made, the outcome of a group decision is more cautious than the risks that individuals comprising the group would have taken.)

Psychologists [2] have identified a factor which they call 'group polarisation' and suggest that where a group inclines towards one alternative or pole, discussion will increase the initial preference. Explanations of why polarisation takes place are varied, but include a suggestion that the people in a group who are the most articulate and persuasive are the ones who may already be most committed to a polar view.

Other factors concerning groups also seem important, especially as many production managers see local group autonomy as one alternative to hierarchical organisations.

1 'Groupthink' can suppress dissent and often brings a measure of cohesiveness.
2 Cohesiveness can produce group loyalty even when an individual in a group seems to be losing by following a group line. The soldier fighting to the death in a hopeless cause is perhaps the extreme example of this. Production managers may see similar though less extreme actions in their own factories.
3 Groups, despite the fairly thin evidence available on work groups, do not always seem to be good at solving problems. The following reasons may apply:
    (a) Personal doubts of knowledgeable individuals are suppressed to achieve group loyalty.
    (b) Discussion is limited to that of the knowledge and experience of the group. Despite the wide use of consultants and other specialists, groups tend to rely too much on their own internal knowledge otherwise the nature of the group will change. This seems to be why some groups would prefer to face extinction rather than accept outside help.
    (c) Supportive statements which do not challenge proposals made by 'opinion leaders' are the rule rather than the exception. If this takes place at Board meetings and at other senior management groupings where most group members should be knowledgeable and articulate, how much more might it happen on the shop floor where people may be neither of these.

17.5 LEADERSHIP

With its association with military command and public school training, 'leadership' is not something that most production managers seem to consider very deeply. Yet a production manager is a leader of a group. He has a commitment to achieve specific company objectives by ensuring that his group performs specific tasks in a requisite way. He may well be in competition with other 'leaders' who have emerged on the shop floor. These may be unofficial in that they are opinion formers or unofficial spokesmen. (Where shop stewards seem to have compromised themselves too much with management, unofficial voices tend to strengthen.)

While successful leadership can be partly due to personality, other more solid traits seem to be needed if a production manager is to gain the loyalty and commitment of his workforce to help to gain corporate objectives.

So it is useful to explore the idea of leadership a little more deeply than that propagated by military commanders.

1   Has the production manager any rivals as leader of the production group? Why do these exist? Is it possible to have dual leadership?

2   While the shopfloor leaders will be chosen usually through a democratic ballot or even through the emergence of a strong man with considerable charisma, the production manager will nearly inevitably be imposed upon his group. How in these circumstances can he legitimise his authority?

3   Leadership has to be seen to be related to the tasks which the group has to perform. The production manager might gain leadership status by ensuring that he is seen to be facilitating the achievement of group objectives. If the group is problem ridden then an overt problem solving role may best serve to promote 'leadership'. The production manager acts in a supportive rather than an authoritarian way. If a major objective of the group is job security then the production manager should be seen to be doing everything to promote this. It should be fairly easy for example for the production manager to be seen to be 'taking on' sales personnel at every opportunity to ensure that sales are maintained to keep the factory employed.

4   To be a leader implies the possibility of influencing the group over which leadership is claimed. Production managers need to be seen to be more knowledgeable about the group's objectives and how they might be achieved than any other actual or potential leader. A key factor in this might be an ability to articulate objectives and problems in a way which makes sense to the group.

5   As he is obviously imposed on his group and may be faced with democratically elected competitors, a production manager should consider how far he can behave in an authoritarian way. Is it possible — or desirable — to take decisions which directly affect group interest without explaining the need for them? Without some charisma or outstanding

personality, is it possible that a production manager can really compete with shopfloor leaders who may have such traits?

6   The production manager has an apparent rational/legal right to be obeyed. His leadership is based on the threat of the sanctions which he can deploy. However it should be asked whether production managers need to believe that the only way they can gain leadership is through this method.

7   It is interesting to witness how often shop stewards become authoritarian in their particular leadership role. In such situations the full application of 'supportive management' may do much to ensure that the voice of management is listened to.

17.6   GROUP STRUCTURES

Groups can form anywhere within an organisation where group norms or behaviour apply. They can be small or large. They can be functional or departmental. Often local technology will determine the size of the group — a flow line, key process such as production planning, work study or quality control.

Production management might guide group structure by:

1   Relating an activity to a given set of resources and instituting some input/output measurements which might generate group cohesiveness.

2   Sponsoring direct workers and supportive personnel to operate as one team. For example, maintenance personnel might be seconded to work permanently on the shopfloor with one group of workers. Work study people may be asked to work in one part of the factory only. Planning and scheduling staff could be established for one part of the production process only.

3   Management should be seen to be supportive to particular groups that it wants to foster. For instance it should be fairly easy for production management to build up production facilities (by good maintenance), to ensure that high wages can be earned. Planning and scheduling might be directed towards the same end.

4   It might be useful also to generate local group decision making to ensure that the group acts cohesively. Introducing payment schemes which mostly relate to the group should have the same effect.

17.7   DESIGNING GROUP JOBS

How far is it possible to redesign a job or jobs to accommodate group psychology and perhaps 'group dynamics' in the widest sense on the shopfloor? The following list is not exhaustive but provides a possible framework for group job design.

1   Role

Within a team or work group there may be several different jobs or roles to be performed, often demanding different skills and effort. Are members of a group to be allowed to organise themselves so that the group's members choose or organise their own roles, to provide for maximum efficiency in the group, individual job satisfaction or generally to relate skill and effort to individual capacities?

Two aspects of role are therefore important:

(a)   Job allocation
(b)   Job rotation.

Either could predominate in a role distribution. Experience suggests that where job allocation and rotation have become the prerogative of the group, commonly little job rotation actually occurs. Individuals within a group can dictate a misallocation of roles.

2   Rate of output or production

This is largely group or individual dominated anyway, especially where incentives are employed. (Most workers will come to a tacit agreement about what is the maximum output they will achieve.) However, it may be novel and worthwhile officially to allow a group to set its own norms of output if added value or other forms of productivity payment schemes are in operation.

3   Manning levels

Again where added value or some other form of incentive allied to overall company performance is in operation, it may be advisable to allow a group to establish its own manning level — if sufficiently good controls over quality, machine utilisation, etc. are in existence or can be introduced if they are not.

4   Composition of working groups

In industries such as coal mining it was long the practice for self-selecting groups to exist. Workers chose a 'marra-group' with which to share work tasks and rewards. The problem in industry generally in having 'marra-groups' is that it takes away essential flexibility and might breed insularity and resistance to change.

5   Problem solving

Problem solving customarily has been the preserve of first line supervision, e.g.

pay problems, lack of tools, inadequate service from maintenance staff. Are members — or is one member — of the group allowed to contact other personnel outside the work group in order to solve a problem facing the group? If so, what are the chances of a multiplicity of complaints and requests (perhaps at odds with each other) being made?

6   Hours of work

It has become traditional in some industries for one man to 'stand in' for a fellow worker, if the latter does not want to work overtime or wants to go home early. Flexibility at shift changeover times often includes a man on the afternoon shift working later than 10 p.m. (or normal finishing time) in order to allow a colleague to complete some social engagement. If machines are fully manned and normal production is proceeding, is this detrimental to the company?

How great should the flexibility be? To what lengths might it be taken? While 'flexi-hours' may be impossible on the shopfloor, should a working group largely split up working hours to suit themselves?

7   Quality

Normally, quality control is a basic function in most manufacturing units. Is it feasible that a working group could be allowed to carry out its own quality control and inspection, with the certainty that no defective products will be sent to customers?

8   Capital investment

New equipment is often a bone of contention in industry and is occasionally not accepted unless increased rewards are offered. The purchase of new equipment is usually a management decision with a rigorous method for capital expenditure evaluation. Is it possible for a group both to demand and subsequently take part in the evaluation of capital equipment?

9   Rewards

It may be possible within a group to allocate the group's rewards in any one of numerous ways — by job, seniority, apparent effort, skill, overall worth to the team. Is it possible or even desirable that the money the group earns be split up in a way which the group as a whole believes to be equitable and just?

10   General organisation

'Who does what' is usually decided by a line supervisor. Should the group be allowed not just to allocate jobs, but generally to organise the group's activities — for example, when material is to be moved, the materials handling equipment needed, the production procedures to be followed?

11   Reporting to management

This is usually a first line supervisor role. Reports on order status, rejects, clocked hours, achieved standard hours, machine breakdowns — are the kind of things which would form the basis for management control. Is it likely that a working group would report as accurately as is needed?

12   Method

In most organisations where fairly complex manufacturing activities are carried out, methods are established in a 'making particulars' book. Precise instructions are then given to operatives. Within many, perhaps most, incentive schemes, operatives tend to follow their own method even though an official one has been stipulated. Are groups to be allowed to follow their own method provided it gives high productivity, low rejects and does not contravene any safety rules?

13   Order sequencing

Most production scheduling systems will use a disciplined scheduling technique for machine and operation loading, order priority establishment and batching. This should help to ensure that orders are produced on time at minimum cost. Should a group be allowed to influence batching and order sequencing rules?

14   Machine set-ups

In many engineering workshops, machines are set up by skilled personnel. Is it possible that semiskilled people could be trained to carry out the set-up task? There would obviously be demarcation disputes in some industries and organisations.

15   Repair of breakdowns

This could be an extension of 14 above, involving even more complex training and activities. To some extent, it is the type of breakdown that will be the determining factor.

17.8   IMPACT OF NEW JOB DESIGN

Traditionally, management's role has been to 'measure, plan, control and motivate'. What the previous section has implied is that if work organisation and jobs are changed so that the shopfloor is given 'job enrichment' in some way (or perhaps in all the ways suggested) then management's role must also change if it is not to become permanently diluted.

It is perhaps the role of first line supervision which will change most if more autonomy is given to the shopfloor. Some, perhaps most, of the function which supervisors traditionally might have undertaken could be taken away from them. If their team or workforce is enriched then they might be impoverished.

It is possible that first line supervision will resist changes in work organisation which will diminish their role. So what role might they take? Perhaps the following:

1   Supportive management

Instead of issuing commands, as in a conventional hierarchy, first line (and perhaps other) management acquire a supportive role. They might set out to help their unit to achieve high productivity or added value. In this way they could be consultants, available perhaps on request, to provide professional services. The conventional hierarchical pyramid might be turned upside down.

2   Elected team leader

The work group may require a spokesman to negotiate added value or other objectives as well as to determine group requirements for the services of maintenance, training or other services personnel. The first line supervisor may come to be accepted (if not elected directly) as the team member who carries out this kind of function.

3   Team member

The first line supervisor becomes a member of the team with no more or no less status than other members but is employed to carry out certain functions — perhaps organisational — for which he has the requisite skills.

4   Role of service functions

Service functions may lose much of their role if greater autonomy is given to the shopfloor. A quality controller may be needed outside a work group, but equally, quality control may be established as an intrinsic part of the group's operations. All operatives could be quality controllers.

Maintenance engineers also may be dispossessed of some of their traditional activities. Interunion squabbles may result from this demarcation and other associated disputes arise.

Methods and time study (work study) personnel might also need to adapt their role, becoming (like first line supervisors) consultants to autonomous groups.

Although many of the new roles may be debatable, an indication has been given of how service functions should be considered generally. Too often they have been allowed to grow with little measurement of the value which they give. Turning them into consultants where their services have to be bought by working groups should help to indicate their true value to the organisation. But like all consultancy activities, the service offered has to be appreciated by potential users. This may mean some training for the work groups in the use of techniques which could help them.

5   Role of shop stewards

The primary working group has often been a rich ground for industrial relations troubles. If pay problems and other grievances are largely eliminated within the primary work organisation, there will be less need for shop steward intervention. However, a newer and perhaps more important role may emerge — linking groups together, solving intergroup problems and demarcation disputes with services personnel and perhaps ultimately in helping to decide upon the strategies which the various units in the work organisation might follow.

Shop stewards should be active in discussing and then establishing new forms of work organisation. Like first line supervision they might obstruct rather than help progress if they believe that any change will undermine their position.

NOTES

1   See for example:
   (a)   I. Sarnoff and P. C. Zimbardo, 'Anxiety, fear and social facilitation', *Journal of Abnormal and Social Psychology*, Vol. 62, 1961.
   (b)   S. Schachter, 'Deviation, rejection and communication', *Journal of Abnormal and Social Psychology*, Vol. 46, 1951.
2   C. Fraser, C. Gouge, M. Billig, 'Risky shifts, cautious shifts and group polarisation', *European Journal of Social Psychology*, Vol. 1, No. 1, 1971.
3   I. L. Janis, *Victims of group think: a psychological study of foreign policy decisions and fiascos*, Houghton Mifflin, 1968.

18

Recruitment, training and manpower planning

18.1 INTRODUCTION

Recruitment, training and manpower planning may appear at first sight to have little congruence. In reality recruitment and training are essential parts of manpower planning. The latter can be used to pull recruitment and training into a coherent pattern, along with job study, group and corporate organisations and other factors which have been discussed in this part (IV) of the book.

This chapter ends with a section on redundancy, regrettably a subject of growing importance for many production managers.

18.2 RECRUITMENT

In many organisations, recruitment is still carried on in an *ad hoc* manner. A vacancy occurs and the Personnel department is informed. Those who are currently available to work are examined. A short list is drawn up from which the line manager — often reluctantly — chooses one.

Steps in recruitment

With the Employment Protection Act and other legislation plus trade union power, recruiting someone could be the beginning of a lifelong relationship. Some trouble spent on eliminating potential poor workers is well worthwhile.

1 Job description
The minimum job description for a shopfloor operative is shown in Fig. 18.1. For management positions a job description of the type described in Chapter 16 will be needed.

FROM   DEPARTMENT   TO   PERSONNEL DEPARTMENT   DATE

Please initiate recruitment to fill the following vacancy:

HOURLY PAID	STAFF		
OCCUPATION/JOB TITLE	OCCUPATION/JOB TITLE		
C.C./JOB NUMBER	DEPARTMENT OR SECTION		
INCENTIVE	GRADE		
ANCILLARY			
HOURS OF WORK – Please tick Days	HOURS OF WORK – Please tick Days (Office Hrs. 8.30 – 4.30)		
Nights	Days (Factory Hrs. 8.00 – 4.30)		
Two Shifts	Two Shifts		
Three Shifts	Three Shifts		

QUALIFICATIONS REQUIRED:
     Essential
	QUALIFICATIONS REQUIRED:
	     Essential		

Desirable	Desirable		
PREVIOUS EXPERIENCE REQ'D	PREVIOUS EXPERIENCE REQ'D		
	STAFF POSITION	ESTABLISHMENT	ACTUAL
	Section		
	Department		

REASON FOR VACANCY – Please give full details

PERSONNEL DEPARTMENT USE	AUTHORISED BY	Signature	Date
Requisition Checked	Initiated by		
Fill by Internal Transfer	Dept. Manager		
Advertise Internally	Dept. Head		
Advertise Externally	Director		
Appointment offered	Joint M.D.s		
Appointment accepted	or Chairman		
Successful candidate	Ref. No.		

Fig. 18.1   Employee requisition – job description for shopfloor operative

The job description or specification should enable a match to be made between job and candidate.

A list of desirable attributes in the candidate may eliminate non-runners fairly quickly:

Preferred age

Personality — essential/desirable

Education, technical and professional qualifications — essential/desirable

Experience — essential/desirable

Special aptitudes and other requirements — essential/desirable

Salary and fringe benefits to be offered.

2   Where to recruit

In most organisations trade unions now demand that all vacancies be first advertised internally.

Much time can be wasted in interviewing internal candidates — purely for the record. A strict application of 'suitability' could eliminate unnecessary interviews.

Externally, recruitment might come from family or other contacts, job centres and, if they have been developed, from informal contact with schools and colleges.

For senior positions the Professional and Executive Register may be useful. Otherwise the national and local press are to be preferred.

3   The application form

Most jobs need an application form, if only to act as a record of the personnel who are taken on. The form should contain the maximum amount of verifiable information. The form should be set out so as to facilitate the recruitment interview.

For junior or middle management jobs the following information might be requested:

Name

Home address

Date and place of birth

Nationality

Marital status

Number and ages of children

Height

Weight

Past illnesses

Disabilities — past and present

Education — School, University, Technical College; years and qualifications

Work experience — dates, employers, nature of employment, salary, reasons for leaving

Reference
Photograph
Dates available for interview
Publications — if any
Interests
Highlights of life to date and future ambitions.

The last item might be contentious, but it could provide a character insight which the rest of the application could hide. Present employment might be set out in greater detail than previous jobs. Some indication of current job responsibilities would have merit.

4   Short lists
Any job of even comparatively minor importance should have a short list drawn up for it. The short list should be chosen by weighted desired attributes and these compared with those the candidates apparently have.

5   The interview
Interviewing is not easy and there are principles which should be followed.

Prepare for the interview. Never 'play it off the cuff'. The interviewee will notice even if you do not. Prepare a list of pertinent questions — Why do you want to work for us? Why do you want to leave your present job?

Take two courses of attack. Determine the candidate's technical ability. Then consider his social attributes.

Have a form prepared which can be used to mark down a candidate's characteristics — personality, manner, appearance, attitudes, academic attainment, technical skill. Give a mark for each — say out of ten.

Get the candidate to do most of the talking, if this is possible, but keep control over the interview.

Allow plenty of time for the interview.

Close the interview in a friendly way, even if the candidate is obviously unsuitable.

6   References
References should always be verified. It is unlikely that referees given by the candidate will give a bad reference but some salient points might emerge. Companies for which candidates have worked often reveal key strengths and weaknesses.

7   Choice of candidate
Often the candidate who best seems to fit the company is chosen. This is not wrong if no 'boat rocking' is required.

If no suitable candidate appears to be available, then it is probably better not to recruit at all.

8   Success of recruitment
The interviewer will be biased in some way towards candidates. For example, there may be more or less emphasis on paper qualifications. Not, did the candidate go to university, but what university? Did the candidate do well at games?

An assessment of the performance of new recruits and how long they stay in the company is important in deciding how good recruitment has been.

18.2.1   The induction course

Most recruits of whatever standard will need some form of induction course. Where several recruits start on one day a general course on the company can be established. The following may provide the basis for the course:

A history of the company

The products made

A visit to all parts of the factory and offices

A booklet should be issued, and discussed, which contains a plan of the works and offices, a list of departments and names of associated managers and other factors relating to employment (a full list is given in Chapter 24)

18.3   TRAINING

18.3.1   Why train?

Training should be seen as a means of ensuring that job performance at all grades within a company reaches required levels. It is an important aspect of manpower planning.

Why training is necessary might be analysed as follows:

1   What job performance of what people or groups of people needs to be improved by training?
Merit rating, performance appraisal, failure to achieve agreed targets, obvious deficiencies in skills or conduct should suggest where training is required.

2   To improve employee potential
Current job performance may suggest that an employee is capable of developing new skills needed for promotion to a different job.

3   Current job skill enhancement
The environment is changing so quickly that many managers and skilled operatives quickly become obsolescent. Training is needed to maintain job performance and match new demands posed by environmental changes.

The type of training required might be developed as follows:

4   Job performance training

Two analyses are required. Firstly what is the extent of the gap between current job performance and targets which should have been achieved? Secondly, why have the targets not been achieved? This second analysis might quote deficiencies under the following headings:

Technical skills
   i.e. accounting — budgeting,
   cost control engineering,
   general management skills.
Motivation (self)
   i.e. lack of self discipline,
   laziness.
Social skills
   i.e. ability to communicate,
   leadership

5   Employee potential training

To improve or develop an individual for promotion will need analysis of current skills and knowledge and the requirements of a new job. Comparison between current and required skills will indicate the gap which exists and which training should fill. As in job performance improvement, training might be considered under three headings:
technical
motivation
social skills.

6   Current skill enhancement

The required analysis may be slightly more difficult than in 4 and 5. Environmental changes which will influence how jobs should be done need to be recorded. The new skills demanded might be assessed under the following headings:

General skills, e.g.
   EDP
   Manpower motivation
   Mathematical programming.
Government and trade union, e.g.
   Legislation — e.g. health and safety participation
Technological, e.g.
   Microprocessor use
   New products
   New distribution or marketing modes.
General environment, e.g.
   Raw material supply (decline)

Problems with power.
Economic, e.g.
    Inflation
    Depression
    Competition.

The analysis suggested will help to select the type of training which is necessary.

Training should provide further benefits than those already stated. It should reduce the time an employee takes to become effective after he has been recruited or moved compared with no training being given.

Training should also decrease the need to recruit people with special skills. Consequently morale and job satisfaction should increase. Maximum use should be made of intellect, character and dexterity of employees.

18.3.1   Types of training

Some indication of the types of training which will make up a training plan are given below.

1   Social skills
Social skills are often neglected when considering training. Yet for management and supervision such skills are often a key factor in job effectiveness. 'Coverdale' and 'T group' training are both used to improve social skills. Each is a form of group training. In the former a group of individuals is given tasks to carry out. At their completion, the group is asked to analyse how the tasks were achieved — who contributed, who did not, who was obstructive, who constructive, etc. As a result social skills should be improved.

Variants on this pattern are covered by the 'T group' philosophy, sensitivity and interactive skills training.

2   Creativity
One training technique often used to increase 'creativity' or lateral thinking in management is synectics. This technique was born out of the brainstorm idea, where a group of people is asked to freewheel mentally, in the hope of producing radical ideas.

Synectics extends this idea by using five themes:

Deferment — look first for viewpoints around a problem rather than its immediate solution.

Autonomy — let the problems have a life of their own.

Use of the commonplace — move from the familiar to the unfamiliar.

Involvement/detachment — move between deep involvement with the problem and standing back from it.

Use of metaphor — suggest analogies which will promote new viewpoints.

The synectics group's thinking is structured around these five themes.

3   Action learning

Action learning is based on the idea that only by tackling real life problems which involve more than one aspect of an organisation will training be really effective.

'Clinics' are established where a set-leader or chairman plus trainees consider a problem. The clinic is sponsored by a senior member of the organisation who ensures that a solution will, if produced, be implemented.

Problem diagnosis is stressed, fostering the pooling of ideas.

The 'set' or mix of people brought together to carry out action learning is important. Technical and administrative personnel are often mixed together to provide the requisite skills.

4   In-company training

In-company training is conducted within an organisation usually by company personnel, occasionally by outsiders. The benefits of such an activity are that the interaction of participants is likely to increase organisational team spirit; it is normally cheaper than going outside the organisation and training can be directly orientated towards the organisation and participants.

5   External courses

These are useful to meet individual specialist needs. Their use, however, should be limited. They are expensive and occasionally not worth the money spent. Choosing an external course is often a gamble. External course reports similar to that in Fig. 18.2 should be completed.

6   Non-specific training

An important part of training may have nothing to do with training as such. This sounds paradoxical but the following examples prove the point:

Job rotation
Group discussions
Special assignments
The playing of business games.

7   Programmed learning

This approach uses teaching material, usually in book form, where question and answer routines are set out in such a way that they take a trainee from having little or no knowledge of a subject to being competent in it.

18.3.2   Operative training

The analysis suggested so far is largely directed towards management or

A. THE COURSE

Title: _____

Run by (name of Institute, College etc.) _____

Brief description of syllabus: _____

_____

_____

Principal Lecturer(s): _____

_____

Dates: _____ Nos. attending _____

Fees (residential or otherwise): _____

Venue: _____

B. THE COURSE MEMBER

Name: _____

Age: _____

Job Title: _____

Department: _____

Location: _____

C. OTHER COURSE MEMBERS

Majority of course members were at:
*Same Job level/Higher Job level/Lower Job level
*Delete as appropriate

D. SUMMARY REPORT

Please grade the course on a 0 – 4 scale where:
4 = Excellent   3 = Very good – minor points of detail could be improved
2 = Satisfactory – but room for improvement   1 = Weak   0 = Extremely weak

	Tick (as appropriate)				
	0	1	2	3	4
General achievement of objectives					
Lecturing efficiency: name of lecturer					
name of lecturer					
name of lecturer					
name of lecturer					
name of lecturer					
name of lecturer					
Supporting Paperwork (handouts)					
Discussion Sessions					
Group Work/Syndicates					
Administration (timekeeping, food, accommodation)					

Fig. 18.2   External course report

supervisor training. A large proportion of any company's training budget will be directed towards apprentice, or operative, training.

An apprentice was, at one time, given little training except 'on the job'. Now regular attendance at external educational establishments is usually part of the apprenticeship.

Block release or day release is common. These are systems where employers allow apprentices and other young people to attend courses during working hours without loss of pay.

Continuous assessment of day release personnel is usually made by a member of the training department and anyone not meeting required standards has the day release terminated.

Sandwich courses are also used for training junior personnel. The individual has periods of some months at an educational establishment alternating with similarly lengthy periods of work experience.

On the job training is normal for shopfloor operatives. Training is undertaken by a member of the instructor force who may revert to being an operative once the training is over.

18.3.3   The learning curve

When given a new job, a person will take some time to become proficient in it. The period needed will depend upon the aptitude of the person involved but mostly on the nature of the job itself. For some shopfloor jobs a few weeks or even days may be all that is necessary. For some highly skilled technical occupations or some parts of management, years may be required for the relevant skills to be acquired.

The learning period can be graphed. At the beginning, learning is intense. As time passes only marginal increases in skills are gained until finally skill acquisition peters out altogether. This 'learning curve' is often used when a person is transferred to a new job to forecast when the requisite new skills will have been gained. It is usually part of the negotiated allowance when an operative is brought into an incentive scheme.

18.3.4   The Industrial Training Act, 1964

The three main objectives of this Act were to ensure that there was an adequate supply of workers with appropriate skills, to ensure that training standards were improved generally and to institute methods to spread the costs of training equitably across all organisations which had training needs.

A Training Board was set up for each major industry and was made responsible for ensuring that appropriate training was carried out within the industry. A system of levies and grants was introduced which was designed to stimulate training.

A levy on each member of each organisation was made and a refund given on training undertaken. The training has to satisfy the requirements of the Training Board.

18.4 MANPOWER PLANNING

The various components of manpower planning have been discussed throughout this part of the book and in this chapter. As a result of applying job study or training, understanding group dynamics or carrying out organisational analysis, a manpower plan should be derived. Often, pulling all these factors together may not be undertaken, mainly because of the complexity of the task.

It is recommended that what appears to be crucial to the organisation be considered under the general heading of manpower planning and appropriate plans made. The process is shown as a system in Fig. 18.3 and now discussed further.

1 Environments
The system has environments which production management should analyse carefully:

Technical — New technologies such as microprocessing will indicate where new skills are required and training needed.

Business — Future trading conditions will indicate where redundancies may be forced on the company or changes in capacity and capital investment will be required.

Government — Legislation such as Equal Opportunities and Employment Protection Acts should be observed.

2 Inputs
The inputs will be people (numbers), skills, experience and the effectiveness of individual and organisational performance.

3 Influences on inputs
This part of the system will be concerned with influences which can be brought to bear on the inputs. Training, redundancy, recruitment, job study, organisational change will be the kinds of activity to be carried out. Normally they might each be the basis of a sub-plan within the manpower plan.

4 The organisation and its processes
This will comprise the production and other activities which go to make up the business.

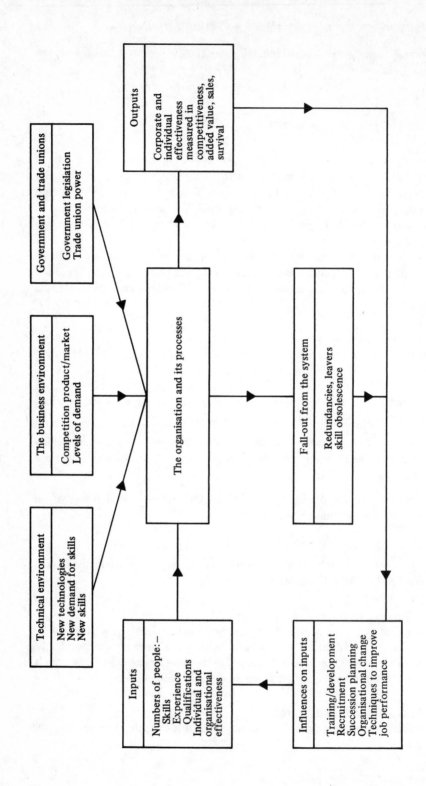

Fig. 18.3 Manpower planning as a system

5   Fall-out from the system

'Fall-out' will include leavers and redundancies, but also people whose skills are no longer appropriate to meet the environment the company faces.

6   Outputs

These will include the effectiveness of corporate and individual performance when compared with competition or some measurement such as added value.

The manpower plan will embody a number of sub-plans:

Organisation
Job study activities and associated management development
Succession
Training
Recruitment.

Manpower planning can never be a mechanistic process where numbers can be manipulated like figures on a balance sheet. It should pull together all the activities which ensure that people are used effectively. Personnel managers may claim to be its progenitors and guardians. However, production management is largely about the use of resources of which people are often the most important and potentially the most troublesome, so manpower planning is a principal production management function.

18.4.1   Redundancy

'Redundancy' is covered by legislation in the Employment Protection Act 1975. The rights which employees gained under this Act were:

Guaranteed payments. Employees who lose pay through short-time working are entitled to guaranteed payments for a limited period.

Medical suspension. Employees who have been suspended from work through statutory medical regulations are entitled to normal wages for a maximum of twenty-six weeks.

Maternity pay. Employees are entitled to various maternity rights. Pregnant employees cannot be dismissed, for example. Employees away from work having a baby can claim pay for the first six weeks of absence. An employee who has had a baby can claim her job back up to twenty-nine weeks after the birth.

Job security. An employer planning redundancies must consult the appropriate trade unions. If this is not done the trade unions can apply to an industrial tribunal for a protective award.

An employer must inform the Department of Employment of redundancies affecting more than ten people for more than one month.

1. Head of Department (See also 4 below)

    Full name _____ Date of birth _____

    Address _____

    Position _____ Dept. _____ Commenced _____

    Date of leaving _____

    Keys and other company property_____

    Letter of authority (internal audit only) _____

    Luncheon vouchers _____

2. Cashier_____

    Money outstanding (loans, expenses, etc.)_____

3. Payment officer

    Final payment of salary arranged _____

    P.45/Insurance cards returned_____

4. Head of department
    Summary of employment

    Starting salary _____ Finishing salary _____

    Ability _____

    Character _____

    Would you re-engage? _____

    Reasons for leaving_____

    _____

5. Company secretary

    Board notification (where appropriate) _____

Fig. 18.4   Termination form

Unfair dismissal. An employee can appeal to an industrial tribunal following dismissal. The tribunal will hear the case and can require re-instatement or a compensatory award if the dismissal is proved to be unfair. An employee who is dismissed is entitled to a written statement of the reasons for dismissal.

Where dismissal appears to be a result of trade union activities an employee can apply to a tribunal for an interim remedy under a special emergency procedure. An interim order may be issued by a tribunal which insists on reinstatement or re-engagement.

The Act also covers:

Trade union membership and activities. An employer may not victimise an employee for wanting to join a trade union or for taking part in union activities.

Time off work. Employees are entitled to time off from work for:
Trade union duties and activities
Public duties
Looking for work.

Insolvency. An employee whose employer becomes insolvent will not lose money owed to him by the employer. Outstanding money will be paid by the Department of Employment.

18.4.2   The exit interview

A form similar to the one shown as Fig. 18.4 should be completed for each voluntary leaver. The exit interview is often important in determining company morale and levels of staff motivation. Considerable time might be spent on determining the real reason why a person wants to leave.

19

Organisational development and the management of change

19.1 INTRODUCTION

Organisational development or 'OD' is a term which is used to cover changes in individual job descriptions and role, and in group and corporate organisations, in order to increase overall effectiveness while accommodating changes in the environment.

This has been the main theme of this part of the book and rather than recapitulate what has already been said, 'change' and how it might be accommodated generally will now be discussed. Then some indication of the experiments and philosophies which have been applied in Sweden (where perhaps the most advanced thinking on organisational development is taking place) will be recorded.

19.2 THE MANAGEMENT OF CHANGE

The most successful production managers appear to be those who are able to introduce or at least cope with change yet at the same time keep their production units operating at near maximum efficiency. The one constant factor in the 1980s must be 'change', so those who can accommodate it will be in a strong position.

The management of change — analysing the need for it, recognising what has to be done and successfully introducing the result — is something which does not come easily to many people. It needs training and the acquisition of special skills.

19.3   CHANGE AND STRESS

It may be possible, as Toffler [1] suggests, to 'create an environment in which change enlivens and enriches the individual but does not overwhelm him'. To achieve this happy state he suggests that we must 'employ not merely personal but social strategies'. To formulate such strategies may not be within the function or perhaps even the competence of many production managers, but unless a situation is brought about where change does not overwhelm, then resistance to it — with consequent poor results for everyone in an organisation — will be common.

Stress is a substantial ingredient in most production managers' lives. Change only seems to increase the amount of stress which they suffer. The greater the degree of change the more likely that severe stress will occur. If too much change takes place the recipient could even die as a result. Holmes and Minoru [2] for example, have suggested that there is a limit to the number of common life events — such as the death of a spouse or losing one's job — which a person can cope with in a specific time period.

Howard [3] records some particularly stressful jobs and suggests that one of the worst is for those whose function lies between activities or people with conflicting demands. The production manager with competing demands for low cost production and high output from his boss and job security from his workforce typifies this situation.

19.4   WHY CHANGE IS RESISTED

The following factors seem important in considering why change is resisted:

1   Organisation and tradition

Experience suggests that the organisation with the greatest tradition and perhaps even personnel who are imbued with that tradition is the hardest to change.

2   The clash of employer- and employee-needs

If change is seen to be antipathetic to individual goals then it is likely to be resisted. Why should anyone calmly accept a worsening of job and pay because of change which is not under his control?

3   Social values of the people concerned

It is possible that people with certain social values due to class, age, sex and educational attainments will be more ready to accept change than others. They may trust the change makers more and generally feel more secure.

4   Individual characteristics, attitudes to work, education and qualifications

Some line managers seem more ready to accept change than others. It is always wise when a change is required to search out such people (especially if they have influence over others) and win their approval for the change.

It is perhaps paradoxical that, occasionally, the people most likely to resist change are those who are giving a good job performance. They often resent having a career investment negated in some way. Conversely the poor performers may welcome change especially if they see it as a means of breaking out of a boring occupation.

There is evidence that some of the most obstructive people are 'professionals' such as cost accountants or work study personnel, who may feel that their professionalism is under attack if change of a specific type is introduced. 'Luddism' is not confined to machine operatives.

Normally the people most likely to accept change are those who are comparatively young and well qualified.

5   How change has been handled in the past

If past changes have been handled crudely and without much thought for the people affected by them, it is unlikely that further change will be accepted readily. If an authoritarian approach has been taken with the excuse that the change had to be done quickly, it is more likely to have caused more resentment than if it was done comparatively slowly, through the use of work groups with plenty of adaptation.

6   Performance of the company

Usually the more efficient and well managed the company the more likely that change will be acceptable. Trust is a large element in accepting change. A well managed organisation generally gives the impression that it can handle even complex change situations competently.

7   The consequences of change

These should be known — job transfers, redundancy, etc. The consequences of changes have to be seen to be fair, while the plans for change must be based on reality.

8   The mental and emotional inertia of the individuals who are affected

Each group of people develops its own social system. Change may only impact on one or two people within the system, but the whole group may react. Whether there will be a group response or one by only one or two individuals might largely depend upon mental and emotional inertia.

19.5 CONSIDERING CHANGE

The following precepts might be adopted in considering change:

1 Look at change through the eyes of people it affects

It is likely that suitable analysis on this point will take the following lines:

How people will be affected by the proposed change —
  considerably
  moderately
  only in a minor way
What kind of people are affected? What are their personal objectives? What
is their overall —
  ability
  education
  profit consciousness
  training
  competence
  experience
  history
  temperament
  aggressiveness
  subservience
  social values
  attitudes towards the company, including loyalty to its style
  verbal fluency
  ability to influence others by their actions and attitudes
  attitudes towards systems development?
What are the likely reasons for rejecting change —
  habit
  alliances
  security
  lack of information
  tradition
  general fear
  lack of knowledge?
If change is to be opposed, in what form might the opposition occur —
  verbal opposition
  general mistrust
  holding back of information
  withholding co-operation
  active dissociation with the project
  sabotage

failure to carry out procedures once written
carrying out new procedures wrongly?

2 *Change, if possible, has to be seen to offer something of value to the people*
   affected

People will more readily accept change if they see that they will gain something
from it. This 'something' can refer to the company objectives of the personnel
concerned — career and promotion — or they could be private and personal
objectives such as home, family or hobbies. For each person who could
possibly obstruct the proposed change, the following analysis might be made:

What are the business ambitions of the person concerned —
   increased security
   promotion
   greater freedom to make decisions
   increased autonomy
   improved paperwork systems
   to be noticed by superiors
   to be right more often in taking decisions
   improved salary?
What are the business requirements of the person concerned —
   security
   need for training and experience
   need for less authority and decision taking
   to be provided with more information so as to improve control over subordinates and become less vulnerable to criticism from superiors
   to be seen to be doing a good job
   to be able to do a better job?
What are the personal objectives of the person concerned —
   greater ego satisfaction
   more social contact
   improved job variety — increased travelling or less routine work, for
   example
   more money and fringe benefits
   to have superior fringe benefits — office, desk, etc?
What are the family objectives of the person concerned —
   job security
   security of pay and pension rights
   status in the eyes of neighbours
   the material possessions that status can bring (company cars, for
   example)?

Where no match can be achieved even though negative advantages are stressed, then it is unlikely that the change will be sold easily or even sold at all.

3 People will want to influence change

It is likely that change will be more readily accepted if the people concerned have had some influence in formulating it. Unfortunately there is a paradox in this truism. Many people lack the experience, knowledge and conceptual vision to be able to play a leading role in influencing change. Yet without their help, it is unlikely that change will be brought about appropriately.

This situation has been the breaking point for many desirable changes. If a senior manager takes the lead then ordinary personnel may resent him and his ideas. If junior personnel are given command progress could be slow and often not very revolutionary.

19.6   VEHICLES FOR CHANGE

Appreciating the need for change and understanding why it is often resisted will be the cornerstone of the management of change.

The production manager must then develop the vehicles through which change can be carried out — e.g.:

1   Help from management services personnel. Bringing in an internal consultant could be advantageous if he has the requisite skills and behavioural sensitivity. It is important that such personnel remain advisers or consultants. Their leadership of a project could be disastrous if local line personnel do not feel committed to what is going on.
2   Outside consultants. The same applies — but outside consultants are usually more expensive.
3   Self-generating change groups. The use of local personnel with an input of knowledge and motivation is one of the best ways to activate change and ensure its successful introduction.
4   Company style may inhibit change. Motivation must still start from the top.
5   Organisational development, where greater autonomy and knowledge of the business is developed, is often another useful vehicle to develop change.
6   Occasionally the development of a management information system or a single technique could produce general change. However, the best way seems to be the view change from the standpoint of the systems framework described earlier in the book (Part III) — i.e. motivation, resources, systems and work organisation having an interdependent relationship.

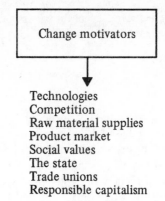

Change motivators

Technologies
Competition
Raw material supplies
Product market
Social values
The state
Trade unions
Responsible capitalism

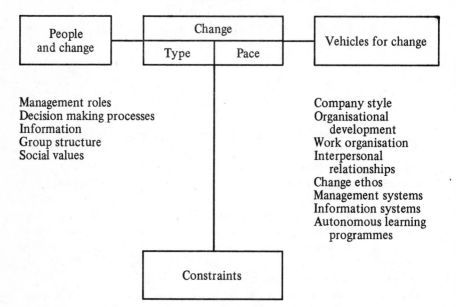

People and change	Change		Vehicles for change
	Type	Pace	

Management roles
Decision making processes
Information
Group structure
Social values

Company style
Organisational
   development
Work organisation
Interpersonal
   relationships
Change ethos
Management systems
Information systems
Autonomous learning
   programmes

Constraints

Tradition/history/style
Socio-psychological barriers
Managerial competence
Organisational rigidity
Wrongly defined objectives
   and strategies

Fig. 19.1   Motivators for change

19.7 CHANGES IN ORGANISATIONAL STRUCTURE

In the traditional organisation with a firm hierarchy requests tend to flow upwards, decisions and advice downwards. With change increasing in pace the hierarchy seems an endangered species. Its reaction time is slow. People high up in the hierarchy may not possess the requisite new knowledge needed to handle current-change events. The volume of data now needed may overwhelm the hierarchy completely.

This section in the book has attempted to analyse current organisations and to suggest some options. In this context it is interesting that the Swedish Employers' Confederation in their book entitled *Job Reform in Sweden* [4], which is based on considerable organisational innovations, comes to the conclusion that there are no final truths about job design and new work organisation.

Anyone who is tempted to see Sweden as a model for the UK might consider the following:

1 Sweden has long-established harmony in labour/management relations.
2 Technology is advanced.
3 There is a strong democratic tradition.
4 There is a high receptivity to new ideas.
5 There is strong, responsible unionism (95 per cent of all industrialised workers are unionised and 70 per cent of all white collar workers).
6 Sweden has considerable Government legislation covering industrial activities of all kinds.

The Swedish experience may not, therefore, be relevant outside that country, but even so some brief analysis of Swedish experience might be worthwhile.

19.7.1 The approach taken in Sweden

Rolf Lindholm [4] states that the approach to discovering organisational alternatives in Sweden has been as follows:

1 A search was made for production units of moderate size having sub-units which could operate independently if need be.
   The sub-units were determined by considering:
   (a) Whether it was possible to break up a production line or department without detriment to the overall efficiency of the department or line.
   (b) Whether it was possible to rearrange the manufacturing process so that sub-units could perform a complete cycle of work or perhaps assemble a major part of the total product being made.
   (c) The degree of independence which was possible.

(d)   The degree of stability in the production system.
It seemed that the degree of stability was important. This was helped by:
(e)   Simplifying and improving material flow patterns.
(f)   Improving the reliability of production equipment and processes.
(g)   Designing work organisations which were not sensitive to production changes. (The possibility of having parallel production processes was explored.)

2   It was decided that work organisations should be designed to include the following:
(a)   A variety of tasks requiring differing skills.
(b)   Groups and teamwork which broadened and enriched jobs.
(c)   The size of the work group was established so that visual and social contact was possible.

3   Environmental factors were improved:
(a)   The shopfloor, it was felt, should be a pleasant place on which to work. Perhaps both administrative and physical workers would share the same floor space.
(b)   Health and safety hazards were eliminated.
(c)   Noise was reduced to minimal levels.
(d)   Well equipped rest rooms were provided.

4   Technological approaches used in designing new work organisations included:
(a)   The product design was changed to allow new work organisations. A 'building block' approach was used where complex products were broken down into smaller pieces which could be produced in small work groups.
(b)   The factory became brighter, smaller, quieter.
(c)   Factory layout — flow processes and materials handling were often key factors in deciding upon a work organisation.
(d)   Technology was changed to accommodate smaller work groups, individual workplace design and individual job design.

5   Participation in the changing of work organisations. Throughout all the published literature on work organisation changes in Sweden, participation is strongly stressed. It is suggested that all available knowledge about processes and machine usage should be harnessed through participation. Workers' opinions are sought from the start.

Participation is usually generated inside the new or proposed work organisation to be concerned with day to day operations. (Participation, it is said, works best when it is deeply rooted in the line organisation. Establishing participation for its own sake runs the risk of not providing anything of great value.)

Works councils (which are mandatory in Sweden) have been used by Swedish industry to help introduce new methods of work organisation. (The tendency in works councils is to discuss working environments, employee facilities, training and expansion, rather than day to day industrial problems.)

Project groups have also been used to help to design and then introduce new methods of work organisation.

6 Has it been worth it and has it succeeded? The literature gives evidence that the degree of consultation and participation which has been generated in Sweden has been very costly to local industry. As might be expected the results seem to vary. Some companies have benefited considerably, others not at all.

A leading contributory cause of failure seems to be over elaboration. Labels are given to everything. The programme is launched with immense written documentation and kept separate from the normal running of the company.

Those activities which have succeeded have usually been relatively unimportant and with a simple programme on a small scale with formal rules kept to a minimum.

Job design has gone hand in hand with new work organisations. Work cycles have been extended, sometimes by as much as thirty or forty times. Jobs that used to cover one or two minutes' activity endlessly repeated have expanded in the same proportion.

However, while job satisfaction appears to have increased considerably, production costs have remained more or less as they were.

Job rotation, when it has been either scheduled or 'rolling', has usually been a failure. However, job rotation based on multi-skill training has been successful.

19.8   RESOURCE UTILISATION TEAMS

The experiments in Sweden prompt the question 'how should new work organisations more suited to changing environments be designed?' The analysis and subsequent design might be based on the production framework — resources, systems, motivation and work organisations. The first three elements are important in designing the fourth. All elements act and react on each other. One should not be looked at in isolation.

From such an analysis the most appropriate work organisation might be 'resource teams' designed as follows:

A business uses resources of all kinds in its activities of producing goods and services. The business will only continue if the value of output is greater than the value of input to the business.

Many businesses use return on investment as a measurement of performance, but this is not possible at fairly low levels in an organisation. Even so there is a need to measure the performance of resources in a company and also the working groups which are employed to operate them.

A group operating a substantial resource can be utilised to improve the performance of the resource — either its contribution or added value. Measurement and control can be established accordingly.

Such groups or teams could be formed around a product line or part of it where these factors can be determined.

1   All variable costs associated with the production resource or resources can be identified and measured separately from the variable costs of the total line.
2   Net sales revenue can be determined — or at least a standard transfer price (if further operations are required).
3   Contribution or added value earned can be established quickly enough to enable corrective action to be taken if anything goes wrong.
4   Personnel associated with the product line are able to have an impact on the contribution or added value they can earn.

Normally a resource utilisation team would be directed to maximise the contribution it earns. For a product manager this would, theoretically, need a knowledge of the variable costs of the products he makes and an authority to discuss and determine the product mix which will help maximise contribution. (Production resources should, in effect, be sold to the customers and products which yield most contribution.)

Resource teams should be allowed or given authority to maximise contribution, perhaps as below:

(a)   Reduce variable or direct costs, for example, by improving material utilisation.
(b)   Alter the product mix.
(c)   Concentrate all management effort on the current constraining or limiting factor. The organisation of the resource teams, therefore, has to be adaptive to outside influences such as:
       Technological change
       Raw material supply situations
       Changes in the product market.
       In the short term the resource team leader should ensure that he maximises his contribution against the current limiting factor.

The benefits of using resource teams are:

(d)   The wage payment system can be based either wholly or in part on contribution or added value earnings.
(e)   There is a strong possibility that participative groups can be formed where joint employee/management decisions can be made with meaningful and measurable results.

(f)   Management in part has to become 'enabling'. It enables its resources to improve their performance. Pressure should stem (once appropriate training has been given) from the resource team on management to improve the team's performance.

(g)   Junior management and first line supervision can have an independence and autonomy which management by objectives techniques has always implied they should have, but which are rarely achieved in practice.

Within the resource team, sub-units might be tried out and jobs enlarged along the lines suggested by the results of the experiments in Sweden.

NOTES

1   Alvin Toffler, *Future Shock*, Pan Books, 1971.
2   Thomas H. Holmes and Masudru Minoru, 'Psychosomatic Syndrome', *Psychology Today*, April 1972.
3   John H. Howard, 'What is our Capacity to Cope with Stress?', *The Business Quarterly*, Winter 1973.
4   *Job Reform in Sweden*, Swedish Employers' Federation, 1975.
5   P. Torner, *The Matfors Report*, Swedish Employers' Federation, 1973.
6   S. Agura et al, *The Volvo Kalmar Plant. The Impact of New Designs of Work Organisation*, The Rationalisation Council, SAF/LO, 1976.
7   H. Lindestad and A. Kvist, *The Volkswagen Report*, Swedish Employers' Confederation, 1975.

PART V

Motivation and Payment Systems

20

Motivation

20.1 INTRODUCTION

It is probably true to say that most industrial managers still regard money as the most important, perhaps the only, factor in motivating their work force. They are frequently sceptical of the sociologists and psychologists whose studies of motivation in industry often seem unreal.

There is a danger that sociologists project their own feelings, perhaps beliefs, into their experiments and studies concerned with industrial societies. Perhaps they see the shopfloor as a rather noisy extension of a university or polytechnic senior common room; a place where people have the same value systems and aspirations as themselves.

Yet in the mid seventies it did appear that industrial psychologists were having some success in selling their ideas. Even veteran production managers suddenly became aware of 'Theory X' and 'Theory Y', 'Maslow's hierarchy of needs' and 'job enrichment'. Even so, the difficulties of applying such ideas were daunting. Some who tried found that they had little reward for plenty of hard work. When the dust subsided productivity had risen very little — if at all — and all the old problems of trying to ensure that the shopfloor produced what it was possible to produce from the equipment it had remained.

20.2 IS MONEY THE ONLY MOTIVATOR?

Anyone who has first-hand experience of the production planning function will be aware of a situation where weekend overtime is necessary to complete urgent orders or to keep work in balance on the shopfloor. Everything has been laid on — shop services, the canteen, internal transport, security at the factory gate. Then only a small proportion of the required work force actually turns up. The rest have exercised their right to say that there is a limit to the amount of leisure they care to lose for more money, especially when high tax rates apply.

What other evidence could a hard headed production manager require before he considers that there are other motivators than money? Perhaps the following:

1   The nature of 'Taylor type' financial rewards suggests something funda-
    mental about the nature of a shopfloor worker. First of all his services need
    to be bought. He is basically mechanistic and will respond like Pavlov's
    dogs to a direct stimulus — in his case, money. The contract between
    employer and the worker is purely a financial one.

    Yet many senior (even middle) managers see their own jobs very
    differently. Many would state that giving them more money will not make
    them work harder or more effectively (though declining differentials may,
    conversely, make them work less effectively in some instances).

    The intrinsic nature of the shopfloor worker, it appears, differs from that
    of a manager. Is this really true? Or is it what has come to be expected, so
    that behaviour is adjusted accordingly?

2   Even if many shopfloor workers respond to the direct application of more
    money for greater output, does everyone? To treat everyone alike is to
    assume that there are no differences between people. Yet among shopfloor
    personnel there is usually a wide variety in age, family responsibilities and
    outlook. The man with a young family and a house on mortgage is likely to
    think more highly of money than perhaps an older man with neither to con-
    sider.

3   The evidence that shopfloor workers can be motivated by factors other
    than money is by now extremely wide. The classic study which deserves to
    be mentioned is the well known 'Hawthorne experiment'. The 'Hawthorne
    effect' has passed into management folklore as an indication that in certain
    circumstances a workforce can be motivated by social conditions rather
    than money.

4   Few production managers would dispute evidence that individual piece-
    work incentives rarely provide independent individual motivation. As
    Argyle [1] suggests, the standards of work output set by groups on a
    shopfloor have been found to override the effect of financial rewards.
    Groups, he suggests, set 'norms about how fast people work, how hard and
    how long, what standard of workmanship should be attained, safety regula-
    tions, etc. Group norms include the permissible limits of time wasting,
    scrounging, cheating on incentive schemes etc.; management is compelled
    to go along with these practices, condoning them and attempting to
    manage them.' This seems to ring true for many factories.

5   Why people work is an interesting question. The fact that many people do

not want to retire, whether at the regulation age or if they have won or inherited enough money to stay at home, says something about not working as opposed to working. Despite the irksome conditions which exist in many factories, is it possible that many people see the shopfloor as a social institution, from which they derive social satisfaction?

6   Money is important. Yet how many times is it possible to see in individual incentives that there is some manipulation not to produce high earnings but to produce wage stability? Steady work and steady wages, as Kahn [2] suggests, is very high up the requirement list of most factory operatives.

7   Finally, most industrial relations problems seem to arise because of disputes about money and particularly incentive payments. This seems to support the 'money motivation theory' — yet does it? Money is a convenient thing to demand. It is a measurable gain (or loss) in the battle with management. It is often the only factor which can be legitimately argued about in a factory which is dominated by piecework incentives.

Management has chosen the weapon with which it negotiates with its workforce. Is it unreasonable when the workforce replies in kind?

20.2.1   The external environment and motivation

In some degree every organisation is a prisoner of its own environment. It is impossible for it to act as a free agent and ignore what is happening in the world beyond the factory gates. What happens nationally — in Government or the economy or even in education or social conditions — is sooner or later reflected in some way on the shopfloor.

How hard people are prepared to work and their attitudes to work generally could have as much to do with local or even national value systems as the skills, techniques and determination of management.

20.2.2   Why people work

As Balchin [3] suggests, there are three reasons why people work:

Because they must
Because they want to
Because they feel they should.

The first reason is mainly an economic one — 'we work to live'. The second concerns the non-economic satisfaction which work can bring. The third reason is ethical in content.

20.2.3   Productivity, wealth creation and motivation

One of the key problems in establishing any form of wage payment system has been how to relate wages paid to factory productivity and eventually to the wealth created by the organisation.

Greater participation in company affairs by workers should generate a greater inclination to consider the wider economic aspects of running a business, its security, survival and success. To help to achieve this will probably need a positive method of relating pay to productivity. Equally a method is required which gives the workforce a share in the prosperity of the organisation for which they work.

20.3 THE INDUSTRIAL PSYCHOLOGISTS' APPROACH TO MOTIVATION

The fascination of work and why people do it has affected many sociologists and psychologists. It seems a perennial topic for theses and books and many shopfloor operatives must be getting quite practised at answering questionnaires and giving their opinions about work groups or production lines.

The ideas of two of the leading writers in this field — Maslow and Herzberg — have already been mentioned (see Chapter 14) in the context of industrial conflict.

Maslow [4] put forward a needs hierarchy to explain why people are motivated. A man's basic requirement, Maslow suggests, is physiological, followed by safety. Belongingness is next and then esteem and finally — as the supreme requirement — self-actualisation.

If Maslow is right (and this is debatable) then financial rewards serve only the lowest needs in his hierarchy. Status, achievement, the possibility of using all talents and capacities, which are the highest needs, could have little to do with monetary incentives.

20.3.1 Job enrichment

1   The approach

In previous books [3] the author has expressed a degree of scepticism about 'job enrichment'. Anything that is (or perhaps was) regarded as a universal panacea must be suspect.

Herzberg suggests that the psychology of motivation is tremendously complex. There are, he states, several myths about motivation. Amongst these he lists the following apparent motivators as really negative in their application:

(a)   A shorter working week. The problem still remains of getting people to work when they are actually at the workplace.

(b)   Increasing wages. Whoever remembers when one wage rise did not automatically lead to the next?

(c)   Fringe benefits. The cost of fringe benefits — holidays, sickness pay, subsidised canteens, overalls, etc. — has reached very high levels, yet they still do not motivate.

(d) Sensitivity/human relations training. Saying 'please' to a machine operative still does not motivate him to work hard.

(e) Communication. Telling a shopfloor worker about the condition of the company may produce more rather than less animosity. Informing people about profitability (or lack of it) does not encourage them to think about how it can be improved if they cannot do it constructively within their own jobs.

For Herzberg these approaches to motivation are 'hygiene' factors. They are factors extrinsic to a job — and could include company policy and administration, supervision, interpersonal relationships, working conditions, salary, status and security. If they are not present there will be demotivation. If they are they will be accepted, but they do not motivate (at least these are the conclusions Herzberg has reached from his experiments).

Real motivators must be related to unique human characteristics — the ability to experience psychological growth. So motivators should be related to 'achievement, recognition, work itself, responsibility, advancement and growth'.

Jobs therefore, should be restructured so that psychological growth can be gained.

This approach is contrary to the notion that a worker is really 'economic man' and can be bribed by higher wages to increase his output. It is also contrary to a method study approach — i.e. that a good working environment and the best possible method to carry out a task will produce high productivity. Finally it is against the human relations approach to motivation, whereby it is hoped that attitudes to work can be changed by creating an appropriate social and psychological climate.

True motivation must lie in giving greater responsibility and providing the possibility for greater achievement and growth and recognition for performance. Many companies try to do this by enlarging a job — for instance by providing new and more difficult tasks, introducing self control and monitoring, giving greater autonomy and authority, instituting the possibility of acquiring new skills.

2 Problems and criticisms of job enrichment ideas

It seems possible that it is the nature of work which is a prime cause of much job dissatisfaction and industrial unrest. However, there is considerable evidence to suggest that job enrichment has not been widely applied. If the ending of dull monotonous meaningless jobs raises productivity without raising costs, one wonders why job restructuring is not a priority task for all industrial managers. Could it be that job enrichment is not easy to apply and that when applied the results are not as good as theorists suggest can be achieved?

The following need to be considered:

(a)   Technological. Many factories use a technology which restricts the possibilities for job enrichment, even when management is keen to apply it. Some jobs defy enrichment.

(b)   Do workers want it? Job enrichment has been largely propagated by industrial psychologists and taken up by senior managers but rarely — if ever — by trade unions. 'Improvements in our working lives' requested by shop stewards are mainly about increased wages and shorter working hours. While these are what negotiations have been about for decades, and so somewhat stereotyped, their predominance is a crucial factor.

(c)   One man's job enrichment could be a junior manager's job poverty. The least enthusiastic people about job enrichment are those who are likely to be detrimentally affected by it. This may have serious repercussions on the application.

(d)   'Work itself', one of Herzberg's motivation factors, has always been tied up with salary, job security and personal relationships.

It is difficult on occasions to divorce hygiene from motivation factors. They often seem to act and react on each other.

(e)   Establishing jobs so that job enrichment is possible is a leap in the dark. The implications are very wide. If it is to work effectively the whole pattern of management styles, attitudes, even hierarchical organisations, must change. There are not many organisations which would happily allow this to happen.

(f)   If job enrichment works then the wholesale changes required may be worthwhile. If it fails to work then management might find itself in a frighteningly dangerous situation where anarchy may rule.

(g)   The evidence of job enrichment making a positive and valuable contribution to increased profit is sparse. Workers may feel greater satisfaction but if this cannot be converted into higher added value or profit, then the company may end up making fine but fairly worthless gestures. From a profit/efficiency viewpoint it may still be better to allow the division of labour to continue despite the attendant industrial relations problems.

(h)   Job enrichment implies that each and every worker wants responsibility, authority and participation in decision making. This is far from being proved.

20.4   THE LINKS BETWEEN FINANCIAL AND NON-FINANCIAL MOTIVATION AND THE EXTERNAL ENVIRONMENT

The proponents of financial and non-financial motivators have put forward their ideas as if it were necessary for production managers to make a clear cut decision between one or the other. It has to be 'X' or 'Y'. It has to be individual incentives or a plant-wide scheme. Money is the sole motivator or it is not.

If individuals differ so do organisations and factories. The history of one company is totally different from another's. Local environments, organisational style, the type of work performed, the conditions under which it is carried out all seem to contribute.

What could be right for a textile mill in Lancashire could be totally wrong for a factory making shaving cream on the Slough trading estate. What must be realised, however, is that there is a link between the type of financial and non-financial motivational system, management style, company organisation and history. Motivation has to be viewed within the total framework of the production system.

20.5 CONCLUSION

So there seems no one right motivational system which will suit all occasions and situations. There is no universal solution.

A production manager should aim to get the best fit between the history of an organisation and the type of production process he is involved with, the local and national cultural environment and the motivational systems which have served him well so far.

In deciding upon the best fit a starting point might be the local work organisation and not the motivational system. It is how people see their job, their role, their authority, the power they can wield (as opposed to times when they actually wield it) and their local environment which needs analysis.

Motivational systems therefore, should be discussed within the overall corporate policy of the organisation.

It is possible that organisations have tended to see their workforces as being generally homogeneous, motivated economically, exhibiting similar work values and attitudes and having uniform needs. Yet the same workers would probably say, individually, that they were each unique with attitudes and personalities of their own, owing nothing to their fellow workers except their social relationships and perhaps when management intervene too much, loyalty to their working group.

It is perhaps not too surprising that some academics have taken up this idea (for example those at the Manchester Business School) and now suggest that it is only possible to consider the problem of motivation through the study of individual situation. (They have even given a term to the approach — contingency theory.) Only by analysing the variables in a situation and providing a 'best fit' will appropriate motivational procedures be discovered.

NOTES

1   M. Argyle, *The Social Psychology of Work*, Penguin, 1972.
2   R. Kahn, 'Human Relations on the Shop Floor', in Hugh Jones, E. M. (ed)
    Human Relations and Modern Management, 1958.
3   N. Balchin, 'Satisfaction in Work', *Occupational Psychology*, Vol. 21,
    1947.
4   A. H. Maslow, 'A Theory of Human Motivation', *Psychological Review*,
    Vol. 50, 1943.
5   For example see B. H. Walley *Management Services Handbook*, Business
    Books, 1973, Chapter 35.

21

Work measurement

21.1 INTRODUCTION

No matter what method of motivation or incentive is applied good work measurement is essential. Traditional time study based measurement has formed the basis for individual payment by results incentive schemes and also for many measured day work systems.

Work measurement is defined in BS3138 as 'The application of techniques designed to establish the time for a qualified worker to carry out a specified job at a defined level of performance'.

21.2 TRADITIONAL WORK MEASUREMENT AND WORK STUDY

Work measurement has formed one of the twin pillars of work study (the other is method study). Carrying out work measurement and applying subsequent incentives has often been equated with 'work study' in many organisations. This limited view has drawbacks, not least that method study or some other form of productivity improvement may provide greater benefits than the application of individual payment by results schemes.

Work study practitioners have attempted to enlarge the scope of their discipline by including other facets of improving production efficiency apart from work measurement and method study. For example, production systems and the application of what are generally thought to be operations research techniques such as linear programming, have been listed by some as being part of the work study function. This tendency is not recommended. Having well rounded individuals in a management services unit where interdisciplinary teams can be established is a much better way of diagnosing and improving production efficiency.

A work study engineer will normally have the following duties. To:

1   Ensure the most economical use of labour, materials and equipment by studying methods procedures in existence on the shopfloor or other areas designated by management through method study and work measurement.
2   Issue instruction sheets (job descriptions) for all new methods where incentive schemes are to be applied.
3   Ensure that operatives are working to the method set out in the job description before the commencement of work measurement.
4   Devise, develop and install bonus incentive schemes using accepted work measurement techniques for as many operations as are considered suitable and practical for such applications.
5   Prepare and/or update work value sheets.
6   Provide a work study service to other departments and divisions as directed by work study department.

21.3   REASONS FOR REQUIRING WORK MEASUREMENT

Some of the following reasons will be important in most cases. To:

1   Establish equitable work distribution among operatives.
2   Establish targets or output rates on which production scheduling and control can be based.
3   Provide the basis for incentive payment.
4   Determine the need for improvements in production processes and to measure their effectiveness once the improved methods or equipment have been introduced.
5   Train or develop staff in some way.
6   Help in environmental studies.
7   Generally improve the use of manpower.
8   Provide the basis for manpower budgeting and product costing.

In many respects work measurement is the measurement of the ineffective use of machines, labour and services within a production environment.

21.4   WORK MEASUREMENT. TIME STUDY

21.4.1   Starting the study

The process of work measurement is recorded in Fig. 21.1. This shows that the start of the activity is the completion of a study sheet and that the figures produced will normally be supported by production studies. An important

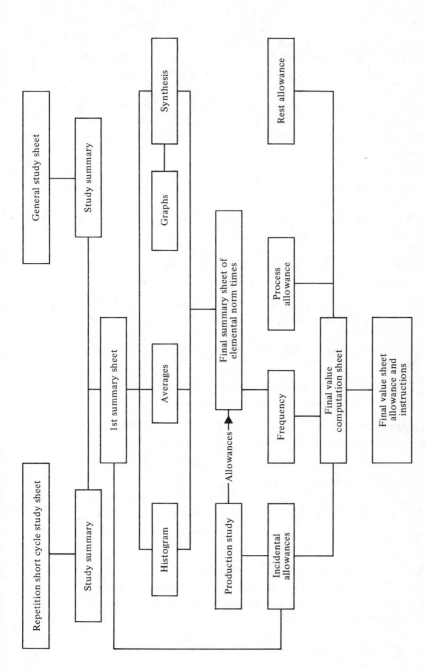

Fig. 21.1 Work measurement – the general approach

factor in the procedure will be the establishment of allowances of various kinds which will be added to the work measurement data before the final value sheet is produced.

To gain acceptance for a study it is usual to agree with local unions the overall work measurement programme and the reason why individual studies are required — for example, new jobs have been or will be introduced, methods have been or will be changed, standards for some reason have become out of date. Occasionally, operatives or unions ask for a study to be carried out. Normally, however, management agree a programme of work measurement, necessary, they believe, to enhance production. Work study personnel will, therefore, be utilised on priorities (as far as possible) and their work planned.

The relationship with method study is emphasised and the two are often complementary.

21.4.2   Job analysis

An essential part of the work study activity is to gain all appropriate knowledge about the job being studied. For example:

Methods used: These have to be those laid down in any 'making particulars' or 'operating instructions'.

Tools: These will need to be checked. Are they appropriate, sharp and in generally good condition? Are any misuses of tools observable?

Servicing of the job: How much of the operative's potential effectiveness is conditional on servicemen?

Variances in output: Are these due to the machine or the operative? How far is the work which is performed machine paced?

Environmental conditions: How far do these affect the rate at which the operative can work — e.g. heat, dust, position, etc?

Extraneous activities: Often some machines need a preparation period or changeover times. These must be measured.

The operative: Is he properly trained?

21.4.3   Element breakdown

A key part of most work measurement studies is the element breakdown. An element (BS3138 — 1959) is 'a distinct part of a specified job selected for convenience of observation, measurement and analysis'. Why consider elements? The following factors are important:

1   Abnormal processes are detectable which are not in keeping with the laid down method.

2   Ineffective or idle time in the total process could be discovered and so lead to a new and better method being devised.
3   Some parts of the job may be done by the operative in a better way than the others. Training might be introduced for the less good parts.
4   Timing is proved to be more accurate when established at element level.
5   Rating is also improved in the same way.
6   When the various elements are identified these may aid the application of relaxation and rest allowances.
7   The use of element analysis is essential in the application of some methods of work measurement — e.g. motion time measurement.

Over the years various standard elements have been recognised. These are:

Repetitive — these are main elements which recur in every work cycle.

Occasional — elements which do not occur in every work cycle, but are necessary for completing the job.

Irregular or non-competitive.

Constant — elements for which a standard time can be applied, no matter when or where they are performed.

Variable — elements for which the standard time will vary dependent upon some characteristics of the product being made, machine used or process performed.

Manual — elements carried out by the operative and not associated with the machine.

Machine — elements performed by the machine alone.

Governing — elements which dominate the job, often occupying a major part of the time incurred.

Work study practitioners will have been trained to recognise 'elements'. These will be as short as possible (perhaps between 18 and 30 seconds) and often occur when tools are changed or the machine obviously finishes one operation. Handling times are normally separated from machine or operational times. The various element types should be recognised and used in the study.

The normal way of establishing elements is to determine 'breakpoints' in the process.

Elements are considered further in discussion on motion study (21.4.5–9) and PMTS (21.5) systems of work measurement.

21.4.4   Time recording equipment

Usually a stop watch of either the centiminute or milliminute type is used. Both continuous and flyback methods of time recording are used. The latter is the

Observation sheet   Study sheet no:—
                                                     Study no:—

Observation being undertaken   Observer:—
Department   Date started:—
Section   Date stopped:—
Product   Study agreed by:—
Operation
Operative

Element	Rating	Obs. Time	BMs	Element	Rating	Obs. Time	BMs

Comment:—   On method:—

              On timings:—

              On operative:—

Fig. 21.2   Observation sheet

most common. The watch is observed at the end of an element while the hand is still moving. After reading, the winding knob is touched and the hand returns to zero, ready to record the next element. No calculations are needed to obtain element times, so the eventual clerical work needed to produce the standard time is reduced.

Continuous recording gives the element time and also an overall time for the operation.

Work study personnel normally have a clipboard with an observation sheet (see Fig. 21.2) and a stop watch on the board to facilitate recording.

A study summary of the type shown in Fig. 21.3 is used to consolidate the readings.

C.C. _____

Job No. _____

Job Description _____ Study No. _____

Standard Class _____ Type of Product_____ Quality Symbol _____

Finished Size (Final)_____ Size at Op. _____

Machine Type _____ M/C No. _____

Machine R.P.M. _____ Feed _____ Operator _____ W.S.E. _____

Equipment _____ Procured from _____

_____ Assigned to _____

Operation:–

Ele.No.	Element Description	Tot N.Min	Occ's	N.Min/Occ

Additional information:–

Use reverse side of sheet for Workplace layouts, Plans, Sketches etc.

Fig. 21.3   Study summary

An extremely accurate form of work measurement uses a ciné-camera which can simultaneously record and time the elements.

21.4.5   Statistics in work measurement

It is normal in work measurement to accept that many, perhaps hundreds, of readings must be made before a standard time is derived.

Accuracy in taking studies may be disturbed by:

1   Errors in stop watch reading.
2   Errors in considering the elements being timed.
3   Variations in operating conditions — materials, methods, lighting.
4   The pace at which the operative works (this could be deliberately variable).
5   Failure to take account of some non-repetitive element which occurs.

While this kind of disturbance can be eliminated or reduced by the standardisation of method and control of the job, the variations which still exist must be taken into account in the study.

Bias may also occur through the expertise (and lack of it) of the work study practitioner.

The readings taken are samples of a job activity. They must be taken randomly over the predetermined length of the study as with activity sampling. A recommended procedure is to take small groups of readings at random over a long period of time.

Readings should continue until statistical stability is achieved. (A weighted average of basic times is calculated for each element.)

21.4.6   Rating

Recording of the type described is obviously inadequate to deal with the wide variations in operatives' performances. Naturally they will not work as hard as they can while being studied. So work study personnel often have a consider-able problem in determining what is a fair time in which to do a job. What a standard time should be, can be the subject of endless debate with trade unions.

'Normal performance' has been established as a man walking without a load along a level road at three miles per hour. This idea is not particularly useful in determining how fast a man might operate a grinding machine or a mixer except that it produces a relative view of effort.

So in attempting to determine standard times determination of what is normal performance is required. Then the observed times have to be adjusted to normal by some form of scaling or numerical index. Since this has to involve some evaluatory perception, rating a job does not have scientific accuracy — as many work study personnel claim it has.

Two rating scales are used — 60/80 and 100. (The latter is the BSI scale.)

The 60/80 scale conveniently mirrors 60 minutes. A '60' is normal performance and is equivalent to a man walking along a road at 3 mph. The equivalent rating on the BSI scale is 100.

A fast, brisk or standard performance is rated at '80' on the 60/80 scale and 133 on the BSI system. This is the traditional 'time and one third' to which most incentives are geared as achievable by operatives.

The fact that in many schemes operatives regularly earn over 80 on a 60/80 rating is disturbing. This could be due to numerous factors:

1 Poor rating.
2 Excessive allowances.
3 Non-incentive time booked in excess to boost the incentive part of the job.

Experienced work study personnel are aware of the difficulties of rating accurately. They are usually trained by 'training films' where rating of several different types of job is shown. However, long experience with definite mental bench marks for rating purposes is needed so that rating in part becomes subconscious.

What should work study and production managers be looking for in considering a standard rating? Perhaps the following:

4   Well trained operatives.
5   A brisk businesslike performance.
6   Body motions at a minimum and generally rhythmic.
7   A smooth fast activity.
8   Work is done to methods laid down using all appropriate tools correctly.
9   Equipment is correctly placed.
10 Work is done accurately with little need to check consistently for quality.

Normally each element in the activity is rated (only effective work being included).

The rating system outlined compares actual speed with standard speed. There are others — e.g.:

Bedaux's original skill and effort system.

The Westinghouse four-factor system (skill, effort, conditions, consistency).

Synthetic rating — comparison of timed values with synthetics.

Objective rating — against a standard allowing for job difficulty.

Physiological evaluation of performance level (heart rate changes etc.).

21.4.7   Allowances

This is another area where negotiations over time standards often produce lower values than work measurement might determine.

Fatigue at some stage will affect most operatives. There are obvious needs for personal breaks, so a major allowance which is usually negotiable is for relaxation. While some standards for 'RA' have been established debate will usually centre around the effort required, posture, the different motions the operative has to undertake, and the factory environment (particularly thermal and atmospheric conditions). These can all be used to suggest the suitable amount of relaxation allowance.

Fig. 21.4 gives some of the more common relaxation allowances and suggests some percentages which may need to be built into the work measurement. A brief list outlining some relaxation allowances follows:

Personal needs — these would include allowances for sitting, idleness in machine cycles and handling of light weights.

Posture — standing or walking unladen, bending or stretching, crouching or kneeling, lying on back, side or face.

Effort — in, for example light sedentary work, walking upstairs or pushing an empty wheelbarrow, hacksawing or filing, handling heavy weights.

Motions — might comprise normal, limited or awkward, extremely awkward, dextrous.

Air conditioning — good, fumes and dust requiring protective clothing.

Temperatures — ranges, highs and lows.

Visual — normal, medium, high.

Aural strain — normal, medium, high.

Monotony/Tediousness — disagreeable with little variety, disagreeable with little satisfaction and no end product.

While relaxation allowances are the most important allowances, there are others:

Contingency allowances — these usually cover small amounts of work which are undertaken but have not been included in the study.

Process allowances — it may be possible for rest from manual work to be taken during the machine or process cycle time.

Policy payments — these are used in conjunction with incentive schemes either to start up the incentive or to give standard bonus for less than

Cost Centre _____ Job No. _____

Machine _____

Operation Description _____

_____ Date _____

El. No.	Element Description	Weight	Volume	Length/Width/Thickness	Area	Personal	Standing	Abnormal Position	Dexterity – Use of Force - Weight Lifting - Arduousness	Air Conditions	Lighting Conditions	Visual Strain	Aural Strain	Mental Strain	Monotony	Tediousness	TOTAL
Excessive						7%	2%	–	25%	7%	–	–	–	8%	–	–	
High								5%	20%	5%	5%	5%	4%	6%	4%	5%	
Medium								2%	10%	3%	2%	2%	1%	4%	1%	2%	
Low								–	5%	–	–	–	–	1%	–	–	

Fig. 21.4 Selection of rest allowances

standard performance. They are a favourite bargaining factor with trade unions.

Synchronisation allowances — these compensate an operative for possible simultaneous stoppages on several machines tended by one person.

Training allowance — operatives under training usually receive a gradually reducing allowance to compensate for their original lack of skill.

Average earnings allowance — when, in situations (where new methods are being developed for example) which are out of the control of an operative, standard performance cannot be paid, average earning allowances are given in compensation.

21.4.8   Extension of observed times

Following the taking of the required number of readings and making out a rating for each element on the job, the observed times are extended. This process is often called 'normalising the time study'. So to achieve the extended time it will be necessary to carry out the following simple calculation:

$$\text{Extended time} = \frac{\text{Observed time x operative's rating factor}}{\text{Reference rating factor}}$$

Thus if an operative completed an element in 30 seconds and was given a rating of 80 (on a 60/80 scale) the extended time would be:

$$\frac{30 \times 80}{60} = 40 \text{ seconds}$$

Selecting a representative reading for each element may present something of a problem. Arithmetical averages can be used for the purpose, though plotting a histogram may show variances more clearly. The reciprocal graphical method may be better still.

The various allowances which management and unions have agreed are necessary for the job being studied, have then to be added to the rated element times.

21.4.9   Comparison with a reference period

The next chapter deals with payment systems. It is useful however at this stage to suggest how the result of work measurement and the application of an associated payment system can be determined.

A reference period fully representative of the conditions which prevailed before the study began is chosen. Three pieces of data need to be collected:

Output — record of output and quality
Hours — including lost time
Payment — gross pay including overtime, allowances, and payment for lost time.

The amount of work done in the reference period is converted into work units by using the new standard time values. The following calculations will then determine if savings have been made and if so how much.

Reference period (operators paid on time basis)
A Measured work (in work units on new values)
B Unmeasured work (clocked time only)
C Lost time (stop notes) (clocked time)

$$\text{Minutes credited} = \text{Total clock minutes}$$

$$\text{Work units} = A + B$$

$$\text{Cost per work unit} = \frac{\text{Direct wages}}{A + B}$$

(where direct wages = hours x rate).

Period after application (operators paid on piecework basis)
A Measured work (in work units)
B Unmeasured work (clocked time)
C Allowed minutes on unmeasured work (allowed minutes)
D Lost time (clocked time)

$$\text{Minutes credited} = A + B + C + D$$

$$\text{Work units} = A + B$$

$$\text{Cost per work unit} = \frac{\text{Direct wages}}{A + B}$$

(where direct wages = payment for work done, allowed time and lost time).

The work done is analysed to arrive at a cost for direct work which includes any payment for lost time etc.

Indirect work
A separate comparison is generally made for indirect work (such as supervision, servicing etc.) over the period.

Summary of results
A typical example is shown below:

For reference period: (10 operators working 40 hours per week)

Average weekly output   = 20,000 (including unmeasured units)

Average weekly hours worked = 400

Average weekly direct wages = £80

Department unit-hour $= \dfrac{20,000}{400} = 50$

Cost per 1,000 units $= \dfrac{8,000p}{20} = 400p/1,000$ units

Operator's hourly earnings $= \dfrac{8,000p}{400} = 20p/hour.$

Period after application

Average weekly output   = 37,500 (including unmeasured units)

Average weekly hours worked = 400

Average weekly direct wages = £100

Department unit-hour $= \dfrac{37,500}{400} = 94$

Cost per 1,000 units $= \dfrac{10,000}{37.5} = 267p/1,000$ units

Operator's hourly earnings $= \dfrac{10,000}{400} = 25p/hour$

Resulting in:
1 Increase in performance (50 to 94)   = 87½%
2 Increase in hourly earnings (20p to 25p)   = 25%
3 Reduction in cost per 1,000 units (400 to 267) = 33%
4 Reduction in hours (in this case same hours) = Nil
As total weekly savings will be saving in cost per 1,000 units x quantity produced in an average week after application, then:
5 Total weekly saving at new level of production $= \dfrac{£37.50}{1,000} \times 133 = £4.98$

21.5   OTHER FORMS OF WORK MEASUREMENT

1   Predetermined motion time systems (PMTS)

Next to time study, predetermined motion-time systems of various kinds are the most popular method of work measurement. Though no accurate evidence seems to be available, the use of PMTS appears to be on the increase.

The basis of PMTS is that fundamental motions are recognised within the activity being measured. These motions are usually similar to those shown in Fig. 21.5 (therbligs). The motions represent the elements used in conventional time study.

Motion analysis designed to establish the elements in the activity is the first requisite in a PMTS study. It is assumed that the motion patterns are universally descriptive and applicable.

Once sufficiently accurate motion patterns have been discovered and recorded, predetermined times are applied to the motion and the total time taken is calculated. The predetermined times are taken from tables which have been prepared for the purpose and which represent an accurate assessment of how long a motion should take whatever the activity, whatever the industry and, perhaps, the country.

Included in the times will be the rating elements and work variables so that the times will fully represent the standard time for the activity.

Motion-time study therefore, is a direct challenge to the operative to perform against what could be a worldwide standard. Obviously such an approach is usually regarded with considerable suspicion by many trade unions. Whereas the stop watch they believe can be manipulated and the rating aspect is not scientific, in motion-time study there seems to be a lot less to argue about. PMTS has other advantages. For example:

(a)   In determining times before a job is even introduced there can be a synthesis of existing data if the motion elements are described accurately.

(b)   It should be possible to study motion patterns and eliminate unnecessary movement.

(c)   Product design might be influenced beneficially if direct operatives' time can be synthesised.

(d)   The selection of equipment might be improved.

(e)   Training supervisors to be cost conscious will be made easier.

(f)   Settling grievances with shop stewards and operatives could be less difficult than with time-studied work measurement. Rating is part of the 'times'. Times have been produced from a very large number of studies. Short cycle work is more easily timed.

Symbol	Name
⬯	Search
⬯	Find
⟶	Select
∩	Grasp
⌓	Hold
⌣	Transport load
9	Position
#	Assemble
U	Use
⧣	Disassemble
◊	Inspect
⧸	Pre-position
⌢	Release load
⌣	Transport empty
ℙ	Rest for overcoming fatigue
⌂	Unavoidable delay
⌐	Avoidable delay
℘	Plan

Fig. 21.5   Therbligs

Tables of data have been developed for the following movements:

Reach
Move
Turn and apply pressure
Grasp
Position
Release
Disengage.

The motion time can be determined by the following:

Distance moved
Weight lifted
Visual attention required
Precision required
Muscular control in stopping motions.

As with time study, cameras and chronocyclograph equipment to photograph motion patterns and apply times to them will help in PMTS.

There is a fairly large number of proprietary applications of PMTS. Many independent consultancy companies have developed their own standard data:

Methods, time measurement (I) and (II) and (III)
Work factor (and simplified WF)
Ready work factor
Basic motion-time study
Basic work data
Motion-time analysis (MTA)
Motion-time data for assembly work
Dimensional motion times
Simplified PMTS.

Universal maintenance standards (UMS) have been developed to measure maintenance work. Various clerical applications have been made (e.g. master clerical data).

The differences between PMTS methods are largely in:

Whether normal, standard or another level of time is used.

Whether relaxation allowances are embodied in the times.

The time units adopted.

The degree of accuracy of the application.

The applicability of the systems — i.e. universal, general or specific.

The motion patterns used.

2   Activity sampling

This is a work measurement technique in which a large number of instantaneous random observations is made over a period of time. Each observation is used to record what is happening at the instant it is made.

The technique uses the statistical theory that by taking a sample of the whole it is possible to infer certain characteristics of the whole.

From activity sampling it is possible to obtain knowledge about the activity of people or machines. For example, it may be necessary to determine how much a particular machine is operated, or a group of workers needs to be studied to ensure that they are all equally occupied most of the time.

In carrying out activity sampling the following process is used:

(a)   Define the activities to be observed. For example an operative may be working or not working, he may be changing his machine or perhaps is absent from it. Each activity is given a code letter or number and this is recorded when appropriate.

Eight to ten activities appear to be a maximum which can be covered in activity sampling.

(b)   Choose the period for the technique to be applied. This has to be representative of the work as it normally occurs, taking in periods of idleness, starting and finishing times, and work fluctuations. Seasonal, daily or weekly peaks and troughs should be covered.

(c)   The record sheet. This should show the time when the observation was taken, the machine or operative being observed, the coded activity observed.

The coded observations are counted and expressed as a percentage of the total.

(d)   Number of observations. The greater the number of observations the more certainty can be felt about the result. Two factors are involved — the limits of accuracy (L) and the confidence which can be put into the limits of accuracy. Normally (L) will be accurate to 95 per cent confidence limits.

The number of observations required can be found by using the following formula:

$$L = 2\sqrt{\frac{P(100 - P)}{N}}$$

where P = the percentage of time observed taken up in a particular activity; N = the total number of random observations on all activities; L = the percentage of accuracy of P plus or minus.

This formula will give 95 per cent confidence limits if applied to a homogeneous population. However, various rule of thumb tables have been devised. The following specimen has been taken from *Work Sampling* by R. M. Barnes.

Type of work sampling study	Approximate number of observations
1 Help determine general objectives (general trouble spots)	100
2 Help determine specific management objectives (causes of down time, idle time etc.)	600
3 Appraise specific conditions (set-ups, delays)	2,000
4 Appraise machine utilisation	4,000
5 Set time standards, determine allowances up to	10,000

Often in carrying out observations a random number table is used to ensure that true randomness is achieved.

3 Analytical estimating

This is a method of work measurement where the past knowledge of times is used to determine the likely time a job will take in the future. Maintenance is a usual subject of application.

Syntheses of operations and partial times are also used to build up a measurement of work.

4 Work scheduling

This is more a method of work control than of work measurement, as it is based on issuing work to operatives in controlled batches. Records of average times are taken and used for control purposes. See also 'short internal scheduling'.

5 Corporate estimating

This method uses times which have been proved useful in other operations with an apparently similar job content to that being studied.

21.6   WORK BOOKING

An integral part of any work-measured payment scheme is to ensure that the times and allowances are not overbooked by operatives. The problem grows greater where a variety of relaxation, policy and other allowances has been negotiated.

Harried local supervision occasionally allows some work booking malpractices to go by default. This is either because they do not have time to check every claimed allowance or perhaps they see allowances as a means of operatives earning money falsely and at the same time obtaining an easier life, so workbooking fiddles are condoned.

Such practices are often a major cause of wages drift and low productivity.

Two documents are normally used for workbooking verification:

1   A daily work card

An example is given as Fig. 21.6. The orders involved, the operation carried out, time on and off are all completed by the operative who also books claimed allowances. Time study clerks record the values per 1,000 and calculate the standard minutes earned.

The card, once verified by the local supervisor, is passed forward for payment purposes.

2   Stop notes

Once an operative ceases to perform measured work it is important that this be recorded. The stop note is used for this purpose. It also records the allowances claimed and is signed by the supervisor as they occur.

It is not always possible to keep accurate control over workbooking, where many products are handled each day on a batch basis. 'Set-ups' may be over-booked, for example, when actually several *products of the same size* have been run together.

Where a production schedule is issued it is possible to calculate both the allowed standard minutes and allowances which should be taken. The figures can then be compared with those achieved — or booked.

Fig. 21.7 shows a practical example of determining operatives' performances.

21.7   TRADE UNION ATTITUDES TOWARDS WORK MEASUREMENT

This brief outline of work measurement does little justice to the skill required in applying most work measurement techniques. The skill will only come from

Week No.

Ending

Shift

Card Type 1–3

L21

Shift Ind. 7   B/A Ind. 8   Clock No. 9–14

Date (Cols. 4–6)

C/Centre & Job No. 15–22

Standard Classification	Order No.	Order Card No.	Type	Size/Operation	Die or Jig No.	Quantity	Value per 1000	TIME On	TIME Off	C/O S/U Clean M – UM 23 – 30	Standard M – UM 31 – 38	Non-Standard M – UM 39 – 46	Rectification M – UM 47 – 54	Stop UM Code 55-58	Pt. Hr.	Allowed Mins. 59 – 62	Serial No. Form 52

TRANSFERS   CERTIFIED CORRECT

ELAPSED

TO/FROM TIME   C C   JOB No.   TO/FROM TIME   C C   JOB No.   MEASURED

UNMEASURED

TOTAL

PA

– ATTENDANCE RECORD

CARD TYPE 13	STD IND 15	DAY IND 16	TIME ON 17-20	TIME OFF 21-24	DAY IND 25	TIME ON 26-29	TIME OFF 30-33	DAY IND 34	TIME ON 35-38	TIME OFF 39-42	DAY IND 43	TIME ON 44-47	TIME OFF 48-51
L43			52	53-56	57-60	61	62-65	66-69	70	71-74	75-78		

TARGET   Rate

AVERAGE   Rate

Performance   Stabiliser/Make-up 71-75

HOURS NORMAL 63-66

HOURS OVERTIME 67-70

Total Credits 76-79

IND 80

Checked by: DAILY WORK CARD ACCEPTED FOR PROCESSING

Fig. 21.6   Daily work card

Week no. 43

Day	Mfg. hrs.	%	Non mfg. hrs	%	*Non mfg. hrs	%	Total hrs	Achieved units	Man hrs	Total credits	Performance	1000 units per man hour
Sat.	95.5	90.5	10	9.5	9	8.5	105.5	85,474	36	7,403	293	2.37
Mon.	334.5	90	41.5	10	32.5	8.5	376	302,451	138.5	26,166	271	2.18
Tues.	314.5	90	35	10	26	7	349.5	271,408	131	24,472	267	2.07
Wed.	243	87	36	13	28	10	279	223,444	102.5	19,214	272	2.18
Thurs.	218.5	88	30.5	12	24.5	10	249	184,463	96	17,300	259	1.92
Fri.	200.5	90	22.5	10	17	7.5	223	212,702	88	15,577	253	2.42
Total	1,406.5	89	175.5	11	137	8.5	1,582	1,279,912	592	110,132	267	2.16

*Excluding meal

Fig. 21.7 Analysed daycard achievements

considerable practice, after a thorough training. Some work study practitioners never become totally proficient. Union officials and shop stewards usually know those who provide tight or slack ratings; those who are prepared to compromise and those who are not.

The booklet 'Plant Level Bargaining' issued by the Transport and General Workers Union gives some useful insights into the use of work measurement from the union viewpoint.

Rating, it is stated perhaps with some justification, is always subject to human error. So in some degree the standard performance must always be negotiable.

Management's standard times are always to be regarded as management's, never the operative's says the booklet.

They should always be queried along these lines:

The operator was too skilled (or unskilled) to operate properly.

Job descriptions are incomplete.

Element break-points are not clear enough to allow standard times to be determined.

Allowances of all kinds are inadequate.

The study did not cover enough job cycles.

The sequence of motions is unnatural.

The standard time cannot be kept up throughout the working day.

There is no table of rest allowances which are applicable in every situation.

PMTS is the 'cardboard stopwatch' and should be treated with caution. Time values under such systems have been set by outside consultants and not negotiated locally. All PMTS times should be subject to negotiation, either through a percentage uplift or by individual operatives or both'.

Anyone who has been involved with union negotiations over work measurement will recognise the arguments. What can be done, if anything to cut down the weary hours of negotiation and renegotiation?

Any chance that slack values will be introduced should be avoided at all costs. It is far too easy to give way to a belligerent shop steward and build in allowances or compromise times just to gain agreement. This could be highly dangerous.

Work measurement must be seen to be equally applied irrespective of job, department or shop steward involvement. There must be comparability between effort and reward. If this is compromised every job that has been studied and the outcome accepted will again be open to negotiation.

Times and perhaps rating therefore need to be sacrosanct to some extent. If any compromise has to be made then it may come from the allowances offered.

As Chapter 24 suggests, negotiations with the unions must derive from a considered policy. Being hard one day and soft the next will not produce reasonable solutions to the problem of 'selling values'.

Work study personnel must be well trained. The studies must be impeccably carried out, the results beyond doubt.

Some companies have tried to teach work study to shop stewards and in some instances this appears to have produced a more sympathetic attitude. Having negotiators who can understand the studies and the rating made must be beneficial to some degree.

22

Production studies

22.1 INTRODUCTION

A production study according to BS3138 is 'a continuous study of relatively lengthy duration, often extending over a period of one or more shifts, taken with the object of checking on existing or proposed standard times or obtaining other information affecting the rate of output'.

Production studies are often linked with work estimation which is defined in BS3138 as 'a means for assessing the time required to carry out work based on knowledge and experience of similar types of work without a detailed breakdown of the work into elements and their corresponding times at a defined level of performance'.

22.2 THE NEED FOR A PRODUCTION STUDY

At first glance production studies may seem to be competitive with standard work measurement. This is certainly not the case. The purpose of using production studies shows that the two are complementary.

1   The study should be used to check the accuracy of the rating used in work measurement, so minimising the issuing of false values.
2   It should ensure that laid down quality standards are maintained.
3   The standard time should be verified through a production study, with the object of eliminating any disputes that may arise otherwise.
4   The study will provide a record of the production unit against which past, present and future performances can be matched.
5   Current production methods should be checked and then compared with the work specification.
6   The study should show where improvements in current performance might be made.

22.3   APPLICATION

A continuous record is made of the job being studied over an extended period.

A stop watch is used with the normal time study framework.

The stop watch is started and ratings made every half minute or so. As this happens an analysis is made of every event that occurs during the study. (This can be compared with activity sampling.)

Rest allowances, unmeasured work and waiting time are all recorded. The net working time is then calculated by deducting these factors from the elapsed time recorded on the stop watch.

Production for the elapsed time is counted and the ratings which have been made are summarised.

Gross working time is then determined by deducting the net working time and rest allowances, given in the original work measurement, from the elapsed time on the stop watch.

The following calculations are then made:

$$\text{Standard minutes of work produced} = \frac{\text{average rating}}{100} \times \text{gross working time}$$

$$\text{Standard time} = \frac{\text{standard minutes of work derived in the study}}{\text{actual production}}$$

These figures are then compared with the original values determined. Where there are discrepancies, an investigation will obviously be required.

23

Traditional wage payment systems

23.1 INTRODUCTION

It is perhaps a truism that systems of wages payment often reflect the ability, desire or even opportunity of managers to manage. Piecework or payment by results systems, for example, appear to be self managing and production supervisors usually adopt a 'leave well alone' posture. Plant-wide schemes on the other hand, need a more highly trained and involved line management which can ensure that the workforce will operate effectively without the need for rigorous incentives.

23.2 HISTORY OF PAYMENT SCHEMES

Payment systems have traditionally comprised one, two or all three of the following:

1   Base wage: Usually these were determined by the supply and demand of labour in large degree, until the advent of strong unions to force up base wages or maintain them when employers might have had them reduced. (In reality the proportion of wages to sales appears to be remarkably stable over the long term.)
2   Production bonus: A reward was paid for achieving output beyond a specified level. F. W. Taylor was one of the first to introduce payment for pieces or products made.
3   Fringe benefits: Gradually these have become more important — holidays with pay, pay for sick leave, cheap canteen facilities, free overalls, etc.

23.2.1 Piecework plans

1 The general characteristics of the first of the piecework plans were:

(a) Largely they were designed for individuals or at least based on as small a group of workers as possible; the philosophy being that motivation had to be as direct as possible for the people concerned.

(b) Reward was proportional to effort. Wages of operatives were directly geared to output. If a graph was drawn of an original piecework scheme it would show a straight line rising from zero output and zero pay.

(c) The shortest possible operating period for the incentive was introduced. This was either a day or a week.

(d) Incentive schemes were as simple as possible; simple enough to allow operatives to calculate their pay easily.

(e) The schemes were applied to workers who could directly affect their output.

(f) Two basic pieces of data were used — standard time per unit and normal time per unit. Schemes were normally geared to allow a one-third bonus plus basic rate to be earned. At normal time no bonus was earned.

(g) Direct labour costs, therefore, were constant for all levels of output. The actual unit cost was the same as the standard labour cost.

(h) Two workers operating the same equipment producing the same output were paid the same. Other factors such as seniority or consistency in output were not rewarded.

(i) Occasionally when loose standards were given or when a downturn in company sales occurred, employers attempted to cut the rates arbitrarily. This often led to strikes and other industrial unrest.

(j) Once a job rate had been agreed, operatives had a vested self interest in maintaining the way in which the job was carried out. Innovation or change of any kind tended to be resisted. If it was accepted then a special 'buying out' payment was usually made.

(k) Many schemes were (indeed still are) subject to some form of manipulation of output rates and work booking by operatives. Production management often failed to control malpractices because of the considerable effort needed constantly to monitor and renegotiate established output rates. A more serious failing has been high work-waiting time and unmeasured work embodied in a payment-by-results scheme so engineering high payments for little results.

(l) Quality often suffered when piecework was applied, especially when the schemes allowed payment for bad as well as good production. Allocating blame for rejected work was not always easy, especially if many operatives were making the same products on different shifts.

(m) It was often difficult to prevent plant-wide repercussions when one time-rate was changed.

(n)   The most widely known and commonly used method of payment was for output only — i.e. the system was a 'mono-factor' one.
(o)   A scheme once negotiated was not open for renegotiation unless the method changed or some governing environmental factor altered.
(p)   Facilities were available to ensure that the bonus was achievable — e.g. correct type of work, sharp tools, good maintenance.
(q)   Basic hourly rates were guaranteed.
(r)   Each scheme was 'made to measure', not stolen from some other part of the factory — or from another factory altogether.

2   Usefulness of individual PBR schemes:

Direct incentives appeared to be most useful where:

(a)   Large numbers of employees were engaged, doing roughly the same kind of work.
(b)   There was a large degree of product homogeneity.
(c)   The operations carried out were based on individually manned machines and not team groups.
(d)   Output was relatively easy to count and control.
(e)   Work content of various products did not differ significantly; operations mainly had a short cycle and were easily measured.

3   Defects in PBR systems:

Such systems often had the following defects:

(a)   Industrial relations suffered, occasionally severely, owing to the constant niggling inherent in negotiating the initial payment, and subsequent problems which arose when operatives could not manipulate the system as well as they would like.
(b)   There have been occasions where workers competed against each other and 'dog-eat-dog' situations developed.
(c)   As counter to (b) trade unions and shop stewards often felt the need to ensure that all operatives tacitly agreed an overall performance which tended to equalise pay between similar machines and jobs, irrespective of the true desires of operatives.

   While the past tense has been used in describing original PBR incentives, most of the factors quoted still apply where such schemes exist.

4   Alternatives to 'straight line' piecework:

Various options to the straight line mono-factor system were quickly devised — the straight lines, for example, were transformed into curves, ellipses, hyperboles and differential axial intercepts. Among the more commonly applied derivatives are:

(a) Standard hour plan. In this system the operative is allowed a standard time to complete each unit of production. Normally the operative is paid at base rate for a standard performance. If he achieves a unit of production in less than the standard time the bonus paid is usually:

$$\text{Standard time} - \text{actual time taken} \times \text{base rate}$$

Such payment schemes can be applied to group activities as well as for individuals. Standard minutes earned is often a less emotional debating point than money.

(b) Differential time plan. These are useful where work is difficult to measure. A simple way of introducing such a system is to determine a standard performance or task level; then pay a low base rate for output below the standard performance and a high rate for production beyond standard. So what occurs is a stepped bonus scheme with the step being adjusted to suit local conditions. A series of steps can be introduced at various performance levels, if this appears necessary.

Such systems are appropriate where sustained and fixed levels of production are required. In its approach therefore, it has many similarities to measured day work. A key factor is the performance where the step occurs and the height of the step. The bonus paid can be calculated as follows:

$$\text{Below target performance} = \text{hours worked} \times \text{base rate}$$

$$\text{Above target performance} = \text{step} \times \text{rate per hour}$$

(c) Taylor differential piece-rate plan. F. W. Taylor was one of the early payment systems specialists in the USA who soon recognised the inherent motivation to produce more implicit in the differential time plan. A generous reward could be made to those who achieved a specified level of production and 'punishments' given to those who did not.

Taylor established a high standard performance (task) and then used high hourly rates to ensure that wages were (say) 125 per cent of standard. He might have set a rate of (say) one dollar for standard performance. For less than this, the operative might be paid seventy-five cents. For above standard performance one dollar twenty-five cents.

Payment therefore, could be established as follows:

$$\text{Pay} = \text{output produced} \times \text{function} \times \text{base rate}$$

The 'function' was the elements in the scheme which established the levels where pay rates changed.

(d)   Merrick differential piece-rate plan. Taylor attempted to divide workers into high and low earners. Merrick (and many workers) disliked the punitive nature of the Taylor system. Merrick, therefore, devised a system where basic rate was paid up to eighty-three per cent of standard task performance (i.e. up to normal output). Between this point and standard task performance a ten per cent step in payment rates was introduced. Above standard task performance twenty per cent extra bonus was paid.

Merrick's plans, like Taylor's, paid the rate earned for all output achieved, not just for the extra output.

The Merrick plan proved useful in situations where operatives were transferred from daywork to piecework. It limited the severity of the Taylor plan and as such is more applicable in a more enlightened age.

(e)   Halsey constant partial sharing plan (premium plan). Fixed minimum time rates were not part of the Taylor and Merrick plans. These came with the Halsey plan. Halsey suggested that past performance could be used as a basis for establishing a standard level of performance (low task standard). Above this level payment would be equal to base rate × actual time worked plus base rate × 50 per cent of the time saved.

The incentive is obviously less than in either the Taylor or Merrick differential time plans. Actual output rates could vary considerably. It is a plan which has been used fairly widely where many of the factors which influence output are not under the control of operatives.

(f) . 40–60 constant sharing plan. The 40–60 plan provided a minimum payment of 60 per cent of time rates at a zero performance. The 50 per cent share in the Halsey scheme is replaced by 40 per cent. The scheme is useful for learner operatives who require a fairly long training period.

(g)   Bedaux 100 per cent sharing plan. This has proved to be one of the most durable and popular payment systems and in many ways is a standard hour plan of the type mentioned earlier.

Bedaux used the 60–80 rating scales and the plan guaranteed base rate up to a 60 rating. Operatives gain full bonus for all savings made from extra output. The formula used in the standard hour plan would apply in this system.

(h)   Rowan variable sharing plan. The plan which has been popular in the engineering industry attempts to divide hours saved so that the company and the operative gain more or less at various performance levels. The share to the operative is high at low efficiencies and gradually sinks as higher efficiencies are gained.

The scheme is effective where standards are loose for various reasons. Wages drift should be curtailed to some extent. Galloping incentives are avoided.

A formula which pays $33\frac{1}{3}$ per cent bonus at a 100 performance (on the BSS scale) has been given the title of the 'modified Rowan plan'.

The formula for calculating pay under the standard Rowan plan is:

$$\text{Pay} = \frac{(\text{Rate per hour} \times \text{hours worked}) + \text{hours taken} + \text{hours saved}}{\text{Hours allowed}}$$

(i)   Variations on the plans briefly quoted above were devised by Barth and
        Emerson. The former introduced a variation on the Rowan plan that uses
        a horizontal parabola as a payment line. It rises more quickly than piece-
        work at lower levels of output and then declines at higher levels.
             Emerson introduced a plan which gave base wages at low tasks and
        then continued on a parabolic curve.

23.2.2   Other payment systems

Either because PBR had been tried unsuccessfully or perhaps because the
production process did not lend itself to piecework systems, other methods of
payment have been developed.

1   Multi-factor incentives

Incentives with a single output measurement (i.e. production units) have serious
drawbacks. Quality and reject considerations, for example, often are very
important. Lateness, absenteeism, and timekeeping generally become significant when group organisations are needed for production purposes.
     To answer these problems some incentives are designed to take account of
factors other than output. Multi-factor incentives satisfy this requirement.
     Modern industrial technology is forcing the pace towards multi-factor
incentives:

Group as opposed to individual jobs are now common;
Material is an ever increasing cost and high utilisation is important;
High versus continuous machine utilisation in many process industries is
important.

Multi-factor incentives provide the basis for:

Enlarging the incentive, making it more compatible with company requirements;
Greater flexibility can be engendered which will allow improved attitudes to
be fostered;
The nature of the incentive can be more closely related to the 'output' of the
company, if not the 'value';
Administration costs might be lower than with single factor incentives.

The incentives might cover some or even all of the following:

Production
Machine utilisation
Material utilisation
Absenteeism
Process control
Quality
Consumption of services — power, packages, maintenance, etc.
Orders delivered on time
Orders produced in the right sequence
Punctuality

The usual methods of applying multi-factor incentives have been through multiplication, addition and modification methods.

The multiplication method gives an equal potential bonus to each factor by setting a standard for each in the same way as for 'production', i.e. a fallback or base rate level and a bonus level. Points then are given for the achievement of each factor, to be converted eventually into money, by multiplying together parts achieved for each factor.

It is possible to stress the importance of particular factors by setting higher standards.

The addition scheme apportions bonus requirements between the factors as desired by management and agreed with unions. A basic weakness is that bonus could be earned from one factor alone (unlike the multiplication method).

In the modification method a man-bonus scale is set for the main factor which in turn would be multiplied by the percentage achievement of a second factor. It lacks the flexibility of the other two methods.

The extra factors must, of course, be measurable and, following normal PBR practice, controllable by operatives and not by other agencies. Normally no more than three factors are built into the system (it being impossible for the operative to emphasise one of the factors at the expense of the rest). It may be necessary to train operatives in the ways in which material can be saved or machine utilisation improved.

2 High day rate

Where machines or processes dominate production activities, as in many chemical plants, the need for direct incentive payments is not always crucial in achieving high productivity. In these circumstances high day rates are often paid. Any differentials in pay are usually based on the application of job evaluation.

There can be considerable advantages to management in applying high day rate in appropriate circumstances. These include:

(a)   There should be few squabbles about differentials — or even about what rating a particular job should have.
(b)   Wage payment is simple and should involve minimum administration.
(c)   Deployment of labour, particularly in moving people from one job to another, should be easy.
(d)   Methods changes should not be obstructed (except perhaps where these have a clearly adverse effect on the labour content of a job).

There are obvious weaknesses. These include:

(e)   As such, high day rates do not motivate — i.e. there will have to be other inducements (status, work content, job satisfaction) to act as motivators.
(f)   While merit rating or job evaluation can be employed to provide the means for differentials, inevitably some squabbles will arise.
(g)   Potential conflict could also arise from having jobs needing unequal effort.
(h)   Management has to be sure that it can gain requisite production levels from using machine and other controls. This may not always be possible.

3   Measured daywork

As an alternative to individual incentives, many organisations have introduced measured daywork. This is a method where operatives, shop stewards and trade unions enter into a bargain or contract with management, whereby a certain level of output is to be maintained. Output can be established at a particular level or on an output curve.

At regular intervals, checks are made to ensure that contracted performance is being obtained. Pay gradings are determined from actual performance and can be based on a bonus graph, with a built in provision for failure to meet a contracted requirement. In this latter case, the pay of operatives is reduced.

Normally work measurement is used to help to arrive at contracted production levels, but there are occasions when management assessments of the required production level are used (e.g. the speed of a vehicle building track).

The advantages to management include:

(a)   Many of the industrial relations problems which occur with individual PBR disappear (though others might take their place). A more mature negotiating situation is likely to develop.
(b)   Management is able to forecast the output which will be achieved, so making production planning much easier than it occasionally is under individual PBR schemes.

(c) Control of earnings is facilitated. Wage drift can be mostly eliminated.
(d) Opposition to change, particularly technological change, is often reduced.
(e) Administration is limited.
(f) Labour deployment and redeployment are facilitated.

For employees, the advantages include a guaranteed take-home wage, more sustainable and perhaps easier to earn than in an individual PBR scheme.

However, many measured daywork schemes have been abandoned owing to lack of management control. The scheme is not so self-managing as individual PBR and needs constant monitoring by management and particularly the application of downgrading when contractual production is not achieved.

4 Premium payment plan

This is an incentive payment similar in many ways to measured daywork but performance is calculated at quite long time intervals — e.g. monthly, so that pay stability is very high.

5 Plant-wide incentives

Disenchantment with individual payment by results schemes and to a lesser extent measured daywork, led to consideration of plant-wide incentives. The main element in such schemes is the degree of economic knowledge if not discipline which must play a leading part in determining incentive payments.

The schemes have been given various names:

Scanlon type plan, share of production plan, Rucker plan etc. depending upon the details of the application.

However, each scheme has the following general attributes:

(a) The payment of incentive is based on the overall economic success of the organisation. This can be measured as added-value, sales revenue or profit.
(b) Production and non-production personnel can share equally well — or one section only can participate.
(c) Outside influences (e.g. inflation or raw material price rises) can be taken into account. They can be used in the calculation of economic results or discounted with the personnel taking part in the scheme.
(d) Calculation of results is largely done through the accounting system. There is no need for accurate work measurement.

The benefits to management include:

(e)   A certain degree of understanding of the business is required of participants in the scheme. This, it is hoped, will produce more rational thinking and debate in wage bargaining.

(f)   The administration costs should be low.

(g)   Improvements in:
      Product quality
      Materials productivity
      Delivery performance
      Factory services utilisation
    should emerge.

(h)   Co-operation not rivalry between production and service units should be fostered.

(i)   Communication must inevitably improve and a sense of participation be engendered.

However, there are drawbacks:

(j)   Traditional PBR schemes tend to insulate the work force from direct competition — e.g. if a competitor produces a better product, overall company profit may decline but PBR results (for those still in employment) remain the same. Under a plant-wide scheme corporate failures have a direct impact on wages payment.

(k)   Individual skills or effort are not rewarded as such. This could depress some people's earnings and perhaps output generally. This breaks one of the canons of Taylorism. The relationship between effort and reward is often a tenuous one.

(l)   The stimulus for action must come from an industrial relations climate where co-operation and the drive to participate is high. Many organisations have not got this degree of IR support.

(m) Management must be both sincere and adept at explaining the basis of the schemes. This is not always possible. A demanding style of management which encourages co-operation is required.

(n)   Where there is a likelihood that there will be a decline in added value or sales revenue, such schemes will inevitably run into some trouble.

Chapter 24 — Second generation incentives — carries the debate further.

6   *Group as opposed to individual incentives*

In some production activities group incentives are necessary because of the work organisation. Production lines or flow process industries are inevitable candidates for group incentives (though many work study people of long standing would still plump — nearly automatically — for individual schemes despite their administrative cost and all their drawbacks).

The following aspects need to be considered in thinking about group schemes:

(a)   Group schemes should ensure smaller administration cost.
(b)   Is the group scheme to be tried out on an interdependent team?
(c)   Will the group be so established as to provide pressure on lazy team members?
(d)   Will the group be a natural one and reasonably small?
(e)   Will the group be able to calculate its earnings easily?

7   Merit rating

Not all employees work equally hard or conscientiously and in many organisations some are more valuable than others.

It has happened, however, that merit rating, no matter how well constructed, caused jealousies and petty friction of all kinds. Usually a merit rating committee is established where at least one union representative or shop steward sits. Employees are then rated against established criteria; points being awarded for diligence, good quality work, good time keeping, co-operation, etc.

23.3   OTHER FACTORS IN WAGE PAYMENT SYSTEMS

There could be many elements within a payment system additional to the kind of payment systems which have been briefly described. Among these are:

1   Attendance money. It seems faintly absurd to have to pay people to come to work, but when absenteeism runs at ten per cent or more, it starts to make sense. The bonus — which is what it is — is paid for lateness or absence below a specified limit.

   However, where workers already feel that they are paid sufficient for them to take one or two days off fairly regularly, paying an attendance bonus may have little effect.

2   Conditions payments. Occasionally workers may be asked to work in conditions or situations which are abnormal. Maintenance personnel could work inside boilers or machinery of some kind. It is usual that extra payments are made in these situations.

3   Shift allowance. Most companies will pay an allowance for workers who regularly work shifts.

4   Training allowances. Until an operative is fully trained and can achieve a standard performance, a training allowance is paid. This is fairly high at the

beginning of the training period and gradually declines as proficiency is gained.

5   Mobility pay. To ensure that operatives will be willing to operate more than one machine, payment for mobility is made. An operative will train to become proficient in several types of activity.

6   Overtime. This is another normal payment which in some instances would form a considerable part of total pay.

7   Lieu bonuses. Where operatives are unable to earn a bonus or their work is incapable of having an incentive applied for it, lieu bonuses are paid as a compensation. Otherwise operatives may be unwilling to work on the operation.

8   Average bonus. Where an operative is taken off an incentive job for some reason, he will normally be paid the average bonus of the shop if the removal is at management's convenience.

9   Job grading. This often provides a differential payment which more skilled people will gain. Companies might use job grading as a means of raising pay rates in times of wage restraint.

23.4   GENERAL COMMENT ON PAY SYSTEMS

1   Why change a pay system?

Perhaps the following are the principal reasons:

(a)   Increased productivity is required as well as increased output.
(b)   Administration of the current scheme is too expensive.
(c)   Current schemes are a major cause of poor industrial relations.
(d)   Incentives need to be extended to other personnel in the company as well as those currently having incentive earnings.
(e)   Manipulation of the current scheme is on a large scale.
(f)   The scheme is out of control — e.g. wages drift is considerable.
(g)   Change is restricted, especially the introduction of new methods and equipment.
(h)   Payment is not sufficiently influenced by the operatives taking part in the scheme.
(i)   Loss of earnings through factors outside the control of the operatives has increased.

   Not all these reasons need a new system. It is likely that increased control will solve some of them but in practice it is often reasonable to have a new system which will provide a new start so avoiding the tensions associated with tightening up a scheme which has developed serious defects.

2   Trade union attitudes to incentives

Experience suggests that operatives look for the following in the pay schemes they accept:

(a)   Their take-home pay from week to week should remain fairly constant. This seems to be reasonable when most people have fixed outgoings — rent, mortgage, food, etc.

(b)   There is ability within the scheme to ensure that the fixed take-home pay can be manipulated — i.e. an operative can work hard or not in order to produce earnings which are acceptable to him. He is able to balance the need for effort with the reward it brings him along fairly well-defined lines.

(c)   The scheme is simple enough to allow an operative of even moderate academic ability to calculate the relationship between effort and reward.

(d)   The system should be seen to be equitable between jobs requiring differing skills and efforts. No-one wants to work on a job which he knows is rated low in the payment system, where timings are tight and control too close.

(e)   There is some evidence to suggest that the negotiations inherent in arriving at a compromise in a payment system (i.e. in the standards established) are used as part of the industrial relations activity. The negotiations relating to the payment system are usually no worse or better than the current IR situation allows.

(f)   There is evidence that the wage bargaining system has, in many plants, been the means whereby a worker–management dialogue is carried on. Without it joint consultation would have been meaningless. Wage payment negotiations provide a forum for a debate on a whole series of matters which otherwise might not have been raised. This side effect could be important in looking at and perhaps revising wage payment systems.

3   Management and wage payment systems

(a)   It would obviously be useful if wage systems could be devised which help to engender co-operation from shopfloor personnel and a feeling that the economic success of the company is of equal importance to workers and managers alike.

(b)   The initiative for wage increases largely stems from organised labour. This puts management at a disadvantage in the subsequent negotiations — they are usually on the defensive. A wages system where management and workers negotiate without duress would be beneficial.

(c)   Many if not most PBR schemes concentrate on the quantitative rather than qualitative aspects of production. A situation where each factor is given its due importance would have merit to many production managers.

(d) Wage payment systems should be such that they generate co-ordination and co-operation between individuals, units or groups, departments and functions within the organisation.

(e) The system should engender change, particularly the introduction of new methods and equipment.

(f) Schemes should be comparatively simple from two points of view. The workers should understand them. Management would obviously like as little administration as possible.

(g) Schemes should help to achieve overall company objectives. For example, an incentive should not hinder the production control process.

4   Wages drift

Unfortunately many companies (perhaps most) who have introduced payment or reward systems based on work study values suffer from wages drift. This, briefly, is the condition where an increasing amount of money is paid for the same level of output. It can be measured in several ways. Direct wages per standard hour or standard time measurement is the usual one. The drift can be graphed and perhaps issued on a monthly or quarterly basis.

Drift can be an important problem and a major cause of economic decline.

There are three main reasons for drift:

(a) The schemes themselves. Loose values will be the main factor. Either the original studies were badly carried out or too much was given away during negotiation concerning either the values or the rating. The result will be seen in high earnings and 'high point hours'.

The schemes may be corrupt in some way. The payments curve could be badly or inadequately drawn. Some factor may have been missed out when the curve was designed. 'Padding' could have been built into the scheme.

The wages structure generally is too complicated and has built in anomalies which allow the unions constantly to renegotiate the 'wages package'.

(b) Failure of management control. Lack of a good work booking system is often crucial in containing drift. If various irregularities are allowed to creep into the scheme — like extra teabreaks or allowances which were not originally negotiated, then they quickly become 'custom and practice' for the union and so unchangeable.

'Fiddling' often becomes a way of life for many operatives. A boring job will push many reasonably intelligent workers into the only really intellectual challenge they face — fiddling their work booking sheets.

They become experts at it — far better than management who have many other intellectual preoccupations.

Management control is often lax over the 'allowances' elements which have been negotiated. For example in:

Payments for waiting time (normally at average bonus)

Payments for unmeasured work (normally at average bonus)

('Average bonus' for all sorts of conditions, from activities where development of some kind is occurring to visits to the surgery, is usually a major negotiating factor for unions and shop stewards.)

(c)   Unforeseen factors. While all circumstances should be foreseen to some extent, there are factors which it might be difficult to take into account when negotiating wages, such as levels of output. The economics of production are often such that a minor downturn in business will push up wage rates as a ratio of output very quickly. This is especially true when direct labour has to be viewed as a fixed cost. Payments for 'waiting time' could rise dramatically.

5   A wages structure

A wages structure is a collection of differential wage rates, paid to people in an organisation, which has been determined (it is hoped) by some soundly based and accepted criteria. The judgement might reflect differential skills, responsibilities, authorities, long service, qualifications, job conditions, age, and experience.

The structure may reflect the comparative power of the negotiating parties — one trade union or several, management or the people with specific skills who maintain a closed door on recruitment.

It seems rare to find a wages structure which has been determined solely by the logical application of job evaluation or some other equally sound method. The external labour market will influence the pay rates of certain types of labour. The national agreements achieved by certain unions will have to be introduced locally.

It is important in reviewing a wages structure and the pay differentials within it to determine what constitutes a wage being paid, i.e. base rates, overtime, shift premium, condition money, incentive, etc. Skilled people on day shift and working without an incentive should not really complain if semiskilled operatives working on a three shift basis on incentives earn more from a lower base rate.

6   Factors influencing payment systems

Why companies choose one form of payment system in preference to any other often appears an arbitrary decision. Lupton and Gowler [5] have put forward what appears to be a logically structured 'sieve' from which it should be possible to determine the most suitable type of payment system.

In practice company history and the general industrial relations climate often appear to be the most dominant determinants. The kind of incentive which would have been applied in a factory making nuts and bolts in 1900 is neither appropriate nor necessarily acceptable on a semiconductor production line in the 1970s.

Perhaps the following should be considered in thinking about payment systems.

(a)   Management. Its competence. How much power and authority it still holds. The degree of control over work activities of all kinds which is exercised by management. The more control, the more likely that measured daywork and factory-wide incentives will be appropriate.

(b)   The products manufactured. If these are homogeneous and made with short cycle operations where the operative can influence output considerably, then some form of payment by results could be required.

(c)   The manufacturing technology. The more process- or line-orientated the manufacturing technology is, the less likely that individual payment by results schemes will be suitable.

(d)   Cost components. The cost of labour may only be a small part of total factory costs. Maximising the use of labour through an incentive could be counter productive.

(e)   The external and internal environment. Among the more important of these will be:
       Trade union attitudes — what is acceptable
       Supply of labour — skills and age
       The need for change. The stability of the industry
       National agreements. Government policy and legislation
       General payments.

(f)   Company problems and opportunities:
       Absenteeism
       Labour turnover
       Difference between standard output and current output rates
       Mobility — actual and needed
       Age of workers and composition (female and male)
       Number of trade unions
       Job stoppages (strikes) and duration
       Disputes over pay.

23.5   RECENT TRENDS

Since the 1939–45 war the advance of mass production techniques and increase in capital investment has led some industries to believe that plant-wide payment systems such as measured daywork have benefits over individual incentives. Taylor-type payment by results schemes, it was suggested, perpetuated individual self-interest, and failed to promote the factory-wide flexibility which large scale investment needed.

Individual piecework schemes seemed to have many anomalies. Wages drift was nearly normal and the perpetual crises which individual PBR schemes seemed to generate made industrial relations very difficult to handle. 'Rationality', it was thought, would reflect the increasing intelligence and sophistication of workers at all levels.

Partly as a consequence of the failings in PBR many organisations in the UK in the late sixties decided to introduce productivity schemes or bargains for which the Fawley scheme set an example.

At that time the National Board for Prices and Incomes countenanced such agreements and for a while productivity bargaining was the only way a pay rise could be given.

Various principles governing such agreements were stipulated:

1 Workers had to make clear and demonstrable contribution to increased productivity.
2 Work measurement was to be used to measure productivity gains.
3 Even when new investment was taken into account unit costs had to decline.
4 The bargain had to be appropriately controlled.
5 The consumer had to gain from the bargain in some way.
6 An agreement had to bear any consequential cost which was incurred elsewhere in the organisation.

As in multi-factor incentives, productivity bargains were designed to buy out bad practices — poor timekeeping, low product quality, overmanning, lack of flexibility, inability to recruit key workers.

However, once it was realised that it was the 'bad boys' — those who had kept restrictive practices and could bargain with them — who gained most, the activity went into decline. A variety of non-productive 'productivity' bargains was also made which sent it into greater disrepute.

Shortly after productivity bargaining was in vogue some organisations put their faith in measured daywork. But like productivity bargaining, measured daywork often produced less benefits than were anticipated, mainly, it seemed, because managers did not manage the system.

It was nearly inevitable that output fell when operatives realised that they still received a guaranteed wage no matter how hard they worked. The benefits to them of stable earnings and more job security were apparently largely taken for granted. So backward glances at the days when piecework was in operation were made and in some companies measured daywork has been abandoned.

Yet at the same time there has come a slow realisation that there has to be an improved relationship between pay and productivity. Many organisations, for example, use added value as a means of monitoring pay and productivity, if not for the actual basis of wages payment.

23.6 INCENTIVES IN THE FUTURE

Like so much futurology, guessing about the future of incentives could be dangerous, most of all when set in a British context. However, some comment on the current and possible future state of incentives seems essential.

A recent survey in the USA [2] suggests that wage incentives generally are holding their own. There is no significant trend towards a disenchantment with such schemes. A shortage of industrial engineering personnel is the main factor preventing an increase in wage incentive applications.

In manufacturing industry in the USA the survey suggests that ninety-five per cent of the companies surveyed use work measurement while fifty-nine per cent have wage incentive applications. Even union leaders are thought to favour incentives by two to one, though this shows a decline from a survey carried out seventeen years earlier. The standard hour type is the most popular type of incentive.

Over two-thirds of the schemes had been introduced more than twelve years ago and most use time study as the basis for determining standards. Most schemes are audited on a random or continuous basis.

(Production managers might like to know that from the survey sample forty per cent of the respondents said that they had management incentives. Largely these were based on profit sharing.)

The Swedish Employers' Confederation [3] considered the future of wage systems quite deeply, in the light of all the changes in work organisation which have occurred in that country. They suggest the following:

1   Wages in manufacturing will continue to consist of some form of payment by results, though fixed take-home pay will increase as a proportion of the total.
2   Bonus systems will be based increasingly on production groups or entire shops, reinforcing the objectives embodied in the work organisation.
3   Wages will be based partly on job evaluation data and partly on the competence and skills of individuals. Wages within a group will be related to the degrees of difficulty of the tasks performed and the ability shown.
4   The system of relating jobs to wage determination will still be based on job evaluation. But it will be necessary to develop new forms of this technique to allow (and to pay for) job flexibility and even the spontaneous movement of workers.
5   Stressful working environments and physically demanding jobs must be seen to be essential parts of the reward system. This can be done best by a separate wage supplement.

6   The wage system will need to accommodate factors other than 'effort' in an individual's attempts to improve his pay. Knowledge of new technologies or the economics of his company should provide the basis for wage rate improvement.

7   Production profit sharing has already been widely introduced in Sweden, based on a simple efficiency index (not the classical profit sharing system).

8   The wage system developed will be applied equally to blue and white collar workers and also management.

Everyone who works in a self contained shop or on a production line should have a fixed monthly wage with a bonus based on shop or line performance.

These are Swedish views and the warning must again be given that what will serve one nation, industry or company well, will not necessarily suit another. There is no one method of ensuring co-operation and high output which is applicable for all organisations. The scheme or schemes chosen will depend upon production methods, type of product made, management skills and style, local and national cultures, work organisation, the development of relationships in the company and perhaps above all its incentive history. It is likely, however, that the following points will need to be taken into consideration when discussing wage payment systems and incentives:

9   Where mistrust and low productivity exist and current incentives seem to be failing to motivate, a productivity bonus may be effective, especially if it links together production and other factors normally excluded from individual payment by results. 'Productivity' could be plant-wide, line or even part of a production line.

10   Two-tier incentives may be useful. A bottom layer based on PBR might be overlaid by a plant-wide bonus scheme.

11   Over the next few years change is likely to accelerate rather than decline. What kind of payment system will help to foster change rather than prevent it?

12   Incentives and wage payment systems might' be used for improving productivity and also to become part of the life style of people within an organisation [4].

13   Will advancing the status of shopfloor workers — as has happened in ICI and other companies — reflect how pay and productivity relationships are established? Is there a possibility of moving from high performance incentives to full salaried status?

14   Why not ask working groups what method of payment would suit them? This is not suggested facetiously for many shop stewards have ideas on payment systems which are worth listening to.

15   Wilde [1] comments on a survey covering 316 companies and the experience they have had with using incentives over the last fifteen years. Seventy-eight per cent of these companies said their incentive schemes

either had failed completely or had major weaknesses. While no strong conclusion can be drawn from such a sample, it does show that the past application of (it is assumed) PBR incentives, is fraught with some danger.

NOTES

1   Some useful descriptions of these payment types, their weaknesses and applications, appear in *Work Study Magazine* from September 1977 to January 1978. (Author E. Wilde)
2   R. S. Rice, 'Survey of Work Measurement and Wage Incentives in the USA', *Management Services*, January 1978.
3   *Job Reform in Sweden*, Swedish Employers' Confederation, 1975.
4   P. J. Butcher and F. T. Mountford. 'Problems of Productivity', *Management Services*, November 1977.
5   T. Lupton and D. Gowler, *Selecting a Wage Payment System*, Engineering Employers' Federation, 1975.

24

Wages policies and associated negotiations

24.1 INTRODUCTION

It is perhaps paradoxical that wages seem to cause the largest number of strikes and industrial relations troubles (though other hidden causes may be the real problem) yet not all organisations develop a coherent wages policy. A policy by definition needs to be well considered and widely understood by all those who are covered by it. It is nearly axiomatic that the policy should be 'open' — that is a knowledge of pay rates and salaries should be available to everyone.

24.2 ASPECTS OF WAGES POLICY

A wages policy should cover all the following factors if it is to be seen to be fair:

1 It must engender trust. No-one must feel that he is being treated unfairly or that others are being given better treatment. 'Relative deprivation' should be eliminated.
2 Rewards for skill, effort, responsibility and achievement must be seen to be awarded equitably throughout the organisation, whether on the shop-floor, office, laboratory or Board Room. It seems particularly important that fairness is seen to operate cross-functionally as well as within a function. There should be a basis for establishing relativities which will provide appropriate rewards for skill etc.
3 Job pay rates should be comparable with similar jobs in other industries of the same type. Workers must feel that their company pays as well as others for the same skills.

4   A living wage should be paid. Definition of this varies throughout the world but within one national economy wage levels should match economic reality and material aspirations.

5   There should be an inbuilt means of improving individual wage levels, either through productivity incentives, salary progressions or promotion prospects. A concomitant of a wages policy, therefore, is a promotion structure which will provide an appropriate degree of opportunity for wage/salary advancement.

6   The wage has to be seen to be fair in relationship to what shareholders receive.

7   Fringe benefits may provide a considerable part of an income. This factor should be recognised and discounted for people who are not able to achieve fringe benefits.

8   Conditions of work must be taken into account in providing income levels. Hazards of all kinds should be recognised within a job and appropriate rewards paid for them.

9   Perhaps controversially, wages should be kept within the hierarchy which has been established by national trade union negotiations — e.g. if one set of craftsmen gain an advantage nationally it is unlikely that this advantage can be withheld locally for any length of time.

10   Wages are of little use if job continuity is not maintained. While Government legislation will protect a worker from unfair dismissal the complete shutdown of a factory or organisation could be disastrous. The problem of long term employment, the need for appropriate strategies and capital investment should be discussed when wages policies are established.

24.3   METHODS OF ESTABLISHING A WAGES POLICY

1   What can the company afford?

This is not the usual starting point for most wages policies. While it will be impossible to start afresh and suggest that the wages and salaries should only be X per cent of sales revenue or cost of sales, a review of that type should be made. For example —

To maintain the company's profit position a ten per cent return on investment (ROI) is required equivalent to £1 million.

	£ million
Material	5.0
Power	1.0
Packages	0.5
General overhead	2.0
	8.5
Sales revenue will be	15.0
Total costs except wages	8.5
Remainder available for ROI and wages	6.5
(Wages previous year	5.0)

So if the required ROI is to be obtained the extra wages available during the year are £0.5 million.

While this approach will seem naïve to many production managers it is at least a useful starting point in discussing the realities of the wage situation.

Wage budgeting, as suggested in Chapter 25 (second generation incentives) should be an important aspect of establishing and then controlling what the company can afford.

2   *Establishing relativities/job evaluation*

Job evaluation has been comparatively successful in many organisations. Often it has been applied to clerical rather than manual workers as the application appears to be easier in clerical routines. There seems to be no reason why job evaluation should not be used throughout an organisation — on general labourers or a purchasing manager.

The more common method of job evaluation uses a predetermined set of evaluation factors each of which has been allocated a number of standard or reference points. Even this can cause dissension among various employees. For example, an employee on an assembly line will demand the highest possible number of points for manual dexterity or a need to work in poor environmental conditions.

A clerical worker may, equally, consider that educational achievements demand a higher rating.

The standard points allocation, therefore, could distort the whole exercise. Some organisations (like consultants HAY/MSL) have produced standard points allocation packages and it would be advantageous to use these wherever possible — if local conditions do not allow equitable points distribution.

Job evaluation is fully covered in Chapter 16 and reference should be made to this chapter.

3   *Establishing wage levels*

It seems comparatively easy to determine what monetary reward is given for each job point in a job evaluation exercise. In practice, however, this might mean that every job in an organisation has a different job rate. This would present difficulties in salary administration. The normal procedure would be to link various jobs together into grades which provide a common salary band as well as salary progression.

Each job should be given a 'living wage' rate to which the job evaluated points rating should be added. The effect of this should be to limit the effect of job points evaluation somewhat, the differential being applied only to wages/salaries paid above a base wage.

Either as an alternative to the job evaluation points pay method or as a support to it, it may be necessary to bring jobs together in a general way within a pay scale, so determining a wages ladder. It could, therefore, either help to iron out discrepancies in the job evaluation procedure or, conversely, distort it, depending upon the ability of the people or team concerned.

If a money payment is made for each job evaluated point which has been gained, the squeezing of differentials should — theoretically — not occur, unless the proportion of evaluated wage to base rate is changed. However, conversely, flat rises of £X per week, which have been offered by governments over the last few years, will effectively destroy the job evaluated differentials.

4   Incentives

The means for rewarding extra effort have been in operation for a long time on the shopfloor. Individual payment by results has so far predominated.

If, however, incentives or rewards for skill, effort and achievements are needed for services or administration personnel then individual PBR schemes will not be appropriate. For non-shopfloor areas the second generation incentive should be investigated.

24.4   OPERATION OF PAY POLICIES

1   Free collective bargaining

Though lauded by most trade union leaders, at plant level free collective bargaining may only reflect the power structure which exists between different unions and between unions and management. Free collective bargaining therefore may distort and corrupt any wages policy based on relativity of skills and effort etc. Various industry unions — newspaper publishing is probably one — seem to be able to extract wages and conditions far in excess of the true worth of the jobs being performed.

Power therefore, has to be recognised in establishing wages policies. It will distort relativities, cause disruption in settling wage disputes and perhaps hinder the establishment of any kind of policy. Trade union leaders nationally, and shop stewards locally, will always be reluctant to forgo the power they have and the benefits this brings to their members. This should not be an excuse for management not to attempt to introduce methods and policies which provide equity between all employees in an organisation. How far a wages policy can be pushed will show who controls the industrial system.

2   Trade union involvement

Despite the comments in 1, nowhere is trade union involvement more needed than in the establishment of a wages policy. Uncertainty, according to

Brown [1], is a strong motivator for wage demands. To create a situation where uncertainty is lessened if not eliminated seems a useful way of discussing wages policy. Trade union involvement, therefore, should start further back than discussions on wages policy. The state of the company and the consequent need for a policy should be debated first. If general agreement cannot be gained here then debates about wages policy will be meaningless.

Nationally a state has been reached where (to quote Brown again) some dockers are paid twice as much as young teachers as a result of their bargaining power. Moving to a position where social and economic requirements and not power is the main determinant of wage levels must lie largely in the hands of national agencies, and can be little influenced by production managers — at any level.

Locally the design of wages policy might be helped by the trade unions on the basis that there is limited money available — how can it best be split up?

A 'wages council' comprising trade union, management and perhaps even shareholder interests might be assembled to debate the company's present and potential performance. It might come to a conclusion about the split of revenue into capital investment, wages, profit, etc. The split of wages into trades and functions can then be continued, hopefully in line with agreed differentials, worked out through some form of job evaluation.

3   The policy must be a policy

It is the common practice within industry for minor disputes to crop up at any time. Problems over an incentive, poor work from a previous section or operation, changes in the working environment — all might cause a demand for some revision in pay rates. It is extremely easy to solve such disputes (which could be holding up a production line) by paying a few more pence per hour on base rate or adjusting the local incentive. In consequence the immediate problem may be solved, but others will certainly arise. Once it can be seen that the policy is flexible then inevitably the traditional coach and horses will be driven through it with all the alacrity that the shopfloor can muster.

4   Methods of measuring performance

Undoubtedly the best measure of performance to be set against wages paid is added value or profit. Others relating to individual and perhaps group PBR schemes can be useful. Merit rating has also been tried but it has the disadvantage of being manipulated by the rater.

24.5   WAGE AND OTHER NEGOTIATIONS

Little has been written about the negotiations which eventually determine wage levels, particularly incentives paid to a company's employees. Both union and management often seem to see the process as a trial of strength with negotiations being taken to the brink before a settlement is agreed. Only occasionally (far less often than is popularly imagined) the ultimate weapon of physical sanction is used and a strike takes place.

Most management negotiators are aware that a totally rational approach to wage negotiations is often impossible. Politically motivated shop stewards and union officials are not usually influenced by rational argument, no matter how well presented.

Wage and other negotiations cannot be divorced from the past history of the company. If brinkmanship has been fairly constantly practised, then it will be difficult to break away from such measures in the short term.

While bargaining is the essence of wage negotiations and general industrial relations practice, compromise is the usual result. The quality of the compromise will largely depend upon the culture of the organisation and the way it does things (or does not do them) and the comparative strength of the two sides. Where one side has overwhelming strength, a dictated peace is usually arrived at and not a compromise. If a peace is made which is exploitable or damages the long term prosperity of the company, then it can be doubly dangerous.

Any two factories can have different cultures, management style and history of negotiations, but the following points seem relevant in any negotiating situation:

1   There should be a negotiating policy. This does not mean that there should be rigid rules on what to say and how to say it, but basic principles should be laid down and followed. For example, in a 'condition dispute' in which line managers have been involved, it would be detrimental to the organisation as a whole to have the personnel function or senior general management subsequently take a diametrically opposed view to local line management.

2   In addition to 1 above there should be a 'company line' — a style of doing things. This might be an easy friendly approach to union demands or a tougher more abrasive posture. If line managers and services personnel adopt opposing styles it will be easy for union negotiators to play off one set of senior personnel against another.

3   As far as possible, 'policy' should cover a large percentage of the possible areas of conflict between managers and unions. A works employees' handbook might be compiled to lay down precise rules covering work conduct etc. The possible content of such an employee handbook is given at the end of the chapter.

4   Dangers exist where an agreement is apparently reached yet the subject is still held to be negotiable. For example payment by results schemes are often considered by trade unions to have endless possibilities for negotiation and renegotiation. In some ways this may not be a bad thing as the era of productivity bargaining in the late 1960s proved. Then the buying out of

the union rule book (which some managements attempted) had the undesirable side effect of eliminating the negotiable factors which kept shop stewards busy. This tended to take away fairly minor debating points only to substitute major factors for them.

However, with the trade unions gaining more power there needs to be a balance established between responsibility and power. It seems important, therefore, for agreements between unions and management to be seen not so much as compromises but contracts with all that this word implies.

5   It is far too late to consider informing the unions or shop stewards of the 'state of the company' or 'why we can't pay higher wages' when negotiations over wages begin. This should be an ongoing process. The shopfloor should be made aware of the company's financial position by having regular issues of company performance and financial results given to them.

24.6   WORKERS' HANDBOOKS

Many organisations issue a workers' handbook to inform employees of the main terms of their employment and the amenities and facilities which the company provides. It is perhaps fair to state that often such handbooks emphasise workers' rights and soft pedal reciprocal responsibilities.

A workers' handbook should help to reduce the negotiable factors in working conditions, and eradicate ambiguity and the possibility of misunderstanding. Where there is a need for further negotiations to take place the handbook should provide a common starting point for the negotiations. It should improve communication.

A handbook might cover some or all of the following topics:

1   Working conditions

What comprises the working week
Shift working and conditions appropriate to shift working
Overtime — the amount of notice given before overtime is convened
Payment
Rest periods
Meal breaks
Time recording
Lateness and absenteeism
Work-done recording
Incentive schemes — methods of reward
Job rates
Transfer between jobs — reasons and payment
Guaranteed week, layoff pay, occasions when layoff pay will be given at full rates of pay

Sickness payments
Redundancy
Dismissal — disciplinary procedures
Grievance procedures over redundancy and dismissal
Maternity leave

2   *Holidays with pay*

Entitlement
Holiday periods
Holiday payment
Likelihood of not taking holidays during holiday periods
Statutory holidays

3   *Industrial relations and general factory grievance procedures*

Shop stewards — numbers, procedures for elections
Negotiating machinery — stages of negotiations
Trade union and negotiating procedures
Trade union membership — collection of dues
Time off from work to attend union matters
Time off from work for public duties

4   *General*

Education and training
Wages — how these are paid
Safety at work
Fire alarms and precautions
Emergency evacuation of buildings
Suggestion schemes
Long service awards
Social and sports clubs
Pension fund
Parking facilities
Change of home address
Leaving notice.

24.7   CONCLUSION

There may be little that local management can do against Government edict
and wage bargaining of the type which takes place between employers'
organisations and national trade unions. If there is an agreement to pay ten per

cent more nationally then it will be more or less mandatory locally. However, there are other things which can be established within a wages policy:

Wage differentials within a plant
Incentives related to added value or profit
The split of profit or added value gains
Wage levels generally
Grading structures
Merit rating and other performance evaluation procedures.

The benefits of a wages policy should be to:

Keep wage levels under control
Ensure equity in wage earnings
Help prevent wage drift.

NOTE

1   Wilfred Brown, *The Earnings Conflict*, Penguin Books, 1973.

25

Second generation incentives and wage payment systems

25.1 INTRODUCTION

Traditional incentives have, largely, been based on the application of time studied values related to an individual's production of product items, for which payment was made. Developments in using MTM (methods time measurement) to determine standard times, the addition of factors other than output in the wage payment (e.g. product quality or material utilisation) and the application of incentives to small groups have failed to eradicate many of the problems associated with traditional incentives. Innovation tends to be discouraged, restrictive practices encouraged, co-operation with management is not fostered, individual rather than company performance is stressed.

Many organisations are now finding that traditional payment by result schemes are outmoded, often perpetuating low productivity and occasionally counter-productive within the activites needed to raise overall company performance.

25.2 WHY A NEW APPROVAL MAY BE NEEDED

1 Traditional payment by results schemes were introduced at a time when direct labour was a key factor in raising output. Advanced technology where production is machine paced, the comparative importance of related production resources such as materials, the increasing importance of production support services such as production planning and maintenance, all suggest that it is essential to take a team approach to increasing productivity.
2 If achieving profit or added value is the main objective of any business then

incentives and motivation should be directed towards this end. Encouraging individuals to increase their own output may not necessarily result in improving added value or profit.

3   There are high pressures on management to introduce greater participation and consequently, it is hoped, improved co-operation with trade unions. Second generation incentives might be used to support participative activities, making discussions more constructive than they might be otherwise.

4   Government legislation has tended to restrict the changing of shopfloor labour levels to keep them in line with market demand. Incentives which more closely relate revenue earned by product sales to shopfloor performance may provide one alternative to redundancies in times of recession.

5   Changes in production methods, technologies and investment have to be fostered rather than restricted if worldwide as well as national competition is to be met. Positive attitudes to change need to be encouraged at all levels in any organisation, and incentives might help to do this.

6   Performance of industry generally has tended to be bedevilled by antique attitudes. The basis for wage payment may help in creating new and positive approaches to productivity — if the associated work organisations allow it.

7   Return on investment over the last few years has declined considerably when related to other economic changes. Only genuine improvements in productivity or unit cost performance will provide a basis for needed improvement.

8   The increasing power of the shopfloor may force management to make disadvantageous agreements on pay and conditions. A limit on the amount of money available for wage increases should provide a hedge against making spurious productivity deals merely to placate local trade unions.

25.3   CHARACTERISTICS OF A SECOND GENERATION INCENTIVE

Second generation incentives relate employee performance to profit, added value or sales value of production and calculate an appropriate bonus. Normally the incentive is applied to groups rather than individuals (i.e. factorywide, a production line or a working group). Attitude change is a key factor in ensuring a successful application.

25.4   CONSIDERATIONS IN DESIGNING A SECOND GENERATION INCENTIVE

The types of second generation incentives which have been applied need careful consideration. The following factors might be used as a check list:

1   What base will be used for the incentive? Added value, sales value of production and cost improvement have all been used. What information is available to help to decide upon the base? The right formula today may be wrong for tomorrow.

2   Will the incentive be applied across the company, on one product line or even perhaps on part of a section of a product line? What is the likely effect in each case?

3   Applying second generation incentives usually requires changes in attitudes throughout the organisation. How is this change to be brought about? What timescale is envisaged? How difficult is it likely to be? Is senior management likely to change its philosophy? What will be the attitude of junior management? (This could be crucial for the success of the whole activity.)

4   What is the likely response of the workforce to the application of second generation incentives? Is it likely they will respond positively to such schemes?

5   What is the current position concerning incentives? Are the current ones worn out or disintegrating? Do they still motivate?

6   How often will bonus earnings be calculated: weekly, monthly, quarterly, annually? How will the bonus be paid:
    By equalised payments, through a kitty principle?
    In arrears, but equalised through a moving average?
    As it is earned?
    How stable can the bonus be? How stable does it have to be?

7   How are factors not under the control of the workforce to be handled — e.g. seasonality, decline in sales for national-economic reasons, capital investment, inflation?

8   Can individual performances still be recognised within the proposed system? Is it necessary to recognise individual performance?

9   How is the bonus to be shared — between company and employees, management and shopfloor, individual work group and employees?

10 Will the new incentive replace all incentives currently in operation, or will it act as an overlay to them?

25.5   ADDED VALUE

As added value plays a considerable part in many second generation incentive schemes it is intended to describe this measurement of performance and productivity in some detail.

Work study and work measurement have been concerned largely with the output of physical quantities. The fact that output is really wealth or value has often been overlooked.

The use of added value enables changes in productivity to be expressed in value terms. This is especially pertinent in measuring labour productivity. Whatever decisions are made to improve productivity, whether by means of extra capital or increased wages, a true judgement of the result will probably be best made by using added value gained per unit of extra resource spent.

1 Definition

Added value is defined in the Engineering Employers' Federation Handbook [1] as 'the value added to materials and other purchased items which provides, as a result of productive activities in the firm, the sum out of which wages, salaries and administrative overhead expenses are paid leaving any surplus as profit'.

For example:

Net sales revenue		£100
The cost of materials	£30	
Other manufacturing costs (e.g. power, packages, etc.)	£15	
TOTAL		£45
Added value is		£55

From the figure of £55 must be paid:

Wages
Administration costs (including salaries)
Depreciation
Profit

Added value can be calculated, in practice, in several ways. The most popular are:

Net margin + wages, or
Sales — all manufacturing cost less wages and salaries.

(Net margin is profit before various charges have been deducted from it, including depreciation.)

The absolute accuracy of the added value calculated is not important unless comparisons are being made between organisations, manufacturing units or even countries. (Accountants often differ in their treatment of items making up the profit and loss account.) It is important that the same basis be used to calculate added value from one year to another. It may be necessary, therefore, to calculate the effects of inflation on materials and other purchases and also on sales. (It is possible to use standard prices.) However, because inflation influences both sales and costs it tends to be discounted.

2   Using added value as a performance indicator

Fig. 25.1 shows a set of figures for the years 1975–77. These are typical except that added value has been calculated (by deducting materials and general manufacturing expenses from net sales revenue).

Profit which was £1,300,000 in 1975 reduced substantially in 1976, but recovers somewhat to £1,092,000 in 1977. Management has done well to reduce current assets slightly over the period despite inflation. Sales revenue has increased substantially (partly through inflation) while the labour force has actually declined.

Added value has increased substantially (from £12,421,000 to £18,860,000) and the added value per employee has gone up significantly.

How well is the company doing?

Wages and salaries have increased considerably and it is when these are compared with the added value produced that a measure of the company's productivity is determined. The proportion of added value to wages and salaries has declined significantly. It started at a low figure of £1.440 (which is much lower than the UK national average) and ended at £1.290. So that for every £1 of wage paid 44p was earned in 1975 reducing to 29p in 1977.

The proportion of added value which has been paid out in wages and salaries has increased from 69 per cent (once again a high figure in the UK) to 77 per cent. At the same time the proportion of profit to added value has fallen quite significantly.

The company has conceded wage demands without ensuring that there was an increase in added value to meet them. Inevitably this must weaken the company's overall trading position. What goes on wages cannot be spent on new plant and equipment or enlarging the company's trading base.

3   Added value as a measurement of performance

Like other measurements, added value cannot be related solely to labour productivity. It has also to be recorded from a fixed and working capital viewpoint. With this proviso in mind the use of added value as a measurement of performance is important.

E. G. Wood [2] suggests that past productivity measurements have proved inadequate to measure productive performance — e.g.:

Output does not distinguish between profitable and unprofitable products or between capital intensive and labour intensive industries.

Sales revenue may represent no more or less than the value of goods produced even when it does not facilitate comparisons between companies or industries.

Defining 'profit' or 'return' on investment is difficult. Company gearing distorts the picture. Asset valuation is a problem. One company may pay high wages yet gain low profit; another pays low wages and gets high profit. Each may be equally efficient at generating wealth but they share the result differently so producing different return on investment figures.

Added value is not (unlike profit) affected by depreciation, grants, wage levels etc., because all these items are contained in the added value which is calculated.

Added value is a fully stable measurement (unlike profit).

	1975	1976	1977	% average change 1975–1977
Number of employees (total)	2,160	2,020	1,945	
Number of direct workers	872	884	912	
Net sales (including + − changes in inventory)	£25,621,000	£28,846,000	£36,000,000	
Less materials	£10,000,000	£11,721,000	£12,640,000	
manufacturing cost	£2,600,000	£3,300,000	£4,500,000	
added value	£12,421,000	£13,825,000	£18,860,000	+ 51%
Wages and salaries	£8,621,000	£10,461,000	£14,621,000	+ 61%
Administration cost	£2,500,000	£2,750,000	£3,250,000	
profit	£1,300,000	£425,000	£1,092,000	
Fixed assets	£30,000,000	£31,000,000	£30,500,000	
Current assets	£6,500,000	£7,200,000	£6,175,000	
Total assets	£36,500,000	£38,200,000	£36,675,000	
Performance ratios				
A/V per employee	5,750	6,844	9,676	
direct employee	14,244	15,639	20,679	
per £ capital − fixed	414	444	618	
current	1,911	1,920	3,054	
per £ administration cost	4,968	5,027	5,803	
£ wages and salaries	1.440	1.321	1.290	− 10%
Wages and salaries as % of A/V	69%	75%	77%	+ 11%

Fig. 25.1 Added value performance

4   Use of added value in wage negotiations

One of the unsatisfactory situations facing many managers when negotiating wage rates is the lack of suitable information which can be used to suggest how much wages the company can afford.

In Fig. 25.1, there is a downward trend in the return of added value per £ of wages and salaries. It is possible that a target figure for this ratio might be established. In the case of the company concerned — perhaps 1.7 or even 1.8.

The way in which wage increases can then be achieved is to increase added value or reduce the number of employees without reducing the added value.

With the added value produced it will be possible to relate wages to salaries, one department to another, direct workers to indirect workers, operatives to managers, manufacturing personnel to administrative workers, so suggesting where productivity is rising or falling or where salaries and wages are going above or below the company average.

What appears to be happening in the company's figures shown in Fig. 25.1 is that labour productivity as a whole has been falling while productivity of fixed and current assets has been rising slightly. The reward going to labour has been growing and that to fixed assets decreasing.

Companies have a limited amount of money they can pay as salaries and wages. If they are coerced into paying higher wages than can be supported, then inevitably there will be serious economic consequences.

What matters in wage negotiations is not necessarily how high wages are (or indeed how low they can be kept) but what can be gained by paying more. There need (in theory) be no limit on individual earnings, so long as these earnings relate to value of output.

Wage negotiations therefore, should be concerned with the total added value being produced, the way it is distributed and how it can be improved. Wage negotiations are inseparable from the economic state of the company and, in the end, the nation. This fact of life needs to be expressed simply and strongly whenever pay discussions are carried on.

The data set out in Fig. 25.1 should help to establish what wage levels a company can afford. The wages quoted can be related to manual and non-manual workers, departments, functions, or even cost centres and wage budgeting sheets prepared as in Figs. 25.2 and 25.3.

For example the following circumstances may apply in one company:

Desired profit on added value earned — 20 per cent

Required depreciation to service fixed capital — 18 per cent on added value earned

Required interest to service current assets — 10 per cent on added value earned.

The following table shows how the wages payable can be calculated:

Net sales	£20,000,000	£24,000,000	£30,000,000
Raw mat'l and mfg expenses	6,000,000	8,000,000	10,000,000
Added value	14,000,000	16,000,000	20,000,000
Profit 20 per cent	2,800,000	3,200,000	4,000,000
Depreciation 18 per cent	2,520,000	2,880,000	3,600,000
Interest 10 per cent	1,400,000	1,600,000	2,000,000
TOTAL	6,720,000	7,680,000	9,600,000
Possible wages payment	7,280,000	8,320,000	10,400,000

It is suggested that at all times managers negotiating wage payments have the following company data for the last three years at least. (Trends are very important.)

Added value per production worker
Added value per £ of direct wage
Added value per £ of direct wage in each department
Added value per £ of direct wage in each production cost centre
Added value per £ of ancillary wage (i.e. services personnel)
Added value per £ of indirect workers' (supervisors etc.) wages
Added value per £ of administrators' wages
Added value per £ of management salaries.

The proportion of added value given to:

Wages and salaries
Depreciation
Profit.

Trends in rewards between labour and capital productivity.
Comparison of added value produced and added value per £ of wages paid between British companies and industries and other similar companies in the EEC and the rest of the world.
A negotiated standard added value ratio per £ of wage paid would obviously have benefits.
For broader control the following may be necessary:

Average hourly earnings per department
Factory average hourly earnings
Sales value per month
Added value per month at constant prices

'Hours earned' per clock hour
Added value earned per clock hour
Added value per £ capital employed
Added value per £ sales
Profit/capital employed ratio

Judging the components of added value (sales, raw material and direct manufacturing cost) will be a problem, but this can be handled fairly simply by drawing a chart similar to Fig. 25.4. The allocation between profit, wages and salaries and depreciation and interest can then be drawn. If the components of added value alter, a new chart needs to be recorded.

5   Using added value as an incentive

(a)   The preceding sections have suggested that increases in wages must derive from increased added value if the organisation is to maintain a sound economic base. The essence of establishing added value as an incentive, therefore, is to ensure that a link is established between value created and wages paid.

(b)   The ways in which added value can be increased are far more numerous than in a physical output orientated incentive system — e.g.:

Product rationalisation — making only those products which yield a high contribution
Improved machine utilisation — a function of the planning system
Improved materials productivity — generally both a technical and an operational problem
Increased capital expenditure
Repricing of products
General cost reduction

Some part of these improvements will be under the control of operatives, some not. This is why it is important that increasing added value be seen as a team rather than a direct operative responsibility.

(c)   The steps using added value as the basis for an incentive could begin by recognising the need for everyone to understand the basis for calculating added value and how it can be improved. This would provide the foundation for an added value team and the degree of management/operative co-operation, participation and information sharing necessary to ensure an improvement.

(d)   Establishing appropriate teams might be difficult. Experience suggests that these should be as small as possible. However, the need to include services personnel of all kinds might make for larger rather than smaller teams. All the costs of the team need to be identified (wages, NHI and other costs) as well as the sales revenue it is generating. This may largely dictate the size and composition of the added value unit.

	Reference period	Current budget	Actual period under review
Fixed assets			
Current assets			
Current liabilities			
Net current assets			
Total			
Net sale revenue			
± Changes in stock			
W.I.P.			
Less			
Raw materials			
Ancillary purchase			
Consumable stores			
Power			
Packages			
Other manufacturing expenses			
Added value			
Wages			
Direct			
Indirect			
Salaries			
Interest payable			
Selling expenses			
Admin costs			
Depreciation			
Total			
Pre-tax profit			
Total added value			

Fig. 25.2   Wage budgeting sheet A

Item	Reference period % A/V	Current budget % A/V	Actual % A/V
Budgeted added value			
Wages			
Direct			
Indirect			
Salaries			
Depreciation			
Admin. costs			
Interest payable			
Profit			
Direct hours			
Indirect hours			
Admin. hours			
Selling hours			
Others			
A/V per hour –			
Direct			
Indirect			
Admin			
Selling			
Others			
Payroll cost per			
Direct hour			
Indirect hour			
Admin. hour			
Selling hour			

Fig. 25.3   Wage budgeting sheet B

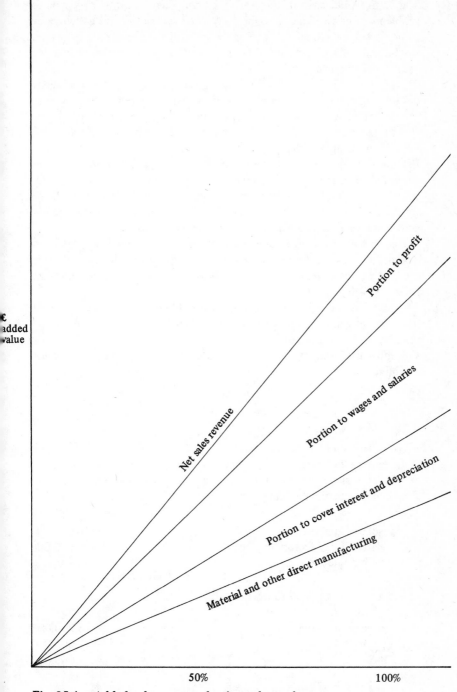

€ added value

Net sales revenue

Portion to profit

Portion to wages and salaries

Portion to cover interest and depreciation

Material and other direct manufacturing

50%   100%

Fig. 25.4   Added volume – production volume chart

(e)   The team would have to be largely self contained and this may lead to problems of control and autonomy. Work organisation and added value could largely go hand in hand. The possibility of giving authority on stock levels, work in progress, hours of work etc. which can alter added value must be considered.

(f)   The need to run the added value unit as a business would need someone on the team with appropriate experience. The added value business should not engage in activities antipathetic to the organisation as a whole and there would have to be a business strategy within which the added value team would operate.

(g)   Establishing 'standard performance' plays a large part in any conventional work measured incentive. In added value schemes it is difficult to determine precisely at what level of added value generation a scheme would start. In practice it seems difficult to move away from a currently achieved level of added value without some incentive.

   Records of past added value performance, especially where peaks and troughs in sales and production have occurred, must be determined. This done, it will be necessary to suggest how the added value the team has produced will be shared.

(h)   Advocates of added value incentives (e.g. Bentley Associates) suggest that the relationship between the wage/salary bill and added value remains fairly constant over time.

(i)   The most useful index to measure productivity and provide a base for incentives is:

$$\frac{\text{Value added}}{\text{Employee cost}}$$

or value added per £ of wages paid.

   Incentives can be established which will ensure that this index always remains the same (as per h). For example the following are the current financial results of a company:

	£
Net sales revenue	10,000,000
Materials and factory expenses	2,000,000
Added value	8,000,000

Added value is split as follows:

Wages and salaries	6,000,000
Depreciation	1,000,000
Profit	1,000,000

$$\frac{\text{Value added}}{\text{Employee cost}} = 1.333$$

A new position might be:

	£
Net sales revenue	16,000,000
Materials and factory expenses	3,000,000
Added value	13,000,000
Wages and salaries	9,752,000
Depreciation	1,000,000
Profit	2,248,000

$$\frac{\text{Value added}}{\text{Employee cost}} = 1.333$$

Usually monthly results are calculated and a proportion of the gain is paid out. The rest is put into a stabilisation account, which can be used to offset occasions when added value declines.

(j)   The advocates of added value incentives suggest that a ratio of value added to employee cost is negotiated which must be seen to be fair to employees, to working and fixed capital funding, and to shareholders. Any improvement in added value is shared in an agreed way.

(k)   In many industries there is a fixed element in wages and salaries irrespective of the added value produced. This needs to be taken into account when considering the value added/employee cost ratio.

(l)   Consultants in the added value incentive field suggest that a committee which will negotiate the share of added value will be needed. In large organisations, more than one committee may be required. The composition of such committees is important.

(m)   Most schemes are based on time related elements — e.g.:

The reference period — the fixed time between the base period and bonus period

Bonus period — the period being compared with the reference or base period

The lengths of these periods might well be a function of the industry or where the incentive is applied. Often a month's bonus is chosen, though weekly periods have been used.

The calculation of bonus payment is made by comparing the base period with the bonus period. Where the latter is less than the former, no bonus is paid. Where it is greater, it is issued on a prenegotiated basis (i.e. percentage of total added value earned).

6   *Benefits which might accrue in using added value as an incentive are:*

(a)   Companies could be enabled to break out of the narrow concept of labour productivity, which most individual payment by results schemes are geared to achieve.

(b)   Generation of co-operation to achieve wealth creation for the organisation — as opposed to individual incentives which tend to promote selfishness and self seeking. An awareness of the need to create wealth should be created.

(c)   Sharing added value seems to be in sympathy with the suggestion that motivation should be self produced, not externally imposed.

(d)   Incentive earnings can relate directly to the value of production achieved, not pieces of production.

(e)   New and more appropriate work organisations can go hand in hand with added value incentives.

(f)   Shared prosperity can be one of the most important factors in any participation which is introduced.

(g)   The approach seems more suited to the social and economic requirements of today and tomorrow.

(h)   Added value indices can be tailored to the economic circumstances of most work groups and incorporated into a business planning and control procedure.

(i)   Undoubtedly one of the most positive results looked for by management would be attitudinal change at all levels in the organisation.

7   *Problems in using added value as an incentive are:*

(a)   The problem of capital productivity is obviously important in using added value. There can be too much concentration on labour productivity and too little on capital (fixed and current) productivity. An index of capital productivity is needed. Added value is usually improved by increases in capital investment. The share of added value going to the company, management and labour, might need to be renegotiated where major capital investment occurs.

(b)   Added value does not measure labour productivity, as such, if this is concerned with the production of physical quantities. It measures increases in wealth or value. It does not, for example, necessarily measure 'effort'.

(c)   Critics suggest that merely by putting up prices, extra added value will be generated, though this cannot really be defined as wealth. But in the end market forces determine whether price rises are possible. Added value still measures the effectiveness of the business.

(d)   Where there are individual payment systems added value incentives can be superimposed on them but there will be problems of dual calculations etc.

(e)   Excessive order fluctuations or sales revenue changes may undermine the whole added value scheme.

(f)   Teams can become too big and the relationship between effort and reward totally lost. Influence over productivity must be identifiable.

(g)   Techniques of work measurement must still continue for manning and planning purposes, whether added value is used or not.

(h)   The application of added value incentives needs an open management style which some organisations may not be keen to adopt.

(i)   Operatives could gain from improvements over which they have no influence (though this happens under any incentive scheme more or less).

(j)   An added value incentive may not act as one and the payment may be too remote from the actions which bring it about. (However, it does emphasise the team concept in producing added value.)

(k)   The long term and steady growth which form the basis of most added value schemes might be missing.

(l)   Inter-company trading may nullify added value production owing to the transfer pricing system.

25.6   APPLICATIONS OF SECOND GENERATION INCENTIVES

Far from being new, incentives based on profit, added value and sales value of production have been available for a long time. For example the Rucker and Scanlon Plans were introduced into the USA in the 1930s.

While some companies have used them with considerable success, there have been dramatic failures.

There seem to be two main reasons why these plans have yielded limited benefits. The productivity index used failed to be a motivator. It may have been too remote from the individual working on the shopfloor. Secondly, either attitudes did not change or there was no serious attempt made to change them — particularly through new work organisation structures.

Experience suggests that requisite organisational and attitudinal changes may take at least a year to bring about, perhaps longer. (Substantial benefits can be achieved, purely through this process.) Unless shopfloor personnel and opinion leaders in particular understand and accept the incentive, it will nearly inevitably fail.

It seems particularly important for productivity teams to understand how they can influence added value — e.g. by improving materials productivity or machine utilisation.

25.7   SECOND GENERATION INCENTIVE AND WAGE PAYMENT SCHEMES

Various schemes have been introduced. The more important are:

1   Profit sharing

An index is negotiated which relates bonus payments to either a pre-tax or a post-tax profit (usally the former). The index also relates either to total profits or profits above a base line (e.g. profit levels which give a net required return on capital. New investment therefore, can raise the level at which bonus payments start to be paid).

Profit sharing schemes normally share the increased productivity bonuses between the workforce and the company. The profit share index therefore, is:

$$\text{Profit earned} - \text{baseline profit} = \frac{\text{bonus}}{2} = \text{employees' share}$$

Even where no baseline adjustment is made for new investment, increased depreciation charges should help to ensure that company benefit from the incentive does not fall. Where wage rises occur, the bonus is self adjusting if the baseline is maintained.

2   Incentives based on added value

Two types of incentive based on added value have been used:
(a)   Where the total wage bill is considered to be a constant proportion of the added value created. (It has been researched that the ratio of wages and fringe benefits paid with added value earned is fairly constant over the longer term.) The historic proportion is guaranteed under the scheme.
      The bonus is calculated as follows:

£

a	Added value
b	Employee labour cost allowed ($x\%$ of added value)
c	Actual labour cost
d	Gain or loss
e	Allocation to the company of added value ($x\%$)
f	Deduct company expenses
g	Bonus available $(d-f)$
h	Amount given or taken from added value reserve
i	Amount available for distribution $(g-h)$
j	Bonus paid $= i/j \times 100 = y\%$

This approach to using added value as a bonus has been claimed by the Rucker and Bentley Plans (share of production plan). Employees can gain only by doing better than they have in the past.

It is, of course, assumed that the value added/labour ratio is correct. This may not be so and before management introduces such a plan, they should ensure that the ratio they want to live with has been obtained.

(b)   Value added bonus schemes

In this scheme added value improvements are usually shared equally between workers and the company. A bonus level (of added value) is agreed and only above this level is a bonus paid. (In the Rucker` or Bentley plans the total wage bill is related to the added value earned.)

While the scheme is responsive to improvements in shop efficiency, inflation or capital investment could distort the result, unless the formula discounts these factors.

3   Sales value of production

The sales value of production can be defined in several ways — i.e. net sales revenue, standard sales revenue etc. The proportion of wages paid is maintained as a fixed percentage or proportion of the sales value of production. The bonus paid is then the difference between the basic wages paid and the amount calculated using the productivity formula.

This incentive or wage payment method is often referred to as the 'Scanlon plan'.

4   Productivity indices

A productivity bonus can be based on added value, increases in product value produced, or cost reduction.

For example, in the last case cost savings could be shared 50/50.

25.8   GENERAL COMMENT

There appears to be no one best index or scheme to suit all situations. Self-help on the shopfloor and improvements in machine or material efficiency can perhaps be motivated best by added value incentives. The product value produced method does not appear to be very responsive to savings made on the shopfloor.

New investment must be taken into account in all schemes with the exception of profit sharing. Schemes similar to the Rucker and Bentley types seem inflation proof and adjust automatically to wage increases.

Whatever scheme is chosen, added value and the ratio of added value to wages paid provide excellent ways of measuring any improvement which is gained.

It may be advisable to see the application as an overlay to a normal PBR scheme and only when it proves effective should it be extended to provide a greater proportion of take-home pay. Skill and effort, as such, are not rewarded and this may cause dissension.

25.9   IMPLEMENTATION

The following seem to be the most appropriate steps to take in introducing second generation incentives:

1   Decide management's objectives and desires and determine how these can be met through the incentive.
2   Determine the attitudes of the workforce to incentives and especially second generation incentives.
3   Carry out an educational programme among the workforce and management so that the reasons for considering second generation incentives are understood and especially the basis for establishing them. Detailed programmes to explain added value and associated production indices will need to be instituted. (Education of this kind is extremely important and the whole application will be in grave danger of failing if it is not carried out.)
4   Measure the current situation very carefully and determine the degree of improvement which the application might produce.
5   Define the incentive, taking account of the following:
The basis — added value, sales value of production etc.
The sharing — between company and employees etc.
Reference periods
How the bonus is to be paid
Factors not under the control of employees.
6   Decide what work organisation needs to be introduced to ensure that the incentive will be effective.
7   Carry out a simulation under varying operating conditions and determine the potential outcome — for the company and employees.
8   Establish a team of management and employees to discuss the proposed plan. (Results of the simulations should be given to the team.)
9   Gain agreement of the plan, introduce a pilot study and evaluate results with the help of the incentive team.
Introduce new work organisations if this has been decided.
10   Make changes which seem to be appropriate and re-introduce the scheme in an important area. Project or area teams might be used for the purpose.
11   Monitor the scheme and report results regularly.

NOTES

1 *Business Performance and Industrial Relations*, Engineers Employers' Federation Handbook, 1979.
2 G. Wood, *Comparative Performance of British Industries*, Graham and Trotman, 1977.

PART VI

Production Resources

26

Production resources and resource usage

26.1 INTRODUCTION

Resources are inputs to the production system. Their use should be determined by their effect on outputs from the system. The measurement of resource effectiveness should therefore be directly related to the system's productivity (say added value or perhaps sales revenue).

The range of resources will include the following:

1 Personnel (Manufacturing)

Direct labour — a term covering operatives directly concerned with production.

Indirect labour — all those who service production:
Storekeepers
Shop clerks
General servicemen including internal transport
Maintenance squads (where these are controlled by production management).

Supervision and management — covering first line supervision and associated management.

Production administrative services — these will be mainly concerned with production systems, i.e. production scheduling, wages payment, shop control systems etc.

Quality control personnel — these would normally include laboratory workers directly associated with production.

2   Machines and equipment

These should be divided between:
Production machines and spares — items directly used in production
Non-production equipment, quality control instruments, equipment for clerical support services.

3   Materials

These might be divided between:

Direct materials which are consumed by production processes. A further breakdown will be required between raw materials and components.

Indirect materials which, while being necessary in production, cannot be directly allocated to a particular machine or process — e.g. lubricating oils, wiping cloths, stationery.

Work in progress — this is often a major cost to production.

4   Power

This will be power mainly consumed by production equipment. It will be useful to be able to allocate power usage between production activities or even individual machines where consumption is significant.

5   Packaging

In many industries packaging is often a substantial resource and its strict control is important.

6   Direct support services

While not necessarily under the direct control of production managers, there are some direct support services which need to be taken into account when considering resource usage in production. These will include:

Maintenance services not under the control of production personnel
Engineering workshops such as toolrooms which provide equipment and spare parts for the production process.

7   Plant and buildings

Such things as rates and insurance and depreciation are kept under this heading.

26.2 PLANNING AND USE OF RESOURCES

1   The resources recorded suggest some categories to use in classifying them. Each category might be given a resource number or code and appropriate budgeting systems established. Where possible it seems advisable that resource allocation or budgeting be made at supervisory and management levels which relate to the work organisation in operation.

2   The planning and use of resources should be based on the productivity of such resources. This implies that a productivity measurement is possible for each resource. For many of the direct resources such as labour or materials, this is a comparatively easy calculation. For others — the toolroom for example — it may be more difficult.

     Although some of the resources are not interchangeable many are. For example, it may be possible to keep a machine running at eighty per cent efficiency with minimum maintenance (either planned or casual). The introduction of a planned maintenance scheme which costs, say, £50,000 may increase that efficiency to eighty-five per cent. It should therefore be possible to relate the extra cost to the enhanced value produced by five per cent more efficiency.

3   Comparative importance of resources. This can be judged in two ways:

     (a)   The proportion spent on each resource to achieve a given level of output.

     (b)   The marginal return earned when further money is added to an already existing resource.

     The first criterion is often the most important in improving resource productivity. For example, in many manufacturing companies material is often two to three times more expensive than direct labour. Yet direct labour is often controlled tightly but materials scarcely at all. Again administration or maintenance is often expensive compared with direct labour and therefore deserves much tighter control than it often receives. A final example is an expensive piece of equipment where the direct labour cost compared to the running cost is very small. Incurring overtime or shift premiums to keep the machine running is therefore of much less importance than keeping it in production.

     The marginal return gained from each resource can best be explained by an example. Production managers have a limited amount of money to spend on improving resource use. Should they increase wage rates (by introducing a more effective incentive) so that machine usage or perhaps efficiency increases, or should they spend the money on improved maintenance or perhaps materials handling? The answers will depend upon the return gained for the money spent.

     The marginal approach to improving resource productivity can result in fairly complicated (and occasionally subjective) calculations which management accounting systems are not always geared to produce. In fact, conventional management accounting may not be appropriate at all.

26.3   THE IMPORTANCE OF MEASUREMENTS

It would appear that insufficient measurements are usually available to carry out the decisions suggested in 26.2. It is recommended that even in comparatively small organisations sufficient data be available on machine output rates (both current and potential), on material yield, on the comparative importance of the various resources used and their relationship to production of a variety of product mixes if these are important, so that appropriate decisions can be made.

26.4   NON-PRODUCTIVE RESOURCES

Conventional management accounting systems have been based mostly on 'absorbed costs'. In such systems non-productive resources are included in costs by 'absorbing' them with the direct production costs. This tends to hide the scale of non-productive costs. Their productivity is misted over.

   While many organisations are well aware of the scale of overheads they have to carry, little is done to measure them in a way that ensures no wastage of money. Every production manager should insist that non-productive resources be as effectively planned and controlled as those in production.

   There are many ways of doing this, for example:

1   A marginal approach may be possible. If money is spent on, say, a computer, what direct return does it give (not some nebulous 'it is acting as a catalyst')?

2   The expense of the resource should be matched with its result. For example the cost of running a purchasing department can be divided by the number of orders it places. If a cost allocation of £20,000 is given to a production department which needs only 100 purchase orders per year placing, the cost of the service given is excessive.

3   'Could anyone do it for less?' is usually a sound question to ask of non-productive services. For example, could an outside contractor provide cheaper and better meals than could an internal canteen department?

4   If work measurement is good for the shopfloor, then why not for administrative personnel? There is a variety of clerical work measurement techniques which can be used.

27

Materials productivity

27.1 INTRODUCTION

Materials productivity in manufacturing units is a vital factor in ensuring a high level of effectiveness and efficiency.

This chapter is based on experience in carrying out several important assignments to improve materials productivity. Though not universally applicable, it is considered that if the approach outlined is followed, considerable improvement in materials productivity will usually result.

27.2 THE APPROACH TO MATERIALS PRODUCTIVITY

27.2.1 The importance of materials productivity

1 Raw materials and bought out components costs usually constitute a high proportion of the total cost of sales of most manufacturing organisations. *Management Today* in December 1976 quoted the following ratios of material to labour cost for these industries:

Textiles	— 3.8
Carpets	— 4.0
Machine tool	— 2.6
Footwear	— 2.3
Furniture	— 2.6

The productivity of materials could be more significant than that of labour. It justifies a correspondingly high degree of analysis and control.

2   Where a concerted effort to improve materials productivity has not been made in the last five years, it can be increased substantially. Gains of 3 to 8 per cent of the total material bill have been achieved frequently.
3   The demanding nature of current production problems leads production and technical management to concentrate nearly inevitably on industrial relations, payment problems and related output.
       Investigations to improve materials productivity do not — normally — raise emotional or fundamental industrial relations problems. In practice, therefore, materials improvement is one of the most easily achieved major savings, even in the most belligerent industrial relations environments.
4   Experience also suggests that the measurement of materials productivity is best done as 'material yield'. 'Yield' is the weight of finished products accepted by customers when compared with the weight of all materials issued for production purposes. Percentage yields should be calculated both for individual operations and for each production line being studied.

27.2.2   Materials productivity — relationships with other measurements and activities

1   Improving material productivity is one of the most direct and important ways of enhancing added value.
2   Gaining information on material losses can help in establishing general data for production control and costing purposes, so providing the means to improve the planning and control of production resources generally.
3   Material losses can be related to incentive payments and help to increase their effectiveness.

27.2.3   The importance of data in improving materials productivity

The data book

Usually where materials productivity has been improved considerably the first step has been to record how much and at what stage in the manufacturing process material loss occurs. Such information is often entered in a 'data book' containing other relevant manufacturing information, which is the basis for standard costs. (So considerable relevant information could already be available.)

Use of materials productivity data

1   By highlighting anomalies that would remain hidden otherwise, data collection often produces immediate benefits. While line managers are usually aware of their materials productivity in some degree, the 'data book' should provide a studied record and practical evidence of where an immediate improvement could be made.

2 Materials productivity data should also provide a means for initiating and guiding action and for measuring and recording improvements.
3 The use of information on materials productivity is therefore invaluable in setting objectives and measuring production performance generally.

27.2.4 Considering improvements in materials productivity

Types of information required

Material losses mainly result from two causes:

1 Technical losses — these are considered to be part of the production process (grinding, pressing, cutting, trimming etc.).
2 Operational losses — these occur during the process of manufacturing and can be due to material quality defects, poor workmanship or machine/manufacturing deficiencies.

Information should be collected under these two main headings, as the approach to improving materials productivity could be substantially different in each case. Problems intrinsic to the production activities may require technical improvements to the plant. Operational losses may emphasise the need for tighter control over production and product quality than has existed hitherto and a systems approach may therefore be appropriate.
It is further suggested that data should be collated to answer three questions:

Do we have a problem? — Often the problem is hidden by a lack of data. For example, 'yield figures' are not regularly produced. Occasionally the comparative costs of labour and material are not known by the managers who control these resources.

Where do we have a problem? — Pinpointing where material losses occur is usually halfway towards improving materials productivity.

Why do we have a problem? — Frequently by far the most difficult question to answer.

Do we have a problem?

A broad indication of materials productivity and the degree of possible improvement can be acquired by obtaining the value of various major materials which are issued, the sales revenue obtained from their use, the associated labour cost and eventually the material yield. This information could be particularly valuable if it could be calculated for the key products which the organisation manufactures.

Material utilisation

Key data

	Year 1	%	Year 2	%	Year 3	%
Product 'A'						
Total material cost						
Labour cost						
Overhead						
Profit						
Product 'B'						
Product 'C'						
Product 'D'						

Fig. 27.1   Material utilisation

Completion of Figs. 27.1 and 27.2 is recommended to provide the initial data which will help to establish whether there is a problem of materials productivity. As suggested earlier, the most important information is that of 'yield' — the difference in weight between what is input to a process or production line and what is eventually sent to a customer.

Where do we have a problem?

1   Technical and operational losses usually occur unevenly both throughout the product range and at operations or processes in manufacture. It is important to determine which products have least yield and at what operations or processes most loss occurs.

   Fig. 27.3 can be used to provide a record (especially for principal items in a product range) of where the need to improve materials productivity appears to be most urgent.

   Each operational cost should be quoted as the further down a production line losses occur, the greater the loss in value.

Material utilisation

Key data required for the total production process

Major products	Total value of material issued by type	Sales revenue	Labour cost	% Mtl to		Material yield %
				S.R.	Labour	

Fig. 27.2   Material utilisation

Material utilisation and cost record

Date: Product:

Stnd quty

Issued weight of materials:

Operation	Process qty per hour	Direct expense		Indirect expense	Material		Operation cost	Material loss		Standard net weight carried forward
		Fixed	Variable		Weight	Cost		Weight	Money	

Fig. 27.3   Material utilisation and cost record

Such sheets as that in Fig. 27.3 should be completed for operational as well as technical losses. Operational losses, by their nature, will normally tend to fluctuate from week to week, but taken, say, over the last three months, should provide a useful record.

There is a need to categorise why material losses occur to gain a rough first indication of 'where do we have a problem' — e.g.:

Technical losses	*Operational losses*
Machine limitations (due to machine design)	Operatives' errors
Methods failure	Machine faults
Raw material quality losses	
General material chemistry	
Product design	
Standards too high for material and products	

2   Possibilities of obtaining speedy results. Only the products comprising eighty per cent of the product range should initially be measured as proposed.

Sampling should be carried out to indicate where major product losses occur. (Process or operation losses should be obtained.)

All available data should be used to indicate the areas where materials productivity can be improved. (Costing information could be an obvious starting point.)

Obtaining appropriate information can be a lengthy and laborious process, but without it signposts will be missing which can direct effort to the most likely opportunities for improving materials productivity.

In practice up to one man year has been spent in preparing appropriate information for one product line of twelve operations with approximately 8,000 part numbers.

It is possible that experiments will have to be made to provide accurate information.

Why do we have a problem?

To determine why material losses occur and establish a cause for each loss is not always as easy as it sounds. The real cause may be hidden until a fairly lengthy technical evaluation has been made. A project team of production, production engineering, quality control and systems/costing personnel is often needed for a 'reasons why evaluation'.

Fig. 27.4 needs to be completed at this stage to provide a record of cause of loss, possible corrective action and the cost of such action. Again, separate records for operational and technical losses will be needed.

Considerable engineering and technical problems may have to be overcome if materials productivity is to be improved. Many of the solutions will need

Material loss evaluation sheet

Date:

Operation	Product type	Total annual loss (%)	Cause of loss	Annual lost value	Possible corrective action	Cost of possible corrective

Fig. 27.4   Material loss evaluation sheet

capital expenditure and the process of implementation may be slow. The total savings to be made will depend upon the type of loss, whether substantial or only minor parts of the loss can be saved and the amount of capital and other expenditure needed to achieve the savings.

However, production personnel with comparatively slight technical knowledge have made significant savings without help once they have produced for themselves, or had produced, appropriate information.

27.2.5   The product mix and materials productivity

Often the product mix and the size of orders have an important effect on materials productivity. One type of product may, owing to difficulties in making it, have a higher material loss than others. Appropriate information is needed.

27.2.6   The team approach to improving materials productivity

The mixture of 'technical', 'operational' and 'mix' classes of material losses which are usually found suggests that a multi-discipline team will have most immediate and long lasting benefit.

27.3   APPROACHES TO IMPROVING MATERIALS PRODUCTIVITY

27.3.1   Materials productivity

Materials productivity is the responsibility of production line managers. It should be one of their principal objectives and appropriate targets should be set up. Their responsibilities should include the establishment of materials productivity improvement assignments.

27.3.2 Control information

1 Input—output records

Fairly simple input—output controls or measurements are required to ensure that continuous record of performance is made.

Material control record							
Batch or order number	Issued weight and re-cycle	Planned units	Standard weight	Achieved units	Achieved weight	Material sent for re-cycle	Overall variance
A	B	C	D	E	F	G	H=B−F+G
Totals							
Comment:							

Fig. 27.5   Material control record

Fig. 27.5 shows a simple sheet for recording input and output on a batch basis. Re-mix, re-cycle or re-batch materials often play a large part in providing 'input' and these have to be included in the record.

Usually a material record card can travel with the batch or order so that an accurate record can be made of material losses. Sequence numbers can be used to ensure that all material issues have been accounted for.

Batch control is recommended — i.e. one batch or load of a particular weight is monitored and the resulting material yield calculated. A count of

Material utilisation report

Product line or department: Month:

Material type	Quantity issued	Standard weight	Standard cost	Achieved weight	Standard cost	Actual cost	Variances			
							Total cost	Good mtl	Total weight var	Reports issued
A	B	C	D	E	F=C×D	G=D×F	H=F−G	I=B−E	$J = \dfrac{E \times 100}{B}$	Yes/no

Total

Data source:

Transfer data to:

Fig. 27.6 Material utilisation report

work in progress, therefore, becomes less of a problem in providing control over weekly or monthly material issues and receipts.

Control over raw material issues must be efficient. No material should be issued without the sanction of a responsible individual and never in excess of that required by the orders being produced.

2 Material utilisation reports

Weekly or monthly reports are required which will record material variances from standard. The input—output records should be used to provide input data for this purpose.

Fig. 27.6 shows an appropriate form where material qualities are controlled.

3 Producing information

Records providing information should be produced at intervals which enable managers to increase their performance by taking action to improve materials productivity. Timing therefore is very important in producing control information.

27.3.3 Operational approaches to improving materials productivity

1 Quality control

Enhancing the policeman role of inspection or quality control will have benefits if the enforcement of well-defined quality rules is needed. This could have limited value, however, if the more fundamental causes of quality defects are not tackled.

Preventing poor quality products reaching a customer is often a negative approach. A positive method of determining why products are rejected and what can be done to achieve higher materials productivity is often decisive in making quality control a key influence in reducing material losses.

The following questions should be answered to provide an appreciation of the effectiveness of the quality control function:

Do we carry out quality control at the key points in the production process which maximise the possibility of preventing material losses, particularly by operative error?

Is the quality control process geared to catch rejected material early enough in the manufacturing process to ensure that the maximum amount of recycling of material occurs?

Are reasons for quality failure so recorded that line managers can take action from time to time?

Do line managers carry out corrective action once they have been told of causes of rejection?

Are rejections brought to the attention of operatives? Is any disciplinary action taken as a consequence of major rejects being caused by operative error?

2   Control of operative performance

The control of operative performance is another vital element in reducing material losses. The following questions need to be answered to ensure that appropriate control is in operation.

Is materials productivity part of the bonus system? Do we use standard scrap allowances indiscriminately so that some operative performance is hidden?

Do we always know which department, shift and individual have caused reject material?

Are agreed disciplinary procedures activated when operative error causes material losses? Do operatives appreciate the value of material? Is operative training conducive to reducing material losses?

'Participation' in improving materials productivity is often beneficial.

27.3.4   Technical approaches to improving materials productivity

Taking a technical view alone of material losses will be ineffective if operational losses are more important and only a small proportion of time is spent on these latter. Often the results of a technically orientated approach to materials productivity are requests for substantial spending on capital equipment or on plant modifications. This may be wrong if output and other factors are not taken into account.

1   Use of value analysis and value engineering

Value analysis and engineering are philosophies, rather than techniques that can be applied to materials productivity. Their intention is to question all facets of products and how they are made, and to determine whether all costs incurred contribute to the final value of the product.

'Ten tests for value' have been determined which ostensibly challenge all non-essential product characteristics and operations. However, the following questions may be more relevant.

Does every facet of the product produce value? Is every one necessary?

Do we use materials which are too expensive?

Is every operation performed essential? Could any operation be combined with another? Why do we need to make the product in the way we do? Are there cheaper ways?

Some of the possibilities of applying value analysis might be:

To challenge the need to add on material, initially, merely to be ground off at a later stage.

To challenge the finish of a product. For example, should the top and bottom surfaces of a product be treated in the same way although the bottom one is hidden in use?

To challenge the need to carry out 'finishing operations' at a stage in the process when material recovery is impossible — e.g. after a product has been baked.

2 Product geometry

In many production processes sheets or blocks are first made from which products are then pressed, stamped or cut. Product geometry analysis should ensure that sheets or blocks are of optimum size — i.e. minimum waste ensues from production processes.

As a rule of thumb it is likely that, for the top eighty per cent of the product range, product geometry calculations to provide maximum material yield will be needed.

However, there may be a wide range of products absorbing marginal production time which could be made from a standard range of blocks or sheets from which two or more products can be made.

'Standard sheets' should be used where the gain in production efficiency exceeds in value the loss in material when using a tailor-made sheet. Such calculations will need the following information:

Material losses — weight or square metres of standard material value taking account of related factory marginal costs.

Cost of handling materials lost in production (dust, offcuts, etc.).

Value of material recoverable when standard items are used.

Gains in efficiency by using standard material, probably measured in better machine and labour utilisation.

Cost of stocking standard materials and risks of obsolescence.

Gains and losses should be calculated in contribution terms if possible. Use marginal costs in any calculation made.

Yearly off-take for each item will also be needed and calculations of annual losses and savings made before a product geometry decision is taken.

3 Scrap control and recovery

In many production units a scrap control and recovery unit is usually extremely valuable in reducing material losses. Its main functions might be:

To provide a scrap collection service. To analyse scrap, grade it and store it for future use, recover it, or dispose of it.

To know what scrap occurs, its cost, weight, shape, size, type and possible treatment which will ensure its profitable use. To understand why scrap occurs and to suggest changes which will improve materials productivity.

If material is to be lost inevitably during the production process, production engineering and production planning should ensure that its future use and/or recovery is, in some way, facilitated.

4 Standardisation and variety reduction

Reducing material qualities and product sizes should have an inevitable result on materials productivity. Fewer tools, fewer changeovers and set-ups will be required, standardised methods of material utilisation and control will be possible.

Variety reduction can be tackled in one or more of the following ways:

(a)   Leaving the 'cosmetic' operations on a product until the latest possible point in the production process.
(b)   Ensuring that the product mix is based (partly) on contribution earnings.
(c)   Ensuring that product rationalisation is based on gradually widening (or enlarging) produce sizes — e.g. using sixteenths instead of thousandths of an inch, providing minimum size tolerances, etc.
(d)   Eliminating as far as possible, low volume and 'one-off' products (volume being one of the many factors in determining the product range).

The comparative importance of each method will differ according to the situation being investigated.

5 Tool control

Properly sharp tools should be available always. Tool control is vital for this purpose. The relationship between tool control and conversion/yields should be known.

Tool control should cover all items likely to have any effect on materials productivity, including:

Jigs and fixtures
Grinding wheels
All cutting equipment used generally in production
Drills
etc.

6   Engineering/machine improvements

New machines and equipment can often be justified by the material savings potential alone.

However, it would be erroneous to believe that this should have a high priority in materials productivity. Steps which might be taken are:

(a)   Review machine/equipment standards. What was the material utilisation standard envisaged at the introduction of the equipment?
(b)   What modifications are possible to improve materials productivity equipment? What will they cost? How long will they take to introduce?
(c)   What new equipment is desirable?

For (b) and (c) DCF calculations might be made.

7   Materials handling/method study

Handling of materials is often a direct cause of low materials productivity. Products are often chipped, broken or scratched through inadequate materials handling methods.

Allied to this will be methods study and how products are handled when in process. Methods study should be used to improve productivity of labour, machines and materials.

27.4   ACTION PLANS

Once appropriate data have been assembled and evaluated an overall plan should be drawn up to achieve the savings. Priorities will be needed if several possibilities of improving materials productivity have been highlighted. Control over the projects raised is essential if savings are to come as quickly as possible. Action plans are needed therefore, listing actions, objectives, timescales, cost and responsibilities. Fig. 27.7 shows an appropriate format.

Action plan

Date: No:

Action proposed	Items, areas, products etc. covered	Cost and man/weeks agreed	Objectives	Responsibilities	Timescale	Reporting procedure

Signed:

Fig. 27.7 Action plan

27.5 CONCLUSIONS

1   Experience in improving materials productivity suggests that the availability of appropriate data is of paramount importance.

Production line managers should take direct charge of materials productivity. At their discretion, technical, costing and other personnel should be utilised to determine how higher materials productivity can be gained.

Improving materials productivity can largely be the result of 'business decisions'; it is important that it remains a 'business function' and the alternatives of capital expenditure and materials saving judiciously weighed.

A team approach to improving materials productivity is often the best.

Much knowledge of material usage is to be found among shopfloor personnel. Properly directed through either multi-factor incentives or participation, such knowledge can be used to make substantial improvements.

2   While better materials productivity leads to considerable profit improvement, the carrying out of a survey might considerably influence the improvement of all aspects of shopfloor productivity.

3   Suitable terms of reference for a materials productivity activity might be:

To determine at each stage, operation or process, an accurate material yield for (initially) the products making up 80 per cent of total throughput — and, eventually, the remainder.

To determine why material losses occur and to establish a cause for material loss, initially under the chief headings of 'technical' and 'operational' losses.

To determine possible degrees of materials productivity improvement and embody these in the objectives of local line management.

To initiate actions which will improve material yield.

A programme for this should be established, with timescales and personnel.

28

Labour productivity

28.1 INTRODUCTION

One of the main relationships between employees and employers is a contractual one. For nearly guaranteed rewards, an employee carries out specified duties. Many of the shopfloor controls which management use are to ensure that employees maintain their part of the contract — required output, an anticipated machine efficiency, a planned cost of achievement, products produced of a desired quality. Many industrial relations problems stem from the desire of employees to have the contract changed or renegotiated — in their favour.

Put in this quasi-legalistic framework, labour productivity and the use of labour generally can be considered to be the result of the power relationships between two contracting parties. In practice the contract is not just about productivity, it is also concerned with the kind of job being done and the environment in which it is carried out. Discussions about labour productivity therefore, especially when concerned with 'labour control' or 'efficiency reports', may not take account of some of the most vital elements in the debate.

28.2 THE ECONOMIC POWER OF LABOUR

Measurements of labour productivity have traditionally tended to be concerned with 'effective hours', 'clocked hours' and 'lost time analysis'. Recent history suggests that a much more fundamental starting point is necessary.

1 Labour as a fixed cost

An important phenomenon of the last few years has been the gradual acceptance that labour of all kinds is becoming a fixed cost, at least in the short

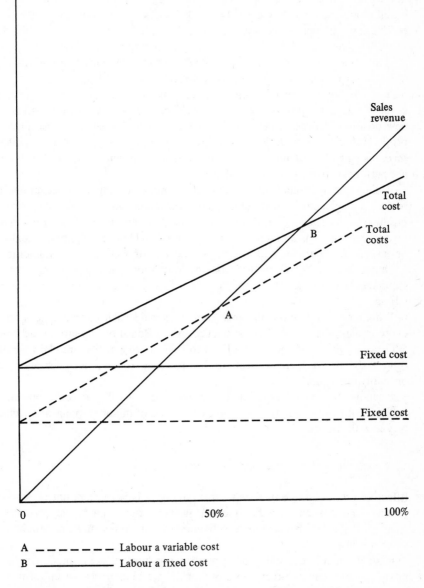

£

Sales revenue

Total cost

B

Total costs

A

Fixed cost

Fixed cost

0   50%   100%

A — — — — — — Labour a variable cost
B —————————— Labour a fixed cost

Fig. 28.1   Break-even graphs with labour a fixed and variable cost

term. Government legislation on employment protection plus the increasing power of the unions has meant that even the arbitrary movement of workers around the plant, let alone their dismissal, has become something which does not happen easily. For management accountants and others to continue to cite labour as a variable cost is an anachronism.

Increasing the amount of fixed cost has a major effect on a trading organisation as a break-even chart would show. In the traditional graph, where labour is still treated as a variable cost, the break-even point could be sixty per cent of production volume. When labour is treated as a fixed cost, the graph shown in Fig. 28.1 gives a break-even point of eighty per cent.

While the figures are not important, the result is extremely important. The message for production managers is very clear.

If production volume is less than 80 per cent no profit will be made. Whereas in the old days, the odd stoppage could be accepted with little or no qualms, the new position enforces a new look at labour usage. The slightest disruption in production is likely to drag down profit very quickly. The production manager recognising this situation is certain to be worried about the chance of labour not performing well — or not at all.

Riding out a dispute until time settles it may no longer be acceptable by senior management even though production management think that it would produce a satisfactory decision. If keeping labour at work and machines turning effectively is a major objective, then this will have weighty implications on industrial relations and wages payment. For example if an additional payment of, say, £120 ensures that a production line keeps going when a stoppage will cost £10,000, the temptation to give in to union pressure is strong.

Whether a production manager should yield in such circumstances could cause endless debate. Will he be backed by his Board of Directors if he does? Will taking the easy course only lead to even more extravagant claims in the future? If management is seen to be an 'easy touch', new demands will probably queue up.

Perhaps the crucial question to be asked is — will corporate objectives suffer most from one major stoppage or a series of minor stoppages stretching way into the future?

2 Production interdependence

Effective production control can substantially reduce the amount of work in progress needed on the shopfloor. However, without work in progress a production line can become extremely vulnerable to either machine breakdown or labour dispute.

High earners and good productivity in one part of a production process might quickly denude other zones of work if productivity is not uniform. The greater the degree of production interdependence, the more important it becomes that labour productivity be established to provide uniform group norms, not individual output rates.

3 Labour productivity, pay and capital investment

With a high break-even point, capital investment becomes increasingly risky. If the new capital equipment is not worked intensively from its introduction then the chances are that the company's profitability is at risk. Labour productivity must improve where new capital investment is introduced, so that unit costs are reduced at the same time that planned improvements in output are achieved. How often with the current political and social environment can such a situation be guaranteed?

4 Free collective bargaining and the labour contract

The foregoing comments suggest that the contract between the shopfloor and the company can often become distorted and biased by the power of the shopfloor and the state of industrial technology. Production managers might like to consider whether government wages policy has helped them in their dealings with shopfloor workers. By mobilising public opinion on incomes policy, is it possible to tip the scales of the labour contract back towards equilibrium? In a free for all, the production manager has much greater difficulty in reaching a reasonable conclusion. Support for a government wages policy therefore may not be a bad idea.

28.3 INFLUENCES ON LABOUR PRODUCTIVITY

Labour is a resource like capital or material. Its productivity is bound up with the use of the total resources in an organisation. The influences on labour productivity therefore include:

(a) Capital investment. Labour productivity is often directly proportional to capital investment.
(b) Product mix. Multi-product manufacture with high machine set-ups will reduce labour productivity below the best possible.
(c) Motivation. National values and local incentive schemes may have, often, an equal impact on productivity.
(d) Planning. Production or operational planning is often a key factor in ensuring high labour productivity.
(e) Control. Without adequate control, especially from well motivated local supervision, work booking is commonly the subject of malpractice; ill discipline of all kinds can creep in.
(f) Work organisation is often a key factor in ensuring conformity to agreed productivity levels. Group conformity will normally operate.

28.4   MEASURING LABOUR PRODUCTIVITY

In earlier chapters added value has been proposed as a means of measuring company performance and, with some reservations, labour productivity. The reservations have concerned the amount of capital available (and its use), the measurement of inputs and outputs and the variations in sales revenue.

The measurement of labour productivity in a conventional type of bonus system will be different. The 'standard performance' will be determined by work measurement of some kind and is used to calculate a 'standard output'. The conventional formula is:

$$\frac{\text{Units of work produced}}{\text{Standard units of work expected}} \times 100$$

or

$$\frac{\text{Standard hours earned}}{\text{Hours taken or clocked}} \times 100$$

The standard hours or minutes are determined by converting units produced into time, using the standard output rate obtained by work measurement. Comparing hours earned with hours clocked seems particularly useful, no matter what method of motivation or control is used.

Usually most measurements will need information on the following, to support the conventional formula:

Hours spent on measured work
Hours spent on unmeasured work, e.g.:
    Cleaning
    Change-overs and set-ups
    General non-productive time
Manning levels utilised
Overtime worked.

The degree of unmeasured work undertaken or booked (the latter is important) will be produced by:

Management controls
The planning/scheduling system
The incentive method applied.

No-one should be ashamed to admit that in most, if not all, incentive schemes some work booking fiddles go on. If an operative is allowed twenty minutes to carry out a change-over he will (normally) be on the lookout for ways and means of maximising the use of such an allowance. While some moralists may regard this as 'theft', it could be part of the ethos that Taylor-type incentives tend to foster and production managers should be aware of it.

Work booking carried out by operatives must always be suspect to some extent. It's all part of the game between management and the shopfloor.

Even where second generation incentives are in use or indeed where no incentives operate at all, it is important that work-measured standards are available for all operations. These should enable a comparison to be made between standard and current output rates as suggested in Chapter 2. It may not be possible to sell a work-measured standard performance to operatives but no-one should hide this fact by suggesting that what is sold is 'standard productivity'. The reasons why standard capacity cannot be achieved must always be known in case circumstances change and the possibility of reselling the scheme recurs.

A great danger with incentives is that they constrain production at levels well below standard capacity.

There are also dangers in measuring productivity in units or even hours. For example:

Section 1 produces 100 tons per week of product A and uses 100 man hours.
Section 2 produces the same quantity of the same product but only uses 50 man hours.

It is clear that section 2's productivity is twice as high as that of section 1 — section 2 has considerably newer and better equipment with which to work.

Such measurements as direct hours per ton produced are only valid if the situations are comparable. For example capital investment and incentives may remain the same on section 1 for a year, yet better production control or a different sales mix could improve labour productivity. A comparison between the beginning and end of the year is valid.

Where a sound costing system exists and standard costs are accurately determined, a useful measurement of productivity is the standard cost of output as a proportion of actual wages paid. The standard cost includes all costs which should have been incurred in making a product. Dividing this figure (which is in essence a credit to the operatives who have produced the associated products) by the actual wages which have been paid will provide a good indication of labour productivity.

Many years ago Tippett, Ewart Smith and Beeching [1] produced various labour productivity measurements. The use of added value and the measurements suggested above appear to be as good as theirs.

28.5 IMPROVING LABOUR PRODUCTIVITY

Many of the preceding chapters have been concerned with ways and means of improving labour productivity so only some of those which have not been mentioned are quoted below.

1   Avoiding lost time

Lost time is time that an operative does not spend at his machine or other workplace. It can be due to sickness, holidays, general absenteeism, lateness in coming to start work, or breaks in the routine.

Queues at the clocking out station, five or even ten minutes before finishing time, seem to be the rule in most factories. How realistic is it to hope to prevent this? An incentive which penalises such happenings is very difficult to devise.

A new and perhaps greater problem for production managers is absenteeism. As wage rates have increased, the response of many operatives in industry has been to take the odd day off each week. The money earned in four days is sufficient for their needs. Consequently where standard manning has been rigorously enforced, team strength is often below that planned. Where machines are individually manned as in a jobbing shop, this may not be so serious except that overall production is reduced. Where teamwork is needed, absenteeism may substantially reduce a team's effectiveness.

A point seems to have been reached in many factories where it is totally uneconomic not to run expensive plant as much as possible. As Fig. 28.1 shows, there is often a need to keep production at very high leveis if any profit is to be earned at all. Against all conventional wisdom, it may be necessary to overman on key machines rather than accept absenteeism and its consequent effects. More 'relief operatives' or 'factory casuals' may have to be employed than hitherto.

In some organisations payment for attendance has been used to tempt people to come to work. The results have not been encouraging. If absenteeism occurs because people have enough money and prefer leisure to work, paying an attendance bonus may have only marginal results.

2   Non-productive time

Non-productive time is any time when an operative is available for work but is not employed productively. 'Waiting time' or 'idle time' is a key factor in gaining or losing labour productivity. Some causes have been mentioned already — cleaning, setting up, waiting for work. The major cause may well lie in the production scheduling system. Unless this is effective, especially in determining the trade-offs between comparatively high work in progress and the chances of running out of work, then non-productive time will remain a problem.

Some factories have now reached a state where it is essential to provide stage or zone balance of work load, at the expense of low work in progress or even deliveries on time. Otherwise industrial relations suffer.

3 Scrap and rectification. Quality control

Any organisation with a scrap rate above five per cent could be in trouble over productivity as well as losing the benefits of good production. Depending upon the sequence in the production process where the reject is found, the loss in profit could be from one half to the total of the amount rejected.

Rectification of a substandard product, though preferable to throwing it away, has to be fitted into the production process, either by rewriting production programmes or providing production time for the process on an 'allocated basis'. In either case labour productivity is diminished.

It seems that in many factories, quality control is either not founded adequately or wrongly directed. Arresting delinquent items before they leave the plant is to be commended. Stopping the delinquency from occurring is even more important. It may be necessary to divide the quality control function between 'final examination' and 'process quality control'. The former can perhaps come under the command of a separate quality controller; the latter could become part and parcel of the production process.

4 Manpower planning

Most production managers are aware that in some areas or processes they have overmanning, and labour is generally under utilised. The reasons for this are often justifiable. For example, a definite time limit is needed to make changes where overmanning occurs. Retirement or resignations may make some room, but as a rule changes have to be negotiated with the unions and this takes time. Consequently there are many production managers who devoutly wish that manpower planning in all its aspects could be introduced.

5 Technique usage

Some of the more conventional ways of improving labour productivity include:

(a) Incentives of various kinds
(b) Product rationalisation and possibly increasing batch sizes to reducing the need for set-ups and change-overs
(c) Production planning and control, in all its aspects, particularly when it is used as operational planning
(d) Rota systems
(e) Fatigue study
(f) Method study
(g) Value engineering and value analysis
(h) Better maintenance
(i) Improved materials handling
(j) Improved shopfloor control
(k) Allied with (j), improved management.

All these factors should be reviewed within the production framework — systems of resource planning and control, work organisation, motivation systems and resources.

NOTE

1   L. H. C. Tippett, *Indices of productivity*, BIM, 1949.
    Sir Ewart Smith and R. Beeching, *Measurement of the effectiveness of the production unit*, BIM, 1949.

29

Capital resources management

29.1 INTRODUCTION

The design, acquisition, use and disposal of capital assets has been given a variety of names: resource management, cost of ownership, terotechnology, cradle-to-the-grave management. Each describes the process of optimising the life cycle of capital equipment. The process of acquisition and use of capital assets is perhaps one of the most crucial factors in maintaining and improving the economic position of a company. The quality of the associated management decisions must be very high and anything which assists the process must be welcome — technique, procedure or skills.

The expenditure of large sums of new manufacturing capital has possibly more risk now than at any time. For example, the situation where direct labour can be treated as a fixed cost has moved the break-even point for many organisations to a very high level. This has an effect on new capital investment as the usage of the equipment must be equally high. This suggests that no new capital equipment should be obtained unless its planned utilisation is, say, 80 per cent. Where the extra plant capacity being acquired provides large, new, discrete chunks of production, extremely carefully co-ordinated production–marketing actions will be required.

The use of discounted cash flow and other techniques might appear to have removed most of the risk in acquiring major pieces of plant. This is certainly not true. Such acquisition is still a gamble — on the borrowing rate of money, inflation, taxation rates, growth and profitability in the company, as well as on factory costs.

The use of any technique should be subordinated to the strategic considerations involved in making capital decisions. A decision must be seen as part of a 'trade-off'. If one choice is made, it is because another has been forgone. Money spent on new plant is not available as wages or increased dividend to shareholders.

Discounted cash flow — assessment of expenditure

Originator: Request no:

Request: Date:

Outflow		Inflow						Discounted at								
								5%		10%		15%		25%		
Year	Expense	Cost saving	Tax for year (−) @ %	Net cost saving	Tax saved	Capital recovery (grant)	Net inflow	In	Out	In	Out	In	Out	In	Out	
								1.00		1.00		1.00		1.00		
								.952		.909		.870		.800		
								.907		.826		.756		.640		
								.864		.751		.658		.512		
								.823		.683		.572		.410		
								.784		.621		.497		.328		
								.746		.564		.432		.262		
								.711		.513		.376		.210		
								.677		.467		.327		.168		
								.645		.424		.284		.134		
								.614		.386		.247		.107		
								.585		.350		.215		.086		
								.557		.319		.187		.069		
								.530		.290		.163		.055		
								.505		.263		.141		.044		

Total

TOTAL Factor Out
In

Caculation of solution rate

A = Factor above unity
B = Factor below unity

2) 1.000 − (Factor B) ÷ (Factor D)

Factor	%
A	=
B	=
C	÷
D	

= % (E)

3) Solution rate

B% + L%   %

Reported as:—   %

Calculated by: Checked by:

Fig. 29.1 Discounted cash flow — assessment of expenditure

The decision must be seen to influence the overall production system — whether, for example, it distorts the existing work organisations or makes the current motivational systems obsolescent.

29.2 CAPITAL INVESTMENT — THE TRADITIONAL VIEW

It is uncommon now for a costly piece of plant or equipment to be acquired without the use of the discounted cash flow technique. DCF uses a form similar to the one shown in Fig. 29.1. Forecast cash outflows are compared with cash inflows — i.e. cash generated through having the equipment and cash lost through having to purchase or rent it. Tax is important and plays a substantial part in the calculation.

The further on in time that cash is generated the less importance it has, so it is discounted. The discounted rate used each year varies according to the overall discounted figure being used. So if 10 per cent is the target rate, projected cash flows in the second year of the life of the plant should be discounted by 0.909, in the third year 0.826 and so on.

The project is discounted so that in X years a 'present value' can be calculated. The original capital sum or rental can be deducted from the present value, so providing a net present value or NPV. The NPV therefore, will show after X years how valuable the project might be or, in retrospect, has been.

Any important project, therefore, should initially be deemed financially sound through the use of appropriate techniques, and then introduced in the best possible way. The difference between an introduction which is on time and one delayed by as little as six months could be crucial to success. Post-completion reviews are an essential element in capital investment, mainly in determining what went wrong in the project and, of course, what went right. This should not only apportion blame — if this is needed — but also build up capital investment and project expertise.

A post-completion review should therefore comprise the following:

1   Cost of project installation versus budgeted cost

Items should be listed as follows:
  Equipment cost
  Building cost
  Services cost (power, water connecting, etc.)
  Labour cost
  Costs under control of local management
  Costs not under control of local management.

2   *Time scales:*

Actual versus budget
Delivery of equipment
Engineering of facilities
Service connections
On stream.

3   *Effectiveness:*

Production versus budget
Running costs
General efficiency
Manning levels
Sales.

4   *Return on investment:*

Anticipated
Likely.

5   *Changes from plan:*

Sales mix
Inflation
Costs
Delivery of equipment
Sales revenue
Tax.

6   *Comment required on:*

Project control and effectiveness (management skills)
Technical skills required, used and their effectiveness.

7   *Advice for future projects*

The DCF technique can also be used either as a means of assessing the NPV of a project after X years at a given percentage return or alternatively of discovering the true rate of return after discounting.

The problems of using DCF start with required information. While the logic of the approach is sound, any falsity in the data will make the whole exercise invalid. The use of target rates of return implies that a company has endless cash to support projects if they apparently achieve those targets. In practice the technique should produce a priority list of potential investment which can be used to test various hypothetical strategies within the overall business.

Discrimination between high and low risks is also needed. A manager who has consistently failed to reach required target rates of return on investments should probably have higher DCF returns to achieve than others who, historically, have done better. Having a standard rate of return does not take account of the comparative risks involved. Once the DCF sheets have been completed it is usual to subject them to sensitivity testing. Each of the components of the return is amended and the final result recalculated, so determining which of the components is important in achieving the target return. This discovery can then motivate greater control for vital factors.

29.3   POST–COMPLETION REVIEW

While most accounting systems will provide some mechanism for appraising the result of capital expenditure, it is rare to find a rigorous evaluation of an entire project. Installing expensive new equipment is not commonplace in many companies, and the opportunity to gain experience of managing such activities is infrequent.

29.4   INVESTMENT DECISION MODELS

One of the more successful applications of modelling has been in capital investment appraisal. Computer suppliers and software houses market such models through which the DCF technique and sensitivity testing can be applied to investment decisions.

If profit planning routines are well established the model will need to be run once a year when appraisal and ranking of competing projects can be carried out. This approach is strongly recommended.

29.5   TEROTECHNOLOGY

1   Introduction

Terotechnology is defined in the relevant Department for Industry booklet [1] as follows:

A combination of management, financial, engineering and other practices applied to physical assets in pursuit of economic life cycle costs.

It requires no new techniques or disciplines, but uses those already in existence in a coherent and well-planned way. The practice of terotechnology is

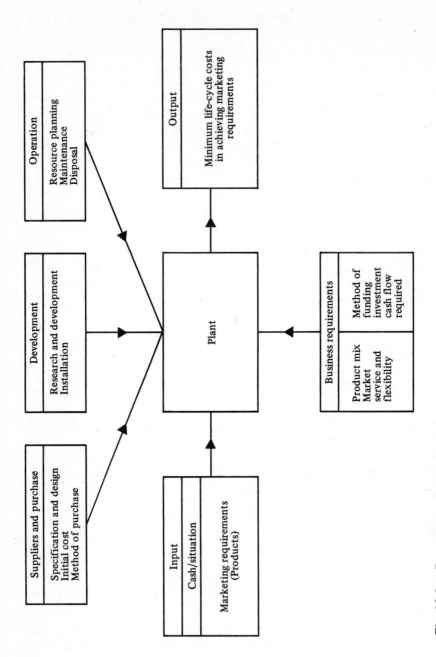

Fig. 29.2   Resource management system

concerned with the life cycle of capital equipment — its design and specification, development, acquisition, introduction, maintenance, modification and replacement. It is a resource function in a total sense.

2 The application

This is largely set out in Figs. 29.2 and 29.3 where all the relevant activities and techniques are quoted.

3 The approach

The approach is cross-functional, needing the skills of many specialists — engineers, accountants, purchasing and materials handling specialists, as well as production managers. If a production manager is chosen to head up the terotechnology application he should be aware of the special skills required of participants. A company style which facilitates communication and cross-functional co-operation will be advantageous.

4 Costing

Life cycle costs are all 'costs of ownership' with the exception of all variable costs associated with the use of the equipment. Excess costs may arise from:

Poor specification of the equipment
Inadequate development
Subsequent redesign
Inefficient use due to slow installation and commissioning, poor specification or inadequate development
Poor maintenance/low reliability
Unsuitable siting of the equipment
Inadequate use of raw materials
Poor disposal.

Life cycle costing should help trade-offs to be established between the initial cost of the plant and its reliability during its working life.
'Costs' will be mostly concerned with establishing the range of target performance expected from the proposed plant:

Operational:
    Utilisation and down time per 168 hours per week
    Output per hour
    Manning levels
    Power consumption
    Material utilisation

LIFE CYCLE FUNCTIONS		SYSTEMS SPECIFICATION	PLANT DESIGN	PLANT MANUFACTURE	COMMISSION INSTALL	PLANT OPERATION	MAINTENANCE	REPLACEMENT
PERFORMANCE	TASK	Define parameters for technical performance	Balance performance against time and cost	Evaluate prototype performance		Assess performance to specification and reliability		Assess future performance need
	TECHNIQUES	Performance evaluation	Environmental planning	Tribology, corrosion				
QUALITY	TASK		Carry out value engineering study	Set quality limits	Commission and test to quality limits	Check quality to specification	Assess influence of maintenance on quality	Determine future quality need
	TECHNIQUES	Marketing factors	Probability theory, sensitivity analysis	Quality assurance, value engineering		Quality assurance, sampling	Corrosion, tribology, sampling	
RELIABILITY	TASK	Specify realistic limits	Assess failure probabilities		Test reliability	Set maintenance schedule	Maintain to schedule and assess reliability	Determine future reliability
	TECHNIQUES	Marketing forecasts	Value engineering, simulation	Value engineering	Forecasting		Preventive maintenance, probability analysis	
DOWNTIME	TASK	Collect data from previous plant records	Assess maintenance need in light of specification	Snags carried forward	Snags carried forward	Establish actual downtime		Evaluate progressive future downtime
CONTROL	TASK	Evaluate project, set control parameters and reporting	Control design schedule time and cost	Control manufacture, schedule, time, cost, quality	Pre-planning implemented control schedule and cost	Control cost and progress	Control maintenance cycle and cost	Collate life-cycle cost for appraisal
	TECHNIQUES	Project appraisal	Network analysis		Network analysis	Linear programming	Network analysis	Project evaluation
COST	TASK	Calculate whole life-cycle cost	Allocate design costs	Allocate manufacture cost, set price	Allocate installation cost	Assess cost of operation and downtime	Assess cost of maintenance	Assess and evaluate economics

	TECHNIQUES	Life-cycle costing, investment appraisal, sensitivity analysis	Financed, cost accounting, management accounting	Cost and management accounting	P E R T (cost)	Cost and management accounting	Marginal costing	Cost forecasting D C F, investment appraisal, cost benefit analysis
SCHEDULING	TASK	Request schedule as part of quotation	Produce manufacture and installation schedules	Set work flow based on schedule	Install based on schedule	Set work flow for production	Set maintenance schedule	Schedule replacement phase
	TECHNIQUES	Planning	Resource scheduling	Work study, resource scheduling, materials handling	Work study, resource scheduling, materials handling	Work study, materials handling, linear programming	Work study, resource scheduling, materials handling	
TIME	TASK	Set design plan	Utilise feedback to reduce design time	Work study production process	Value of long-term commissioning	Investigate economic runs	Evaluate maintenance load	Determine economic life
	TECHNIQUES	Marketing factors	Critical path analysis	Critical path analysis		Critical path analysis		
FEASIBILITY	TASK	Carry out feasibility study to set specification	Use feasibility study data	Test operating feasibility				Assess project feasibility
	TECHNIQUES	Probability theory	Probability theory	Modelling, synthesis	Simulation			Cost benefit analysis
RECORDS	TASK	Specify records to be kept (up to delivery)	Determine future records needed	Maintain process and manufacture records	Keep commissioning log	Keep production, downtime, cost records	Keep maintenance records	Collate records
	TECHNIQUES	Information systems, information theory	Systems analysis	A D P	Network analysis	A D P	A D P	
FEEDBACK	TASK	Keep specification up-to-date	Modify design in light of feedback	Feedback design	Feedback to design and sales	Feedback to purchasing and design	Feedback to previous stages	Feedback to all previous stages
	TECHNIQUES	Information theory	Behavioural science					

Fig. 29.3 Some examples of relationships between life-cycle functions and relevant techniques

Revenue to be earned: product mix per year
Total operating costs per machine hour.
Non-operational:
Design and development cost
Installation cost
Servicing and general maintenance
Need and cost of spares.

Costs should be built up for each major piece of plant. The usual standard costing or financial accounting system does not follow this course and separate accounts for major pieces of plant may be necessary. Some costs — maintenance spares, for example — may not be identified in the system. The indirect cost penalties for downtime or below standard performance are not always stated as clearly as they should be.

Operating costs should be channelled back to the design engineers.

Design aspects of terotechnology

The physical design of the plant will be beyond the scope of terotechnology. What will be needed, however, will be the parameters of the design as follows:

(a)   The performance required from the machine:
Output rates
Utilisation
Downtime
Tolerances
Material utilisation
Power consumption.
(b)   Environmental factors:
Location
Temperature and humidity
Safety
Corrosion
Noise
Atmospheric pollution — smoke, dust
Type of workforce needed to operate plant safely.
(c)   Company strategy:
Date on stream
Capacity usage
Product mix
Quality of production
Adaptability
Interchangeability with plant already installed.

(d)   Other factors:
        Expected life
        Resource capacity
        Installation difficulties
        Technologies — training requirements.
(e)   Cost:
        As stated under 'cost' heading.

Supportive data should include:
   Corporate plan
   Test data on installations already made and user data
   Product specifications of suppliers
   Material quality standards
   Feasibility study reports

Comment and advice should come from:
   Corporate planning
   Production management
   Maintenance management
   Other users.

Trade-offs should be established to help ensure that maximum contribution is gained throughout the life of the plant. Contribution in this instance will be the difference between sales revenue gained by the plant and all the costs it incurs during its lifetime.

6   Maintenance in terotechnology

(a)   Maintenance management should provide an input at the plant design stage to ensure that maintenance costs and spares replacement costs are considered in the investment appraisal. The design should consider trade-offs between increased plant cost and decreased maintenance costs.
(b)   Condition based maintenance should be developed. This implies:

   Instituting sensing mechanisms (occasionally human) to indicate the state of a piece of plant — e.g. vibration analysis, spectrographic oil analysis and infra-red photography.

   Relating maintenance costs to the condition of the plant.

   Ensuring reliability studies and statistical appreciation of potential breakdowns are made.

7   Purchasing

Purchasing managers should:

(a)   Ensure that an adequate specification is drawn up on which suppliers can quote.
(b)   Not assume that first cost is so important that other considerations can be excluded.
(c)   Form a team with design and production engineers to explore tenders or quotations.

8   Installation and commissioning

Many problems which subsequently disturb operational performance stem from faulty installation.

9   Benefits from taking a terotechnological approach

These appear to be:

(a)   Lower total cost of the ownership of plant
(b)   Greater plant reliability
(c)   General improvements in operational efficiency
(d)   Lower maintenance costs
(e)   Better cross-functional communications which should enhance company performance.

NOTE

1   *Terotechnology: An introduction to the management of physical resources*, Department of Industry, Committee for Terotechnology, 1975.

30

Plant layout

30.1 INTRODUCTION

A useful definition of plant layout is 'the arrangement of machinery and associated services and the flow of materials and components, which provide the fastest production at least cost, while taking account of all the environmental factors which influence the layout'.

A good plant layout will minimise cost by helping in:

Reducing:
    The effort needed by operatives to carry out their tasks.
    The number of operatives needed.
    Handling movements within the production process.
    Walking and other non-production activities by operatives.
    Operative fatigue.
    Work in progress.
    Material losses.
    The use of services of all kinds:
        Power
        Maintenance
        Tooling
        Inspection
        Storekeeping
Improving:
    Material quality
    Cost control
    Supervision
    The morale of operatives by providing good working conditions.

Improving production control:
  Shortening lead times
  Providing consistent output
  Ensuring less rejects
  Stabilising lead times
  Minimising order loss (i.e. orders going astray during the production process).
Aiding control generally:
  Enabling production counting and measuring of performance to be simple and effective.
Minimising and improving the use of capital investment by:
  Providing facilities for change of product mix.
  Maximising machine utilisation.
  Maximising output per machine.
  Reducing the number of operatives per machine.
  Reducing the floor space needed.
  Reducing the materials handling equipment required.
Taking account of legal requirements:
  For example the provisions of the Health and Safety at Work Act.
Providing for:
  Security
  Prestige.

It will be seen that some of the factors quoted could be mutually exclusive.

30.2   CARRYING OUT PLANT LAYOUT CHANGES

Few production managers will ever have the opportunity to design a manufacturing unit from scratch. Even where this does arise, it is usually done by a team — architects, engineers, methods, personnel, materials handling specialists, etc.

Once a factory is built and in operation, there is limited freedom to modify the existing plant layout. The principal savings should have been gained at the planning stage.

A survey of an existing layout might begin by looking at the following:

1   The layout, by plan or blueprint.
2   The production processes performed; the flow of materials — in numbers and weight. A movement diagram of material flow would be useful.
3   Operational activities:
      Machines and machine utilisation (maximum and minimum).
      Operatives per square foot.
      Services and how they are brought to the production process.

Bottlenecks.
Storage areas, especially in-process storage.
Materials handling equipment.

The analysis recommended is then

4   How much space is taken up by:
    Production machinery
    In-process storage.
    Non-production functions:
        maintenance, offices of various kinds.
5   What working conditions exist:
    Hazards.
    Space problems.
    Bad working practices.
6   What constraints are imposed on the plant layout by:
    The building — one floor, two floors.
    The site.
    Space.
    Light.
7   What money is available for a revised layout? How can adjustments or changes be justified?
8   Apply general principles and state:
    If interdependent operations, activities and departments are in general proximity.
    If the layout facilitates flow process type manufacturing operations.
    Whether the layout follows one of the following plans:
        Straight line.
        U-shaped.
        Divergent process.
        Convergent process.
        E plan.
    Are the most widely used services (maintenance, stores) located centrally?
    Are all obnoxious and dangerous stores isolated?
    Are materials handling procedures and warehouses an integral part of the layout?
    Is arduous or delicate work separated from general production?
    Is noise a problem?

By using a three-dimensional model layout, scaled drawings or other media, the following might be attempted:

The use of different layouts e.g. U-shaped, E form etc.

The different flows of materials which seem possible.
Different locations for:
  Key machines.
  Warehouses.
  Stores.
  Service areas.
  Receiving and despatch areas.

Power and service lines of all kinds need to be shown on any diagram, plan or model made, and also possible potential improvements.

Complaints concerning heating, lighting, ventilation, congestion etc. should be collected and reviewed. Information concerning production activities should include:

Volumes of production.
Types and variety of products made.
Hours of work normally planned for different parts of the plant.
Whether the products can be made as standard items up to a specific point in the process. This information will be important in establishing in-process buffers.
Whether sub-assemblies dictate the relationship between main assembly and sub-assembly areas.

30.3   MATERIALS HANDLING

Plant layout and materials handling procedures are complementary in their effects on shopfloor activities. The materials handling procedures will help to determine:

Aisle widths.
Storage areas.
Transfer equipment and space between production equipment.
Production flow.
The number of operatives required to handle in-process materials.

30.4   FUNCTIONAL RELATIONSHIPS

A travel chart (Fig. 30.1) should be used to indicate functional relationships. Each area or unit which receives or despatches products or materials should be listed. The numbers or weights of despatches should then be shown against the units or areas receiving them. A numeric system should be used to indicate

		From							
	A	B	C	D	E	F	G	H	I
A		31	12		11	12	10	–	–
B	11			40	12	13	–		
C	21	–	61					17	
D	13			60		70			
E	41		20					16	
F	11		20			24			
G	21								
H			60					21	

(To, at left of rows)

Fig. 30.1   Plant layout travel diagram

the amounts passing between two points. The higher the number the nearer together the points should be.

That principle may not apply if gravity is used in the transfer process. In that case downward rather than horizontal flow can be used to move items considerable distances, provided power is not needed to raise them later.

30.5   ENVIRONMENTAL FACTORS

These are obviously important and reference should be made to Chapter 4.

30.6   PROCESS VERSUS PRODUCT LAYOUTS

Process and product layouts are often in contention in optimising plant layout. A process layout is one where flexibility can be obtained in the manufacturing activity. Like activities are put together. One machine may make several different products. The process therefore is specialised and can be subjected to efficient supervision and maintenance.

Product layouts are typified in car assembly plants. Such layouts should reduce handling costs and production time. Work in progress should be minimised.

In many instances a combination of product and process layout is desirable.

30.7   PLANT LAYOUT AND WORK ORGANISATION

The importance of work organisation may dictate change of plant layout to accommodate new ideas in primary work group structure:

1   Work stations may be established which enhance social exchange.
2   The work unit and associated production equipment should aid autonomous work group activities.
3   Job enlargement, if not enrichment, could in part dictate the design of production flow processes.
4   More space may be needed for relaxation and other non-working activities than has been allocated in the past.
5   Operator environment may have to be improved.

31

Materials handling

31.1 INTRODUCTION

The Financial Times of 10 May 1977 gave the annual cost of materials handling and storage in the UK as £8 billion. It went on to quote a Department of Industry [1] study of thirty engineering companies completed in 1976 which showed that approximately £90 million might be saved through improved methods of storage and materials handling.

Materials handling is clearly an important area for improving cash flow, reducing costs and raising productivity.

31.2 PRINCIPLES

As in most other technologies there are basic (materials handling) principles; the majority of these are listed below:

1 Materials handling is a service function — it is not an end in itself. There is a danger of becoming carried away with the potentialities, neatness, automatic and other features of handling systems at the expense of the overall requirements of the company.
2 There are two ways of considering a materials handling system. First design an ideal system and then modify it as little as possible to meet local constraints — structural walls, fixed machinery, etc. Secondly, start with the existing layout and other 'unalterable' features of the factory — e.g. shift system worked, downtime due to poor maintenance, machine technologies, capital investment.
3 Safety requirements must be considered — no overloading of equipment,

safe operating practices, satisfactory lighting, condition of floors, structural limitations, aisle widths.

4   Movement should be reduced in time and distance wherever possible.
5   Materials should be deposited as near as possible to their point of use and if possible prepositioned so that no further movement is needed.
6   Handling and rehandling of all kinds should be minimised or eliminated.
7   Continuous movement is more efficient than irregular movement.
8   Equipment should set a uniform pace.
9   Equipment utilisation should be as high as possible.
10 It is usual to establish fixed routes for all handling devices — e.g. fork lift trucks.
11 Wherever possible flowline principles should be used.
12 Motion economy should be applied wherever human work is involved.
13 Equipment should be as simple as possible, consistent with the material or products to be moved and speed of movement — e.g. gravity rollers might be used instead of powered conveyors where material moves down inclined planes.
14 Equipment should be standardised if possible.
15 In all cases, use method study and work simplification.

31.3   UNIT LOADS

The unit load principle is one to have in mind wherever materials handling and storage is considered. Perhaps the most telling example of the principle in use is 'containers' in road, ship and rail transport. As far as possible loads are built into a container which is not opened or repacked until the final destination is reached. The load, irrespective of composition, is handled as one unit and all materials handling equipment and systems are designed accordingly.

31.4   TYPES OF EQUIPMENT

Types of materials handling equipment will not be discussed in detail. Many useful magazines and books give such information [2]. Briefly the main types are:

1   Aerial ropeways and cableways

2   Conveyors

The more common types are:

Chutes
Roller conveyors

Belt conveyors
Drag links
Bar or slot
Tow
Screw
Pneumatic
Bucket or tray elevators
Car and chain conveyors
Monorails.

Most conveyors are expensive to install, cheap to run, reliable in operation, require little maintenance, are inflexible and restrict plant layout changes. There is, however, a useful family of small portable conveyors usable to great advantage for various purposes.

3   Hoists and lifts

4   Cranes

It is difficult to define cranes precisely as they shade in one direction into hoists and in the other into conveyors. The possibilities are:

Portable or mobile
Travelling (fixed track)
Fixed
Other sub-types including
    job
    gantry
    bridge
    derrick.

5   Trucks and tractors

These will include:

Straddle
Pedestrian controlled
Hand operated
Industrial tractors.

6   Pallet handling trucks and pallets

Perhaps the greatest impact on materials handling in the last forty years has been through the advance of palletisation and associated equipment. A pallet is a portable platform on which goods are placed to form a 'unit load' for handling and stacking. A stillage is a simple form of pallet, usually disposable and therefore cheaply constructed.

A variety of trucks has been designed for handling pallets, including:

Fork lift trucks — a generic term covering all types of truck capable of using forks to lift pallets.
Reach trucks — where the forks are telescopic to facilitate stacking.
Stackers — designed to operate from batteries or mains in a fixed position.
Hand pallet trucks.
Stillage trucks — hand operated single fork trucks.

Various devices can be used with fork lift trucks:

Side shifter attachments for correct lateral positioning
Special loading and offloading attachments
Clamping arms and grabs
Tilting, rocking and rollover devices.

7   *Earth moving equipment — which need not concern us.*

8   *Various miscellaneous equipment:*

Van and lorry loaders
Lorry floor conveyors
Lifting tail gates
Vibrating screens
Hydraulic bridges.

9   *Automatic transfer equipment*

This category is undergoing more rapid development than any other at the present time, because of the general trends towards automation.

31.5   OBJECTIVES OF A MATERIALS HANDLING SYSTEM

The objectives of the materials handling system will help determine its design, its interaction with the many production activities and the ultimate cost of moving material.

Objectives which might be pursued are:

1   Improved production performance by speeding up material flow. Fewer hold-ups due to lack of material. Lower unit cost of production.

2 Less work in progress and so an improvement in cash flow.
3 Reduced labour costs of handling material.
4 Better utilisation of shopfloor and warehouse.
5 Fewer breakages.
6 Reduced fatigue of operatives and other shopfloor personnel. Better facilities, better jobs and chances to make higher bonus.
7 Reduced accidents.
8 Improved product quality.
9 Better customer service.
10 Generally increased safety.

The objectives, therefore, can be divided in two:

Improvement of production performance and reduction of costs.
Improvement of conditions for shopfloor personnel.

Feedback from the production system is a vital part of designing materials handling systems.

31.6 ANALYSIS

Analysis of the production system must be concerned with the overall system and the cost and efficiency of the materials handling sub-system.

As Fig. 31.1 suggests, all the elements affecting materials handling need to be identified and reported:

The environment
Inputs
Objectives
Feedback.

Taking a traditional view, the cost of materials handling might be the first piece of the analysis. As *Materials Handling Costs* [1] suggests, the majority of the companies investigated by a pilot study in the engineering industry did not know their true handling costs and had higher materials handling costs than necessary. These costs might be broken down as follows:

Materials handling equipment
    depreciation
Labour costs
    direct
    maintenance
    purchasing
    other.

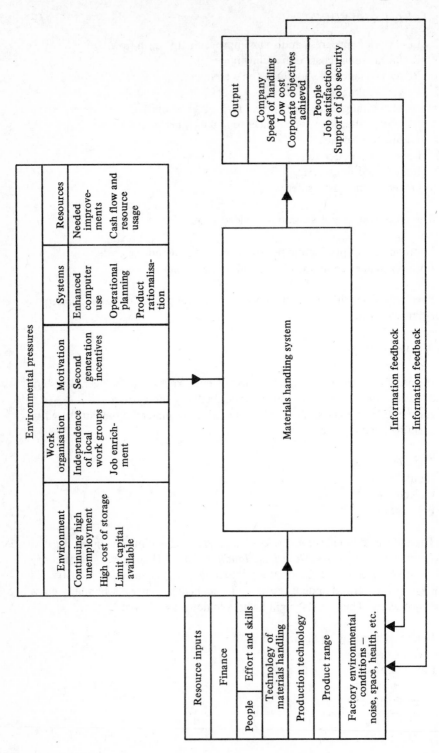

Fig. 31.1   The materials handling system

Space utilisation/building utilisation
  offices
  production
  gangways
  storage.
Storage equipment
  racks
  bins
  pallets
  etc.

Running costs and depreciation are needed in each case.

The losses caused by the materials handling system should then be calculated:

Holdups and bottlenecks
Inadequate use of storage space
Poor customer service
Breakages
Misused labour.

In improving the materials handling system then, there is a need to consider the approach shown in Fig. 31.2. The factors quoted may appear to be trite in themselves but they emphasise the need to relate the materials handling system not just to the techniques normally associated with good handling practice but with the production system as a whole. Inputs to the system are finance (how much is available for new equipment or systems changes); people — their skills and effort; production technology; the product range and the factory environment. Corporate objectives would also be added usually — customer service, cash flow, etc. The technology of materials handling may have to accommodate the pressures on the system — general environment, motivation, systems, resources and work organisation.

Group technology

Group technology provides a suitable example of the relationship required between a materials handling or plant layout sub-system and its environment. (Group technology has been well described in many books and articles [3]).

It is based on the assumption that grouping manufacturing resources such as machines and making them interdependent in a cellular fashion has many advantages over the functional layout which has normally been found in batch shops.

Functional layouts where, say, all the lathes in a factory are grouped

Production systems circumstance or requirement	Materials handling requirement
Outside and inside environment	
Continuing high unemployment into the foreseeable future.	Reluctance by workforce to allow any change which produces even moderate redundancy. Major developments may therefore be put into abeyance or developed piecemeal.
High cost of storage.	High density storage. Narrow aisle handling systems. High-bay pallet storage.
Reduction in environmental pollution — dust, noise, health risks, etc.	Equipment designed to reduce environmental pollution, in its widest sense, is needed.
Pressure on customers to buy larger lots of rationalised products.	Possibility of 'bulk handling' and enhancing unit load principle. Container use increase even in smaller lots. 'Warehouse retailing'.
Work organisation	
Local autonomy given to production groups. Shopfloor personnel to play a greater part in organising their own work flow and job structuring.	Materials handling permits job interchange and group co-operation. 'Cellular techniques' may be best — i.e. group technology idea (but see earlier comments on GT).
Need to provide 'job enrichment' for the shopfloor.	Equipment will be needed to help reduce boredom.
Fatigue inducing jobs need to be minimised.	Fatigue lessening equipment — for example, prepositioning of work for machine loading.
Systems	
Growth of operational planning which links various functions together.	Equipment linkage necessary to reduce the need for work in progress and buffering of operations.
Production control/production scheduling.	Use of equipment which helps scheduling and control.
Computer usage in systems.	Control through the activation of control monitoring in the materials handling system — e.g. shopfloor movements, receipts into warehouse etc.
	Process control improved (with distributive processing).
	VDU's for monitoring purposes.

Fig. 31.2   Improving the materials handling system

Product rationalisation.	Rationalisation of materials handling equipment to handle a rationalised product range effectively. Reduction of the number of product lines should reduce amount of warehousing space needed.
Motivation	
Introduction of second generation incentives.	Materials handling must be seen to augment added value or profit gains.
Reduce variable costs (other than labour).	Advance of simple handling and packaging techniques — shrink wrapping and disposable pallets etc.
Resources	
Improvement required in resource usage — machines and material.	Equipment which reduces breakages, improves quality and provides accurate feeding of machines.
Shortage of capital.	Extension of current technologies — pallets, unit loads, simple conveyors, etc.
	Slow acceptance of the need for high cost automation.
Shortage of space in the factory and warehouse.	High stacking densities.
	Narrow aisle systems.
	Better racking design.
	Faster handling of goods between production, storage and despatch.
Reduction in stockholding required to improve cash flow.	Better stock control facilities, allied with visual presentation of stocks to show current levels.
Resource control must be improved.	Greatly increased need to monitor all forms of materials handling activity.

Fig. 31.2   *(Continued)*

together, tends (say the protagonists of GT) to produce extremely complicated product-route patterns, resulting in high work in progress, bottlenecks and more orders delivered late than early.

A 'components analysis' reveals that in most batch processes there are product families which take common routes. Group layouts can be designed to be the basis of group technology.

Group technology, therefore, appears to be a response to environmental pressures — i.e. failings in the production system. Its benefits have been suggested as being:

Reduced setting up time

Less work in progress

Greater job satisfaction (as operatives are encouraged to move about from one job to another in the GT cell)

Production planning and control is made easier
Scrap rates decline
Speed of throughput is increased.

However, some of the most ardent advocates of GT have now reneged [4] and suggest that it is far from being the effective production method claimed, for the following reasons:

Job satisfaction can be less in GT than with a functional layout.

The use of product families constrains rather than helps production planning.

Incentive schemes appropriate to GT are difficult to design and operate.

Under-utilisation of equipment is often high.

So, it is concluded, group technology should not be advocated as a panacea for all the ills of batch production.

31.7   IMPROVEMENT IN MATERIALS HANDLING SYSTEMS

There seem to be four main possibilities for improvement [1]:

1   Elimination. This is a standard method study approach usually applicable with advantage. Elimination of a materials handling movement is ideal. An analysis of the number of movements a product makes during production, storage and despatch should initiate an 'elimination application' questioning the need for such movements.
2   Mechanisation — it may not cost very much to put some mechanical muscle into the system.
3   Better systems design. Methods study may again play a leading part in providing a better materials handling system.
4   Improved organisational structure. Materials handling is usually 'nobody's business'. It is a minor part of a production manager's responsibility, or could be tagged on to a material manager or controller, maintenance manager or someone in charge of internal transport. Centralising the control of materials handling often helps its efficiency.

31.8   DEVELOPMENTS

Like the production system itself the materials handling system is subject to the influences of external and internal environments. Technology is obviously a key factor in materials handling. Automation springs to mind immediately. So far, however, automation has been applied to a restricted group of industries with continuous processes and with fairly uniform products.

It is difficult, then, to determine what materials handling will be like in the future without reference to developments within the production system itself.

NOTES

1 *Materials Handling Costs: a new look at manufacture*, Department of Industry, 1977.
2 For example: *Production Equipment News*; *Materials Handling News*; publications of the National Materials Handling Centre, Cranfield Institute of Technology, Cranfield, Bedford.
3 For example: G. A. B. Edwards, *Readings in Group Technology*, The Machinery Publishing Co., 1971.
4 R. Leonard and K. Rathmill, 'The Group Technology Myths', *Management Today*, January 1977.

32

Quality control

32.1 INTRODUCTION

Most modern systems of quality control use statistical methods to eliminate the need for 100 per cent inspection. Consequently rejects will not be eliminated but reduced to an acceptable level. Quality is not absolute. What would be acceptable for a mass produced car, would not be so for a space vehicle. Quality control and inspection have a price. They should be so set that a quality level determined by production and marketing management is maintained without undue expense. The quality of a product should be a 'standard acceptable to customers at a price they are prepared to pay'.

32.2   100 PER CENT INSPECTION AND SAMPLING

Quality control and inspection are certainly not synonymous. Inspection is the process of examining products in production and determining whether they meet a predetermined standard. Quality control is a 'system for measuring and recording the variables that affect quality in a methodical manner, so that the values and trends can be compared with standard and corrective action taken'. Inspection is part of this process.

100 per cent inspection, if practised by human inspectors, is likely to give less than 100 per cent results. Contrary to popular belief 100 per cent inspection will fail to find all quality defects. This has been proved in numerous experiments. The sheer monotony of measuring or looking at every item produced will eventually allow some defective products to go through undetected.

32.3 WHAT IS QUALITY CONTROL?

Quality control should be established after considering the following:

1 What precisely is quality control expected to achieve? With the majority of manufactured articles, it is unreasonable to expect every product unit made to be without defect. What cost is justifiable to limit faults to an acceptable proportion?

2 The probability of a fault will rise with the number of components in the finished product. (This is why motor cars are unreliable to some degree.) The multiplication law of probabilities shows that if there are six components in a product, each of which is 90 per cent reliable, the reliability of the product will only be 53 per cent (0.9^6).

3 Quality standards should be set after establishing quality control objectives. They should include:

(a) The engineering specification. This defines the limits of acceptability from an engineering or processing point of view and will normally be set by the design office.

(b) The operating standard. This is a target type standard, based on what careful operators should be able to achieve, e.g. the number of breakages when packing glassware; the wastage of printed biscuit-tin lids due to off-centre stamping. These standards are set by line management from practical experience.

(c) Quality control standards. These standards take account of the limits of accuracy the process can achieve, and the level of quality which management desires based on the product's net sales revenue and customers' quality expectations.

(d) How to inspect. The standards of product acceptance will help to determine the methods of inspection, the equipment, and general control principles. For example:

The dimensional accuracy required will determine the use of jigs, micrometers, plug gauges (go/no-go) or other equipment.

Attribute testing may be as important as dimensional quality control.

In high speed mass production regular process charting is essential.

Statistically based sampling should ensure that appropriate confidence limits can be assured.

It is important to correct out of course events as early in the production process as possible. Final inspection alone may be totally inadequate in improving material yield.

Patrol inspectors who carry out tests for quality at any operation have considerable advantages.

Once inspection has been carried out, control reports are required. These should be of two types — process control charts for operatives and quality control reports on numbers rejected and reasons.

The customer is the final arbiter of quality control. Customer reports on quality defects should be routed via the quality control section. It may still however be a marketing problem.

32.4   QUALITY CONTROL ORGANISATION

On the principle that to put the cops with the robbers will only lead to contamination of the police, many companies separate the quality control function from that of production line management. In practice this could cause antagonism between line and quality control managers.

At the core of the debate is the problem of who is responsible for quality — operating management or quality control. Where they are separate should an inspector have the power to stop production if he finds that product quality is lower than standard?

Line management is responsible for producing at the right cost and quality. Quality control seems a key part of the production function.

In practice, where there is separation of function, quality control personnel could easily concentrate on trapping deficient material before it is sent to the customer, rather than on improving the product reject rate or material yield. While a quality longstop is important, it is much more important that product defects be stopped as early in the process as possible. Machine defects should be caught as soon as they occur. Maximisation of material yield is a prime quality objective.

32.5   QUALITY CONTROL PROCEDURES

Two basic statistical laws apply in quality control:

1 The law of statistical regularity. This states that if a fairly large number of items is taken randomly from a much larger group, the items taken will, on average, possess the characteristics of the larger group.
2 The law of inertia of large numbers. This suggests that where one part of a group varies statistically in one direction, it is likely that the other part of a group will vary in the opposite direction. The total change therefore will be small.

These laws are the foundation of statistical quality control. Sampling techniques which are devised will largely follow activity sampling procedures.

The statistical measurement normally used is the deviation from a predetermined level of acceptance. This measurement is normally called 'standard deviation', and is determined as follows.

From a sample of products needing quality inspection the arithmetic mean of the quality measurement is determined. The deviation from the arithmetic mean is found for each item. The deviations are squared and the arithmetic mean of all the squares determined. Finally the square root of the mean is calculated.

The root mean square deviation (to give it its other title) can be established as follows:

$$S = \frac{SD}{\sqrt{N}}$$

Where   S = standard error of the mean
       SD = standard deviation of the products in the sample
       N = number of products in the sample

Sampling needs to be done randomly and confidence or control limits are normally established.

The results of the sampling are recorded on control charts. If practical, such charts should be posted alongside machines — not in the quality control office. They can be changed daily or at some other suitable frequency and the completed sheets kept for further analyses forming the basis of weekly or monthly reports.

The chart is in the form of a graph (see Fig. 32.1) on which the measured value (weight, thickness, etc.) is plotted against the sample number. The chart will carry several pairs of horizontal lines. Inside the band enclosed by these two lines is a second pair — the action limits; these are sometimes called the upper and lower control limits. If a sample average measurement strays outside these limits action is taken at once. Inside this inner band is a pair of lines called the warning limits. Measurement beyond these inner boundaries calls for extra watchfulness and possibly resampling. At the centre is the process average line. It is possible to plot individual results rather than sample averages if the process is reasonably stable. If sample averages are plotted it will also be necessary to plot the range within each sample on an accompanying chart; this chart will contain the twin pairs of action and warning lines. These two control charts are called 'mean' and 'range' charts respectively.

This type of charting is very easy to prepare if a process is stable and measurements tend to drift slowly through the permissible range. Warning and action limits, if desired, can be set empirically, e.g. with the warning limit sufficiently far from the action limit to allow resampling before the process passes the action limit.

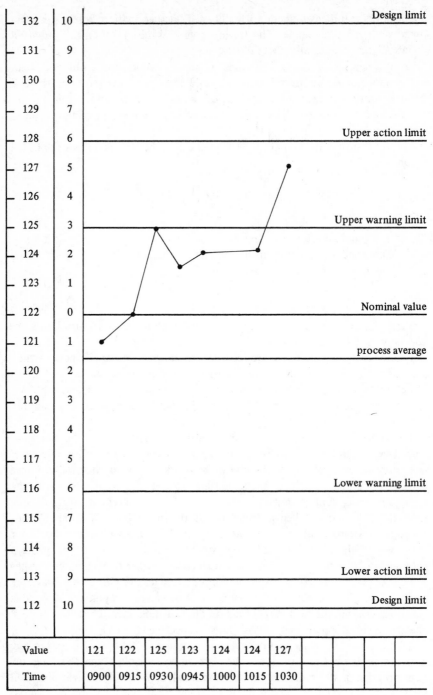

Fig. 32.1   Quality control chart

32.6 IMPROVING QUALITY

Many of the appropriate analyses and controls for improving product quality are given in Chapter 27 — Materials productivity — and will not be repeated here. However the following factors are still relevant:

1   Reports to management. Examples of the type of quality control report given to management are:
   (a)   Analysis of defects by type and cause.
   (b)   Comparison of defect levels with previous periods and standard levels.
   (c)   Comparisons between processes and departments.
   (d)   Long term trends in quality — say over six months.
   (e)   Reports on customer complaints and evaluations of returned articles.
   (f)   Basic quality control data — number of measurements taken, level of production sampled, cost of operating the function.
   (g)   Developments in quality control — new processes embraced, changes in inspection density, new attributes used.

2   A quality control audit. An audit might be covered by the following questions:
   (a)   What is the rejection level — in items, material losses (yield), cost?
   (b)   How many customer complaints are received each month, year?
   (c)   What complaints about quality do the marketing people make?
   (d)   How does the company's quality compare with competitors', especially from overseas?
   (e)   Looking at the company's quality control function, are the following aspects appropriate?
       Standards — too high or too low?
       Cost of quality — down time, adjustments, delivery delays.
       Knowledge and attitude of quality control personnel.
       Equipment for testing and measurement.
       Inspection techniques.
       Procedures for reporting quality drift.
   (f)   What improvements in quality have been made over the last five years?

33

Storekeeping

33.1 INTRODUCTION

Storekeeping often has an indeterminate existence. Few people are adequately trained for the function. It has a blurred place in many organisations. Responsibilities are not usually adequately defined. Yet good storekeeping is a vital part of the production activity, including prevention of misuse and theft of tools and equipment.

33.2 ORGANISATION

The storekeeper can report to the local production manager, works manager, production controller, maintenance manager, even the purchasing manager. The appropriate place in the organisation should depend upon its main accountabilities, e.g.:

To keep tools in good order
To give a good service to the production activity
To keep records of materials and re-order when necessary.

The predominance of an accountability such as die and jig control and the need to ensure that all are in good repair, might lead the stores to being part of the engineering function. Where the chief issues are raw materials and there is a need to keep stock levels under review with a detailed stock recording system, then purchasing department may be an appropriate home. Otherwise there seems no reason why production management should not be in control, though the production controller could be more suitable than local production management.

33.3   CASH WASTAGE

The stores are often a cause of cash wastage. Some of the reasons for this are:

1   Stocks are too high when measured against demand, cash flow requirements or return on stores investment.
2   Stocks are too low for the service levels offered and the restrictions or stoppages in production caused by too little stock of some or all stock items.
3   Too much writing off of stock through deterioration caused by poor stores control, bad housekeeping or inadequate storage area. Rusting, breakages, materials going beyond normal standing time may all occur.
4   Ordering of wrong stores, resulting in obsolescence.
5   Frequency of ordering too great and administration costs consequently too high.
6   Loss of cash discounts, demurrage, loss on returnable packages, etc. owing to inefficient system.
7   Pilferage. The stores is usually a happy hunting ground for the light fingered.
8   Excessive control. Too much control can often be as bad as too little. Too elaborate stock control systems may be expensive to administer. But it is better to have a complicated but good control if these complete the storeman's normal working time.
9   Over issues. Frequently material is over issued but unused material not returned to stores.
10   Wastage caused by poor stores layout; excessive heating and lighting is always a possibility.
11   Wrong type of storing and materials handling systems, which are too costly for the use to which they are put.

Space planning and location is often a key factor in ensuring that the stores will give an appropriate service to production.

33.4   SECURITY

It is sad to record that one of the most important aspects of storekeeping will be to minimise pilfering. Often the 'shrinkage' among tools usable at home is in excess of 20 per cent and is very costly to the organisation. The objects of stores security will be:

Not to put temptation in the way of employees.
To protect stores so that there is an irreducible minimum of loss.

The various elements in ensuring stores security might be:

1 Choose stores personnel of good character, known honesty and trustworthiness.
2 Physically isolate all stores vulnerable to theft. This may mean erecting wire mesh or even brick and steel partitioned stores which can only be entered through a lockable door.
3 Employees other than storemen should not be allowed into the stores. (Occasionally stores are used as a canteen area during lunch breaks and at other times. This should be forbidden.)
4 All receipts and issues should be covered by proper receipted and numbered records with duplicates.
5 As far as possible standard, prepacked quantities should be received and issued to permit a 'minimum load' of stores which need not be opened before use and so should reduce possibilities of theft.
6 If possible, a continuous inventory system (where a number of stock items are checked each day or each week) should be introduced, especially on items where pilferage is likely.
7 The number of people who can sign requisitions for stores items should be a minimum. Operatives should not be allowed to draw items on their signature alone.
8 The senior storekeeper should have a clear cut accountability for his stores and their losses.

33.5   STORES RECORDS

The following documents should be used in a storekeeping/stock control system if it is felt necessary. Records and recording should be kept to a minimum with, if possible, only one stock record.

1   Bin cards

Materials and stores items are usually kept in racks or bins. A bin card records receipts and issues and the running total of what remains in stores. Often a reorder minimum is quoted on the card and when this level is reached its correctness is checked against actual stock. A re-order note is then sent to purchasing department.

2   Stores requisitions

Usually these are in duplicate books and are only signed by senior personnel.

3   Material receipt or goods received notes

Often these are completed in triplicate. One copy is sent to purchasing department as evidence of receipt. A second copy goes to quality control for inspection purposes and a third retained.

4 Inspection clearance notes

In many companies where quality is stringently maintained an inspection clearance note has to be issued before any material is used.

5 Material transfer notes or credit notes

Stores requisitions will quote the material required, perhaps the catalogue number if used, the number or amount required and the cost centre on which the stores will be used. The management accounts related to the cost centre will be debited with the stores issue. Where material is transferred from one cost centre to another or is returned to stores for some reason, a material transfer note is completed to ensure that appropriate crediting and debiting takes place.

33.6 ACCOUNTING PROCEDURES FOR STOCK

33.6.1 Stock categories

Stock is usually categorised under the following headings:

1 Raw materials — any item which needs to be processed to make it into a sellable product.
2 Bulk stocks — stock which is kept in bulk, such as iron bars or cement.
3 Part-finished stock — work in progress which is awaiting further processing.
4 Components — usually bought out items which are fitted to company products.
5 Finished stock.
6 Consumable items — cleaning rags, cutting oils etc. consumed during production, but not as production material.
7 Jigs, tools, fixtures — these are tools needed in production.
8 Machine spares — general machine spares kept for breakdowns.
9 General maintenance — lighting, fittings and other items kept for factory maintenance purposes.

Each stock category is coded and given a separate entry in the stores ledger.

33.6.2 Valuing stock

There are various methods of valuing stock. Among the most common are:

FIFO

'First in first out'. Materials or stock are issued at actual cost. Issues are made in strict age order. It may, however, lead to 'under costing' of factory production during times of high inflation.

LIFO

'Last in first out'. Material or stock is issued in reverse order to FIFO. However, 'unfair' costing of production may still result when actual costs are used.

Average cost

All stocks are valued on an average basis. As new stocks are bought at higher prices, the average changes. In a period of high inflation, a 'profit' may be made on fairly old stock.

Weighted averages

In the average calculation weight is given to more recent purchases so that current production costs may truly reflect current stock costs.

Standard cost

A predetermined valuation of stock items is made at the beginning of the financial period. This is then used as the cost of stores to production. Actual costs are compared with standard and a variance determined where necessary and carried forward to the stock ledger.

33.6.3   Stores coding

Most storekeeping practice will embody some form of product coding for costing, valuing, or general recording, re-ordering and identification purposes. Codes are usually of three types:

> Alphabetic – A, B, C, etc.
> Numeric — 1/2462141 etc.
> Symbolic — Star, crescent, kite mark etc.

Often one or more types are used together. Alpha-numeric coding is used widely in computer activities.
Examples of coding are:

Arbitrary

A stores item is given a number or number and letter irrespective of its type, size, quality, use.

Designated

The stores item can, in part, be identified by the coding. For example, the letter A may give the quality of a material used in an item. The item may then be given a size coding — e.g. 300 mm × 300 mm × 150 mm may be 300300150. Finally the use of the item may be important — so a transmission spare part may be coded TR. The whole code may be, therefore, A/300300150/TR.

33.7 STORES LAYOUT, SPACE PLANNING AND MATERIALS STOCKING AND HANDLING EQUIPMENT

1 Finished goods

Finished goods are normally stored away from the shopfloor, adjacent to despatch bays.

2 Raw materials

Though raw materials also are normally kept clear of the main production area, it is not easy to introduce an ideal storage system. The following factors should be considered:

The means of receipt of raw materials — road, rail, water.
The method of receipt — bulk carrier, container, tanker, etc.
The type of material — liquid, solid, corrosive, gas.
The available space.
The point of receipt — one or several.
The point(s) of issue to production — one or several.
Whether special skills are required in unloading and loading.
The equipment needed for unloading and storing.

3 Consumable stores

Consumable and other stores required for issue to production will present several problems — e.g.

Centralisation versus decentralisation

The centralised store will require fewer people to run it; all storekeepers should become familiar with all stores stocked, making job interchange easy; better control and improved security are possible; less total space will be required.

The decentralised store will be closest to its production unit (crucial perhaps in giving a good service), consequently materials handling equipment may need to be improved or increased. Queueing may be less of a problem.

4   Space requirements

Space requirements will depend upon:

What access to the items stored is needed?
How flexible must the stores be?
What protection is required for the stores which are held?

Methods of storing are often crucial:

Stacking height
Bulk stacking possibilities.
Row stacking
The use of bins, shelves, and racks
The need to store in bulk through pallets
Type of materials held.

5   Other storage requirements

It will be important to consider:

Good lighting

The logical arrangement of stores — i.e. those items in most demand should be stored nearest to the queueing point.

Aisle space will be determined by access requirements — e.g. the use of high stacking equipment.

Racks, shelves, and bins.

Racks should be adjustable if possible and even portable. Wooden racks can usually be knocked up on site and have a softer surface than steel so should be more useful for storing delicate items.

Steel shelving can normally be erected easily, is adaptable and flexible. It is not a fire hazard and usually will need thinner supports than wood.

Bins can be fixed or movable. They provide the facilities to operate a 'two bin system' where a safety stock can be kept in one and normal stock in the other. When the normal stock is exhausted, the item is re-ordered. The replacement supply should arrive before the safety stock is used completely.

33.8   INVENTORY POLICY

Chapter 10 suggests that inventory control should be regarded as a principal part of the production control function. However, that chapter largely referred to finished goods inventories which normally would comprise the largest store by value in a manufacturing company. The policies needed for consumable stores could be different.

1   Type of stock control system

For consumable stores, it is likely that the more traditional forms of stock control will be used:

(a)   Maximum and minimum stock levels. A 'maximum' represents the most items which should be in stock at any time — based on weeks of use. Normally about twelve weeks' use is a maximum but this will depend upon order policy. Minimum stock will be a quantity determined by analysis of demand and lead time replacement (i.e. how long it will take for an order to arrive in the stores and be ready for use, after requisitioning).

(b)   Two bin systems — these could operate within a maximum and minimum system. The safety stock kept in the second bin is usually the minimum quantity.

(c)   More sophisticated systems will use the traditional re-order level method of determining when to re-order. The re-order level is the point to which stock must fall before a replacement batch is ordered.

(d)   Re-order quantities and appropriate theory (see Chapter 10) should also be used.

2   Budgeting stocks

Cash flow requirements may dominate inventory policy and dictate the levels of stock to be carried.

In this situation it will be a problem to allocate the money available for stocks of all kinds. Stock categorisation will help (see 33.6.1). Factory raw material supplies will probably receive the highest priority, followed by vital consumable stores such as cutting oils or drills.

The maximum quantities (if used) and re-order levels should be adjusted to take account of budgeted stock value. Erratic lead times may dictate adjustment to this general approach.

3   *Make or buy decisions*

In many factories it may be possible for the local production unit to make some stock items which might otherwise be purchased outside the company.

Where this can be done there can be direct comparison between the variable cost incurred and the price charged by a supplier. If the latter is less then buying out may be appropriate if no other policy needs (like keeping the factory employed) are being followed.

Where the factory is already fully occupied buying out may appear to be the only course of action for stores requirements. This may not be true if the sales revenue being obtained for the use of a stipulated amount of factory capacity is less than the supplier's price for items which would utilise the same capacity.

34

Maintenance

34.1 INTRODUCTION

There are indications [1] that maintenance costs in the UK are possibly £5,500 millions per year. These costs cover the value of maintenance materials held and used, direct labour costs, indirect labour of all kinds and work sub-contracted. Nearly a quarter of the costs appear to be in stocking maintenance tools — an indication of the need for good stock control.

Maintenance can be considered as part of capital resources management as Chapter 29 suggests.

34.2 OBJECTIVES

Objectives of a maintenance manager should not be to minimise maintenance costs or indeed to minimise machine downtime or stoppages. Like the use of many other production resources, maintenance should help to maximise the difference between the variable cost incurred on the plant and the sales revenue obtained from selling the products — i.e. 'contribution'.

This is more easily explained if the contribution hourly rate of a machine is calculated (which will be lost if the machine is idle). If the loss exceeds the cost of maintenance which could keep the machine in repair maintenance is advisable.

This marginal approval is often used in a formal way as Fig. 34.1 suggests. This line status report shows that it should be possible to increase the current capacity by 10,000 D/L if maintenance were better. If this output equalled twenty hours, and if extra maintenance costs were less than, say, £3,500 per week and breakdowns were eliminated, savings would be made.

Machine group	Tech max	Standard	Current capacity	Standard contribution hourly rate	Current capacity hourly rate	Reason for difference between standard and current capacity
Mixing Baking	10000 D/L	80000 D/L	60000 D/L	£190	£220	Breakdowns 10000 D/L Absenteeism 5000 D/L Product mix 5000 D/L

Fig. 34.1 Line status report and related maintenance costs

Unfortunately the work of a maintenance department will include many activities where the marginal approach will not apply — for example in repairing environmental equipment such as heating, ventilation or lighting, or the painting and repairing of buildings.

Various overall ratios for particular industries might be obtained and used to judge the effectiveness of local company maintenance teams. Even so, accurate comparisons may not be possible. Ratios might be:

Maintenance cost as a ratio of value of production machinery
Maintenance cost as a ratio of value of production buildings
Maintenance cost as a ratio of value of non-production buildings
Maintenance personnel as a ratio of direct operatives — total labour cost.

34.3 ORGANISATION OF THE MAINTENANCE FUNCTION

Maintenance can cover several functions and needs many different crafts as follows:

1 Building construction and maintenance. Maintaining the fabric of the building and its internal environment will be the most important activity. The craftsmen required will include painters, bricklayers, joiners, plumbers, glaziers, electricians plus general labourers to act as mates and to carry out general cleaning.
2 Mechanical engineering. Activities directly related to the production equipment and the associated service will be dominant. Steam and power equipment, steam heating, pipework, heat treatment, welding and sheet metal work will all come under this general heading. Fitters, turners, toolroom men, millwrights, will be the main craftsmen involved.
3 Electrical engineering. Electrical equipment of all kinds including power plants, switch boxes, wiring, transformers, motors, electronic control apparatus, recording devices, will come under this heading. Electronic engineers will probably gain greater importance over the traditional electrical engineers and electricians.
4 Site maintenance. This category should cover yards, roadways, railways (if one exists) outdoor cranes and other equipment, site fencing, rigging, drainage and water supply, collection and disposal of waste.
5 Plant safety. This fifth heading might usefully be introduced into maintenance, as a response to the Health and Safety at Work Act and would normally cover all the inspection and correction of defects which ensure safe working conditions.

A further division will be between those maintenance personnel who are workshop located — i.e. in the toolroom or fitting shop and those who are peripatetic. The toolroom will be an area where normal workshop or factory practice should apply with appropriate production control and management controls such as labour efficiency reports, material utilisation sheets etc.

Centralisation versus decentralisation may pose a real dilemma for anyone considering the organisation and control of the maintenance function.

Decentralisation fits in with the idea that work organisations of the future will have greater local autonomy and a wish for local people to carry out maintenance activities themselves. This seems to make sense of seconding to the work organisation maintenance men who perform normal production duties when not engaged on maintenance and share in the bonus scheme which the work organisation enjoys.

If spares are available locally it is likely that breakdowns will be repaired more quickly than with spares from a centralised unit.

Centralisation will provide rare specialist skills which can be deployed at crucial breakdowns. If much maintenance can be transferred to a central workshop, specialist equipment (which may be immovable) can be provided. It is likely that maintenance personnel can be brought under tighter control than if they were spread throughout the factory. Work output can be checked.

However, if the central site has to be located some distance from the production or other equipment which needs maintaining, then maintenance personnel could spend an inordinate amount of time journeying from central location to the area or machine needing attention.

Flying squads of mixed crafts may be one way in which maintenance of all types can be carried out.

34.5 PLANNING AND CONTROL OF MAINTENANCE WORK

As will be discussed further in section 34.5.1 control in maintenance must include a measurement of performance. The difficulties of measuring maintenance activities are:

1 A multiplicity of skills are used, often at widely differing parts of the factory, mostly on dissimilar jobs.

2 Jobs may appear to be repetitive to some extent — for example replacing an identical broken part in a machine at frequent intervals. But the conditions may be different — the machine more worn and the replacement harder to fit than on a previous occasion.

3 Many jobs occur in places and positions which are far from ideal. External work is frequent. Noise and dirt are usual companions to on-site repair jobs.

4 Direct supervision is often a problem. Many jobs are undertaken at one time in different parts of the plant, making supervision of any kind difficult.

5 Jobs tend to have an indeterminate work content — or so maintenance personnel would allege.

In considering 'control' what really is intended? Tighter control over the time taken on jobs is one consideration; ensuring that jobs are performed effectively is another. Improved co-operation between trades and a better use of tradesmen generally could be required.

34.5.1 Control procedures

1 A record of the plant to be repaired is a first step in gaining or improving control. A plant inventory will be needed which shows:
   Type of plant — a description of its design and use
   Plant capacity
   Current and potential utilisation
   Age
   Spares required
   Spares carried
   Some idea of the likelihood of breakdowns based on past performance. (A record of past breakdowns would be useful.)
   Any peculiarities of the plant — use of specific trades for example.
2 A record of maintenance carried out should be kept. This should quote:
   Type of machine or equipment involved
   The maintenance carried out
   Time taken to carry out the maintenance (both in absolute terms and in man hours of trades involved).
3 A record of maintenance personnel is then needed. Skilled craftsmen are usually difficult to obtain if less than average wages are paid. The record should show:
   Numbers by trade
   Turnover by trade
   Average pay by trade
   Where personnel are mostly deployed
   Average local pay for tradesmen
   Average national pay for tradesmen.
4 How maintenance is requested and carried out is a useful systems investigation.
   Who requests maintenance (i.e. who has the authority)?
   What documentation is used (e.g. a maintenance request form)?
   Is the cost of maintenance calculated by ensuring that a budgeted hourly rate is made for each tradesman and labourer? The hours spent on maintenance should be recorded on a maintenance job ticket and multiplied by the budgeted hourly rate. It should then be debited to the cost centre where the maintenance took place.
5 From an analysis of past maintenance activities and the time taken to do them does it seem possible to calculate job standards?
6 From a knowledge of the plant and machinery is it possible to standardise

methods of performing major tasks in the maintenance function?

7   An analysis of maintenance carried out in the plant may help to establish how maintenance personnel might be deployed and eventually trained.

8   A monthly work programme which sets out the main maintenance (planned) function can be used once a deployment has been agreed.

9   Toolroom, fitter shops and other workshop areas should be subject to the same production control philosophy as normal production activities.

10 General maintenance control might be improved by using:

    (a)   Planning boards. These can designate:
        Jobs being done
        Jobs requiring to be done
        Craftsmen or tradesmen's activity
        Time jobs started
        Times jobs might finish.

    (b)   An indication of the kinds of maintenance being requested/carried out — i.e.:
        Emergency — to be repaired immediately
        Emergency — to be repaired immediately, dangerous situation
        Repair — equipment or machine is broken down but repair is not required immediately
        Routine
        Planned.

    (c)   A category code (with sub-divisions where necessary).

    (d)   Cost centre coding which can be used to 'absorb' maintenance costs and give a useful indication of the costs of maintenance set against its value.

    (e)   Maintenance requisitions — completed by line managers.

    (f)   Job cards — issued for each job to be done. These should list:
        The job to be done, in as much detail as possible
        The standard or predetermined time for doing the job
        The number of men to be involved — by trade
        The stores to be used
        Time started
        The maintenance code
        The cost centres to which the maintenance cost should be debited
        The foreman, chargehand or senior craftsmen should record when the job has been completed and also:
            The time taken
            The stores actually used
            The actual personnel involved.
        Comments about the difficulty of the job, which may affect the standard time if this was in use. The maintenance manager or

clerk can then calculate the cost of the maintenance process. Recalculate the job standard if this seems necessary. Pass the cost to the cost office for debiting the appropriate cost centre. Update the planning board.

(g)   Departmental budgets. These should be completed to show:
Budgeted cost by trade or craft, materials, power, capital investment, clerical support, management and supervision, tooling requirements.

(h)   Reporting controls. These should include:
Actual costs set against the various budgets
Jobs carried out
Standard job times versus actual job times (an efficiency should be calculated)
Work backlogs (queue)
Absenteeism
Labour turnover by trade or craft.

34.6   TYPES OF MAINTENANCE

The following list of different types of maintenance might form the basis for a maintenance activity and its associated organisation and control.

1   Maintenance. The glossary of general terms used in maintenance organisation BSI 3811–1964, defines maintenance as 'work undertaken in order to keep or restore every facility (i.e. every part of a site, building and contents) to an acceptable standard'.

2   Planned maintenance. This is defined in BSI 3811–1964 as 'maintenance organised and carried out with forethought, control and records'. This is not very explicit and perhaps the following will be more acceptable. 'Planned maintenance is the studied evaluation of all plant and buildings with the intention of carrying out any maintenance before it is actually needed through breakdown or obvious deterioration in performance, with the aim of reducing emergency maintenance and the associated costs in machine stoppages.'

3   Corrective maintenance. This is really 'demand maintenance' requested by local line management when they need some repair to a machine or equipment.

4   Emergency maintenance. As distinct from corrective maintenance emergency maintenance has a very positive degree of urgency about it. A dangerous condition might have arisen or the repair needed may be vital in getting production back to normal.

5   Spare part reconditioning. This is often the function of personnel in the fitters' shop or tool room.

6   Tool repair. This can be needed because of normal tool wear, tool mal-
    function, or tool misuse. Tool wear can be embodied in a plan (e.g. after
    making X thousand products the tool is withdrawn automatically for
    repair); the others may demand emergency attention.
7   Capital work. This item is covered in Chapter 29 — Capital resources
    management. The main concern is that capital work, though not
    undertaken on a regular basis, is carried out effectively. This needs careful
    planning and control.
8   Plant and machinery installation. This in many respects is merely a
    secondary function of 7 above.
9   Waiting time. Unfortunately there is usually a high degree of maintenance
    waiting time. Some organisations operate a bonus system based on
    machines' running and utilisation, rather than maintenance time spent on
    them. This may increase waiting time.

34.6.1   Planned maintenance

Planned maintenance has had some acceptability but is now falling into
disrepute because the effort expended has not always been appropriately
rewarded.
    The advantages of planned maintenance are:

1   There are numerous operations which should be carried out regularly. In
    a chemical plant, for example, they are necessary to prevent corrosion or
    building up of scaling. Few people would run a car without some
    maintenance to avoid breakdown.
2   It should help to prevent breakdowns.
3   It should aid the planning of maintenance personnel.

    The disadvantages which have been found include:

4   The result is often not worth the effort. No commensurate improvement in
    production is gained.
5   Occasionally the most serious of breakdowns cannot be covered by
    planned maintenance. Metal fatigue for example could cause the breakage
    of crankshafts or key parts of a machine.
6   It may be better sometimes to allow a machine or part of a machine to
    break and then replace the damaged part instead of carrying out
    maintenance. Suppliers of domestic appliances often operate on this
    basis.

    Manuals for planned maintenance can be built up from drawings,
manufacturers' catalogues, plant records, photographs and sketches. They
should describe:

7   Standard maintenance procedures — what should be done.
8   How the maintenance should be carried out. If possible standard times for the various procedures should be introduced.
9   Training required.
10 The method for ensuring that the maintenance has been done effectively.

34.7   MAINTENANCE BONUS SCHEMES

The standard methods of measuring work are mostly unsuitable for maintenance activities. There is a variability in maintenance which seems to defy them. However, three systems have been devised to provide measurement. These are:

Universal maintenance standards
Methods time measurement-2, maintenance data
Basic work data.

1   Universal maintenance standards
    It is recommended that organisational improvements be introduced before the UMS approach is attempted.
    UMS, though based on MTM to some extent, uses 'time range slotting'. This method is developed from an analysis of patterns of repair work and establishing ranges of times for various maintenance jobs. The medians of the range are used as time standards. Small orders of less than one hour's duration tend to predominate in maintenance and local supervision is asked to time-band such jobs and keep a record of them.
    To find a slot for each job the planning/time study official compares the job with a 'bench-mark' timing. While a median time will not be accurate, the negative and positive times will probably cancel each other and give a realistic time.
    The two techniques used in UMS, therefore, are time range slotting and comparisons of work content.
2   MTM2 — maintenance data
    This method is based on MTM2 and uses hand-held tape recorders combined with 'data blocks' and simple verbal codes. It is a visual system, where the analyst classifies the behavioural characteristics of the movements of the work being done. The tapes are transcribed onto standard MTM2 analysis sheets. Time band categorisation is also used.
3   Basic work data
    The parent system of basic work data is simplified PMTS. It has been designed largely for maintenance work involving the assembling and disengaging of parts using typical maintenance tooling. Common patterns used in this process have been grouped into various combinations to

produce basic elements usable in maintenance work. The 'work data' has been simplified to give broad coverage of times for performing maintenance tasks.

34.7 CONCLUSION

The higher the plant value, normally, the higher the cost of maintenance. It is difficult to determine the precise ratio between the two as the age of the plant, the skill of operators, the need to keep the plant in operation, will be vital in measuring the need for maintenance and the justifiable costs.

With automation and microprocessors the skills required by maintenance personnel will change. The future of maintenance may depend, therefore, on the following:

1 How far production processes will change (e.g. through automation and microprocessors).
2 The availability of skilled personnel.
3 The differentials in pay between production personnel and craftsmen.
4 The build-up of local work organisations where operatives and first line supervisors take on some responsibility for maintenance activities.
5 The incentive schemes which maintenance personnel will accept or which can be introduced.
6 The gradual obsolescence of some maintenance craftsmen and whether they can be retrained.
7 The improvement in diagnostic tools to determine where maintenance is needed.
8 The changes in the ratio between variable and fixed costs and the need to keep production machines turning over.

But no matter what the future holds, maintenance should always be seen as a trade-off between its costs and the savings in production costs which good maintenance can produce.

NOTE

1 See *Works Management*, April 1978.

35

Tooling and tooling control

35.1 INTRODUCTION

The aims of tooling control are:

1 To ensure that the requisite numbers of tools are available for production purposes when required.
2 To order tools to accommodate current and future production demand, which will make products to agreed specifications.
3 To ensure that cost/performance ratios are rigorously applied in tool design.
4 To record tool availability and life.
5 To make sure that the tooling which is available will function for a stipulated period.
6 To provide an adequate tool repair service.

Among the more important problems often associated with tools and tooling and for which tool control should provide an answer are:

7 Tools of all kinds are often left on the shopfloor. It is usually nobody's business to ensure their return to the tool store.
8 Tools are wanted in a hurry to accommodate an urgent order; the system of tool checking and preplanned repair then fails.

'Tools' can be conveniently divided between:

Tools — any device which is designed to cut, or remove unwanted, material under guided conditions.

Jigs — any device which supports or holds work or guides tools.
Fixtures — any device which supports or holds work when tools are used.

'Tooling' in this chapter covers all three divisions.

35.2 NUMBERS OF TOOLS

What precise number of tools is to be stocked is a direct relationship between tool cost and customer demand.

It seems simple to say that the annual demand for a product will be 20,000 and sufficient tools will be made available for this quantity. But at what time intervals will the 20,000 be needed? All at once or at equal intervals throughout the year?

In the latter case it is likely that tooling numbers will be less than if the 20,000 were needed at once. In determining numbers, therefore, the following should be considered:

1 Tooling capacity per hour, per week, per month
2 Product demand — weekly, monthly, annually
3 Cost of tooling to meet product demand weekly, monthly or annually.

35.3 FUTURE DEMAND FOR TOOLING

Economic use of tooling will be found only where the market is predictable or where tool recovery costs can be embodied in the charge to the customer. In batch processing this is rarely possible and the economic use of tooling is much more difficult to determine. How should a tool such as a jig which could cost £1,000 or more be ordered? Should it be on the basis of one firm order where it is only possible to recover a fifth of the cost? Or should there be much more certainty that the full cost will be regained?

Tooling is an increasing cost as more sophisticated production techniques are introduced. Should it be enlarged on the chance that sufficient products will be made sometime to cover the cost or is something much more definite required?

35.4 COST-PERFORMANCE OF TOOLING

In considering tooling costs it is important to calculate costs other than the bought out or made cost. These will include:

1 Setting up costs. Some tools take longer to set up and break down than

others. This increases lost production time and could be important. It is always useful to compare set-up costs when considering different types of tooling.

2   Working costs. The time a tool takes to do a job will certainly affect production costs — cutting speeds for example may vary between one tool and another.

3   Repair or refurbishing costs. The cost of refurbishing some tools may be more than for others.

These three types of cost should be determined and added to the purchase costs. A normal DCF approach (see Chapter 29) might then be taken to evaluate one tool against another.

35.5 TOOL AVAILABILITY AND LIFE

Tool availability can be decided by the hours it is in use. Normally this calculation can be complicated, depending upon:

1   The total time of a machine cycle and the percentage of that time that the tool is in operation.
2   The actual time the tool is in use (from 1).
3   Volume or quantity of work done.
4   Speed in use.

Various tool life indicators can be obtained by using Brinell-hardness speed ratios. In practice, the numbers of pieces produced may be an adequate indication of how long the tool can be serviceable.

A tooling record card will be needed to record all tooling, including refurbishing occasions.

35.6 TOOL QUALITY

Quality can be defined as the tool's condition and capacity to carry out its required purpose. Regular inspection of tools may not be necessary if a stipulated refurbishing time has been established.

Regular quality control checks on product dimensions and general quality performance may not show that a tool needs refurbishing until rejects appear.

With some tools — dies for example — products could be made which will get progressively larger through die wear but which may be unnoticed if the extra size is ground off at a later operation.

Where tool life records are kept, a regular relationship between tool wear, refurbishing costs and quality of products made is possible. This should help to determine whether tools of the requisite quality are being obtained.

35.7   TOOL REPAIR SERVICE/TOOLROOM ACTIVITIES

Most sizeable industrial units will have their own tool refurbishing or repair service. The toolroom unfortunately is not usually a highly efficient area of a company. The reasons for this are:

1   The nature of the service given is such that the planned use of either people or equipment is rarely attempted.
2   Like maintenance activities, the toolroom does not seem to lend itself to standard activities with standard times.
3   The highly skilled personnel in the toolroom do not take kindly to being treated like production workers.
4   The toolroom is usually small compared with production units and does not appear to have the same need for good production control. Costs do not appear to be excessive. Yet it is a very real cost which should be tightly controlled. The man hour cost is usually much greater than on the shopfloor. Equipment used is more expensive than production equipment. Productivity is normally lower.

There seems to be no valid reason why the same production control principles should not apply to the toolroom as on the shopfloor. The capacity of the toolroom should be declared — technical, standard and current.
An assessment of the workload should then be made:

By type of tool — using current sales/production forecasts to determine at what intervals tools will need refurbishing.

By man hours — an assessment of the man hours, of various trades and toolroom equipment, which will be needed to carry out the refurbishing required.

Next, make a match between workload and capacity. This could be simplified by:
Categorising tools to be refurbished in a way that indicates the equipment to be used in the toolroom and the possible man hours needed. For example:

Jigs, Drilling: Over 170mm, Code A; From 125mm to 170mm, Code B; Under 125mm, Code C.

Dies, Press Cure: Less than 125mm × 75mm, Code D; More than 125mm × 75mm, Code E.

Providing fairly simple scheduling rules for the toolroom. For example, some machines should be nominated to work on drilling jigs only — by size.
Ensuring that capacity, once declared, is kept constantly filled. Evening out the flow of work will be necessary.

Providing (say) 10 per cent of all toolroom capacity for emergency work.

Scheduling as much as possible on a regular basis. For example a preplanned number of jigs or dies should be refurbished each week.

35.8 CONCLUSION

When labour costs are constantly rising tooling may not appear to be expensive if it permits specialisation and better worker productivity. There are many ways however of keeping tool and tool refurbishing costs at a minimum:

1 By using the cost-evaluations which have been briefly outlined in this chapter.
2 By tool standardisation. Proliferation of tooling will follow from product proliferation, but tools could also increase numerically from a constant desire to experiment and use new kinds of tools. While it sounds retrogressive, it could be better in the long run to standardise and maintain such standardisation for some time to come.

PART VII

Performance Improvement

36

The approach to performance improvement

36.1 INTRODUCTION

Peter Drucker once wrote [1] that managers should be involved with opportunities not problems. Such aphorisms should infuriate production managers, harassed by their superiors for greater production at less cost, by their shop stewards for more pay for less work and their subordinates for more status and power.

Yet, difficult though it may be to accept, the application of many of the procedures, activities and systems recorded in this book have, from practical experience, solved many of the more obvious problems which face production managers. The production planning and control activity is typical of the problems which have to be faced. Often, misapplied planning principles, the inherent lack of planning discipline and the apparent need for flexibility, produce urgent orders which must leapfrog over all the others. These in turn foster other urgent orders, further weakening the application of good planning and scheduling until most orders become urgent as they are not being produced on time. Getting any orders out in a planned and disciplined way becomes a nearly intractable problem. A common sight in such situations is bodies of order chasers haunting the shopfloor in numbers nearly equal to the operatives actually turning out the orders.

Such 'problems' can be solved by the rigorous application of planning and scheduling rules enforced by a rigid determination that such rules will be adhered to, no matter what contingencies occur. 'Problems' of a production control nature are not intractable.

36.2   IMPROVING LONG TERM PRODUCTIVITY

Solving such problems as how to produce orders on time will obviously provide some company benefits; long term improvements in productivity, sufficient to ensure the survival and prosperity of the company may not be one of them. For this, it is proposed, a much more fundamental approach to performance improvement is required.

1   How are we doing?

Chapter 2 gives an indication of the kind of measurement needed to determine local production performance. Such data needs to be collected for the last three to four years.

The information should show:

Where there are intrinsic weaknesses in performance, e.g.
   in material yield,
   in machine utilisation,
   in output rates.
Where there has been a decline in performance, e.g.
   in wages as a ratio of added value,
   in labour productivity,
   in absenteeism,
   in orders delivered on time.
Where there are possibilities of improving performance, e.g.
   in reducing unit costs,
   in better use of maintenance facilities,
   in reducing the consumption of gas or electricity.

2   What environmental influences are affecting us or will affect us?

Some of the more important of these were set out in Chapters 3 and 4. The analysis should be tackled under three headings:

The environmental activity
This comprises events over which production management will have little or no influence. National and international economic circumstances, cultural and social change, decline of world resources are some of the more pertinent ones.

The impact on production
How the environmental pressures will or might affect production, should be recorded. For example, where a raw material is used, such as asbestos, which has a predictable finite supply, the potential effect should be known.

The possible response

Some environmental activities will need no response at all, others certainly will. For example if inflation is to rise beyond 10 per cent the response in terms of capital investment or stock holding strategies needs to be carefully defined.

3   Making a plan

While the plan to improve productivity should stem from the analysis proposed in 1 and 2 the following should be key elements:

Production as a system. Looking at the analysis of environments and past performance will be helped by regarding production as a system. What effect, for example, will the environment have on production objectives and the way these are achieved? Is it possible for the system to be under control or will it career onwards without brakes or even knowledge about how it works?

The production framework. This should provide the structure within which changes will need to be made:

What can be done to make people work better or more effectively, if not harder?

What organisation or sub-organisation will best match environmental circumstances?

What resources will be required and can be made available to ensure that the production system operates effectively?

What methods of planning and control are needed to keep the production system on course to meet agreed objectives?

It will not be possible to change one part of the production framework without affecting the other three sections. Each interacts on all the others.

4   Alternatives

It may be possible to suggest various alternatives, as shown in Fig. 36.1 (The relationships between the four parts of the production framework are shown.)

Once a broad outline has been recorded, the plans can be made in finer detail as shown in simple form in Fig. 36.2.

5   Quantify possible results

It may not be possible always to quantify what will result from taking some action. Participation for example may be just a leap in the dark. Many of the potential actions however will result in some measurable change within the production system. For instance, there may be amendments to the inputs to the system or changes in the objectives. The adaptation of the production process will be seen to have some positive result.

	Motivation and reward systems	Work organisation	Production resources	Resource planning and control systems
Environmental pressure	Apply incentives if none exist.	Consider individual and group organisations depending on type of incentive.	Could materials improvement and other factors apart from 'pieces' be included in the incentive?	Plan, measure and control labour productivity.
	Improve working environment.	Include 'participation' in agreement.	Indicate resource use and new expense.	Measure performance before and after.
Improve productivity	Introduce second generation incentives.	Provide appropriate work organisation.	Measure performance of resources and introduce more when proved necessary.	Measure added value etc. and introduce workers' information systems.
	Relate rewards to power to influence events and achievements.	Relate power, authority and responsibility to current work organisation and change if necessary.	Allocate resources to power structure (i.e. make resources and power equate).	Measure relationship of resource usage with work organisation.

Fig. 36.1 Productivity improvement within the production framework

Environmental pressure	Motivation and reward systems	Work organisation	Production resources	Resource planning and control systems
Diminishing supplies of raw material.	Multi-factor incentives which maximise the use of materials.	Orientation towards saving of material in the short term, better strategic use.	Need to relate material input with company objectives and strategies.	Systems which provide limiting factor analysis and measure material use.
Government legislation on participation.	Second generation incentives to create joint problem solving in the company.	Group activities which will ensure that participation is more than just an endless debate about sharing the available cake.	Use of resources in a way which achieves both company and individual objectives.	Systems which plan the use of participation and monitor its results. Worker information systems.
Product-market demands, greater product flexibility and differentiation in product design.	Establish motivation systems which promote flexibility by working on different machines at different times and with a different product mix.	Organisations where flexibility and inter-relationships are possible.	Labour particularly must be flexible. Machine utilisation may be a problem.	Planning and scheduling systems designed to be quickly adapted to cope with new product-market demands.

Fig. 36.2   The production framework and improvement

36.3 INDIVIDUALITY IN PERFORMANCE IMPROVEMENT

Each factory or production unit is in some ways unique. It has its own history, culture, style, competence, relationships, degrees of trust. There can be few totally stereotyped responses to environmental changes. What is appropriate for a company making textiles in Lancashire could be anathema to a unit making electrical components in Southampton. Each production unit should produce a different plan which exactly matches local requirements. There is no such thing as a universal panacea.

NOTE

1   P. Drucker, *Managing for Results*, Heinemann, 1964.

37

Key techniques

37.1 INTRODUCTION

This final chapter will briefly describe some of the more important and relevant techniques which production managers might consider using in improving their productivity.

Techniques are tools by which the production framework might be changed. They are the hammers, spanners and chisels, with which the structure can be tightened, extended or contracted. They are not the nuts and bolts of the framework.

Techniques need to be used with caution. They can be important, occasionally very important, but they need to have limits put on their radius of action. They are not as important as the elements in the production framework.

The application of techniques has often gone wrong for the following reasons:

1   The users of the techniques did not fully understand them. They were either misapplied or the results achieved were misinterpreted. (This is often true with some operations research techniques.)
2   Management services personnel and others who are technique orientated tend to look around for appropriate problems to solve. They are not necessarily problem solvers, sometimes merely technique appliers. Again, this is often true of O.R. specialists. (Every problem becomes a case for linear programming, for example.)
3   Techniques tend to be applied without sufficient regard either for the production framework and the knock-on effect of influencing, say, a work organisation, or for the general behavioural situation associated with the problem.
4   A technique does not always solve the problem as intended. Techniques tend to 'sub-optimise' situations.

37.2   TECHNIQUES

The following list of techniques will obviously need to be supplemented by appropriate literature.

37.2.1   Problem solving techniques

A theory of decision making was developed in the USA in the sixties and 'decision theory' seemed to be a coming method. For a while operations researchers and their research burgeoned and non-mathematical managers saw redundancy or at least demotion as a future prospect.

The quantification needed in problem solving is still important and growing in importance all the time. There are however short cuts to using mathematics in production. For example, model making by computer can be carried out by using packages. The non-mathematical manager, even if he is sensitive to the behavioural problems which exist, can be something of a liability. But often rigorous analysis of the method study type can be used successfully to solve a large number of problems.

So the following suggestions are made about problem solving from a practical rather than a theoretical point of view:

1   Behavioural problems might first be tackled by asking a single question — what does this person (or these people) want out of this situation? A second question might then be posed — can we accommodate him (them) in any way? If both of these can be given positive answers then the problem is a long way towards being solved.
2   Problem solving should be seen in the light of the production framework i.e. motivation, systems, resources and work organisation. A problem in one part of the framework will have repercussions in other parts. A solution which relates solely to a system or motivation could be erroneous.
3   A problem solving routine might be built up. It will be different for all managers in some way but might take the following lines:

    (a)   What really is the problem? Is it real? Can it be written out in one sentence? Often with this kind of initial analysis, the problem will either disappear or become different in some way.

    (b)   Why has the problem occurred? Does it presage other similar problems? What 'knock-on' effect will it generate if it is solved? Is there a time limit on producing a solution?

    (c)   Is enough information available to solve the problem? Can information be found — in time? Often obtaining data is one of the most difficult parts of problem solving.

    (d)   Identify the constraints in the problem. Are these resources — men or money — or are they behavioural?

(e)   Record the various alternatives which seem to offer themselves. Often the use of some technique — method study, or (say) linear programming — may be useful in deciding upon the alternatives. Brainstorming may also be helpful.

(f)   Calculate the value of the alternatives. What do they really give? How much would each of them cost? Can risk analysis help at this stage?

(g)   Choose the alternative which seems to offer the most advantages at least cost.

Following are some useful problem solving techniques:

1   Method study

Though long an essential part of work study, it is curious that most people involved in that discipline rarely, if ever, use method study in the way intended.

According to BS 3138, method study is the 'systematic recording and critical examination of existing and proposed ways of doing work, as a means of developing and applying easier and more effective methods and reducing costs.'

The method study approach is a useful one:

(a)   Select the problem to be tackled (normally a production manager will know what the problem appears to be).

(b)   Record. What really is taking place concerning the problem? What parameters, constraints, costs and failings occur?

(c)   Examine. This is by far the most important element. The questions asked might include:

Purpose — what is necessary? What is achieved? What else could be done? What else should be done?

Place — where does it take place? Why? Where else could it take place?

Sequence — when does it take place? Why then? When else could it take place? When ought it to be done?

Person — who does it? Why? Who else could do it? Who ought to do it?

From the examination a likely new method is often thrown up — or indeed several new methods.

(d)   Develop. The proposed method (or methods) is developed, i.e. worked out in detail, evaluated and tested.

(e)   Install. Installing the new method will also include 'selling it'.

2   Work simplification

Work simplification is the half brother of method study and the philosophies used are often similar. It should be a 'do it yourself' technique practised by production managers and should cover any aspect of work with the object of removing anything that unnecessarily complicates the true purpose of the work.

Work simplification has the direct aim of facilitating many operations and activities, so reducing costs. Like method study, work simplification has useful principles which are largely self explanatory:

Elimination
Simplification
Combination
Rearrangement
Reduction
Substitution.

3   Optimisation techniques

Optimisation covers the activity of achieving the most favourable outcome from a situation where several alternatives can be adopted. Usually these alternatives are resources and the problem is how to use or deploy them so that the most benefit can be obtained. Such problems occur most days of the life of a production manager. For example production scheduling is a constant process of reconciling sales demand with low cost production and keeping the shopfloor reasonably happy. Often rough rules of thumb will suffice to achieve the appropriate balance. No-one should chase after esoteric solutions to problems which hard experience can solve more or less by instinct. There are two optimisation techniques however which production managers should be aware of and apply when necessary:

Linear programming
Model making.

L.P. is a mathematical technique usually used to determine the optimum allocation of resources such as capital, raw materials or plant to achieve a desired objective such as minimum cost of operations. It is only one of a series of techniques which go under the title of mathematical programming. In L.P. the objectives function and the associated constraints are expressed as a straight line form, whereas in non-linear programming this obviously will not occur.

A model, in business, is simply a representation of part of the whole of the characteristics of a real life situation. Usually it will be a series of mathematical equations, which can be used to simulate the decision making possibilities inherent in the real activity.

A model, if correctly designed, should be capable of answering such questions as 'What would happen if ...?' Model making will never give an absolutely correct answer for an optimisation problem, but it will often be better than guesswork. It should provide a dimension or viewpoint which hunch or experience will not always suggest. It is valuable for this aspect alone.

4 Brainstorming

Brainstorming has periods when it is in vogue and times when everybody seems to have forgotten it. There were quite well defined rules for its application when it was first evolved in the USA — people were allowed to 'freewheel', nobody was to be regarded as an eccentric propagating absurd suggestions, and a secretary would take notes and explore every suggestion made. The need for 'brainstorming' is still vital in most factories, whether it is given that name or not. Many problems deserve the attention of a variety of people who can investigate solutions in a free and easy way, relieved of the normal pressures of hierarchical decision making. It does not matter what it is called, but joint problem solving has so many advantages that its practice should be practically mandatory.

5 Check lists

An organisation can be seen to be somewhat akin to the human body and the correction of ailments viewed in the same way. A doctor visiting his human patient usually asks for the symptoms of the trouble, from which he will diagnose what is wrong and then, it is hoped, provide treatment to correct the ailment.

The good manager must become — like a doctor — a good diagnostician. He must be prepared to search for the appropriate symptom — low machine utilisation, late deliveries, high work in progress. He must provide his own diagnosis — poor factory scheduling, lack of liaison between inventory control and production control — and then provide treatment.

Many years ago I thought that it was possible to provide a symptoms diagnosis and treatment chart [2] which would prove useful in fostering this approach. It did imply however that such practice could be formalised and that there are sufficient similarities between organisations to make 'check lists' both useful and applicable.

6 Motion study

Motion study is the systematic investigation of human motion with a view to economising energy and time. Economy can result directly from elimination, simplification, reduction, combination or rearrangement of motions or indirectly from a modification of tools, equipment, product, materials, machines and workplace.

Various principles of motion economy have been devised, e.g.:

The hands of operatives should preferably begin and complete work simultaneously.

Hands, if possible, should not be idle at any time during the work cycle.

The method of operation should have as few motions as possible.

Hands should not work if other body members can perform the task — so long as the hands have other work to do.

The careful application of motion study should increase production, lower operative fatigue, increase machine and equipment utilisation and gain improved control over production.

7   Risk and sensitivity analysis

These are mathematical techniques which will help to evaluate the possibilities and risks associated with decision making. They are often a part of decision theory.

37.2.2   Resource allocation and control techniques

The key activity under this heading is operational planning — really a combination of the production planning and control and costing procedures set out in Chapters 8 and 9. There is an obvious need to cost the decision making implicit in production control, whether this is comparing the amount of work in progress in the system compared with non-machine manufacturing time, or in determining the contribution which each product market gains from the capacity allocation it has been given.

It is possible that either production control or costing production could be introduced alone and substantial improvements take place, but the two together seem essential.

Planning in its widest sense is also required if resource allocation and control is to be effective. While long term plans of, say, over three years, can be of little value to many production managers, shorter term planning is important. Readers may like to refer to my Profit planning handbook [2] for further explanation.

Resource allocation and control can be approached from both an organisational and a technique viewpoint. An example of each of these, not been mentioned previously, is given.

1   Materials management

The ever rising cost of material and its handling within production has led to a view that a materials management function is required to ensure that maximum use of materials at minimum cost is achieved.

This approach has some merit if it aids the recognition of the importance of materials productivity. However, as the philosophy is usually applied, it is cross functional (at least across traditional functions) and this could be a major drawback in setting up an appropriate activity.

The philosophy usually covers the following:

Purchasing activities including:
  Vendor ratings
  Product specifications and alternatives
  Purchase contracts
  Purchase control:
    Stock levels
    Make or buy decisions
    Long term contracts
    Budgets and forecasts.
Forecasting and stock control policies:
  Stock level budgeting
  ABC analysis
  Forecasting, etc.
Materials productivity
Materials handling
Materials management techniques:
  Value analysis
  Product geometry, etc.

2   Product rationalisation

One of the most potent urges in many if not most organisations is to proliferate. It seems too easy to provide a customer with one extra different dimension or 'one-off' change from a standard specification. When sales are comparatively difficult to come by, a minor product change, made just to clinch a deal, will always seem justified. But over the years the modifications and changes go on. The product register fills up. Tooling has to proliferate. Batch sizes decline. Paperwork becomes nearly as extensive as making the product. The company starts to be throttled by the over-complicated administration and manufacturing procedures which are necessary to support the product range.

Calling a halt to such proliferation is often painful. Who will voluntarily attempt to rationalise if many jobs right across the company are at stake?

Anyway, it is possible that sales will decline if the product range is cut — or so the sales force will certainly claim.

The advantages of rationalisation are beyond dispute. Those who have tried it — and many extremely successful companies say that it is the basis of their success — believe it to be vital.

Everywhere in the company benefits — systems become simpler, incentives can be standardised, paperwork is reduced, stocks are brought down, bureaucracy can be contained.

A product rationalisation, or standardisation and variety reduction (if these words make more sense) campaign might take the following lines:

(a) The activity has to be organisation-wide. Communication has to be good, objectives made specific.

(b) A useful start might be to look at the product range, determining the following:

How many items are in the range?
What are their differences of:
  quality
  dimension
  material
  market
  merchandising
  manufacturing/tooling?
How many of the items start from one major item and add cosmetic differences?
What is the cost of carrying the range:
  stocking
  paperwork
  manufacture?
If the range was halved, what kind of savings would there be in:
  manufacturing
  tooling
  stocking and warehousing
  administration?
What are the economics of the current range i.e.:
  turnover per item and per product/market
  contribution per item and per product/market
  profit per item and per product/market.
What sales would be lost if the range was reduced?
This analysis will start to indicate the benefits of rationalisation and also indicate where rationalisation might begin.

(c) Rationalisation. Attempt as follows:
Elimination of all items which give less that X per cent contribution

over variable cost.

Change dimensional sizes so that a standard size range occurs

Leave cosmetic changes to end of the production line or even as a distribution function.

To eliminate colours

    qualities

    codings

    applications

    and all specials

which have a low contribution and are likely to be replaced by standard items.

(d)   Provide a programme of rationalisation of all other aspects of the business which will be affected by rationalisation:

    tooling and materials handling

    manufacturing procedures

    incentives

    paperwork systems, especially production planning and costing

    development

    raw material purchasing and stock control

    quality control

    order sizes.

(e)   Monitoring the result will be necessary to ensure that all the expected benefits are realised and perhaps more importantly that no-one starts to proliferate product items as soon as the rationalisation team has been disbanded.

(f)   Value analysis/value engineering. Value analysis and its derivative, value engineering, are questioning techniques directed towards ensuring that product and engineering costs are directly related to the value obtained.

A test for value check is usually employed by a team of qualified analysts.

A simple looking questionnaire is drawn up, which asks such questions as (for value analysis):

Do we really need a part of the product at all?

Are there any parts of the item which are expendable?

Have the following ever been considered:

    cheaper materials

    cheaper labour etc?

While looking simple the questionnaire can produce substantial results in product engineering and engineering generally.

37.2.3 Manpower development

This is the third heading under which product managers might like to consider how far techniques will help them. A common thread running through many production activities is a dearth of talent. The production function is not attractive. Pay is low — comparatively. Stress is high. Why try to run a factory when lecturing in management studies at the local technical college pays just as much?

While this situation must change if industry is to be even moderately efficient, what talent is available needs to be developed to the full. This means that authority and autonomy have to be given to anyone who shows the ability and desire to take them. But more important, a manpower development programme is needed. Whether this is based on job study in its widest sense with job descriptions, job evaluation, merit rating and performance appraisal or something more esoteric, like action centred leadership programmes, is difficult to assess, but such development is important.

Chapters 16 and 18 largely cover the ground which is needed. Other associated techniques are as follows.

1 Fatigue study

Fatigue study is the investigation and appraisal of the fatigue variables of work with the object of reducing them. It is of importance in both work measurement and method study as it forms a bridge between the measurement of work and its minimisation through method study. In practice, fatigue reduction is seldom attempted for its own sake.

2 Ergonomics

This is derived from two Greek words: ergon — work, and nomos — laws. It is the study of the relationship between man and the working environment with the aim of making work as efficient as possible and minimising fatigue.

Fields of study in ergonomics cover:

The display of information — especially on instrument control panels
Product design
Raw materials
Machine and tool design
Design of controls
Anthropometry
Fatigue.

3 Rota systems

A rota system is a repetitive pattern of shift working designed to cover a specified plant utilisation with a specified number of men present at any one moment. As the amount of capital investment in a production unit increases, equipment must be kept running to the maximum extent.

Rota systems can embrace any range of plant-open time between 80 and 168 hours per week.

NOTES

1   B. H. Walley, *Office Administration Handbook*, Business Books, 1976.
2   B. H. Walley, *Profit Planning Handbook*, Business Books, 1978.

Bibliography and useful addresses

CHAPTER 1   THE PRODUCTION SYSTEM

E. I. Cleland and W. R. King. *Management — a systems approach*, McGraw-Hill, 1972.

G. M. Jenkins, 'The systems approach', *Journal of Systems Engineering*, 1.1, 1969.

F. E. Kast and J. E. Rosenzweig, *Organisation and Management: A systems approach*, McGraw-Hill, 1970.

B. C. J. Lievegoed, *The developing organisation*, Tavistock, 1973.

CHAPTER 2   THE PRODUCTION AUDIT

BIM Checklists (regularly updated).

S. R. Goodman, *Techniques of Profitability Analysis*, Wiley, 1970.

Government statistics – A Brief Guide to Sources (updated annually), Central Statistical Office.

G. Haberland, *Crisis Management: a checklist manual*, Leviathan House, 1975.

J. C. Robertson, 'Some hard questions on management audits', *The New York Certified Accountant*, Sept 1971.

S. A. Tucker, *Successful Management Control by Ratio Analysis*, McGraw-Hill, 1961.

B. H. Walley, *Efficiency Auditing*, Macmillan, 1974.

CHAPTER 3   MAJOR ENVIRONMENTAL INFLUENCES

W. G. Bennis, 'Changing Organisation', *Journal of Applied Behavioural Science*, Vol 2, 1966.

J. D. Daniels, E. W. Ogram and L. H. Radeburgh, *International Business Environments and Operations*, Addison-Wesley, 1976.

T. Edwards, 'Micro-electronics — some social considerations', *Management Services Journal*, Dec 1978.

K. Gill, 'Micro-electronics and the law — a trade union view', *Management Services Journal*, Dec 1978.

J. Morrell and R. Ashton, *Inflation and Business Management*, Economic Forecasters, 1975.

J. Parnaby, *Eclecticism, Change and Dilemma in Manufacturing*, University of Bradford, 1976.

W. Purdie and B. Taylor, *Business Strategies for Survival: planning for political and social change*, Heinemann, 1975.

E. F. Schumacher, *Small is Beautiful*, Blond and Briggs, 1973.

A. Toffler, *Future Shock*, Pan, 1972.

E. Trist, *Urban North America. The Challenge of the Next 30 Years*, Tavistock, 1973.

H. Voegl and J. D. Tarrant, *Survival 2001: Scenario for the Future*, Van Nostrand Reinhold, 1975.

CHAPTER 4   THE INTERNAL ENVIRONMENT

Bowers Egan Safety Policies, New Commercial Pub, 1979.

R. H. Fox, *Thermal Comfort in Industry*, HMSO, 1962.

Guarding of Machinery, The British Standards Institute Code of Practice, 1975.

W. Handley, *Industrial Safety Handbook*, McGraw-Hill, 1969.

J. Harries, *Employment Protection*, Oyez Publishing, 1976.

Health and Safety at Work, T.U.C., 1975.

W. A. Hines, *Noise Control in Industry*, Business Books, 1966.

J. Jackson, *Health and Safety and the Law*, New Commercial Pub, 1979.

E. Mitchell, *The Employers' Guide to the Law on Health, Safety and Welfare at Work*, Business Books, 1976.

Useful addresses

Architectural Association, 32 Bedford Square, London WC 1.
Building Centre, 26 Store Street, Tottenham Court Road, London WC 1.
Building Research Station, Bucknails Lane, Garston, Watford, Herts.
Council of Industrial Design, 28 Haymarket, London SW 1.

Illuminating Engineering Society, York House, Westminster Bridge Road, London SE1.
The Institute of Building, 48 Bedford Square, London WC1.

CHAPTER 5   INFORMATION SYSTEMS

R. N. Anthony, *Planning and Control Systems*, Harvard Business Press, 1965.
R. O. Boyce, *Integrated Managerial Control*, Longmans Green, 1967.
R. A. Johnson et al, *The theory and management of systems*, McGraw-Hill, 1967.
W. McCullough, *Physical Working Conditions*, Gower Press, 1969.
T. W. McRae, *Management Information Systems*, Penguin, 1971.
A. E. Mills, *The Dynamics of Management Control Systems*, Business Books, 1968.
D. Rogers, *Creative Systems Design*, Anbar Publications, 1970.
B. H. Walley, *Office Administration Handbook*, Business Books, 1975.
B. H. Walley, *Profit Planning Handbook*, Business Books, 1978.

CHAPTER 7   PRODUCTION OBJECTIVES AND PLANNING

S. V. Bishop, *Business Planning and Control*, Institute of Chartered Accountants, 1966.
C. Cooper Jones, *Business Planning and Forecasting*, Business Books, 1974.
J. W. Humble, *Improving Business Results*, A.M.A., 1968.
J. W. Humble, *Management by Objectives*, Gower Press, 1975.
P. H. Irwin, *Business Planning — Key to Profit Growth*, Ryerson, 1970.
A. Presanis, *Corporate Planning and Industry*, Business Books, 1968.
B. H. Walley, *Profit Planning Handbook*, Business Books, 1978.

CHAPTER 8   COSTING PRODUCTION

J. Batty, *Managerial Standard Costing*, Macmillan, 1970.
G. Böer, *Direct Cost and Contribution Accounting*, Wiley, 1974.
R. G. A. Boland and J. A. Feathers, *Budgetary Control*, EUP, 1971.
G. D. Bond, *Financial Control for Management*, Butterworth, 1970.
B. Brooks, *Principles of Management Accounting*, Gee & Co, 1975.
Budgetary Control for the Small Company, BIM, 1972.
D. Lock, *Financial Management of Production*, Gower Press, 1975.
L. E. Rockley, *Finance for the Non-Accountant*, Business Books, 1970.
J. Sizer, *An Insight into Management Accounting*, Penguin, 1969.
R. Vause and N. Woodward, *Finance for Non-Financial Managers*, Macmillan, 1975.

CHAPTER 9   PRODUCTION CONTROL

J. E. Biegel, *Production Control — A quantitative approach*, Prentice-Hall, 1963.

J. L. Burbridge, *The Principles of Production Control*, Macdonald & Evans, 1958.

N. Kobert, *Improved Planning, Scheduling and Control at the Supervisory Level*, InComTec.

N. Kobert, *Short Interval Scheduling*, InComTec.

A. H. Lines, *Production Control and Systems*, InComTec.

K. G. Lockyer, *Production Control in Practice*, Pitman, 1960.

R. A. Pritzker and R. A. Gring, *Modern Approaches to Production Planning and Control*, 1960.

N. V. Reinfeld, *Production Control*, Prentice-Hall, 1959.

CHAPTER 10   STOCK CONTROL IN A MANUFACTURING ORGANISATION

A. Battersby, *A Guide to Stock Control*, Pitman, 1962.

G. E. P. Box and G. M. Jenkins, *Time Series Analysis, Forecasting and Control*, Holden-Day, 1970.

R. G. Brown, *Statistical Forecasting for Inventory Control*, McGraw-Hill, 1959.

R. G. Brown, *Decision Rules for Inventory Management*, Holt, Rinehart and Winston, 1967.

J. C. Chambers, 'How to choose the right forecasting technique', *Harvard Business Review*, July/August 1971.

A. H. Lines and J. Beart, *Inventory Control Techniques*, InComTec, 1972.

James Morrell, *Business Forecasting for Finance and Industry*, Gower Press, 1969.

A. B. Thomas, *Stock Control in Manufacturing Industries* (2nd edition), Gower Press, 1979.

CHAPTER 11   USE OF COMPUTERS AND PRODUCTION SYSTEMS

F. F. Coury (ed), *A Practical Guide to Minicomputer Applications*, IEEE Press, 1972.

R. Green, *Using Minicomputers in Distributed Systems*, NCC, 1978.

M. M. Healey, *Minicomputers and Microprocessors*, Hodder & Stoughton, 1976.

D. McKeone, *Small Computers for Business and Industry*, Gower Press, 1979.

P. C. Sanderson, *Management Information Systems and the Computer*, Pan, 1975.

R. Stewart, *How Computers Affect Management*, Gee & Co, 1971.

The National Computing Centre Publications Ltd. *with*
David & Charles Ltd
South Devon House
Railway Station
Newton Abbot
Devon
publishes a variety of books and pamphlets concerning computer use. These include:
Approach to Systems Design
A system documented
Systems documentation manual
Production Control — a survey of computer application packages and services for production control in the UK
Computer guide and production control
The address of the NCC is
Quay House
Quay Street
Manchester

CHAPTER 12 WORK ORGANISATION

J. Childs (ed), *Man and Organisations*, Allen & Unwin, 1973.

L. Davis and J. Taylor, *The Design of Jobs*, Penguin, 1972.

G. K. Ingham, *Size of Industrial Organisations and Worker Behaviour*, CUP, 1970.

D. Katz and R. L. Kahn, *The Social Psychology of Organisation*, Wiley, 1966.

C. Kerr et al, *Industrialism and Industrial Man*, Penguin, 1973.

M. J. Leavitt, W. R. Drill, and H. B. Eyring, *The Organisation World*, Harcourt Brace Jovanovich, 1973.

K. Legge and E. Mumford (eds), *Designing Organisations for Satisfaction and Efficiency*, Gower Press, 1978.

T. Lupton, *On the Shop Floor*, Pergamon, 1963.

J. G. March and H. A. Simon, *Organisations*, Wiley, 1958.

CHAPTER 13 TRADITIONAL ORGANISATIONS

A. Adamson, *The Effective Leader*, Pitman, 1971.

R. L. Bentin, *Supervision and Management*, McGraw-Hill, 1972.

E. F. L. Brech, *Organisation — the framework of management*, Longmans Green, 1959.

R. S. Edwards and H. Townsend, *Studies in Business Organisation*, Macmillan, 1966.

J. A. Litterer, *The Analysis of Organisation*, Wiley, 1965.

P. A. Management Consultants, *Company Organisation*, Allen & Unwin, 1970.

J. March and H. Simon, *Organisation*, Wiley, 1958.

C. Perrow, *Organisational Analysis*, Tavistock, 1970.

J. Woodward, *Industrial Organisation: theory and practice*, Oxford University Press, 1965.

CHAPTER 14   CONFLICT AND ITS POSSIBLE CONTAINMENT

Aims of Industry, *Reds under the Bed*, Aims of Industry, 1974.

H. Beynon, *Working for Ford*, Wakefield EP Publishing, 1975.

R. Blauner, *Alienation and Freedom: the factory worker and his industry*, University of Chicago Press, 1967.

R. Dahrendorf, *Class and Class Conflict in Industrial Society*, Routledge & Kegan Paul, 1959.

J. Goldthorpe, D. Lockwood, F. Bechofer and J. Platt, *The Affluent Worker*, Cambridge University Press, 1968.

K. Hawkins, *Conflict and Change, Aspects of Industrial Relations*, Holt, Rinehart & Winston, 1974.

R. Hyman, *Strikes*, Fontana, 1972.

R. L. Kahn and E. Boulding (eds), *Power and Conflict in Organisations*, Tavistock, 1972.

K. Marx, *Capital* (2 volumes), Everyman, 1930.

K. Marx and F. Engels, *Communist Manifesto*, Allen & Unwin, 1948.

R. Schacht, *Alienation*, Allen & Unwin, 1971.

S. Terkel, *Working*, Wildwood, 1975.

CHAPTER 15   INDUSTRIAL DEMOCRACY

J. Bank and K. Jones, *Worker Directors Speak*, Gower Press, 1977.

Wilfred Brown, *Employee Participation in Management*, Knight, Wegenstein Consultants, 1973.

W. W. Daniels and N. McIntosh, *The Right to Manage*, MacDonald, 1972.

A. Flanders, *The Fawley Productivity Agreements*, Faber & Faber, 1964.

D. Guest and K. Knight (eds), *Putting Participation into Practice*, Gower Press, 1979.

A. E. C. Hare, *First Principles of Industrial Relations*, Macmillan, 1965.
I. S. McDavid, *People, Participation and Motivation*, Work Study and Management Services, Sept 1970.
M. M. Scott, *Every Employee a Manager*, McGraw-Hill, 1970.
R. Stayner and H. Rosen, *The Psychology of Union–Management Relations*, Tavistock Publications, 1960.
Lynda King Taylor, *A Fairer Slice of the Cake*, Business Books, 1976.
G. F. Thomason, *Experiments in Participation*, IPM, 1970.

CHAPTER 16   JOB STUDY AND DESIGN

M. T. Akalin and M. Z. Hassan, 'How Successful is Job Evaluation?', in *Industrial Engineering*, 1971
BIM, *Merit Rating — a practical guide*, (Personnel Management series number 5), BIM, 1960.
BIM, *Job Evaluation — a practical guide for managers*, BIM, 1970.
T. H. Boydell, *A Guide to Job Analysis*, BACIE, 1969.
M. S. Kellog, *What to do About Performance Appraisal*, AMA, 1965.
G. McBeath and N. Rands, *Salary Administration*, Business Books, 1976.
T. T. Paterson, *Job Evaluation*, Business Books, 1971.
H. E. Roff and T. E. Watson, *Job Analysis*, Institute of Personnel Management, 1961.
T. L. Whisler and D. E. McFarland, *Performance Appraisal*, Holt, Rinehart & Winston, 1962.

CHAPTER 17   GROUP JOB DESIGN

W. R. Bion, *Experiences in Groups*, Tavistock, 1961.
R. Brown, *Social Psychology*, Collier Macmillan, 1965.
D. Cartwright and A. Zander, *Group Dynamics: Research and Theory*, Tavistock, 1968.
L. E. Davies and J. C. Taylor, *Design of Jobs*, Penguin, 1972.
J. J. Morse, 'A contingency look at job design', *California Management Review*, 1973.
N. A. Rosen, *Leadership, Change and Work-Group Dynamic*, Staples, 1969.
P. B. Smith, *Groups with Organisations*, Harper & Row, 1973.
R. Wild, 'Groups, Enrichment and Mass Production', *The Production Manager*, October 1973.
R. Wild, *Work Organisation*, Wiley, 1975.

CHAPTER 18   RECRUITMENT, TRAINING AND MANPOWER PLANNING

J. Adair, *Training for Leadership*, Gower Press, 1968.

C. M. Bowen, *Developing and Training the Supervisor*, Business Books, 1970.

D. H. Gray, *Manpower Planning*, IPM, 1972.

M. M. Mandell, *The Employment Interview*, Bailey, Bros & Swinfen, 1965.

G. McBeath, *Organisation and Manpower Planning*, Business Books, 1968.

P. C. Morea, *Guidance, Selection and Training*, Routledge, 1970.

A. Mumford, *The Manager and Training*, Pitman, 1970.

T. H. Patten, *Manpower Planning and the Development of Human Resources*, Wiley, 1971.

A. K. Rice, *Learning for Leadership*, Tavistock Publications, 1965.

E. Sidney and M. Brown, *The Skills of Interviewing*, Tavistock Publications, 1961.

A. R. Smith, 'Developments in manpower planning', *Personnel Review*, Autumn 1971.

R. Stammers and J. Patrick, *The Psychology of Training*, Methuen, 1975.

D. H. Sweet, *Recruitment — a guide for managers*, Addison-Wesley, 1975.

J. Wellens, *The Training Revolution*, Evans Bros, 1963.

CHAPTER 19   ORGANISATIONAL DEVELOPMENT AND THE MANAGEMENT OF CHANGE

R. Beckard, *Organisation Development — strategies and models*, Addison-Wesley, 1970.

W. G. Bennis, *Planning of Change*, Holt, Rinehart & Winston, 1970.

D. Bryant, 'The psychology of resistance to change', *Management Services Journal*, March 1979.

T. Burns and G. M. Stalker, *The Management of Innovation*, Tavistock Publications, 1961.

Honor Croome, *Human Problems of Innovation*, HMSO, 1959.

E. Huse, J. Bowditch, D. Fisher, *Readings on Behaviour in Organisations*, Addison-Wesley, 1975.

S. A. Judson, *A Manager's Guide to Making Changes*, Wiley, 1966.

I. L. Marrigham, *Managing Change — a practical guide to organisation development*, BIM, 1971.

D. Newman, *Organisation Design*, Arnold, 1972.

G. H. Varney, *An Organisation Development Approach to Management Development*, Addison-Wesley, 1976.

CHAPTER 20 MOTIVATION

D. R. Davies and V. J. Shackleton, *Psychology and Work*, Methuen, 1975.

S. W. Gellerman, *Management by Motivation*, AMA, 1968.

F. Herzberg, *Work and the Nature of Man*, World Publishing Co, 1966.

F. Herzberg, 'One more time — how do you motivate employees?', *Harvard Business Review*, Jan–Feb 1968.

F. Herzberg, B. Mausret, B. B. Synderman, *The Motivation to Work*, Wiley, 1959.

R. Likert, *The Human Organisation — its management and value*, McGraw-Hill, 1967.

Douglas McGregor, *The Human Side of the Enterprise*, McGraw-Hill, 1961.

Douglas McGregor, *Leadership and Motivation*, MIT Press, 1966.

H. Murrell, *Motivation at Work*, Methuen, 1976.

W. J. Paul, K. B. Robertson, *Job Enrichment and Employee Motivation*, Gower Press, 1970.

Lynda King Taylor, *Not for Bread Alone*, Business Books, 1971.

CHAPTER 21 WORK MEASUREMENT

R. M. Barnes, *Work Sampling*, Wiley, 1957.

R. M. Currie, *Simplified PMTS*, BIM, 1963.

W. C. Glassey, *The Theory and Practice of Time Study*, Business Books, 1965.

H. B. Maynard, G. J. Stegemerten, J. L. Schwab, *Methods Time Measurement*, McGraw-Hill, 1948.

D. A. Whitmore, *Measurement and Control of Indirect Work*, Heinemann, 1970.

D. A. Whitmore, *Work Measurement*, Heinemann, 1976.

CHAPTER 23 TRADITIONAL PAYMENT SYSTEMS

R. Balyeat, *The Case for Direct Incentives*, Industrial Engineering (USA), Dec 1969.

A. Bowey (ed), *Handbook of Salary and Wage Systems*, Gower Press, 1975.

A. M. Bowey and T. Lupton, 'Productivity drift and the structure of the pay packet', *Journal of Management Studies,* vol 7, no 2, May 1970.

Wilfrid Brown, *Piecework Abandoned*, Heinemann, 1962.

R. M. Currie, *Incentives*, BIM, 1963.

R. M. Currie and J. E. Faraday, *Financial Incentives*, Management Publications, 1970.

T. Lupton, *Payment Systems*, Penguin, 1972.

T. Lupton and D. Gowler, *Selecting a Wage Payment System*, Kogan Page, 1969.

R. Marriott, *Incentive Payment Schemes*, Staples, 1969.

CHAPTER 24 WAGE POLICIES AND ASSOCIATED NEGOTIATIONS

G. Atkinson, *The Effective Negotiator*, Quest, 1976.

F. S. Brandt, *The Process of Negotiation*, InComTec, 1976.

Wilfred Brown, *The Earnings Conflict*, Penguin, 1973.

CHAPTER 25 SECOND GENERATION INCENTIVES AND WAGE PAYMENT SYSTEMS

M. Caley, *Plant Wide Incentives*, Management Services, Dec 1976.

J. G. Moore, *Added Value as an Index of Industrial Effectiveness*, Work Study and Management Services, Jan 1973.

M. F. Morley, *The Value Added Statement*, Gee & Co, 1977.

K. Owen and F. Jones, 'Closing the performance gap: what industry can learn from Japan', *The Times*, 9/1/76.

A. R. Swannack and P. J. Samuel, 'The added value of men and materials', *Personnel Management*, 1974.

D. Wallace Bell, 'Profit sharing, value added and productivity schemes compared', *Industrial Participation*, Winter 1976.

H. A. V. Wilson, 'Added Value and Moving Averages in Company Wide Incentive Schemes', *Management Accounting*, July/August 1972.

E. G. Wood, *Added Value — the key to prosperity*, Business Books, 1977.

CHAPTER 27 MATERIALS PRODUCTIVITY

D. S. Ammer, *Materials Management*, Irwin, 2nd edition, 1968.

P. Baily and D. Farmer, *Managing Materials in Industry*, Gower Press, 1972.

H. K. Compton, *Supplies and Materials Management*, Business Books, 1968.

CHAPTER 29 CAPITAL RESOURCE MANAGEMENT

R. M. Adelson, 'Discounted cash flow — a critical examination', *Journal of Business Finance*, Summer 1970.

A. M. Alfred and J. B. Evans, *Appraisal of Investment Projects by Discounted Cash Flow*, Chapman Hall, 1965.

R. G. A. Boland and R. M. Oxtoby, *DCF for Capital Investment Analysis*, Hodder & Stoughton, 1975.

D. E. Farrar, *The Investment Decision under Uncertainty*, Prentice-Hall, 1962.

A. L. Kingshott, *Investment Appraisal*, Ford Business Library, 1965.

D. L. Lock, *Project Management*, Gower Press, 1971.

T. Lucey, *Investment Appraisal — evaluating risk and uncertainty*, Gee & Co, 1970.

A. J. Merrett and A. Sykes, *The Finance and Analysis of Capital Projects*, Longmans Green, 1963.

L. E. Rockley, *Capital Investment Decisions*, Business Books, 1968.

A. Sykes, *The Lease–Buy Decision*, BIM, 1976.

E. C. Townsend, *Investment and Uncertainty*, Oliver and Boyd, 1969.

CHAPTER 30   PLANT LAYOUT

M. J. Clay and B. H. Walley, *Performance and Profitability*, Longmans Green, 1965.

C. Hardie, 'Plant Layout', *Works Management*, July/August 1971.

R. W. Mallick and A. T. Gaudreau, *Plant Layout Planning and Practice*, Wiley, 1963.

CHAPTER 31   MATERIALS HANDLING

M. Hessey, 'The application of micro-processors to materials handling', *Management Services Journal*, Dec 1978.

G. C. James, 'Mechanical handling equipment', *Works Management*, July/August 1971.

R. Muther and K. Haganas, *Systematic Handling Analysis*, Industrial Education Institute, 1969.

D. Rogers, 'Systems Design in Materials Handling', *Works Management*, July/August 1971.

F. Wentworth, *Handbook of Physical Distribution Management*, Gower Press, 1976.

CHAPTER 32   QUALITY CONTROL

D. S. Desmond, *Quality Control Workbook*, Gower Press, 1971.

J. F. Halpin, *Zero Defects*, McGraw-Hill, 1968.

E. G. Kirkpatrick, *Quality Control for Managers and Engineers*, Wiley, 1971.

S. Weinberg, *Profit Through Quality*, Gower Press, 1971.

CHAPTER 33   STOREKEEPING

J. L. Blackburn, 'Principles of materials storage', *Works Management*, July/August 1971.

H. K. Compton, *Storehouse and Stockyard Management*, Business Books, 1970.

CHAPTER 34   MAINTENANCE

A. K. S. Jardine, *Operational Research in Maintenance*, Manchester University Press, 1970.

E. T. Newbrough, *Effective Maintenance Management*, McGraw-Hill, 1967.

H. M. V. Stewart, *Guide to Efficient Maintenance Management*, Business Publications, 1963.

E. N. White, *Maintenance Planning, Control and Documentation*, Gower Press, 2nd edition, 1979.

CHAPTER 37   KEY TECHNIQUES

R. M. Barnes, *Motion Study and Time Study*, Wiley, 1949.

E. S. Buffa, *Models for Production and Operations Management*, Wiley, 1963.

A. Charnes and W. W. Cooper, *Management Models and Industrial Application of Linear Programming*, Irwin, 1964.

R. M. Currie, *Work Study*, Pitman for BIM, 2nd edition, 1963.

A. Field, *Methods Study*, Cassell, 1969.

R. N. Lehrer, *Work Simplification — creative thinking about work problems*, Prentice-Hall, 1957.

J. L. Livingstone, *Management Planning and Control, Mathematical Models*, McGraw-Hill, 1970.

N. Martin, *Variety Reduction*, British Standards Institute and Institute of Production Engineers, 1961.

B. H. Walley, *Management Services Handbook*, Business Books, 1973.

Index